D1158229

Bohemian Brigade

BOHEMIAN BRIGADE

BRIGADE

Civil War Newsmen in Action

BY

LOUIS M. STARR

NEW YORK ALFRED A. KNOPF

1 9 5 4

071
S796b

119610

L. C. catalog card number: 54-7214

THIS IS A BORZOI BOOK,
PUBLISHED BY ALFRED A. KNOPF, INC.

FIRST EDITION

This Book Is Inscribed to M. B.—my "m. e."

Preface

LIKE MANY of those happy people for whom the multiple attractions of the Civil War are practically irresistible, I have often wondered, in the course of my reading, how much the American people knew about it while it was being fought. Mountains of material are available to us today. What of those whose lives turned on the outcome? Were they aware of the significance of the *Monitor-Merrimac* fight while the guns were still warm? Did they know, in the first days of July 1863, of the epochal events transpiring at Gettysburg and Vicksburg? How did McClellan, Grant, Sherman, and other leaders appear to them? In fine, how was the war reported?

These pages seek to answer that question and, in so doing, to assess some of the effects of newspaper reporting upon the war.

My second and more compelling purpose is, conversely, to illuminate the effects of the Civil War upon the development of journalism. The historical literature of journalism abounds in editorial studies, but the news side, save in the general survey histories, has been largely neglected. We have more studies of Horace Greeley than of all the newsmen in his century. Yet the work of these obscure reporters and managing editors was of far greater moment in the evolution of journalism and, indeed, of our society.

Whether the news revolution, as I have termed it, has turned out to be an unmixed blessing, whether the free and easy reporters of Civil War days were more effective, or more influential in determining the course of events, or more honest, than reporters of the quite rigidly institutionalized press of to-day—these and other such questions implicit in this book are deliberately left unanswered. They involve judgments of the modern newspaper which are beyond its scope; the reader, in any case, will have answers of his own.

In magnitude and complexity of obstacles, in number of participants, in sheer volume of copy, and in total impact upon the American newspaper as an institution, the reporting of the Civil War defies comparison. To tell of such an undertaking in a single volume—to deal coherently with the reporting of major battles, the press relations of Union civil and military leaders, the exploits of individual correspondents, and some of the ramifications of the news revolution—I have had to jettison valuable cargo. The Eastern theater has been given disproportionate emphasis at the expense of others; the background of reporting could stand elaboration; the "provincial" papers deserve fuller treatment. These deficiencies reflect the demands of the narrative form I have chosen, and my own predilections. My design has been to explore facets of the whole enterprise, with that archetype among newspapers of the day, Horace Greeley's New York *Tribune*, providing a focal point, and its tribulations a thread of narrative.

What of Southern reporters? Save in the early months of the war, the Bohemian Brigade had no counterpart in the Confederacy, for manpower and newsprint problems crippled its press. As early as May 23, 1861 the New York *Herald* noted that many Southern papers were reduced to half-sheets, and by the spring of 1863 this was true of every daily in Richmond. Extras were issued on proof slips. The South, moreover, lacked a metropolitan press. Richmond counted but

37,910 souls in 1860; its population increased during the war, but the *Dispatch*, its largest paper, never claimed more than 18,000 circulation, not enough to support a news staff of consequence. New Orleans, the only city of more than one hundred thousand, fell to the Federals in April 1862. Even before that, on January 18, the *Daily Picayune* grieved that all of its reporters had enlisted. Resourceful Southern editors organized the first genuine news co-operative, the Press Association of the Confederate States, to pool their war news, and they got it from official reports, from occasional contributors (usually staff officers) in the armies, and from Northern papers. The latter source was utilized so often that the Bohemian Brigade may be said to have reported the war for both sides.

To avoid inundating the text with footnotes, I have resorted to selective documentation. Often, especially in the case of newspapers and manuscripts quoted, the source and the date will be perfectly evident from the text.

Darien, Connecticut   L. M. S.

Acknowledgments

FOR AN INSIGHT into the workings of the New York *Tribune*, glimpses of Lincoln, some previously unknown Lincoln quotations, and a host of other things, the author of this book owes much to the extraordinary kindness and patience of the grandchildren of Sydney Howard Gay.

In a Staten Island stable, one day in the summer of 1950, Mrs. Elizabeth Kidwell, of New York, was concluding a dusty and unrewarding search with me among a wilderness of old papers and forgotten bric-a-brac when we came upon the humpbacked trunk that historians unpack in their dreams. It yielded batch after batch of letters, perfectly preserved: the Civil War mail of her grandfather, the *Tribune's* managing editor. Mrs. Kidwell and her brother and sisters, Mr. Henry Willcox, Mrs. Elizabeth Gay Pierce, both of New York City, and Mrs. Anna W. Dwight, of Chestnut Hill, Massachusetts, generously permitted me to take the entire collection home for study.

The Sydney Howard Gay Papers include nearly a thousand confidential letters written by reporters with the armies and in Washington. This is about three times the combined total in the James Gordon Bennett, Manton Marble, and John Russell Young collections in the Library of Congress, the largest such hitherto known. I had the Gay Papers at my side as I wrote, and since the book could not well have been written without them, my appreciation will be understood. The collection, which includes letters written to Gay from his early Abolitionist days until his death, has since been acquired by Columbia University.

Mrs. Marion Hudson Wilmot, of Concord, Massachusetts, granddaughter of the *Herald's* great managing editor, Frederic Hudson, was kind enough to allow me to examine Hudson's diaries and scrapbooks, as well as the valuable memoir in manuscript by his son Woodward.

A few months before his death in 1949, Oswald Garrison Villard wrote me a fine letter expressing his interest in my subject and granting access to his father's papers; and Professor Henry H. Villard, Oswald Garrison's son, has been hospitable in making them available. George Alfred Bonaventure, of New York, grandson of George Alfred Townsend, showed me his interesting collection of Townsend memorabilia, and I am grateful also to other descendants of some of this book's leading characters, among them Miss Alice M. Richardson, of South Natick, Massachusetts, niece of Albert D. Richardson; Gilbert G. Browne, of New York City, the son of Richardson's wartime prison-mate, Junius Browne; Homer M. Byington, of Darien, Connecticut, grandson of the *Tribune's* ingenious correspondent; Mrs. Helen Rogers Reid, of New York, daughter-in-law of Whitelaw Reid; and Mrs. Claire G. Salter, of New York, daughter-in-law of "Jasper" of the *Times.*

During the latter part of my work I was especially fortunate in having the kindly encouragement and advice of Professor Allan Nevins, as well as the stimulation afforded by his Civil War seminar at Columbia. (Though I suspect that he is blissfully unaware of most of them, Professor Nevins must hold the world's championship for grateful references of this kind.)

I am indebted to Frederick Hill Meserve for his generosity in supplying pictures from his famous collection. Frank Luther

Acknowledgments

Mott, whose *American Journalism* is a landmark, went out of his way to lend me a hand. William Harlan Hale and Francis Brown, when in the throes of their own studies of Horace Greeley and Henry J. Raymond, respectively, furnished useful information. Harry E. Pratt, Ralph Newman, Harry W. Baehr, Bell I. Wiley, Milton Kaplan, and Earl Schenck Miers, authors steeped in many phases of the period, answered questions and offered advice of value.

Many good people brightened life for me in the course of research, including James W. Shettel, of the York *Dispatch*, who unearthed some details of Homer Byington's adventure in the Gettysburg campaign and even discovered a picture of the telegraph operator; Mrs. Lloyd Lewis, who kindly aided in my search for the elusive Cadwallader manuscript; Miss Phyllis Gordon Demarest, of Hollywood, California, an authority on Richardson's turbulent life; and Miss Josephine Cobb, of the Audio-Visual Records Branch of the National Archives, who went to no small amount of trouble searching the files for illustrations.

To all of them, and to the many librarians and others who have helped these five years, my warm thanks.

I wish also to acknowledge the following permissions for copyrighted material:

To the Abraham Lincoln Association and Rutgers University Press for *The Collected Works of Abraham Lincoln*, edited by Roy P. Basler.

To Appleton-Century-Crofts for *Recollections of the Civil War*, by Charles A. Dana.

To Dodd, Mead & Company for *Lincoln and the Civil War in the Diaries of John Hay*, edited by Tyler Dennett.

To Harcourt, Brace & Company for *Abraham Lincoln: The War Years*, by Carl Sandburg.

To Houghton Mifflin Company for *The Diary of Gideon Welles*, edited by John T. Morse; and *Memoirs*, by Henry Villard.

Acknowledgments

To Little, Brown & Company for *An American Procession 1855–1914: A Personal Chronicle of Famous Men*, by William A. Croffut.

To The Macmillan Company for *The Diary of George Templeton Strong*, edited by Allan Nevins and Milton Halsey Thomas.

To Medill McBride Company for *When Dana Was the Sun*, by Charles J. Rosebault.

To G. P. Putnam's Sons for *Anglo-American Memories*, by George W. Smalley.

To The Viking Press for *Lincoln Talks*, edited by Emmanuel Hertz.

☼ CONTENTS ☼

Contents

☼ *ILLUSTRATIONS* ☼

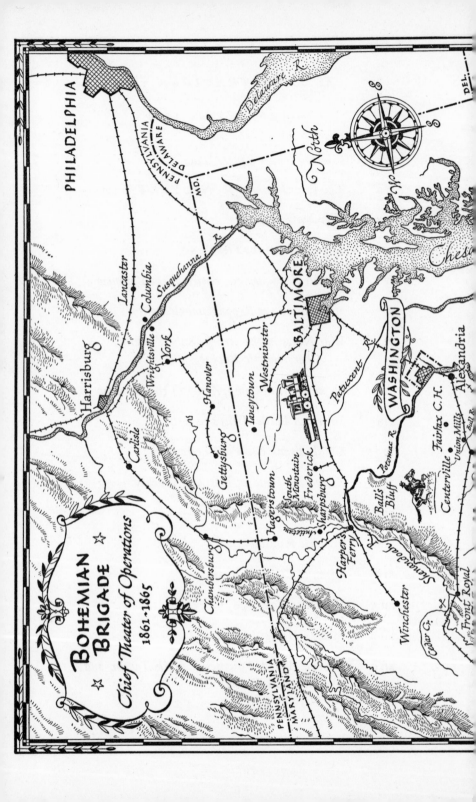

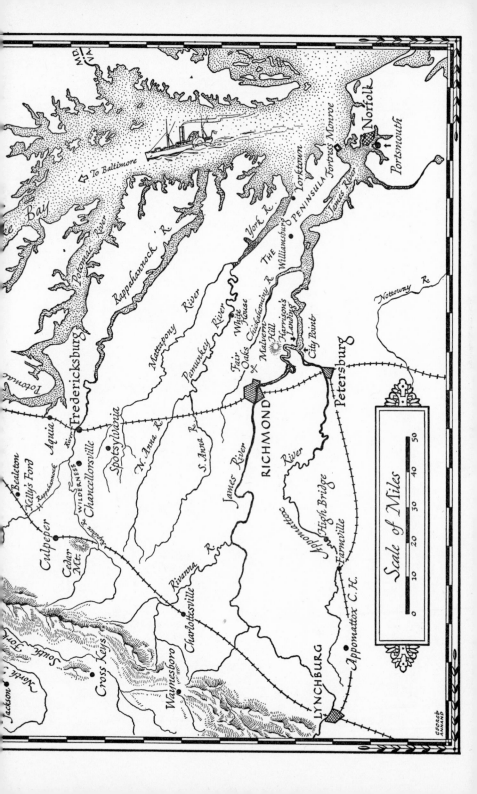

Bohemian Brigade

☼ CHAPTER I ☼

The News Revolution

1. THE CAVE

Pfaff's Cave was crowded as usual of evenings in March 1861, though a few familiar faces were missing. Thomas Nast, the roly-poly fledgling of the *New York Illustrated News*, was in Washington for Lincoln's inauguration. A number of others—who they were was a favorite speculation—had slipped off to Charleston, South Carolina, to report General Pierre G. T. Beauregard's progress in rimming its harbor with guns. For the rest, they carried on as if their days were unnumbered. Charles Ignatius Pfaff, fat and genial, presided at the bar; buxom Saxon girls fetched the succulent sweetbreads, German pancakes, oysters, and lager for which he was famous; and at the long table in the low-ceilinged inner vault, beneath the rumble and clatter of Broadway, the regulars lounged among the hogsheads in an atmosphere of pipe smoke and laughter.

On March 17, the arrival of the eminent William Howard Russell in the city was cause for comment. It was a little disquieting, the New York *World* noted, that the most celebrated war correspondent in the world should make his appearance; *The Times* of London had dispatched him. Russell probably did not visit Pfaff's (none of the guidebooks listed it), but he received an impression of the city that Pfaff's would have done nothing to correct. "New York to my mind," he wrote privately, "is exceedingly gay, insouciant, and even frivolous."

If New York was not dancing on Doomsday, the Cave at 653 Broadway belied it. "We were all very merry at Pfaff's," a *Vanity Fair* concoction by Thomas Bailey Aldrich began, while Walt Whitman celebrated "the vault at Pfaff's where the drinkers and laughers meet to eat and drink and carouse." Regularly toward nightfall, Pfaff escorted any unwary patrons who were sitting in the vault to some other part of his restaurant, Henry Clapp, Jr., took his seat at the head of the table, the initiates appeared, and presently, in Whitman's words, "there was as good talk around that table as took place anywhere in the world." It had been five years since the bright-eyed, witty Clapp, returning from Paris infatuated with Henri Murger's *Scènes de la Vie de Bohème*, set himself up here as "the King of Bohemia." No one, to judge from substantial evidence, was quite sure what Bohemia was all about, but the movement, if anything, was stronger than ever. "The New Theory of Bohemia" was warmly discussed in the current *Knickerbocker*, and the *New York Illustrated News* of February 23, 1861 had a starry-eyed piece on the Pfaffians—"free-thinkers and free-lovers, and jolly companions well met, who make symposia, which for wit, for frolic, and now and then for real intellectual brilliance, are not to be found in any house within the golden circles of Fifth Avenue."

The wit and frolic, at least, were beyond cavil. Charles F. Browne ("Artemus Ward") read a telegram from a California lecture bureau: "What will you take for forty nights?" Clapp sang out: "Brandy and soda, tell them," an answer that endeared Browne to the West Coast. Clapp was asked his opinion of Horace Greeley. "He is a self-made man who worships his creator." William Dean Howells thought it very nearly as well to appear in Clapp's *Saturday Press*, edited (and read) largely at Pfaff's, as to make the *Atlantic*, for while

4

"man cannot live by snapping turtle alone," as one critic had complained, Howells had to own that "the *Press* was very good snapping turtle." The paper had suspended in December 1860, later to be revived by the incorrigible Clapp with the announcement: "This paper was stopped in 1860 for want of means. It is now started again, for the same reason." [1]

It was rather giddy and defiant, this first Bohemian movement in America, a little too self-conscious, perhaps, yet alive with the restless excitement of the city it defied. It resurrected Edgar Allan Poe, less, one suspects, for his art (though Fitz-James O'Brien at his macabre best emulated Poe superbly) than because Poe had lived dissolutely, died spectacularly, and hated Boston. The true *Bohème*, its king taught, should live by his art, spend profligately, spit upon the prim literary gods of Boston, scorn the brownstone respectability of Mrs. Grundy, exalt devil-may-care, cultivate wit and women, affect a pipe and an outlandish peaked cap, and consider the world his own.

Printing House Square drank this heady wine with gusto. A contemporary cartoon showed the *Tribune* building with a peaked cap in every window. Newspaper reporters and artists for the illustrated weeklies flocked to Pfaff's to savor Clapp's ripostes, hobnob with the literati, and pay homage to the "Queen of Bohemia," Ada Clare. Ada, hailed by Whitman as "the New Woman," had returned from a sojourn in Paris aboard a steamer which bore the entry on its passenger list: *Miss Ada Clare, and son.* "A Bohemian is not, like the creature of society, a victim of rules and customs," she explained with candescent charm; "he steps over them all with an easy, graceful, joyous unconsciousness."

Whatever else was to be said of this yeasty philosophy, it offered accommodation for those of a calling sorely in need of it. Newspaper reporters lived on the periphery of a society

[1] Frank Luther Mott: *A History of American Magazines* (Cambridge, Mass.: 1939), II, 39. For Pfaff's, I have drawn chiefly upon Albert Parry: *Garrets and Pretenders: A History of Bohemianism in America* (New York: 1933), and Francis Wolle: *Fitz-James O'Brien* (Boulder, Colo.: 1944).

5

which scarcely understood their function. Dickens, the most widely read novelist of the day, had held them up to ridicule in *Martin Chuzzlewit*. Among American novels of the period, only two of seventeen touching upon journalism mentioned reporters at all; both were by James Fenimore Cooper, and both derogatory.[2] To be a reporter was to be a Paul Pry, a Jenkins, a busybody, a keyhole snooper, a penny-a-liner, a ne'er-do-well. Edmund Clarence Stedman, a reporter on the *Tribune* in 1860, considered that "it is shameful to earn a living in this way."[3] It had been a quarter of a century since the penny papers led the way in broadening the concept of news, but it was their reporting of sex and crime that most impressed the public and left a lingering conviction that reporters were disreputable. Half a dozen of them had gone along with the armies of Scott and Taylor to report the Mexican War; many more had brought the story of "Bloody Kansas" to the country, often inventing the blood; events as diverse as the John Brown raid, the Heenan-Sayers prize fight, the visit of the Prince of Wales, were voluminously reported in a press increasingly aware that, as Horace Greeley put it, "the paper that brings the quickest news is the thing looked to." But the emphasis of the press remained on opinion rather than news, on editorials and editorial commentary, as witness the fame of Greeley himself, of Henry J. Raymond, of Bryant, of a galaxy of editors from Samuel Bowles of the Springfield *Republican* to R. B. Rhett of the *Mercury* in Charleston. The Superintendent of the Census of 1860 reflected the prevailing view when he classified eighty per cent of the periodicals of the country, including all 373 daily newspapers, as "political in their character."[4]

So it was that, as "tails" of a coinage stamped with the

2 James G. Harrison: "Nineteenth Century Novels on American Journalism," *Journalism Quarterly*, Sept. 1945, 217. In contrast, Harrison found that after the war more than half of such novels dealt with reporters, usually depicting them as "unspeakably aggressive in seeking news."

3 Laura Stedman and George Gould: *Life and Letters of Edmund Clarence Stedman* (New York: 1910), 215.

4 *Preliminary Report on the Eighth Census* (Washington: 1862), 103.

names of the great opinion-makers, reporters in the metropolis of journalism were of sufficiently low estate to find in Clapp's Bohemia a certain rationale, and they embraced it with such fervor that the term "Bohemian" would cling to them long after Clapp and his movement were forgotten.[5]

To be a Bohemian afforded license for all manner of youthful exuberances. Howells, on the one night he supped at Pfaff's, noted the arrival of a pair "whom the others made a great clamor over; I was given to understand that they had just recovered from a fearful debauch." Thomas Bailey Aldrich of the *Tribune* and Fitz-James O'Brien (known, for cause, at Pfaff's as "Fists Gammon O'Bouncer") experimented at "sleeping all day and living all night." Improvident to a fault, O'Brien was once refused a loan at Harper's, whereupon he went into the bindery, seized a board on which he printed I AM STARVING in large letters, and picketed the office until the publishers relented. Stedman satirized a *nouveau riche* wedding so pointedly in verse in the *Tribune* that friends had to intervene to avert a duel with the bride's father. Mortimer Thomson ("Doesticks") of the *Tribune* and George Forrester Williams of the *Times* spirited the Prince of Wales from the Fifth Avenue Hotel to a bar on Twenty-fifth Street, where, while tumult reigned in the royal entourage as a result of his disappearance, they introduced His delighted Highness to a mint julep.[6]

Now, drinking their ale in the Cave, these and other buoyant spirits speculated, between witticisms, on the authenticity of the *Tribune's* exciting letters from Charleston. The *Times* and the *World* insisted that they were concocted in the *Tribune* office. It was like Charlie Dana to send men to the very

[5] "The term Bohemian . . . belongs peculiarly and chiefly to the class of reporters." Julius Wilcox: "Journalism as a Profession," *The Galaxy*, Vol. 4 (Nov. 1867), 799. The Bohemian Club, organized in New York in 1868, had the announced purpose of preserving the term as applying to reporters exclusively. Augustus Maverick: *Henry J. Raymond and the New York Press* (Hartford: 1870), 330.

[6] Williams: "When King Edward VII Visited New York," *The Independent*, Vol. 54 (Mar. 6, 1902), 569.

gates of hell if he could talk them into it, but in this case such a feat seemed beyond him. John Bigelow of the *Evening Post* had asked R. B. Rhett of the Charleston *Mercury* about dispatching a reporter to that hotbed of secession a few months before. Rhett's reply was succinct: "He would come with his life in his hands and would probably be hung." Even the proslavery *Herald* had to recall the man it sent on a Southern tour when a vigilance committee came within a hair's breadth of lynching him in Marietta, South Carolina.[7] Later, William Howard Russell of the London *Times* got into an ugly scrape with authorities in Memphis when they learned that Theodore R. Davis, the artist accompanying him, was a Yankee representing *Harper's Weekly*. The *Tribune* was accounted more dangerous than any of these. A Texas sedition law rendered it a felony to receive the paper.[8] Southern postmasters returned it stamped "Undeliverable." (One resourceful lady finally achieved delivery of the *Tribune* to her son in the South by pasting the *Herald's* nameplate on top.) A grand jury in Warrenton, Virginia, returned indictments against local subscribers. A Georgia editor invited Horace Greeley to visit "the land you have lied and re-lied on" in verses ending pleasantly:

> You can lower you chin, and open your mouth,
> While your neck strains the rope you are tied on.

How, then, was the *Tribune* running so much exclusive news from Charleston?

Other matters relating to the imminent dissolution of the United States excited the young men at Pfaff's. Tempers flared. George Arnold, whose burlesques of war correspondence under the name "McAroni" would be a feature in *Vanity Fair*, posed as one of "the chivalry" defending the Southern cause, whereupon Walt Whitman got into a fight with him. Like the millionaires behind gleaming bronze doorplates on

[7] *Herald*, Dec. 30, 1860 *et seq.*
[8] *Tribune*, Aug. 1, 1860.

8

Fifth Avenue, like the secondhand-clothing barkers on Chatham Street, the Germans playing dominoes in the lager gardens of the Bowery, the stevedores on Water Street, the "pretty waiter girls" in the concert saloons of Broadway, the hated Irish in their festering hovels at Five Points, and the million other souls who lived within sight of Trinity steeple, Pfaffians were exposed increasingly to the clamor of a world beyond their ken. Something like a revolution was afoot in the realm of journalism, a revolution that would lift these light-hearted pranksters from their subterranean retreat and whirl them in its vortex. Soon O'Brien, Aldrich, Thomson, Williams, and Stedman, together with others in Clapp's happy coterie—Charles G. Halpine (who stammered to fame at Pfaff's, speaking inadvertently of "H–H–Harriet Beseecher Bestowe"), William Conant Church, William Swinton, E. H. House, Charles Henry Webb, a couple of artists, Frank H. Bellew and Thomas Nast: in all more than half of the identifiable clientele at the Cave—would take the field along with hundreds of other youths of like mind to participate in the greatest undertaking in the history of journalism.

The news revolution, in fact, was already under way.

"The people of the interior," President Buchanan wrote apprehensively to James Gordon Bennett on the very day that South Carolina left the Union, "are kept in a constant state of excitement from what are called 'telegrams.' " [9] Editors themselves were perturbed, as if the wire, now that they were using it more freely, were somehow responsible for the dread news it carried. The Philadelphia *Morning Pennsylvanian*, among many others, thought the telegraph "a curse to the country." "We warn the people to beware of this new power in our midst, more potent than 'an army with banners.' Its whole stock in trade consists in the perpetual excitement of the community." The Erie *Weekly Gazette* had another caution: "Beware of this 'special correspondence' confidence game . . .

[9] Dec. 20, 1860. Quoted in James E. Pollard: *The Presidents and the Press* (New York: 1947), 298.

in the New York or Philadelphia journals. A safe plan is to *believe nothing* you find in a 'sensation' column, however seemingly well authenticated." [1]

There was ample justification for these forebodings. As word came of state after state preparing to follow South Carolina out of the Union in anticipation of a Republican in the White House, of attempts to compromise the slavery issue dying in the last agonies of debate, of a new government rising in Montgomery, Alabama, of Federal installations all over the South falling into the hands of the rebels, of President-elect Lincoln making his way East through crowds of anxious well-wishers at every railroad station, the press began dispensing news, rumors, false reports, and speculations on a scale that left men confounded.

When Major Robert Anderson, U.S.A., spiked the guns of Fort Moultrie and moved his small garrison of regulars out to the more defensible Fort Sumter in the middle of Charleston harbor, the New York *Herald* devoted its entire front page to that electrifying news alone, background stories on Anderson, the forts, the garrison, and two of the Harper brothers' woodcuts going in with the telegraphic dispatches. In January, when Buchanan sent the *Star of the West* to reinforce him, a New York *Evening Post* reporter went along as a stowaway; his account of her voyage, climaxing with the shots that forced her to turn back, was reprinted on every hand. The New York *Times* sent "Jasper"—George Salter, a young New York physician who had been raised in Charleston—to bring its readers word-pictures of the scene as Charleston prepared to blast Anderson and the last vestige of Federal authority from its harbor. Undercover men from the New York *World*, the *Tribune*, the *Evening Post*, the Baltimore *American*, and the Philadelphia *Press* arrived as the tension mounted. Eugene Benson and William Waud, artists "on the spot" for *Frank Leslie's Illustrated Newspaper*, filled pages

[1] Howard C. Perkins: *Northern Editorials on Secession* (New York: 1942), II, 1047, 1049. Perkins prints many such alarums.

with pictures of the city and the forts; *Harper's Weekly* and the *New York Illustrated News* kept pace. Everyone who could read knew by the middle of February that the brick walls of Sumter were eight feet thick, that the Major and his garrison numbered scarcely a hundred, counting workmen and members of the band, and that the fire-eaters in Charleston and Montgomery had decided at last to wait until Lincoln was inaugurated to renew their demands that the flag be lowered and the fort evacuated.

Anderson, a quiet Kentuckian whose chief concern in moving to Fort Sumter had been to get as far from the Carolinians as possible without yielding to them, found himself catapulted to fame—"Our Bob," probably the first American to become a folk hero literally overnight. The *World* compared him to Leonidas at Thermopylæ; "Jasper" interviewed his wife, shopping on King Street; *Harper's Weekly* ran woodcuts of everything from his cot to his candlestick. The good Major was astonished that "the papers are making so much of my position here. . . . I receive, nearly by every mail, letters of sympathy, and many of them from strangers." [2]

Reporting that wakened such a response was a new factor in American life. For four years it would bring home to millions the drama and heartache of the Civil War, raise problems which no government had faced before, and lead to basic changes in the social function of the press. Men of the sort who had laughed away the nights at Pfaff's Cave had work to do.

2. MEET MR. DANA

THE NATION's information system radiated from a small area bordering City Hall Park, the busiest part of New York. Here were ensconced those titans of newspaperdom, Greeley, Raymond, Bennett. Here were published the only eight-page dailies in the United States. Here alone, Senators and solons

[2] *Times*, Jan. 4, 1861.

found they must call on the press; the mountain would not go to Mahomet.[3] In Washington, *Harper's Weekly* observed, the people "actually look to the New York papers for news of their own city." The *Times*, *Tribune*, and *Herald* maintained daily home delivery there. In Philadelphia, the *Inquirer* complained that this trio "literally carries New York over every railway, sets it down at every station, and extends it everywhere." In Albany, Samuel Wilkeson sold his interest in the *Evening Journal* in 1859 in the belief that "the three great dailies of New York would ultimately destroy the newspaper business in the interior of the state." In Charleston, the *Mercury* fumed that "we have to go to the New York papers for news of our own affairs." In Cincinnati, Murat Halstead recalled, he would get the New York papers off the 1:00 a.m. train, then run to the office to slice them up for waiting printers so the *Commercial* could go to press. "From the *Herald*" or "From the *Tribune*" at the head of an article in such journals left no reader in doubt; the practice of reprinting from these two was so common that "New York" was taken for granted.

A dingy little building on the corner of Broad and Wall streets housed the only formal news network in the country, the New York Associated Press. Here, amid clacking telegraph instruments, half a dozen manifolders copied the dispatches in longhand for delivery by runner to each of the city's newspapers. At a second row of battered oak desks, another crew sifted the incoming wires and scanned the local papers to make up the skimpy twice-daily news budget for the rest of the country. "A very large majority of outside papers," Daniel H. Craig, General Agent of the Associated Press, assured the stockholders even after the war began, "require only very brief reports." [4] Craig had some fifty agents posted around the country to cull "outside" papers for news,

---

[3] Amos J. Cummings: "How Newspapers Are Made," *Packard's Monthly*, I (Nov. 1868), 108.

[4] *Annual Report of the General Agent, N.Y. Associated Press, for 1861*, 9.

plus a few full-time reporters and two bureaus, in Washington and Albany. The organization was owned by the seven leading papers of New York, and it was protected from competition by a five-year contract, signed in 1860, with the American Telegraph Company and the Western Union Company, providing special rates in exchange for a guarantee of all its telegraph business as well as that of its members. But the Associated Press was not the only reason for New York's dominance.

On the northeast corner of Nassau and Spruce streets squatted "an immense dry-goods box, surmounted by a flag-staff." THE TRIBUNE, in enormous block letters of gilt, was all that caught the eye, save rows of windows so be-grimed with soot that staffers habitually raised them to read the City Hall clock.

One day in February 1861 a lightly bearded, handsome young correspondent named Albert Deane Richardson, fresh from the gold fields of Colorado and adventures with Kit Carson in New Mexico, went in the Spruce Street entrance of this Rookery, as staffers called it, and ascended the circular iron stair for the first time. The place reeked of ink and sweat, chemicals and scorched paper. Charles Craske, as Richardson would discover later, was conducting some mysterious stereotyping experiments on the top floor. From the third floor came a low bumble: "num-num-num-*tuition*, num-num-num-*catation*, num; num-num-*olition*, num-num . . . "—the everlasting ode of the proofreader. A tri-colored sign stared at the newcomer from an iron door: EDITORIAL ROOMS OF THE TRIBUNE. RING THE BELL.

A face appeared in the grated window, the door opened, and the *Tribune's* Western corespondent made his way among a dozen small green desks in the map-plastered city room to a gate in a ground-glass partition. This gave admittance to what appeared to be "a lurking place for owls." Apple peel, clippings and crumpled paper, bits of tobacco and dried paste littered the floor. Three cases of reference works, a dozen ink-spattered desks, a row of gas burners with their shades askew, and, banked under the windows beneath signs reading: *This File MUST Not Be Mutilated*, dusty volumes of the weekly, semi-weekly, and daily editions—this was the main editorial room.[5]

Here, the stranger must remind himself, was published the most influential newspaper in the United States; here was Mecca for thousands across the land. They came daily, during the afternoon visiting hours, hoping for a glimpse of Greeley's fabled white coat. On Thursdays they would line a balcony rail in the cavernous, hissing basement to marvel as ten blue-shirted pressmen, ranged in tiers around the type-revolving drum of a Hoe Lightning that towered thirty-four feet from the floor—"the fastest newspaper press in the world"—rolled off the weekly edition at twenty thousand impressions an hour all through the day. That was a sight more suggestive of the *Tribune's* glory, but our man did not see it, nor did he see Greeley: the editor was off on a lecture tour. Richardson waited on the managing editor, Mr. Charles Anderson Dana.

Dana sat at his desk in an office off the editorial room, looked up, and went right on "going through a great pile of letters one a minute—some ruthlessly thrown in the waste-basket; others, with a lightning pencil stroke, to indicate the type and style of printing, placed on a pile for the composing room. Two or three glances appeared to decide the fate of each . . . while he kept up a running conversation." Richardson's later rendition of it, faintly suggestive of the novels then in vogue, went this way:

"I received your letter," said Dana. "Are you going to New Orleans?"

"Not unless you send me."

"I suppose you know it is rather precarious business?"

5 Drawn largely from Cummings, *op. cit.*, and James Parton: *The Life of Horace Greeley* (New York: 1855), 403, *passim*.

"Oh, yes."

"Two of our correspondents have come home within the last week, after narrow escapes. We have still six in the South; and it wouldn't surprise me, this very hour, to receive a telegram announcing the imprisonment or death of any one of them."

"I have thought about all that, and decided," said Richardson. "How long shall I stay?"

"While the excitement lasts, if possible." The managing editor leaned back in his chair. "Do you know how long you *will* stay? You will be back here some fine morning in just about two weeks." [6]

There is a ring of authenticity in that parting shot: that was Mr. Dana talking.

The first managing editor to hold that title in American journalism, Dana set a pattern of behavior since emulated by many an "m.e." of fact and fiction. Blunt, decisive, by turns profane and charming, a Brook Farm idealist annealing into a man of the world after years of exposure to Greeley's irascible ways and the bitter disillusionment of a trip to Europe during the revolutions of 1848, he ran the paper with an iron hand. On more than one occasion he had thrown out Greeley's abstractions from Washington to make way for news—once for a divorce story. It was the talk down in Pfaff's that he edited Greeley's editorials as well, and the *Sunday Mercury* hinted that he had been known to veto them. [7]

Walt Whitman had seen him often, striding across the park from his quarters at 90 Clinton Place on his way to the office:

A straight, trim-built, prompt, vigorous man, well-dressed with strong brown hair, beard and moustache, and a quick, watchful eye. He steps alertly by, watching everybody . . . a man of rough, strong intellect,

[6] Albert D. Richardson: *The Secret Service, the Field, the Dungeon, and the Escape* (Hartford: 1865), 19.
[7] Issue of Feb. 24, 1861.

tremendous prejudices fully relied on, and excellent intentions.[8]

Dana once defined a managing editor: "a being to whom the sentiment of remorse is unknown." One of his men began a battle dispatch later: "To God Almighty be the glory! Mine eyes have seen the work of the Lord and the cause of the righteous hath triumphed." Dana wrote him one sentence: "Hereafter, in sending your reports, please specify the number of the hymn and save telegraph expenses."[9]

In appearance, the newspaper for which this man was responsible was no more prepossessing than its office. The front page was solid with advertisements. Pages two and three, six and seven, were loaded with "time" copy—essays and verse and book reviews mingling indiscriminately with letters from various special correspondents at home and abroad—for newspapers could print but one side of a sheet at a time, and this was "the first run." Page four was devoted to editorials; they were set, significantly, in larger type than the news dispatches. The main news page, opposite them in the center spread, was dominated by a standing headline long since discarded by other papers as superfluous:

THE LATEST NEWS
RECEIVED BY
MAGNETIC TELEGRAPH

Under this, in no perceptible order, were sundry items sent by its Washington men or the Associated Press. The chief news of the day came under "THE PRO-SLAVERY REBELLION," followed by quiet secondary heads. Adjoining was an account, "From Our Special Correspondent," of Lincoln's reception in Buffalo, offering brief glimpses of the President-elect through

[8] Emory Holloway and Ralph Adimari, eds.: *New York Dissected by Walt Whitman* (New York: 1936), 132.
[9] William A. Croffut: *An American Procession 1855–1914: A Personal Chronicle of Famous Men* (Boston: 1931), 265.

a torrent of verbiage about the reception. ("When he shakes hands, he does it with a hearty will, in which his whole body joins.") Under a Washington date line appeared the daily indictment of Buchanan by James Shepherd Pike, a redoubtable editorialist: "It is dreadful to have such a loose-jointed, decaying piece of mortality at the helm of state at such a time as this." Alongside a column of local items came a long verbatim report of debates in Congress.

The impression one might gather was that of a rather haphazard potpourri, seasoned with considerable pamphleteering. Yet there were characteristics, as steady readers came to know, that made the *Tribune* unique. The paper seemed to suggest that its readers were as sophisticated as its editors, and that they shared the world between them. Along with this sense of intimacy and a relatively high literary standard, another attribute came to be distinctive. "FIGHT was the word from the start; FIGHT has been the word ever since; FIGHT is the word this day!" James Parton exulted. Backed by Greeley's willingness to give battle for a cause, his broad humanitarianism, and his remarkable talent for getting himself on newsprint, the paper's fighting qualities kindled something like personal devotion. The *Tribune* was scarcely a newspaper in 1861; it was an article of faith. Fanny Fern, writing of the tattered street vendor who declined to part with his copy for a dollar because "I ain't read it yet," E. L. Godkin, considering it "an institution more like the *Comédie Française* than anything I have known in the journalistic world," Bayard Taylor, writing that "the *Tribune* is next to the Bible all through the West," were testifying, each in his way, to a measure of prestige and influence no mere newspaper ever achieved.

Already the myth of Horace Greeley, the moralist in shining armor, the poor Vermont boy with a hatful of type who had worked hard and lived right and made good, the homely philosopher, the eccentric personality, the national oracle, towered almost frighteningly over the man himself. "His entrance into a tavern, much more into a lecture hall, raises gratulating shouts," Ralph Waldo Emerson wrote, "and I could scarcely keep the people quiet to hear my abstractions, they were so furious to shout Greeley! Greeley! Greeley! Catch me carrying Greeley into my lecture again! . . . I had as lief travel with . . . Barnum." [1]

People thought Greeley still edited the *Tribune*, and every word that went into it—"including shipping news," Charles Congdon added wryly. But the *Tribune*, with 212 employees, including twenty-eight editors and reporters in 1861, was no more pure Greeley than was the myth he had become. "The paper would probably have suffered from his want of education and general knowledge," said Godkin, "if he had not surrounded himself with writers who made ample amends for his defects." That was Greeley's forte—attracting to his Rookery men of talent, and creating an atmosphere in which they thrived; yet, in a sense, he was their prisoner. It was his staff, under the direction of his managing editor, which had kept the *Tribune* relentlessly crusading against the extension of slavery. Greeley wavered. Go easy on the South, he begged Dana in 1857; and for the Republican nomination in 1860 he had given his support to Edward Bates of Missouri, a former slaveholder, a moderate man. But the columns of the *Tribune* bristled with allusions like "the Land of Legree and the Home of the Slave," items on runaways and slave auctions culled from the Southern press, indictments of human bondage by *Tribune* men like Pike in Washington, William S. Robinson in Boston, Samuel Wilkeson, George Ripley, Sydney Howard Gay in the office, and the witty Congdon, penning editorials in his book-lined study in Quincy, Massachusetts—men who lived to destroy slavery, root and branch. "I never opened the paper in those days without a terror as to what they might make me say after eleven o'clock at night," Greeley confessed later. [2]

[1] Ralph L. Rusk, ed.: *The Letters of Ralph Waldo Emerson* (New York: 1939), V, 56.
[2] John Russell Young: *Men and Memories* (New York: 1901), 115.

Their loyalty was not to Greeley's politics, but to his ideal of journalism. "I had rather write for the *Tribune*," Congdon wrote Gay once regarding more lucrative work, "than for all the d——d magazines in creation." Such men gave superb implementation to Greeley's credo: that the newspaper must provide American society with leadership—moral, political, artistic, and intellectual leadership—before anything else.

The news revolution had not gone wholly unnoticed in the Rookery. For years Greeley and Dana had shared a green-carpeted office overlooking the square. One day in 1854, as if in premonition that the managing editor's day would come, Greeley had moved to a more secluded part of the building, leaving Dana in practical command. Gradually "the Prince Regent," as Congdon called him, had taken over.

Now Dana was bent on exposing every facet of the secession crisis in *Tribune* terms. The gossips at Pfaff's need not have worried: there was nothing fake about the *Tribune's* correspondence from Charleston. Dana had chosen Charles D. Brigham—"a subtle and utterly unprincipled rascal," according to Sam Wilkeson—for the assignment and sent him down there in disguise in the third week of November. Brigham, a forty-two-year-old upstate New Yorker and former editor of the Troy *Whig*, may have been a rascal, but he seems to have had a remarkably good nervous system.

The Charleston papers alternately doubted his existence and demanded his scalp. Vigilance committees were alerted, suspects arrested and hustled out of town. In the lobby of the Charleston Hotel, Captain Amos Colt, helpfully arranging arms shipments for the Carolinians, was accused of being the *Tribune* correspondent; a glove was whipped across his face, and a fight ensued. Notices appeared on the doors of a bank on Broad Street, calling on the populace to unmask the *Tribune* man and "administer tar and feathers." The *Mercury* spoke hopefully of a lynching. Brigham responded with a little game of hide-and-seek. "If the *Mercury* is really curious as to my whereabouts," he wrote, "let him look into one of the big guns of Fort Sumter. He may find me there." Such taunts spiced every letter. On several occasions Brigham offered minute observations of the weather and the position of ships in the harbor as proof that he was still there. On others, he thanked prominent Charlestonians by name for unwitting help in providing information. The game had many variations —Dana had used it in reporting a secret Know-Nothing convention years before—and every *Tribune* man in the South played it for all it was worth. From Milledgeville, Georgia, came one correspondent's explanation that "circumstances over which I had no control" had prevented him from writing: he was sharing a hotel room with a red-hot secessionist. From New Orleans came Richardson's variations on the theme: "The *Crescent* is exercised at the presence here of 'correspondents of northern papers, who indict real falsehoods and lies as coolly as they would eat dinner at the St. Charles.' The *Crescent's* rhetoric is a little limping, but its watchfulness and patriotism are above all praise. The matter should certainly be attended to." Illuminating as many of these letters were, *Tribune* readers at times got the impression that all the Southern excitement revolved around a serialized spy hunt for *Tribune* men.

In February, Brigham fell into the hands of the Charleston police. While a crowd milled outside headquarters, he was questioned for twelve hours by Governor Pickens and others in the belief that he was an agent for the Federal government. Brigham said nothing to disillusion them—a government spy's life was safer than a *Tribune* man's. They gave him a couple of hours to get out of town. If Brigham tarried that long, it was not by choice. "We remember he described the creeping pace of the train that bore him away," a *Tribune* editorial recalled, "and how like water—like water innocuous—was the flask of brandy that he drank the first forty miles. . . ." [3]

Dana's response was to forward reinforcements. By this time he already had Thomas Butler Gunn, an Englishman

[3] *Tribune*, Dec. 11, 1861; and see Richardson, 122 ff.

thoroughly grateful for his British accent, and another man on the scene; but as the inauguration of Lincoln approached, Dana must have three men in Charleston. These and other *Tribune* men in the South sported blue secession cockades in their lapels, wrote in an elaborate code Dana had devised, and addressed their material to New York banks and commercial houses which had agreed to serve as fronts.

The *Tribune* ran more Southern correspondence than any other newspaper during the winter of secession. Perhaps, as Dana decoded it and scrawled "leaded brevier" across the pages before ringing the bell that would send them rattling up the chute to the composing room, he reflected on the state of affairs that made it precarious for a man from one part of the American republic to enter the other. The *Tribune*, the files in the other room would show, had played no small part in bringing it about.

But it is a lot more likely that Dana allowed himself a smile or two at the beating he was giving a rival down the street.

3. MEET MR. HUDSON

AT NASSAU and Fulton streets, the gas jets burned late in the little room on the southeast corner of the third floor. Frederic Hudson was mobilizing "the electric moving paper of the age" for the war he was positive would come. Letters went out enlisting men all over the South as contributors at space rates. New staff men were hired. "Not enough room for writers and reporters," Hudson noted in his diary that January. "Took in another room for them. Ought to buy Barnum's Museum for the *Herald*." [4] Hudson was organizing a "Southern Bureau" in the office to clip and file every scrap that came to hand about the seceded states. He was reading Theodore Dwight's ponderous *History of the Hartford Convention* for background on secession.

[4] Hudson diary, 1861: MS in possession of his granddaughter, Mrs. Wesley P. Wilmot, Concord, Mass.

If Hudson lacked the color and forcefulness of his opposite number on the *Tribune*, he was more than a match for him in efficiency, and at least his equal in editorial acumen. One day in 1851 he had met Dana for the first time and set down a laconic appraisal in his diary: "Mr. Dana is what might be called a scholar. He is full of all the isms of the *Tribune*." Hudson knew no isms save journalism. "To manage a paper properly one must work steadily and perseveringly," another entry noted. "There is no let-up, no rest, no play that is not mixed up with business."

Every day at precisely 9:30 a.m., Sundays and holidays included, Hudson mounted the two stone steps from his home at 56 East Twenty-second Street to the sidewalk, immaculate in his blue jacket with brass buttons, French boots, and shiny black stovepipe hat, and headed for the *Herald*. Coming home at four, he was off to the office again at eight, not to return until past midnight. "In all matters relating to the *Herald* he is a walking file, talking proof-copy and automaton index," a contemporary wrote. "He remembers with affection the name and address of every housemaid who has advertised in its columns since the date of its inception." Tall and slender, with a melancholy droop to his mustache, he was a man apart. "He never attended a political meeting," his brother Edward testified. "Never voted. Had no political prejudices." He joined no church, no club; he knew no hobbies. Mild and polite of manner, Hudson devoted himself with manic single-mindedness to implementing James Gordon Bennett's dream of publishing the biggest, sauciest, newsiest newspaper the world had ever seen.

"Much as Bennett was the *Herald* and the *Herald* Bennett, we who know understand very distinctly that Hudson was the *Herald* too," one of his reporters wrote; "yet he will go down unhonored in the next generation as he was unsung in this." Hudson had no regrets. He took his ten thousand dollars a year, by far the highest salary in the business, and left the notoriety to his idol. Later he would write the first history of American journalism (for which Bennett paid him six thousand dollars) with scarcely a reference to himself in more than seven hundred pages. Considering that the man was one of the founders of the Associated Press, its chief executive officer for a quarter-century, the "chief editor" of the largest American daily, the "head and front of journalism" to Henry Watterson, and to Samuel Bowles one "who did more than any other man to organize and stimulate the collection of news," such modesty seems a little perverse. Hudson could be perverse in other ways. He could never understand, he said, "why anyone could conceive Mr. Bennett to have anything Mephistophilean about him," a remark that put him in a class by himself.[5]

Almost any New Yorker could recite highlights in the life of James Gordon Bennett, for he had had a special knack in his earlier days for lively autobiography. Starting as "one poor man against the world" in a broken-down job shop in 1835, he had literally shocked the city into taking his paper, and the city hated him for it. One of his first big stories concerned the murder of a prostitute, which he exploited for weeks. He had gone in for "spicy" society scandal, allegedly for black-mailing purposes. He was assaulted on the street on at least four occasions by those who had felt his scathing pen, each time turning out a puckish account of the affray that set the whole town talking about him again. Everyone knew the hoary old Scot once had walked the Wall Street beat himself, gathering material for what would become the first reliable financial news; that he had announced his marriage in a florid confession of love on the front page of the *Herald*; that he had been burned out, thrashed, denounced by the Archbishop of his own church ("devilish holy, us Roman Catholics," he leered), boycotted in a "moral" war—an eagle-beaked old curmudgeon with crossed eyes and a thick Scottish burr who had beaten them all.

[5] Woodward Hudson: *Fragmentary Chronicles of Frederic and Eliza Woodward Hudson*, I. (MS in the possession of Mrs. Wilmot.) Hudson is best described in print in the New York *Leader*, May 7, 1859.

Bennett, sixty-five now and living luxuriously at Fort Washington, no longer came to the office every day; when he did, it would likely be to rap some hapless editorial writer on the knuckles and thunder: "What the de'il made ye talk in that way? Dinna ye ken that sich talk will bring the hoos about yer ears? Noo, sit doon, and I'll show ye how to write on that subject." [6]

The old man had taught Hudson years before what he wanted, and let him have his head. Bennett gave the *Herald* its flavor; Hudson gave it substance. The result contradicted the *Tribune* and all its works. It was not simply that the *Herald* generally tagged along with the Democrats while the *Tribune* spoke for rabid Republicans, nor that they were at opposite poles on slavery and almost everything else. Bennett and Greeley, each professing to publish the great American newspaper, had opposite conceptions of what a newspaper should be. Principles were sacred to Greeley's paper. "The *Tribune*," he said, "would rather be right than popular." Bennett might have reversed the statement. If the *Herald* cared about any principle, it was not discernible to the naked eye. None of its Northern critics, and they were legion, hit so close to the mark as the New Orleans *Picayune*: "The *Herald* may be said to represent, in one particular, the genius of the 'universal Yankee nation'—that is, in its supreme regard for what is vulgarly called the main chance."

One of Hudson's visitors to the office in January was Henry Wikoff, a rank impostor who had bilked, on two continents, victims ranging from Fanny Ellsler, the danseuse, to Lord Palmerston. Hudson welcomed him: Wikoff would prove useful in due course. To report on Lincoln in Springfield and accompany him East, the eye for the main chance fell on a sturdy young German immigrant rejected by other editors as not up to the job. Hudson not only hired Henry Villard, he gave him *carte blanche*, permitting him to write tart rebut-

6 Robert Waters: *Career and Conversation of John Swinton* (Chicago: 1902), 29.

tals to *Herald* editorials in his Lincoln dispatches. Villard, the editor knew, had covered the Lincoln-Douglas debates for a a German-American paper two years before, and there was always the chance that his friendly dispatches would win him the inside track with the President-elect.

The main chance was not so evident in the wisdom of running a tedious history of the anti-slavery agitation day after day in the *Herald* during February, but it was almost certainly there. The gratified author was Felix Gregory De Fontaine, a French nobleman's son lately removed from New York to Charleston, and a friend of another gentleman of French descent, Pierre Gustave Toutant Beauregard.[7]

4. "CIVIL WAR HAS AT LAST BEGUN"

AT HALF past one on March 4, 1861 Abraham Lincoln stood on a wooden platform on the east front of the Capitol before a multitude variously estimated by reporters at from thirty thousand to one hundred thousand persons.

"The power confided in me," the high, clear voice said, "will be used to hold, occupy, and possess the property and places belonging to the government."

The tone of the inaugural address was otherwise so conciliatory that editors were inclined to discount such a statement. What, then, would Lincoln do about Fort Sumter, the bastion that the press had done so much to make a symbol?

Hudson had three men in his Washington bureau who already knew Lincoln: Villard; Simon P. Hanscom, the bureau chief, who had written Lincoln chatty letters during the campaign and worked for his election; and Stephen R. Fiske, a lad of twenty, who had accompanied the new President on the last leg of the trip to Washington, only to be locked in a hotel room in Harrisburg on the night that Lincoln made his

---

[7] Article on De Fontaine by John D. Wade, *Dictionary of American Biography*.

famous secret departure to avert foul play in Baltimore. Hanscom caught the first cue from Lincoln, Fiske the second.

Pierce and Buchanan had been ruled by their advisers. The almost universal belief that this system would continue under Lincoln—shared by Thurlow Weed, the wily New York political manager, and Secretary of State Seward, who regarded themselves as the likeliest wielders of power in the new administration—found expression in a *Herald* editorial just before the inauguration, predicting that "Seward will be the master spirit of the incoming Administration."

To correct this misapprehension, Lincoln turned to the *Herald* men he knew. "It is stated in Presidential circles," Hanscom wired on the day of the inauguration, "that Mr. Lincoln will inaugurate a new system in regard to cabinet consultations. . . . Mr. Lincoln has plainly intimated that he will, after having consulted with it, take the responsibility of carrying out his own line of policy irrespective of their opinions."

That night Hanscom sent young Fiske to cover the inaugural ball. Congratulating the President after his evening of handshaking, the youngster asked him if there was any special news he would like to send to Mr. Bennett. Fiske remembered it years later:

" 'Yes,' he replied, looking at me significantly, 'you may tell him that Thurlow Weed has found out that Seward was not nominated at Chicago.' " [8]

These intimations scarcely sounded as if Lincoln would sit back and let others make his decisions for him, but the press lost them in a maze of rumor and report. What little liaison existed between Lincoln and the Washington reporters vanished in the office-seekers' rush.

The nation must have news, and Dana's men were hot on the trail. Pike wired the *Tribune* on March 10 that Fort Sumter would be evacuated. He had learned that old Winfield

[8] Rufus Rockwell Wilson, ed.: *Lincoln Among His Friends* (Caldwell, Idaho: 1942), 311.

"Civil War Has at Last Begun"

Scott had advised it. A *Herald* man sent a similar report, but added a revealing note as to sources: no one could give "positive authority" for it, but the evacuation report "obtained general currency and was eagerly discussed in the hotels." L. A. Gobright, bureau chief of the Associated Press, jumped to the same conclusion on learning that Anderson's provisions were running out. (Eventually Gobright made a last-ditch attempt to learn the true Sumter policy by sending a note to a member of the Cabinet in an envelope marked "NOT an application for office.")

James E. Harvey, the *Tribune's* number-two man, counted himself more fortunate in the matter of connections. A veteran of twenty years in the press corps and active in Washington society, Harvey knew intimately both Seward and Simon Cameron, the sly old fox of Pennsylvania politics who was Secretary of War. After a chat with Cameron he wired the *Tribune* on March 17 that "the Cabinet . . . with one exception, approve the judgment of General Scott and yield to it as a necessity that cannot be avoided." But Harvey pointed out in his opening paragraph that, as Cameron had told him, the decision was Lincoln's alone. Others either did not believe that, or thought they could read the President's mind in the hotel lobbies. On March 20 the A.P. had it that "an order has already gone forward" to abandon the fort. On March 23 a *Herald* sleuth wired that the President had issued an order directing Anderson to leave.

Such reports continued right up to April 6, the day Lincoln finally reached the agonizing conclusion that if the United States government was not to acknowledge complete loss of authority, an attempt must be made to provision Fort Sumter. Harvey found out about it from Seward the same day, and the *Tribune* set forth the plan under fourteen decks of headlines on Monday, April 8. But that day's *Herald* repeated that the fort would be evacuated. So did "Observer" in the *Times*: "This point is now no longer doubtful."

In *Harper's Weekly* there appeared a cartoon of "Mr.

27

Jones, who . . . takes all the papers, and reads them thoroughly." Mr. Jones was pictured, papers strewn at his feet, slumped in his armchair in a coma.

Mr. Jones of the North was not the only victim. These confusing reports, relayed all over the South, fostered the tragic illusion in Southern minds that they had been tricked when on April 8 Lincoln's emissary notified Governor Pickens of South Carolina that "an attempt will be made to supply Fort Sumter with provisions only."

Friday, April 12, 1861, dawned sunny in New York, with a stir of spring in the air. The City Hall and the *Tribune* and the big hotels on Broadway floated the Stars and Stripes in remembrance of the birthday of Henry Clay, dead these nine years. Strawberries were selling in Taylor's window on Broadway—the first of the season, from Louisiana. Here and there, knots of people idled outside the newspaper offices on Park Row. All day the wire from Charleston was still, and Washington dispatches in the evening papers only confirmed what the morning papers had said. Major Anderson had declined General Beauregard's ultimatum to withdraw.

In Charleston that morning General Beauregard's friend Felix Gregory De Fontaine made his way to the American Telegraph Company's office through streets gone mad, aware that the incredible thunder in his ears would echo in others for generations to come. Nothing could be sent; no trains were to leave town. George Salter of the *Times* watched the startling parabolas of fire in the gray light of dawn from his perch atop a cotton bale on the Alger pier. Returning to his hotel toward noon to write about it, he was interrupted by a bang on the door. "Ten rough customers armed with revolvers" escorted him to the city jail. The *Tribune* men lay low. The Associated Press, typically, had no one on hand—its man would arrive a few days late. All the other correspondents had either been expelled or gone home voluntarily long since. Far out in the harbor, B. S. Osbon of the *World* trained his glass on the grim brick walls that a nation had come to love. Strapped in the crosstrees of the *Harriet Lane*, he was as useless to his paper as the little relief fleet was to Anderson. "I have never been able either with word or pen to express my feelings," he wrote of the scene years later. "It seemed to me that the end of the world was about due."

Late in the afternoon the news embargo was lifted. W. H. Heiss, chief operator of the Charleston telegraph office and a loyal Union man, sounded his call letters to alert New York. De Fontaine and one other reporter whose story would go out as "the general report" waited, copy in hand. New York was ready. Heiss took De Fontaine's manuscript and went to work:

Charleston
April 12, 3 p.m.

New York Herald:

Civil War has at last begun. A terrible fight is at this moment going on between Fort Sumter and the fortifications by which it is surrounded. . . .

Breaches, to all appearances, are being made in the several sides [of Sumter] exposed to fire. Portions of the parapet have been destroyed. . . .

The soldiers are perfectly reckless of their lives, and at every shot jump upon the ramparts, observe the effect, and then jump down again, cheering. . . .

The excitement in the community is indescribable. With the very first boom of the gun, thousands rushed from their beds to the harbor front, and all day every available place has been thronged by ladies and gentlemen, viewing the solemn spectacle through their glasses. . . .[9]

[9] *A Treasury of Great Reporting* (New York: 1949) mistakenly credits this dispatch to Osbon, who was in no position to file it. See his biography by Albert Bigelow Paine: *A Sailor of Fortune* (New York: 1906), 119 ff., the New York *Herald* of Apr. 13, 1861, which credits its special correspondent, and the De Fontaine article cited, *D.A.B.*

☼ CHAPTER II ☼

Mr. Warren Calls the Tune

1. The Man from the Burlington "Hawkeye"

Newspapers, H. L. Mencken once observed, are so busy keeping up with today that they are half a century behind times. There are metropolitan editors who still write "minion" and "brevier" to indicate type size, nomenclature that was formally abolished by the printing industry in favor of the point system before most of them were born. In the relentless plodding of day after day and forever, the evolution of headlines, of reporting techniques, of newspaper style, like the ever broadening concept of news itself, has been so painfully slow that a man turning consecutive pages in a hundred-year file is scarcely conscious of progress from one hour of turning to the next.

But even the Mississippi has rapids, far up in its headwaters; and some of them are turbulent.

The Metropolitan Police had to barricade the streets and reroute traffic when Hudson got the *Herald* presses rolling with news of Major Anderson's surrender early on the morning of April 14, 1861. They continued rolling until one o'clock that afternoon, turning out 135,600 copies—"the largest issue of any newspaper that has ever been printed."

All newsdom was in ferment. Even Richardson's miraculous

reappearance—he arrived on April 17, having taken the last train to leave Richmond for the North—could have won no more than passing notice at the *Tribune* office. Dana announced that day that the *Tribune* would publish an evening edition throughout the war. Five days later the *Herald* countered with afternoon editions, issued thenceforth at one thirty, three o'clock, and four thirty daily. The extra became part of everyday life, the *Express* appearing so often that it was said at Pfaff's that no one had ever seen its regular edition. Even in Boston, old Dr. Oliver Wendell Holmes had a friend who sneaked down the side streets on his way to get the noon extra—"he is so afraid someone will *tell* him the news he wishes to *read,* first on the bulletin board, and then in the great capitals and leaded type of the newspaper."

The *Tribune,* the *Times,* the Chicago *Tribune,* and the Boston *Herald* launched Sunday editions within a few weeks of one another in April and May, invading a field which the sacrilegious Bennett had been able to keep virtually to himself for twenty years. Greeley snapped to a protesting clergyman that the public would no longer be denied; the Hudson River and the New Haven railroads instituted special Sunday newspaper expresses, and crowds awaited them at every station. On May 1 the Associated Press moved into larger headquarters, a five-story brownstone at 175 Broadway. And Craske solved his problems in the nick of time: two days before Sumter, the *Tribune* was able to announce that it was the first newspaper printed from curved stereotype plates, cast from a wet papier-mâché mold which was first placed over the type forms and "beaten with a hairbrush." (With somewhat different weapons and a dry matrix, Craske's process is in universal use today.) By casting duplicates, runs could now be made on all three presses at once. The *Herald* mastered the process on July 8; the *Times* was next, three weeks later. ("The daily papers have taken to boasting that everything they print is stereotyped," said Henry Clapp; "we thought this fact had been patent from the beginning.")

Mr. Warren Calls the Tune

For a managing editor, it was something like Judgment Day. The news erupted in "great capitals and leaded type." Lincoln called for seventy-five thousand volunteers; Virginia seceded; the Sixth Massachusetts, on its way to the relief of the undefended capital, was stoned in a bloody riot in the streets of Baltimore; New York's beloved Seventh marched off amid pandemonium on Broadway, Fitz-James O'Brien recording every step for the *Times*; a hundred thousand persons greeted Major Anderson at a rally on Union Square; the Washington line was cut, and "reliable gentlemen" brought reports that Fort McHenry was bombarding Baltimore, and that "Jeff Davis is at the head of an army on the way North." As John W. Forney would thunder to his managing editor later in the war, "When you and I consider that now is the time for *news* in great papers, it cannot be the time for essays." The leisurely days when one might edit with an eye for literary niceties and philosophical disputation were gone. How would the *Tribune* fare in the new era?

For all the extra editions it issued, the Rookery had not changed much yet. Perhaps an old office, well loved, has a refractory effect on its denizens. Greeley and Dana went along serenely running news inside and advertising out; the most exciting paper in politics seemed to be the most conservative in journalism. There was another sign, more momentous, that the *Tribune* would go right on being the *Tribune*, come what may.

Pike and Harvey of the Washington office won appointments as ministers in the foreign service, Pike going to The Hague and Harvey to Portugal. The *Tribune* had shared Harvey with the Philadelphia *North American*, but for eleven years Pike had given Greeley the kind of Washington representative he wanted. A founder of the Republican party in Maine, Pike had remained active in politics there and in Washington, and his ringing letters to the *Tribune* had won a wide following. News revolution or no, Greeley must have a new Pike, and Dana went to Washington to hire one.

The candidate he selected was impressive: tall, with a formidable horselike face, commanding presence, and a tremendous bass voice. As a brigade commander later, Fitz Henry Warren spurned the practice of writing orders; he used his lungs to reach the entire brigade. Warren was volatile, explosive, "given to bitter recriminations against those who thwarted him." [1] "I do not forget a favor," Warren himself once wrote, "and I have the same tenacity for an injury." [2] In other respects, Warren appeared to fit Greeley's bill of particulars. He had been active in Iowa politics as a Republican of the militantly anti-slavery stamp; before that, he had been a Whig, serving as First Assistant Postmaster General in Taylor's administration; he was eloquent; he was a sturdy son of Massachusetts who had gone west to Burlington, Iowa, as a young man; and he had written for newspapers—as editor of the Burlington *Hawkeye*, and, as an occasional contributor, for the *Tribune*.

Along with dozens of others, Warren had received casual mention in the press as a Cabinet possibility. Lincoln offered him his old post, First Assistant Postmaster General. Possibly that nettled him; it was quite a come-down. Warren had just declined the appointment when Dana came along with his offer to make the *Hawkeye* graduate the most important reporter in town, chief correspondent of the New York *Tribune*, at a salary the *Tribune* boasted was "double that of an average Governor."

By the third week in May, men of Warren's mind were growing impatient. It had been almost six weeks since the flag had come down over Sumter, and no real blow had been struck to avenge the nation's honor. They were bringing pressure on the White House for action, as Charles Sumner told Governor Andrew of Massachusetts on May 24. These men—"Radicals," they were soon called—lived in continual

---

[1] Johnson Brigham: *Iowa: Its History and Its Foremost Citizens* (Des Moines: 1918), I, 370–2.

[2] To Simon Cameron, Nov. 26, 1861. Cameron Papers, MS Division, Library of Congress.

dread that Lincoln would not go far enough fast enough to exploit what they considered a heaven-sent opportunity to smash the Slavocracy and subjugate the South. Warren was one of them.

Only three days after the first raw troops had crossed the Potomac to Alexandria, Warren penned a hymn that would thrill millions harking to the voice of Horace Greeley. The real Greeley was not even in the office when it arrived, for he had cut his knee chopping trees on his farm at Chappaqua, and was convalescing there.[3] But here was Dana's meat, and he served it with plenty of lead:

TO RICHMOND! TO RICHMOND ONWARD!

WASHINGTON, May 27—There is quietness and subordination in Alexandria. . . . Mr. President, Lieutenant-General Scott, Messieurs Secretaries, when shall the bayonet flash to the 'Forward' of the Centurion of the conquering line? "Celebrate the Fourth of July there." Ah, God bless you and Amen, gentlemen, for the words. . . .

On to Richmond, then is the voice of the people. . . . Again, we repeat, On to Richmond! . . . Let her still sowing of the wind, have a generous harvest of the whirlwind, and let it be *now*. . . . To Richmond! To Richmond!

Not long afterward—the exact time is not clear—Warren was notified that the President would like to see him. The distance from the *Tribune's* Washington office on Fourteenth Street to the White House, as nearly as it can be calculated at this late date, was no more than three hundred yards, and one might think that any reporter would have negotiated that distance to check such a report. Not Mr. Warren. The day after sounding his battle cry, he wrote (in another connec-

[3] Jeter Allen Isley: *Horace Greeley and the Republican Party* (Princeton: 1947), 331.

tion) what might well have been taken as his answer: "If 'action, action, action' is the quality and sum of eloquence, 'cheek, cheek, cheek' is here the essential of all success."

Weeks passed, still with no action—and with a marked diminution of cheek. On June 21, Warren suddenly cut loose again, reporting that: "Our soldiers have been requested to fire blank cartridges in all engagements with Southern forces." The next day he set off an explosion:

> Shall I tell you, frankly and honestly, what I hear all around me and abroad? It is, that there is no intention to press this suppression of the rebellion—that the patience of the people is to be worn out by delay—that the soldier is to have his spirit wasted in the torpor and inaction of the camp, and when, at length, the nation are disgusted and outraged to a proper point, then we are to run after the old harlot of a compromise.

Secretary Seward issued a hot denial, but Warren was ready for that: "Let the Administration . . . break up the camps on the other side of the river, for an advance to Richmond, and the country will believe him, and discredit us." Warren's report of compromise had other repercussions, specifically in the bosom of his managing editor. The next day the *Tribune's* editorial page roared: "The Nation's War Cry: *Forward to Richmond! Forward to Richmond! The Rebel Congress must not be allowed to meet there on the 20th of July!* BY THAT DAY THE PLACE MUST BE HELD BY THE NATIONAL ARMY!"

Dana ran this flaming message under the *Tribune's* masthead on the editorial page every day for a week.[4]

During that week Fitz Henry Warren was reminded of Lincoln's desire to have a word with him. The Washington chief of the *Tribune* sent a message over to the White House.

[4] It is clear that Dana, not Greeley, was responsible. See Charles J. Rosebault: *When Dana Was the Sun* (New York: 1931), and Isley, 331.

Mr. Warren Calls the Tune

Mr. President:

It will be a pleasure to me, at any time, to have the honor of an interview with you, when you desire it. But a summons lately conveyed to me, to come to your residence, was of such a character in manner and expression, that I could not but consider it as unauthorized by you. With the publication that you could not receive visitors I have not felt myself at liberty to call unless especially invited, which considering my position I did not anticipate.[5]

It seems likely that Lincoln, upon reading this implication that the man representing the most influential paper in the country considered himself *persona non grata* at the White House, invited him to come at once. For on that same day Warren's tone changed abruptly in the dispatch he wrote for the *Tribune*: "Forward to Richmond," he said, was about to become an actuality! Not until the *next* day, June 29, came the Cabinet meeting at which the objection of General Scott to so hasty an advance was overruled, and approval given to the fateful plan to move against the enemy at Manassas. Clearly, Warren must have had inside information of a high order. Did Lincoln yield to *Tribune* pressure and tell Warren about the plan in order to mute that ear-splitting bugle before Congress convened six days hence?

The consensus of historians has been that Lincoln acceded to the general clamor of press and politicians. The indictment should be more specific, so far as the press is concerned. Many papers abstained from "clamor." The *Herald* accused the *Tribune* of "goading" the administration "into premature action." The *Times* was restrained. The *World*, an administration-supporter at this time, conducted a voluble campaign against the impatient, excoriating the *Tribune* daily

---

[5] Robert T. Lincoln Collection, MS Division, Library of Congress.

for "its crazy and bloodthirsty gasconade." Later Greeley himself acknowledged the *Tribune's* responsibility for what was to follow; there were others, but he knew that they were only echoing the cry that one man had raised.

The man from the Burlington *Hawkeye*, it appears, called the tune. Verily, verily, FIGHT was still the word for the *Tribune*.

2. THE RIGHT TO REPORT

LONG before Warren's "On to Richmond" campaign came to its climax, a struggle was developing between press and government on quite another front.

On the evening of Friday, April 19, Ben Poore of the Boston *Journal* and others met the Sixth Massachusetts, the first regiment to reach Washington, as it detrained near the depot. They collected details about its battle with a secessionist mob in Baltimore, and rushed for the telegraph office at the Willard Hotel. There a squad of National Rifles greeted them. There were to be no messages. The reporters hunted up Colonel Charles P. Stone, commander of the troops in Washington. Orders, he said, were orders. They drove to Seward's yellow mansion on Lafayette Square; suavely the Secretary of State bowed them in and offered refreshments. No, said Seward (whose favorite response to reporters was "If I didn't know, I'd tell you"), he had no idea who had issued the order, but it might be well for morale to keep the Baltimore riot quiet.

The Lincoln administration had stumbled into controlling the news almost inadvertently. Reporters discovered later that the riot had had nothing to do with it. Colonel Stone had seized some steamers loaded with flour which he suspected was destined for the Confederate quartermaster's depot across the river, and had persuaded the War Department to silence the wires until he could round up the conspirators. Such was the haphazard beginning of the first formal news censorship in the United States.[6]

Further rioting in Baltimore cut the wire anyway, but when it was restored the newsmen found censors from the War Department on hand—again the incidental result of an order with another end in view. Secretary Cameron had deputized young Thomas A. Scott, vice-president of the Pennsylvania Railroad, to take charge of the telegraph lines as far as Annapolis in order to direct troop transportation.[7] Scott's orders did not refer to censorship, but with control of the lines in his hands and much of the reporters' copy giving details about the troop movements for which he was responsible, he found himself deciding what a nation "raging for news," in the *Tribune's* words, should be told.

Tom Scott's agents instantly antagonized the Washington newsmen. At first the censors threw out entire dispatches that contained a single censorable fact; later they cut them and sent the gibberish that was left without showing it to the senders. "A more stupidly, ill-judged proceeding," a *Times* man choked in ungrammatical rage, "could scarcely be imagined." Already, as he noted on April 28, the chronic dilemma of censorship had appeared—the War Department agents were beginning "to suppress reflections upon the administration of the government" as information of value to the enemy.

Most loyal newspapers supported the censorship in principle, at least, for the first few months of the war, and some, like the Cincinnati *Press* and the Cleveland *Plain Dealer* (both with few correspondents), were even critical of the govern-

[6] Ben: Perley Poore: *Perley's Reminiscences* (Philadelphia: 1886), II, 78, supported by *Herald*, May 24, June 24, 1861.

[7] *War of the Rebellion: Official Records of the Union and Confederate Armies* (Washington: 1880–1901), Series I, Volume II, 600. Cited hereafter as "*O.R.*" A House investigating committee reported in 1862 that "the censorship seems to have been first under the control of the Treasury Department," but dispatches of the time speak of it as under the War Department, and this citation tends to confirm it.

ment later for not going far enough. The problem was unique. Here was an enemy that spoke the same language, on a two-thousand-mile front across which spies and informers moved almost at will. New York papers reached Richmond regularly two or three days, and sometimes only one day, after publication. To censor these of everything the Confederates might not know (a common argument against it was that they already knew everything in them anyway), not to mention censoring all the "provincial" press down to country weeklies with their letters from men in the camps, was patently impossible. The administration blundered, early and often; but no wonder it was bewildered.

In spite of occasional lip service, the metropolitan papers were in no mood to co-operate. Dana reacted in a way typical of others as well as neatly characteristic of himself, when he ran a reply to General Butler's order circumscribing reporters at Fortress Monroe. It noted Butler's complaint that his plans were getting to the enemy: "Whose fault is this? Is the Major General such an old lady that he cannot hold his tongue? . . . Do reporters, eluding the sentinels, attend his councils of war in feminine disguise?" The *Tribune* went on:

> If officers, in violation of military law and personal confidence, are weak enough to tattle, shoot them or hang them, we do not care which; but to suppose that paid men, sent expressly to obtain information, will not use it when obtained, is to exhibit a fatuity unworthy of a Major General. We profess to print a newspaper. . . . Millions of men and women, fathers, mothers, children, wives, sweethearts, who have sent those dearer than life to these wars, look every day at this journal . . . and turn pages with hands made unsteady by emotion. It is quite as important that . . . their apprehensions should be allayed, that these tortures of suspense should be averted, as that Gen. Benjamin F. Butler should keep secret any expedition which he is likely to undertake.

This ingenious argument of July 13, 1861 sounds a bit sophistical today, but there was reason, at the time, for Dana to carry a chip on his shoulder.

The right to report is not writ large in the minds or hearts of Americans, nor widely celebrated in song or story. There is a disposition to accept it as an automatic adjunct of a free press. But the Constitution does not guarantee the right to report; the First Amendment simply protects the right to print.

The right to report has had to be fought for, and it has been fought for, all in the name of the next edition, by thousands of forgotten penny-a-liners, Bohemians, police reporters, muckrakers, Washington correspondents, war correspondents, and their editors through all the mutations of the American experience. Against natural obstacles, against one another, against the many-sided obduracy of public officials, they have gradually established a quasi-legal right which is indispensable to a people who must be informed in order to govern themselves.

Reporters had been barred from the halls of Congress until the forties, when Henry Clay helped them win a fight for press galleries. Clay himself, though enlightened for his era, would not extend their preserve further. He refused to continue a stump speech in Lexington, Kentucky, near the close of his life, until Richard Smith of the Associated Press "had not only dropped his pencil but had left the ground." When Smith secured a secondhand report, Clay was profane at his "impertinence." "Clay would have astonished anyone who attempted to interview him," the editor who recalled the episode remarked.[8] As late as 1859, Emerson was perturbed at the thought of reporters attending his lectures.

Now, just as the news revolution was materializing, civil and military officials seemed bent on checking it.

Tom Scott's telegraphic censors were so arbitrary that by

[8] Melville Phillips, ed., *The Making of a Newspaper* (New York: 1893), "Early Editorial Experiences," by Murat Halstead, 231.

June both Dana and Hudson had their men circumventing the censorship by mail and express. Through the Associated Press came a suggestion "from an official source" that editors meet in Washington to consider a more effective censorship.[9] "Good manners and common sense, on the part of two or three officials, are alone needed to settle the whole difficulty," the *Tribune* replied; the *World* thought the meeting unnecessary; the *Times* and the *Herald* ignored the invitation. Nothing more was heard of it.

Army officers, meanwhile, were reacting to reporters with bristling hostility. A "sarcastic chorus" greeted them at headquarters in Alexandria. Stone's successor in local command at Washington, a fierce-eyed, white-maned old-timer named Joseph Mansfield, announced frequently and with emphasis that all newsmongers should be chased out of the camps. Mansfield threatened to shoot a *Tribune* man, a fate which another reporter said he would just as soon face "and have an end of it, as lead the life of a Washington correspondent these days."

Security violations blossomed daily all spring. The Confederates could scarcely miss them, because editors were forever citing specific examples of what rivals should not have printed. LeRoy Pope Walker, Confederate Secretary of War, appealed to Southern newspapers to restrain themselves by pointing to "the great amount of valuable information obtained by us from the enterprising journals of the North." [1] The government did not seem to know its own mind. Late in June, Tom Scott's hated censors were unaccountably withdrawn.[2] The press had won round one.

On July 7, as Washington began to stir with news of the forthcoming advance on Manassas, Dana ran so much information about it that he woke up old Winfield Scott. Here-

[9] *Herald* Washington dispatch, June 19, 1861.

[1] Reprinted in *Frank Leslie's Illustrated Newspaper*, XII, 163 (July 27, 1861).

[2] *World*, July 11, 1861; Washington dispatch mentions withdrawal of censors two weeks earlier.

after, the General announced wrathfully, no military news was to be telegraphed without the approval of his headquarters.[3] Correspondents gathered at the Capitol for a protest meeting, for it was obvious that unless Scott's staff was to spend the war reading war news, his order meant the end of such news by wire. E. S. Sanford, president of the American Telegraph Company, pleaded with Scott on his customers' behalf. Yielding to mounting pressure, Scott rescinded his order and directed George H. Burns, Washington superintendent of the telegraph company, to see to it that nothing useful to the enemy was sent over the lines.[4] Burns was left to figure out for himself what to do about telegraphing material that had already appeared in the Washington press, still uncensored and nearest to the enemy. Scott, as a *Times* man said, was "stopping a spigot and allowing a bunghole to remain open."

The General-in-Chief's change of orders led Major General Irvin McDowell to decide that reporters might accompany his army as the great day neared. "They should wear a white uniform," he joked a little nervously to Russell of *The Times* of London, "to indicate the purity of their character." [5]

Reporters besieged the War Department, trying to purchase rations and equipage at government rates, "all pulling at cross-purposes, and too many of them wearying politeness with their importunities," wrote one. What was the status of these unmannerly fellows, anyway? The Department was stumped, and declined to accommodate them. Now and henceforth, as far as food, clothing, shelter, and transportation were concerned, reporters, like true Bohemians, would shift for themselves.

[3] *O.R.*, Ser. III, Vol. 1, 324.
[4] *World*, July 13, 1861.
[5] John Black Atkins: *Life of Sir William Howard Russell* (London: 1911), II, 48.

3. ON TO RICHMOND!

THE MOMENT Fitz Henry Warren had prayed for was at hand. "On to Richmond!" echoed through the land.

For the working press, as for McDowell's three-month men, the campaign began as a marvelous lark. Edmund Stedman, now of the *World*, sat on the stoop of a farmhouse the evening of July 17, munching corn-cake provided by a benevolent Virginian and scribbling a note to Laura, his wife: "We had a perfectly magnificent time today. I never enjoyed a day so much in my life. Was in the van throughout, at the head of the army, and it was exciting and dramatic beyond measure. . . ." [6]

In accordance with General McDowell's suggestion that they had best stay out of the way by keeping together, the reporters advanced en masse. Riding through the Virginia countryside with the singing and banter of the troops in their ears was such a cavalcade as had never been seen: Stedman, small, thin-faced, violet eyes sparkling, wearing the gauntlet gloves of an officer; William A. Croffut, in a white linen duster like the photographer Brady's, bespectacled Adams S. Hill, and Edward H. House, dramatic critic and fixture at Pfaff's, ready to give their all for the *Tribune*; big Henry Villard, astride a great black animal, and William B. Shaw, of the *Herald* contingent; Charles H. Webb, Joseph Howard, Jr., George Salter ("Jasper"), Charles L. Brace, and, yonder in a gig, the dapper little editor himself, Henry Jarvis Raymond, all of the *Times*; Richard C. McCormick, quick and nervous, full of Celtic fire, of the *Evening Post*; George Wilkes, editor of New York's favorite sporting sheet, *Spirit of the Times*; Horace White and Dr. Charles Ray, editors of the Chicago *Tribune*; Charles ("Carleton") Coffin, alert and somber, of the Boston *Journal*, with a couple of other Boston newsmen named Babcock and Haskell; Alf Waud, hearty

[6] Stedman: *Letters*, 230.

jack-booted artist of the *New York Illustrated News*, bumping along with Mathew Brady on the "whatisit" wagon; Joseph Glenn of the Cincinnati *Gazette*; a man named Tracy from the Rochester *Express*, a paper that would not have sent a reporter to anything short of Armageddon; John Hasson of the Associated Press, with a messenger jogging beside him; the Philadelphia contingent, Uriah Painter of the *Inquirer*, J. H. Puleston of the *North American*, and, far to the rear, hurrying afoot with a note in his pocket from the Secretary of War to McDowell directing that he receive special attention, a horse, and equipments, twenty-year-old John Russell Young of Forney's *Press*.

Among these, and all the others whose names are lost beyond recall, probably only two had ever seen a battle: Raymond in the Austro-Italian war of 1859, and McCormick of the *Post* in the Crimea. They were terribly excited. Hill, assisting House in a preliminary skirmish, "had one ball whiz by his ear, got frightened, galloped 22 miles to Washington, and there reported 500 killed, and that the press had fled the field," Stedman confided to his wife.[7] Villard, who was with Stedman and House, climbed a cherry tree to pick some fruit, "when a terrific roar burst out from the woods seemingly within a few steps of us," and a reporter with his mouth full of cherries went sprawling on the ground. ("I can truly say that the music of bullet, ball, and grapeshot never had much terror for me thereafter," Villard wrote.[8])

McDowell had invited William Howard Russell to join him, but the famous and rather ponderous Crimean correspondent of the Thunderer, troubled by the War Department's failure to make suitable provision for him, did not launch his own expedition until the fatal day, Sunday, July 21, 1861. About half past nine on that sunny, hot morning he trundled across the Long Bridge out of Washington in a rented two-horse rig, followed by a saddle-horse and a groom, and fortified with

[7] Stedman: *Letters*, 231.
[8] Henry Villard: *Memoirs* (Boston: 1904), I, 185.

a bottle of tea, a flask of light Bordeaux, a bottle of water, a small flask of brandy, a supply of Havana cigars, and a basket of ham and Bologna sandwiches.[9] He had quite a day ahead of him.

Bull Run affords ample ground for the observation that the men who write "history on the run," as some dramatist styled reporters, sometimes make it.

In essence, McDowell's plan called for Heintzelman and Hunter to flank the enemy's left by swooping across Sudley's Ford in the main assault while Tyler and Miles kept him busy along his front. Both Hunter and Heintzelman, as it happens, were friendly to newsmen, but only a few, among them Croffut of the *Tribune*, went along with them. Villard explained later that he was unaware of the battle plan. He and most of the others, mindful of McDowell's wishes, stayed within sight of one another with Tyler on the Federal center. Here they were close to the main road leading through Centerville to the telegraph station at Fairfax, thirteen miles to their rear, but out of touch with McDowell's headquarters, for the commanding general and his staff soon joined the flanking movement.

Roused at one in the morning to join Tyler's advance in the moonlight, Ed House of the *Tribune*, with his friend Stedman and the others, was on hand to witness the opening cannonade at sunrise. Presently volleys of musketry rolled across the low, wooded hills from the direction of Sudley's. Smoke drifting high in the still July air two miles distant sent correspondents clambering to treetops on high ground near the soon-to-be-famous Stone Bridge. With field glasses they caught glimpses through the clearings: men serving the guns, unidentifiable troops moving hither and yon. By noon the flankers had rolled the Confederate left back near the Henry House, on a plateau about a mile in front of the Stone Bridge.

[9] William Howard Russell: *My Diary North and South* (New York: 1863), 164. 165.

Tyler stormed over in support. Correspondents pieced together breathless word of batteries captured, cheers running through the Union ranks, reports that the rebels were beginning to break.

The din was punctuated now by the shrill, incongruous toot of locomotives. Tree-perchers reported the continual arrival of cars on the Manassas Gap Railroad, troops piling out and moving off on the double, knapsacks still on their backs. These, they knew, would be the men of Joe Johnston's army, coming to the rescue of Beauregard after escaping the Union General Patterson's observation at Winchester. Actually, only 2,300 of Johnston's men arrived this late—about 8,700 had arrived the day before—but great clouds of dust raised by Beauregard's transfer of troops to his crumbling left led reporters to believe that a huge army had reinforced him in mid-battle, "at least 50,000," thought Stedman.

Still came tidings of victory. They were genuine: toward 3:00 p.m. General Beauregard found things going so badly that he considered giving up the field. At 3:30, Shaw of the *Herald* galloped off for Fairfax, taking the government operator there this message: "Hudson, Herald—I am en route to Washington with details of a great battle. We have carried the day. The rebels accepted battle in strength, but are totally routed. . . ." Raymond, in Centerville to find a courier, cautiously wrote the *Times* that "the result is still not certain." At 4:30, Hasson sent his Associated Press courier off with news of a complete victory. Young of the Philadelphia *Press* and a second *Herald* man left with similar news at about the same time. Russell, having disposed of his sandwiches and assorted fluids and rested his horses after the twenty-seven-mile trip from Washington, was picking up what details he could from his countryman, Frank Vizetelly of the *Illustrated London News*, before pushing to the front on horseback.

What happened next military historians still debate, but there is no question what happened to the newspapermen. They were engulfed in a wild panic among teamsters, specta-

tors, and horses near the Stone Bridge. From there, confusion
billowed like smoke from the mouth of a cannon. "A perfect
frenzy was upon almost every man," House wrote. "Some
cried piteously to be lifted behind those who rode horses, and
others sought to clamber into wagons, the occupants resisting
them with bayonets. . . . Drivers of heavy wagons dashed
down the steep road, reckless of the lives they endangered all
the way. . . . Every impediment to flight was cast aside.
Rifles, bayonets, pistols, haversacks, cartridge boxes, canteens,
blankets, belts and overcoats lined the road." Ahead of him,
the mighty Russell tried to stem the debacle, his round face
flushed with excitement. "Stop!" he cried to a driver. "Everything is falling out!" "—— you!" shouted a man inside the
vehicle: "If you stop him, I'll blow your brains out!" Others
were in the thick of it, upholding the glory of the Fourth
Estate. Painter saw Stedman grab the standard of the Massachusetts Fifth, "waving it over him and pleading for the men
to rally round him, but it was in vain." The Philadelphia *Inquirer* man lost his mount, seized a wounded Confederate
cavalry horse by the halter, and galloped off bareback. On
the edge of the wood he saw Villard "trying to pacify the
men, telling them it was only a panic."

Villard, House, Salter, Glenn, and others pulled up at Centerville to see if McDowell would be able to check the retreat.
Raymond picked up his gig there and headed for Washington,
only to run into a fresh stampede; his outfit was "crushed by
an enormous Pennsylvania army wagon like an egg shell." The
little New York *Times* editor hopped into another carriage in
which a couple of Congressmen were fleeing. Earlier he had
seen *The Times* of London thundering by, "profoundly disgusted, making all possible haste to get out of it." [1]

Back at Centerville, reporters learned at 11:00 p.m. that
McDowell had abandoned hope of making a stand and ordered

[1] This quotation and those in the paragraphs preceding are from dispatches in the papers of those quoted, July 22–4, 1861. Russell's appeared
in the London *Times* of Aug. 6.

a general retreat. Villard headed his charger for Washington, passing through Fairfax at about the time Young, blissfully asleep on a mattress in the parlor of the inn there, was roused by an officer with a wild story that the whole army was fleeing with Beauregard in hot pursuit.

4. "TELL NO ONE"

"TELL no one." That was the admonition Seward gave the President's secretaries when, finding Lincoln gone on a drive, he told them the first news of disaster at about 6:00 p.m. From the War Department the same order went to Burns at the telegraph office.

At 8:00 p.m. Shaw burst into the *Herald* quarters on Fourteenth Street to write a fragmentary report: "the rebels were flying" when he last saw them. Burns let it go; he also released a message from General McDowell which the operator at Fairfax had relayed at 5:30, about "a great battle fought and victory won." Hasson, minus only his hat, got to the Associated Press rooms a few minutes before nine o'clock, so overwhelmed by what he regarded as an epochal victory that he was unable to write a word. Old L. A. Gobright, the bureau chief, cleared everyone out, locked the door, and sat taking notes while Hasson paced up and down with the stump of an unlit cigar in his mouth, blurting the story out piecemeal.

The first haggard fugitives, Russell among them, reached the moonlit streets of the capital a few minutes before eleven o'clock. "There are ten thousand rumors prevailing . . . of such a contradictory character that it would be idle to transmit them," George W. Adams, the *World's* Washington man, wired. He would have transmitted them gladly, but that was as close to the truth as Burns would permit. Half an hour later Gobright and Hasson were heading for the telegraph office with their story of triumph when they heard a wild-eyed citizen describing the rout to a crowd in front of the Metropolitan Hotel. Instead of writing a new lead, Gobright simply tacked on: "At this point there was a sudden change in affairs," adding as many details as he could muster. Burns sent the original and killed the add.[2] Just after midnight Raymond, "sunburned, dusty, and hardly recognizable," filed his dispatch with the censor, "who, without a word of explanation, suppressed it entirely." For once Raymond exploded. What about all the victory dispatches? Were the censors deliberately deceiving the whole country? "It is too late to countermand dispatches already sent," he was told, though he knew that the forms did not close at the *Times* until 3:00 a.m.

Meanwhile, thanks to the notion that only the telegraph need be censored, the Washington papers were going to press with the disaster story.

B. P. Snyder, Burns's assistant, lacked instructions from the War Department when he opened the telegraph office at 7:00 a.m. on a rainy Monday men and women would remember all their lives. The reporters made him send over an inquiry: "Shall I allow anything to go forward this morning?" Back came word from Tom Scott. The curtain was lifted.[3]

The streets of Northern cities had rung all night with the cries of tatterdemalions with papers on their shoulders: "VICTORY! VICTORY! GREAT BATTLE! DEFEAT OF THE REBELS AT BULL RUN!"—news which the morning confirmed in headlines that ran riot down column one, as in the *Herald*: "HEROISM OF THE UNION FORCES . . . THEY KNOW NO SUCH WORD AS FAIL."

A *Times* reporter noted that "when the first dirty newsboy whirled through the streets, shrieking at the top of his ominous voice, 'Defeat of the Union Army,' no one felt the slightest disposition to buy an extra. It was regarded as a smart commercial fraud, which ought to be put a stop to by the

[2] L. A. Gobright: *Recollections of Men and Things at Washington* (Philadelphia: 1869), 316, 317.
[3] *O.R.*, Ser. I, Vol. 2, 756.

police. But bad tidings travel apace. . . ." The effect was
brutal. By noon the city was "panic-striken at reading the
bulletins." The first dispatches suggested total disaster. Villard's was so grim that Hudson, mindful of a mob that had
threatened the *Herald* office after Sumter, did not dare run it
until heavy excisions were made.[4] Editors telegraphed the War
Department to ask whether the capital would fall. In Philadelphia rumors flew about that the *Press* was withholding
news of "another Waterloo," that eleven thousand had been
slaughtered on the battlefield, and that the government was
fleeing. John Russell Young's mother and sister wept for him,
and his father tried to reach the *Press* correspondent by wire
to tell him to come home at once. Painter's disaster story in the
Inquirer caused such anguish that when it was partially contradicted "the sensation sheet was bitterly denounced and in
some instances carriers were kicked out of homes for attempting to serve it." [5]

Some accounts read like transcriptions of nightmares;
"masked batteries," "demons," atrocities related by delirious
soldiers lurked in every paragraph. A *Herald* man had it that
the Louisiana Zouaves, of whom Richardson had written in
New Orleans a few months before that "they are boyish looking, and handle their muskets as if a little afraid of them,"
had cut off the heads of Union wounded and kicked them
around as footballs. Reporters caught in the panic enormously
exaggerated its significance. Young put the battle five miles
from the battlefield, and devoted his piece to a recital of the
flight from Fairfax to Washington. "All was lost to that
American army, even its honor," *Tribune* readers learned
from House. "The agony of this overwhelming disgrace can
never be expressed in words."

Later stories and reappraisals, indicating that the panic had
been limited to a portion of the army (Croffut's *Tribune*

[4] Villard, I, 200.
[5] G. B. P. Ringwault to Young, July 26, 1861, John Russell Young
Papers, MS Division, Library of Congress.

piece made no reference to it), seem never to have eradicated the impressions burned into minds that had been jubilant with victory. The well-planned and fiercely fought battle, the 481 Union dead, the 1,011 wounded, would be forgotten; the rout, never. The men who wrote history on the run had made Bull Run part of the national folklore.

To the old office at Nassau and Spruce, the mailman delivered a final footnote to the campaign. The letter came from Washington, and it was signed "Fitz Henry Warren." He was resigning, he said, as Washington editor of the New York *Tribune*.

☼ CHAPTER III ☼

Bohemian Brigade

1. TWILIGHT AT THE "TRIBUNE"

THE NEW YORK *World* was "deluged with hundreds of letters" congratulating the paper for its once unpopular stand against the *Tribune's* "On to Richmond" campaign. The letters were gratefully received, but would not be printed, said a small notice tucked in the editorial-page masthead, "for the *Tribune* has confessed its great error and is doing what it can to atone for it."

What was the great error? The strategy the *Tribune* had urged—that Warren and Dana had shouted for and Greeley had reluctantly condoned—was not so unsound as it is sometimes made to appear. There was nothing foolhardy about the way it was carried out; if anything, McDowell had been too cautious, wasting two precious days during which he might have attacked Beauregard before Johnston reached him. The argument that the troops were green applied equally to the Confederates. Moreover, enlistments were about to expire, and McDowell's troops were not so green as the men who would be recruited to replace them. It was no fault of Greeley's that Patterson did not have clearer orders to hold Johnston, or that McDowell frittered away his chance to end the war in the East with one crushing victory before the Confederacy was fairly on its feet.

Now Horace Greeley was a broken man. He took to his bed with an attack of "brain fever," visions of death flitting before him. He wrote Lincoln: "This is my seventh sleepless night." He would "second any movement you may see fit to make," but he despaired of the Union cause. Dana loosed a thunderclap in his absence, an editorial demanding the resignation of the entire Cabinet. Agonized, Greeley publicly repudiated it. Fitz Henry Warren's letter of resignation, assuming the burden of responsibility for "On to Richmond," he quite properly refused to print.[1] Rallying to one of his finer moments, Greeley wrote an editorial titled "Just Once," acknowledging his responsibility for what appeared in his paper, offering himself as a national scapegoat, coming to grips with what was the real "great error" of the *Tribune* in a paragraph that read:

> Henceforth I bar all criticism in these columns on Army movements, past or future. . . . Correspondents and reporters may state fact, but must forebear comments.

To Sam Wilkeson, his new Washington man, Greeley wrote emphatically on this point, his instructions representing a complete turnabout. He wanted no more Pikes or Warrens. "I want a man at Washington to find out all that is going on or preparing and calmly *report* it, writing Editorials separately, to be submitted to criticism and revision here, instead of embodying them in dispatches. . . ."[2]

Objectivity was a principle all but unknown to journalism, but if the results of Greeley's change of heart were difficult to discern in *Tribune* dispatches, the seed had been planted. More effective in helping it to take root in the minds of news-

---

[1] *World*, Aug. 5, 1861.

[2] These words are from a letter of Dec. 9, 1862, in which Greeley says: "I went over all this ground with you soon after you first went to Washington fifteen months ago; but I see that we are both where we were." I am indebted to Ralph Newman, of Chicago, for furnishing transcripts of this and six other Greeley letters to Wilkeson which have just come to light.

papermen everywhere were the consequences of the "On to Richmond" debacle on the *Tribune*. There was a great hue and cry about "General Horace," and cancellations flooded the subscription office. The circulation of the weekly edition, over 215,000 just before the war, plummeted to 189,000 by October 1861, though that left it still the largest of any news publication. The daily barely held its own at 55,000 while its rivals climbed, the *Times* nearly reaching the *Tribune* by the end of the year and the *Herald* moving from 80,000 in January to 110,000 in the fall.[3] The Sunday *Tribune* was quietly discontinued in September for lack of advertising. War maps —expensive woodcuts, which in Bennett's paper were appearing almost daily and sometimes blanketing the *Herald's* front page beneath what probably qualify as the first banner lines anyone had ever seen (e.g., "THE SEAT OF WAR IN VIRGINIA," across the width of the page)—all but vanished from the *Tribune*. Page size was reduced slightly in September, and a cheaper quality of newsprint introduced. For the first time, Greeley admitted that the paper was losing money and added: "I do not see how we are going to live through the War as times go."[4] The *Herald* stepped up to twelve pages ("Triple Sheets") several days a week. "We can't resist poking our slow coach contemporaries in the ribs, now and then," ran a typical *Herald* taunt, "in contrasting their scanty columns of subscriptions and advertising with our heavy battalions."

The heartbroken Greeley wrote Beman Brockway: "Through the faults of several, mainly mine, the *Tribune as a power* is broken down. . . ."[5] Sam Wilkeson, Warren's wily successor, and an indomitable staff would breathe new fight into the paper. But another force was breaking down

[3] These are, of course, unaudited figures printed by the papers. However, press runs were easily timed by rivals on the Square; editors offered to bet one another on the veracity of their figures and open their books to prove it; and, in the case of the *Tribune*, private letters sustain the published figures, all of which suggests that these are tolerably accurate.

[4] Greeley to Wilkeson, Nov. 17, 1861 (transcript).

[5] William Harlan Hale: *Horace Greeley: Voice of the People* (New York: 1950), 250.

power of the kind Greeley represented, a force that no man could stem.

2. "Bread and the Newspaper"

From his riverside window, the Autocrat of the Breakfast Table could see the sparkle of sunlight on the Charles and the verdure of August on the hills north of Boston as he looked up to turn a phrase in his mind. Ticknor and Fields had sent over his proofs—an article for the September *Atlantic*.

"We must have something to eat, and the papers to read," the neat, small type said he had written. "Everything else we can do without. . . . Only bread and the newspaper we must have." Oliver Wendell, Jr., would be leaving for the Potomac front any day now with the Twentieth Massachusetts. "Men cannot think, or write, or attend to ordinary business. They stroll up and down the streets, or saunter out upon the public places. A . . . most eminent scholar told us in all simplicity that he had fallen into such a state that he would read the same telegraphic dispatches over and over again in different papers, as if they were new, until he felt as if he were an idiot. Who did not do just the same thing, and who does not do it still, now that the first flush of the fever is over? . . . The whole nation is now penetrated by the ramifications of a network of iron nerves."

The network was imperfect; the men who fed it could be singularly inept at times. Yet enough was imparted now, in the telegrams, in the awkward, discursive mail dispatches, to waken a sense that Americans have come to know more intimately, perhaps, than any other people: that mystic sense of common destiny which is conveyed by news of great events reported everywhere and in profusion almost simultaneously with their occurrence. It was the sense that moved Dr. Holmes to write his essay. It was the sense that would come to Mrs. Elizabeth Lindsay Lomax, one among millions, as she sat in her Washington flat just a year later writing: "The newsboys are calling, 'Another Great Battle at Manassas!' God help us!'" It was the sense that gave rise to a wartime phenomenon that the New York *Times* noticed as early as August 21, 1861: "We are always on the highest pinnacle of hope or in the lowest depths of despair." Despite the cacophony of editorial dispute, the bitter partisanship of Radicals, Copperheads, moderates, it was so evident that news eclipsed in interest anything the opinion-makers could write about it that men spoke of the emotions of twenty millions as of one. Three years later, on September 19, 1864, Seward would write privately that "the American people now appear to be as resolute and cheerful as on the 29th of August they seemed vacillating and despondent." To the Secretary of State, the American people had become an understandable entity, reacting to mercurial changes of fortune recorded by their newspapers (Sherman at Atlanta! Sheridan at Winchester!) much as he himself reacted.

Immigrants who had never looked at a newspaper before the war spelled out the headlines, scanned casualty lists, or listened to neighbors read the dispatches, ears cocked for a familiar unit. Frederic Hudson came upon a sign of the times which he pasted in his scrapbook: a pen-and-ink sketch of a scrubwoman, mop forgotten at her side, avidly reading a "War Extra." Stedman's vivid Bull Run, which the *World* paraded in all six columns on the front pages of its daily, semi-weekly, and weekly, sold every copy of them, and Rudd and Carleton hastily republished it in a forty-two-page pamphlet. Even George Wilkes's report, which ran in his sporting sheet cheek by jowl with "The Lives and Times of Distinguished Pugilists," reappeared in pamphlet form. So did William Howard Russell's, and if there were doubts that these long battle stories were read, the reaction to his account dispelled them.

Overnight, Russell became "the best abused man in America," as he wrote John Bigelow. The press jeered at "Russell's Run," and "John Bull Russell's Bull Run romance"; its author was "London Stout Russell," "Bombast Russell," "that Cassandra in breeches, Dr. Bull Run Russell," "this bilious LL.D., the snob correspondent of the London Times," all because he had offended national pride in depicting the rout. For three months he was plagued with anonymous letters threatening him with bowie knives and revolvers; once he was shot at point-blank, but the trigger jammed. He was caricatured, lectured upon, insulted in the streets.[6] In England, where Russell's Crimean dispatch on the charge of the Light Brigade had inspired Tennyson, George Otto Trevelyan wrote a relished bit of doggerel praying:

> Stain not a spotless name with useless crimes,
> O, save the correspondent of the *Times*!

Although no American reporter achieved Russell's notoriety, interest in "our own correspondent," as the papers often styled him, was scarcely less intense. No longer was Horace Greeley, symbol of editorial might, indisputably the central figure of American journalism. He was jostled, suddenly, by a man in his late twenties, in mud-spattered mufti or Federal blue, astride the inevitable sway-backed nag—saddlebags bulging with mackintosh, notebooks, Faber No. 2's, field glasses, pipe, sometimes potables—riding among the troops with half an eye out for the provost marshal's men: the American newspaperman, at last come into his own. Sometimes Billy Yanks in the ranks would recognize him: "Halloo-o-o *Jenkins!* . . . Give our captain a setting up, you sir! . . . Puff our colonel! . . . Where's your pass, bub? . . . Three cheers for Jenkins! . . . Give me a good obituary!"[7] Jenkins! He would become as much a part of their world as the cursing teamster, the bearded brigadier, the sutler with his seductive goods, the field telegraphers unwinding their big spools of wire, the bustling staff officer, Brady and his camera

---

[6] Russell: *Diary*, 185-97, *passim*.
[7] George Alfred Townsend: *Campaigns of a Non-Combatant* (New York: 1866), 250.

crews, the illustrated-weekly artist, or T. S. C. Lowe and his implausible balloons, filtering it all into the nation's consciousness dimly, imperfectly, hastily, through his billion-worded pencil.

That October day when Lieutenant Oliver Wendell Holmes, Jr., unexpectedly found himself clambering up a steep clay embankment of the upper Potomac with his regiment and three others under Colonel E. D. Baker, Jenkins would be there—Elias Smith, of the New York *Times*, for one. Smith was busy all night helping to ferry the wounded across the river in a scow; the next morning he wrote enough to fill two and a half columns on the bloody defeat at Ball's Bluff, only to find that not a word of it could go. Bull Run all over again! The State Department had taken over the censorship, and Seward had ordered H. E. Thayer, chief censor, to pass nothing but officially approved Associated Press dispatches.[8] But Jenkins was in Washington, too. Coffin of the Boston *Journal* and H. E. Smith of the Chicago *Tribune* got word of Baker's death, saw bodies floating downstream on their way; Ed Stedman rode forty-five miles to the scene at one clip, "got bilious intermittent fever," pieced the story together, rode back to Washington, wrote six columns with his head wrapped in a towel, and heard that "the government has stopped the *World* tonight and talks of interfering with me, because I got angry and told the truth about Ball's Bluff." [9]

Jenkins was in faraway Missouri, recording the only sustained action in the first year of the war. At Booneville, on June 17, Thomas W. Knox of the *Herald* had gone to work on foot in a gray overcoat, with a notebook and two pieces of bread in his knapsack, accompanied by Lucien Barnes, of the *Missouri Republican* of St. Louis. Brigadier General Nathaniel Lyon mistook them for enemy scouts; sharpshooters were taking aim when a cry from a staff officer saved the press.

---

[8] *Reports of Committees of the House of Representatives*, 37th Congress, 2nd Session, Volume III (Washington: 1862), 3.

[9] Stedman: *Letters*, 251

Knox, a burly, rather sardonic fellow known as "The Elephant," gleefully anticipated a habit that Johnny Reb would develop in due course: he emerged from combat with a horse and all the equipment for the campaign—"overcoat, roll of fine blankets, and a pair of saddlebags filled with clothes 'just my size.'" Barnes, he said, "wasted time in becoming sentimental over two love letters and a photograph of a young woman" found in the Confederate camp.[1] Franc B. Wilkie, whom Raymond enlisted for the *Times* on the strength of a single article in a camp paper, saw them at Forsyth a month later, "two men in citizens' clothes in the front rank of the cavalry . . . shooting as fast as they could cock their . . . vest-pocket revolvers."[2] Albert D. Richardson, west again for the *Tribune* after his tour of duty in the South, joined them with other newsmen at Wilson's Creek in August to report a defeat in which 223 Union men were killed, including General Lyon. The reporters compiled casualty lists all night, set out at 2:00 a.m., rode seventy miles through the foothills of the Ozarks to a log tavern at Lebanon, pushed on the next morning through bushwhacker country to Rolla, and thence took the cars to St. Louis.

After filing a brief dispatch, Wilkie, a country lad who doubted that Raymond really wanted him, personally delivered his full account of Lyon's defeat and death to his old paper in Iowa, the Dubuque *Herald*, which stunned the country with it.[3] "Retain place—will write," Raymond telegraphed him, and it was this correspondent who then brought off one of the most remarkable beats of the war.

Franc Wilkie was twenty-nine at the time, a hard-drinking, poker-playing homespun with abundant contempt for what he called "Cairo war correspondents"—those who reported the war in the West from the St. Charles Hotel in the little town at the confluence of the Ohio and the Mississippi chiefly

[1] Thomas W. Knox: *Camp-Fire and Cotton-Field* (New York: 1865), 49, 50.
[2] Franc B. Wilkie: *Pen and Powder* (Boston: 1888), 24, 25.
[3] *Ibid.*, 32–4.

because it was handy to the telegraph office. He debunked the When-Knighthood-Was-in-Flower speeches they put in the mouths of dying men, and on one occasion he wrote the *Times* with reference to sundry heroics they had forwarded: "There has never been a battle in the West where hand-to-hand conflict occurred. No bayonet charges received or given. When the opposing forces reach within forty or fifty yards of each other, one party or the other is sure to yield ground." [4] Wilkie accumulated his evidence on the firepower of small arms at first hand.

Early in September 1861 he went along with a relief column under Brigadier General Sam Sturgis which set out for Lexington, Missouri, where Major General Sterling Price, C.S.A., had cornered about eighteen hundred Federals. Sturgis's column, not equipped to handle Price, turned back; Wilkie felt cheated. "Under the inspiration of the situation and possibly that of a few bottles of wine," he went down the Missouri, crossed the enemy lines, surrendered himself to the Confederate pickets, and presented his card. General Price, scarcely expecting the New York *Times* to drop in, put him down as a spy for Sturgis. Wilkie spent the night in the guardhouse—standing up, inasmuch as there was "mud and tobacco spittle on the floor." Released on parole, he collected impressions of Price and the Confederates, went over the battleground after the Federals' surrender, and came away shocked by the failure of either side to bury its dead: "They lay there just as they fell—one man on his face and knees, and with his hands thrown forward as if to prevent his fall—all with countenances black and putrid with decomposition." His head was full of such images, images that would bring the war a little closer to people sewing pretty havelocks back home. He got to St. Louis, overcoat gone and broke, turned down Richardson's sly offer of a hundred and fifty dollars in gold to give his beat to the *Tribune*, touched Knox for a loan, sent his story,

[4] *Times*, May 18, 1862. Wilkie wrote as "Galway."

and on October 3 moved the *Times* to an editorial: "We do not believe any instance can be cited of similar courage and devotion on the part of a newspaper correspondent. . . ." There would be others.

In the first year of the war nearly every young man who had ever written a line for print, it seemed, had boned up on Hardee's *Tactics* and taken the field as "Vagabond" or "Slingshot" or "Bonaparte" to tell the folks back home about it. Counting "occasionals" who were paid at space rates, Albert D. Richardson estimated that five hundred men reported the war for the North; of these, perhaps two hundred were full-time reporters. They comprised a curious sampling of American life. Augustus Cazaran, a Boston reporter, had served time in Sing Sing; Henry Norman Hudson, of Bryant's *Evening Post*, was an eminent Shakespearean; Thomas Morris Chester, a Negro leader, came home from Liberia to work for the Philadelphia *Press*; Joseph B. McCullagh, a tough little Dublin urchin, sallied forth at the age of nineteen for the Cincinnati *Gazette*. Mostly they were young: two thirds of seventy-one whose ages have been ascertained were still in their twenties in 1863. Four out of five had been in newspaper work of one kind or another before the war. A surprising number for the time had attended college—nearly half of a group of fifty. And in a predominantly rural age, better than half of them were urban-born.

Rural folk with whom they were often obliged to take pot luck regarded this strange breed with bewilderment. Thomas W. Knox of the *Herald* recalled the incredulity of rustics at a Missouri inn at the rapidity of reporters' writing.[5] At Warrenton, Virginia, George Alfred Townsend "enjoyed the staring of the citizens, who pondered as to my purposes and pursuits, as only villagers can do," and when they "found me out to be a Newspaper Correspondent, they regarded me with amusing interest . . . confounding me with all the pa-

[5] Knox: *Camp-Fire*, 89.

per—editorial, correspondence, and, I verily believe, advertisements." [6] Major John Beatty took W. S. Furay to visit a farm family near Mitchellville, Tennessee, and "introduced Mr. Furay as the correspondent of the Cincinnati *Gazette*; but the good folks, not understanding this exactly, dubbed him doctor." [7] A farmer greeted Junius Browne of the *Tribune*: "War correspondent, eh? Why, they're the fellows who fought in the Revolution!" [8]

They were a race apart, and rather delightedly conscious of it. Comparatively few had savored Charlie Pfaff's lager or Henry Clapp's witticisms, but as New York set the fashion in all things journalistic, a certain diluted Bohemianism percolated among newsmen in the armies. Townsend, who had written a play titled *The Bohemians* in the Philadelphia *Press* office, gloried to count himself one of them when he took the field: "for be it known, I loved Bohemia! This roving commission, these vagabond habits, this life in the open air among the armies, the white tents, the cannon and the drums, they were my elysium, my heart!" [9] As Browne, a Cincinnatian, absorbed it, "a Bohemian generally means an ill-fated fellow, of aesthetic and luxurious tastes, born out of place, and in opposition to his circumstances."

A larger number of reporters than had congregated anywhere since Bull Run thronged Jefferson City early in October when it seemed at last that Major General John Charles Frémont, the illustrious commander of the Western Department, would get his army into action in one piece against Price. As they waited, reporters from all the major cities got acquainted with one another, with results that Richardson described later:

They styled themselves the Bohemian Brigade, and exhibited that touch of the vagabond which Irving chari-

[6] Townsend: *Campaigns*, 228, 229.
[7] John Beatty: *Memoirs of a Volunteer* (New York: 1946), 142.
[8] Junius Henri Browne: *Four Years in Secessia* (Hartford: 1865), 14.
[9] Townsend: *Campaigns*, 95.

tably attributes to poetic temperaments. They were quartered in a wretched little tavern. . . .

The Bohemians held high carnival, to the astonishment of attachés of the inn. The one who dressed earliest in the morning would appropriate the first hat, coat, and boots he found, remarking that the owner was probably dead. . . .

There was little work to be done, so they discussed politics, art, society, and metaphysics, and would kindle into singing, reciting, "skylarking," wrestling, slinging saddles, valises, and pillows. A couple roared imitations of the "chorus of fiends" into the small hours, declaring with each repetition, that it was now to be given for positively the last time, and at the very special request of the audience.[1]

The place became as uninhibited as Pfaff's. Tom Knox catalogued the missiles flying around him: "overcoats, bridles, books, stove-wood, bed-clothing, chairs, window curtains, and ultimately the fragments of bedsteads."

Frémont is a fascinating enigma to historians today, and he was no less so to the Bohemian Brigade as it waited in the tumble-down inn at Jefferson City. Perhaps no commander save McClellan would provoke such disagreement among them. Richardson saw in him a romantic after his own heart, the Pathfinder, the first standard-bearer of the Republican Party, the bold leader who tried to liberate the slaves of rebel Missourians only to have Lincoln amend his proclamation as impolitic. "I believe in him and love him," Richardson wrote privately a year later. In the *Tribune* of October 11 he paid eloquent tribute to "the greatest woman in America," the General's high-spirited wife, Jessie. On the other hand, McCullagh, bright, belligerent, a little fellow who went about "cursing like a seven-foot pirate," poured out tirades on Frémont, Jessie's influence, corruption in the Department, and

[1] Richardson: *Secret Service*, 189, 190.

the proposed advance, which he predicted would bring disaster.

Hard-headed Franc Wilkie was inclined to go along with McCullagh. Wilkie never forgot the time he had arrived in St. Louis. "Well, boys," he had said to Richardson and Knox at the hotel, "I believe I'll go around and call on Frémont." "Yes, that's right," Knox had said. "You ought to have done that before. Frémont will not like it when he learns that you have been in town for several days without calling on him." The sarcasm mystified Wilkie until he had waited five hours in three successive reception rooms of the elegant mansion Frémont had chosen as headquarters—never getting to see him.[2] "Let me say that General Frémont is supposed to be in St. Louis," the country boy wrote the *Times* September 5. "I say 'supposed'—no one that I have heard of knows him to be here as a certainty." He described the majors, colonels, Congressmen, scouts, and newsmen who were turned away. "It is not thought that the messengers who bore him the intelligence of our reverses . . . have reached him." Now at Jefferson City things were no different, and Wilkie, confronted by a dilemma similar to one General MacArthur presented newsmen generations later, resorted to Bohemian tactics:

> May it not be that General Frémont is too much embarrassed by the etiquette of war—with a cumbrous and unwieldy staff—with the panoply and externals of conflict? There may be use of private secretaries *of* private secretaries *of* private secretaries—of certain ceremonies, headquarters approachable through a pathway lined with glittering swords, bands making the air sick . . . with the stirring music of silver instruments, red tape formalities; . . . yet their effect, although brilliant to friend and observer, is of doubtful utility upon the rugged secessionists

[2] Wilkie: *Pen and Powder*, 49.

who hide themselves and their shotguns in every bush in Northern Missouri.[3]

The *World* man sided with Richardson, taking a swipe at Wilkie and McCullagh: "Correspondents accustomed to rushing up to brigadiers and shouting, with jovial slaps-on-the-back, 'Anything new, Old Boy?' are disgusted."

On October 7, the defeat which Wilkie had witnessed at Lexington having come on the heels of that at Wilson's Creek and others elsewhere in the strife-torn state, Frémont had written to General Scott: "I am taking the field myself." Thirty-eight thousand men were assembled at Jefferson City, and it seemed that the General had awakened from his dreams of marching all the way to New Orleans and would face the reality of a Missouri already half lost to the enemy.

But when would he move? The Bohemian Brigade, for whom his gaudy Hungarian staff officers were obligingly arranging special tents, thought never. Then in mid-October he did move—to near-by Tipton, and who should appear but the silver-haired Secretary of War, Simon Cameron; old Lorenzo Thomas, Adjutant General of the United States Army; and Mr. Samuel Wilkeson of the New York *Tribune*. Something was astir, but not what the Bohemians anticipated.

[3] *Times*, Oct. 5, 1861.

CHAPTER IV

Dress Rehearsal

1. INSIDERS

THE DEVIOUS trail that brought Sam Wilkeson to Tipton, Missouri, in such distinguished company went back just two months. On August 15, 1861, when Wilkeson chuffed into the Washington depot, it was beginning to appear that, Dr. Holmes to the contrary, the nation would have to live by bread alone. Major General George B. McClellan, in a press conference at his headquarters, had entered into what he called a "Gentleman's Agreement" with reporters: they agreed "to refrain from publishing . . . any matter that may furnish aid or comfort to the enemy," in return for which "Little Mac" would "afford the press facilities for obtaining and immediately transmitting all information suitable for publication, particularly touching engagements with the enemy." [1] But McClellan, busy organizing the Army of the Potomac while the press built him up with all manner of lore ("He has been known to take a two-shilling piece between his thumb and forefinger and bend it double"), made precious

---

[1] House Report, *op. cit.*, 2. The agreement was signed Aug. 2, 1861 by McClellan and twelve reporters acting on behalf of "all newspapers in the loyal states."

little news. "All Quiet Along the Potomac" became a standing headline that would ultimately mock him.

Moreover, the censorship, administered now by the State Department, now by the War Department, sometimes by both, and once, for a brief interval, by the Treasury Department, became more capricious week by week. The Washington papers were brought under the censor's ægis at last on August 14. Gradually Seward and Tom Scott, now Assistant Secretary of War, tightened the wires against ungentlemanly revelations. By the end of September, S. P. Hanscom of the *Herald*, replying to Bennett's query whether Frémont was to be removed, found that not even a private wire would go through. Nor was that all. Only five days after the "Gentleman's Agreement," Cameron, with Lincoln's approval, had invoked the Fifty-Seventh Article of War, providing the death penalty for giving information about the army without the sanction of the general commanding [2]—an order which, had it ever been enforced, would have trussed up most of the newspapermen in the field.

Wilkeson's arrival as chief Washington correspondent of the *Tribune* in the unlamented Warren's place is something of a landmark in journalistic history. He introduced the era of the inside operator, the man who sought not merely to report news, but to find out about everything he was not permitted to report, to make arrangements for getting confidential information, and to keep his editor posted on what was going on and what was likely to happen next. The insider's reports, as Hervey Calkins of the *Herald* put it, were "used to give tone to editorials," and they were indispensable in arranging for coverage of naval expeditions and army campaigns; but they were usually marked "private and strictly confidential."

Warm, vibrant, intelligent, in the *Herald's* view "a fanatical, impertinent revolutionary fellow, who will bear watching," Wilkeson cut a striking figure. The proud, high fore-

[2] *O.R.*, Ser. III, Vol. 1, 390, 445.

head, tousled hair worn long, the sharply chiseled profile, knowing eyes, firm lower lip, erect bearing, suggested an intellectual and a man of parts. A Radical in the contemporary anti-slavery sense, son of one of Buffalo's pioneer families, he was above all a newspaperman. For some years he had edited the Albany *Evening Journal*; later he served as Albany correspondent of the *Tribune*.

Wilkeson at once called on Secretary of War Cameron, presented a letter of introduction from Dana,[3] and exchanged pleasantries. To his friend Sydney Gay in the home office he wrote: "[I] soon shall fasten my grapples on the necessary influences here. I *shall have* them Sydney."

These were the "Days of Shoddy." Washington whispered that the War Department, under Cameron's haphazard regime, would buy almost anything at any price. In the light of that, Wilkeson's first move is a revealing commentary on the insider's tactics, to say nothing of ethics. "Secretary Cameron gives day and night to the service of his country," he wrote in the *Tribune*. "The contracts made by him will defy the most unfriendly scrutiny. . . ." He clipped the piece and sent it to Cameron with a note: "The satisfaction of doing justice to a wronged statesman, is not equalled by the pleasure with which I sincerely pay a tribute of respect to a maligned good man." [4]

The old man was delighted. He invited Wilkeson to his farm near Harrisburg for a two-day visit. Wilkeson accepted —"to study him among his neighbors and in his family," as he wrote Gay. Then, to Gay on September 5:

> Three of the Departments here are about secured to us. It will take me a week longer to finish the conquest. Then I shall advance on two others, and by detail & in time get them all. Then the Herald & the Times will be smilingly defied to a competition.

[3] Dana to Cameron, Aug. 15, 1861, Cameron Papers, MS Division, Library of Congress.
[4] Cameron Papers, Aug. 25, 1861, with enclosure dated Aug. 24.

Smiling Sam went about with eyes and ears open. There was a little of the "main chance" of the *Herald* in his own blood; a beat for the paper he loved became his obsession. The *Tribune's* Washington news picked up wondrously. When editors bungled his copy, he exploded:

> Do me the favor to show this slip to Mr. Greeley. The horrible blunder of running two separate items into one, and of commingling a passionate call to arms with a gauge of the soldier's stomach, and of double-leading a paragraph about Rations!! could happen no where else than in the Tribune office.
>
> I don't know who your Night Editor is now—but . . . I was so ashamed of his work that in going to my tea last evening I took a back street. . . .
>
> Study the Telegraphic arrangement of the *Herald*. See how *always*, not casually, *but invariably*, the important items are placed first, and the minor gradually go last. I have to send the matter as I get it. . . .
>
> Faugh! Look at that double-leaded stupidity. It turns my stomach.

October 5, 1861 was a red-letter day for the censorship. That evening, Simon P. Hanscom of the *Herald*, egged on by Bennett in New York, had a long talk with E. S. Sanford (president of the company which was collecting as much as fifteen hundred dollars a week from the *Herald* in Washington-New York tolls alone) and Tom Scott "about annoyances of the last week," by which he meant the censoring of private wires to Hudson and Bennett. "Sanford, as well as Scott, assures me that we will have no more such trouble," Hanscom reported.[5] But it was an even better day for Sam Wilkeson and the *Tribune*. From the War Department a special message went to H. E. Thayer, chief censor:

[5] Bennett Papers.

October 5, 1861

My Dear Sir—

It is my wish that you neither suppress nor alter the telegrams of Mr. Samuel Wilkeson. Please send them as they are written and signed by him.

Respectfully,

Simon Cameron [6]

The "conquest" was finished.

It was immediately thereafter that Cameron and Adjutant General Thomas departed on their tour of the Western departments. With Congress adjourned and McClellan inactive, Wilkeson sensed that the news went with them. The *Tribune* correspondent caught up with the special train at Pittsburgh, where his suspicions were confirmed. "Cameron bore in his pocket a sealed order to Frémont, to surrender his command to the officer next to him," Sam wrote Greeley. The President had left it to his Secretary of War to decide whether to deliver it. Wilkeson had only to see it through to score a beat that would stun the country.

The party arrived at Tipton. Frémont, in full regalia and alive to his peril, immediately proposed a review in honor of the Secretary. Knowing all too well Simon Cameron's susceptibility to flattery, Wilkeson tried to forestall it; but "the delay I sought of demanding that we should at least breakfast was defeated by a jest about my age and the Secretary's tough youth." Wilkeson, alas, was train-sick and unable to go along. "A twelve-mile ride side by side with Frémont, without my countervailing influence, was a necessity. Boots and spurs! Amid laughter and the rattling of sabres and trampling of horses off went the Sec'y. I went to bed feeling that our mission was lost." Cameron did relieve the General; then, "exhausted and without nerve," he allowed Frémont to talk him into suspending the order. Wilkeson, writing Greeley that Frémont "dreams, as men do who take opium . . . surrender-

[6] *Herald*, Mar. 23, 1862, Washington dispatch.

ing the Commissariat and Quartermaster's department of an army for 70,000 to a gang of the damnedest villains I have met since I left Albany," knew that ultimately "Frémont will be removed. That is inevitable." [7] (Frémont was deposed seventeen days later.)

The *Tribune's* special agent came close to sealing the fate of another Union general on the return trip. At Louisville the party stopped off to confer with Brigadier General William Tecumseh Sherman. The bristly, fierce-eyed commander glared at Wilkeson and asked Cameron for a private interview. Cameron joshed him; Wilkeson remained. In the course of the discussion Sherman blurted that he needed two hundred thousand men. After the conference Wilkeson repeated this figure to Henry Villard, who was in town representing the Cincinnati *Commercial*, having quit the *Herald*. Wilkeson said Cameron thought the general must be unhinged. Villard reported this to his editor, Murat Halstead, and Halstead agreed. (Sherman later contended that he meant two hundred thousand for the entire area between the Alleghenies and the Mississippi, not, as those who heard him thought, for Kentucky alone.) So it was that on December 11—Halstead having waited until Sherman was removed from command to say so—the Cincinnati *Commercial* broke the news: "GENERAL SHERMAN INSANE." [8]

That was only one of the hornets' nests Wilkeson stirred up. On October 29, having returned to Washington, he took advantage of his immunity from censorship to telegraph the *Tribune* two major beats. They were official documents, neither of which the President had laid eyes on.[9] One, old Adjutant General Thomas's highly confidential report to him, bears strong internal evidence that Wilkeson had a hand in

[7] Wilkeson to Greeley, Oct. 15, 1861. Greeley Papers, MS Division, New York Public Library. "I guess he is a bad general," Greeley replied, "but he writes capital proclamations." Newman transcript, Oct. 23, 1861.

[8] Villard, I, 212; Halstead: "Recollections and Letters of General Sherman," *The Independent*, Vol. 51 (June 22, 1899), 1610.

[9] *Times*, Nov. 1, 1861, editorial; *Herald*, Nov. 2, editorial.

writing it. Frémont was described as "more fond of the pomp than the realities of war," and it concluded that "in the opinion of most intelligent men" he should be removed from command.[1] Sherman was put down as "gloomy." If the Thomas report was not directly responsible for the removal of the two commanders, its publication made their positions all but untenable. Wilkeson's second beat, a document for which editors had been waiting with mounting impatience, caused even more of a furor. It was General Stone's report of his defeat at Ball's Bluff.

The *Times* and the *Herald* howled. Wilkeson had put Horace Greeley back in the newspaper business, with a vengeance. Rival editors had to look to the *Tribune* for their cues. When Wilkeson predicted that McClellan would remain inactive until spring, the *Times* reprinted his dispatch in full, explaining: "The confidential relations which the *Tribune's* Washington correspondent is understood to sustain to the Secretary of War give this letter more importance than it would ordinarily possess." [2] Privately, Raymond and Hudson were worried. The day the *Tribune* beats appeared, Raymond sent A. S. Mitchell to Cameron with an urgent call to come to New York. Mitchell, the *Times's* entrant in the inside-information sweepstakes, "is eminently intelligent, thoroughly familiar with every phase of public affairs," the editor assured Cameron. "You can speak with him just as freely . . . as you would with me." [3] The Secretary brushed off the summons to New York, whereupon the *Times* said testily that if the government was going to hand out secret information, "it belongs equally to all." The *Herald* demanded Wilkeson's arrest as a common thief, and a few days later Hudson, too, sent his emissary to Cameron.

With that, the Secretary bowed to protocol: he hastened to New York to mend his editorial fences. Meanwhile, Hud-

[1] Other sections are close paraphrases of Wilkeson's letter to Greeley.
[2] Issue of Oct. 29, 1861.
[3] Raymond to Cameron, Oct. 30, 1861. Cameron Papers.

son and Raymond put their heads together to forestall future
Tribune beats. Between them they comprised the executive
committee of the Associated Press. The result of their work,
described in the *Times* on November 21, 1861, was an important step in establishing the modern working relationship
between government and press:

> Arrangements have been completed between Heads of
> Departments in Washington and the representatives of
> the New-York press by which . . . all *official* docu-
> ments, of whatever kind, emanating from the Depart-
> ments, be delivered to the general agent of the Asso-
> ciated Press in Washington—and to him alone—for
> prompt and simultaneous transmission.

This procedure was generally followed thereafter. But it
did nothing to break Sam Wilkeson's profitable hold on the
War Department. Sam still dined with Cameron, early in
December smiling his approval with Ed House of the *Tribune*
and John W. Forney of the Philadelphia *Press* while the Secretary assured his guest of honor, Russell of the London *Times*,
that "the press rules America." [4] There was some truth in it.
Wilkeson's next beat ultimately blew Cameron clear out of
the War Department and all the way to the embassy in St.
Petersburg. The Secretary's annual report to Congress advo-
cated the arming of freed slaves—an issue that Lincoln thought
the country unprepared to consider. Wilkeson, as usual, got
hold of it before Lincoln did, and the President had to order
Cameron to rewrite the offending section after it had been
published in the *Tribune*.[5]

That winter, old-timers in the Washington corps, like Ben:
Perley Poore of the Boston *Journal* and Eliah Kingman of
the New York *Sun* and old Colonel William Seaton of the
National Intelligencer felt like strangers in their own home

[4] Russell: *Diary*, 215.
[5] Carl Sandburg: *Abraham Lincoln: The War Years* (New York: 1939), I, 435.

town. The drowsy Southern community of prewar days had burgeoned into a great, seething mass of contractors, confidence men, soldiers, sutlers, nurses, Bohemians, spies. The lobbies of the Willard and the National and the Metropolitan swarmed with so many visitors that reporters lost track of the notables they were supposed to be trailing. They were waylaid themselves by inventors, commission men, and other favor-seekers bearing "applications for about everything," Wilkeson noted, including "a man with a portable battery of nine pistols, to be worn as a girdle," and another with "a cannon that would keep firing just as long as anyone would turn the crank."

"Honest George" Adams of the *World* estimated that a quarter of all the second floors on Pennsylvania Avenue were dedicated to faro, roulette, poker, and "grog of South Street quality . . . dispensed at San Francisco prices." Adams, known as "the jolliest" correspondent in town, livened his dispatches with vignettes of the social scene:

> A sleigh full of shouting prostitutes goes swishing by the gaslights of the National—a dozen of them, drawn by eight horses in a huge cutter. Though young, gay, and sufficiently picturesque and melodious, I take it that few, even of our young officers who have longest aired their epaulettes in Washington, would have cared about taking a seat among them. But the number of their unfortunate class now congregated in Washington is almost beyond belief. They have come from every city in the North, and even from across the ocean, occupying a hundred houses, crowding into the hotels, silk and feathering along the pavements.

Such was the milieu in which the insider flourished.

Among the swirl of purchasing agents, souvenir-hawkers, officers and their paramours in the lobbies, *Tribune* men kept a nervous eye out for a tall, overdressed dandy. One of them spotted him at McClellan's gala review early in December:

"the saintly Wyckoff," and, on his arm, the first lady of the land.[6] Henry Wikoff had accompanied Mrs. Lincoln that summer to Long Branch, writing the *Herald* of her every move. "I myself heard him compliment her upon her looks and dress in so fulsome a way that she ought to have banished the impertinent fellow from her presence," Henry Villard wrote many years later.

Wikoff had a positive genius for notoriety. Ten years before, his headlong pursuit of a wealthy spinster from England to Genoa, where he abducted her to his suite and compelled her at gun-point to sign an agreement to marry him, had ended in a trial that titillated newspaper-readers on both sides of the Atlantic and landed him in jail. There had been many other peccadilloes. Yet Wikoff managed to sidle back into the good graces of practically everyone who counted. "He pretended to be on familiar terms with every politician of note in his own country, and to know half the statesmen of Europe intimately," an outraged creditor in England explained; and the exasperating thing was that he did know a good many of them, from Lord Palmerston to Queen Isabella of Spain, who had decorated him.[7] "Wyckoff is, so to speak, an intimate of Seward's house and office," Count Gurowski noted in his diary. "His nonchalance, sangfroid, and uniform good humor demand and receive our sincere admiration," said the *Herald*. Ironically, one of his favorite parlor recitals was a richly brogued imitation of James Gordon Bennett in action.

It was Wikoff, so the story went, who put in a good word for Daniel E. Sickles, the Tammany politician, when Sickles's commission was "wavering in Lincoln's mind." [8] It was Wikoff, according to Sickles, who broke up a scheme to oust Cameron by talking Bennett out of it, since "the union of the *Herald*, *Times*, and *Tribune* was deemed indispensable to suc-

---

[6] *Tribune*, Dec. 7, 1861, Washington dispatch.
[7] Henry Vizetelly: *Glances Back Through Seventy Years* (London: 1893), I, 262–8.
[8] Philadelphia *Inquirer*, Feb. 14, 1862, Washington correspondence.

cess." [9] Thus, as the *Herald* had it, "that mysterious but omnipresent being the Chevalier Wikoff, useful alike as a political go-between or the bearer of bouquets and perfumed billets," flitted in and out of important places.

Just after Wilkeson scored with Cameron's report in the *Tribune*, Wikoff engineered his most sensational beat for the *Herald*: excerpts from the President's annual message to Congress, delivered to *Herald* readers before Congress knew a word that was in it. How had he done it? The House Judiciary Committee subpœnaed him in February. He refused to testify. He was brought before the entire House, but remained impassive. Wikoff was cited for contempt and escorted to Old Capitol prison, where, the *Herald* quipped, "he has got just what he wanted—comfortable board and lodging free of all pecuniary charge."

The episode was no joke to Lincoln. Tongues were busy, Mrs. Lincoln's good name was at stake, and the Committee, loaded with Radicals who were hostile to her, remained insistent. The President conferred with some of its members in the committee room.[1] Dan Sickles, acting as Wikoff's counsel, peregrinated between the prisoner's cell and the White House. Suddenly Wikoff yielded. He said John Watt, the White House gardener, had memorized portions of the document and recited them to him. Watt substantiated this unlikely tale and the case was closed, but the rumors persisted. "Friends of the *Herald*," a *World* reporter noted, "openly boasted that the Chevalier Wikoff obtained it through the medium of the highest lady in the land." [2]

However dubious Watt's role had been, no alert insider would overlook him thereafter. "Watt the gardener and your subscribing friend are forming a friendship under the flower pots," Wilkeson wrote Gay, "that will blossom and fruit in

[9] Sickles to Cameron, undated. Cameron Papers.
[1] *Tribune*, Feb. 14, 1862.
[2] *World*, Feb. 14, 1862.

season in beautiful minion." With editors contending for
news under tremendous pressure and in constant fear of being
beaten, "pick-lock journalism," as the *Tribune* called it, had
become the order of the day.

General McClellan's "inscrutable plans," Wilkeson noted
caustically, remained a mystery to all, including "such sub-
ordinate persons as the President and his cabinet." Shortly
after succeeding Winfield Scott as commander-in-chief, Mc-
Clellan simply ignored the President when he came to call.
What went on in the "Little Napoleon's" mind? Here was a
problem for the inside operator, and Frederic Hudson knew
just the man.

Dr. Malcolm Ives appeared at the Willard a day or two
after New Year's, 1862: "a tall, slender, black-eyed, pale-
faced, Italian-looking person of insinuating, serpentine address, of considerable learning, quick and impetuous in his
temper, and prone to difficulties." The son of a New York
physician, Ives had studied for the priesthood in Rome and
Vienna, returned to take a parish in Milwaukee, published an
unauthorized defense of the Spanish Inquisition, lost his parish,
then got himself appointed Vicar-General of the state of Mississippi. Next he appeared on the staff of the New York *Journal
of Commerce*, was discharged, bobbed up on the *Times* as an
editorial writer, married a schoolteacher who left him on finding herself wedded to a priest, was unfrocked, discharged by
the *Times*, and, in 1858, hired by the *Herald* as an editorial
writer. Being "an ultra Pro-Slavery Democrat, and, at the
same time, a professed believer in the divinity of monarchical
institutions," Ives had delighted Bennett with his rabid editorials, one of which called for the arrest and imprisonment
of Henry Ward Beecher, Wendell Phillips, and Greeley.
Ives had also held a succession of Customs House jobs on the
side.[3]

In Washington, this sinister-looking individual shortly got

[3] *Tribune*, Feb. 12, 1862; *New York Illustrated News*, Mar. 1, 1862.

wind of a report that Cameron was through as Secretary of War, and that Lincoln was appointing Edwin M. Stanton in his place. Ives knew Stanton, and he hastened to his office to break the good news. Stanton, then posing as a friend of every faction, said joyously that "if he *did* receive the appointment, he would show that he was no middle measures man, but should throw overboard the rest of the press and cling to the *Herald* alone." And he agreed to introduce Ives to General McClellan. One hour later Stanton was sent for by the President. That was on January 10.

On January 12 there was a Cabinet meeting to discuss the military situation; General McClellan had been invited, but failed to appear. There was another on January 13. This time McClellan did appear, but was distinctly heard to remark, *sotto voce*, that if he divulged his plans to the President, "they would be in the New York *Herald* the next morning." [4]

The following evening, at McClellan's house on H Street, Secretary Stanton introduced "Doctor" Ives ("You see the Pope's titles come into play here," Ives joked to Bennett later) to the General-in-Chief. "Now, General," said Stanton genially, "we will show Dr. Ives what we think of the course of the *Herald*." Stanton excused himself shortly, and there followed one of the most remarkable interviews on record. McClellan locked the door and motioned Ives to a chair. He told him about the Cabinet meeting. "What I declined communicating to them," he said dramatically, "I am now going to convey through you to Mr. Bennett and Mr. Hudson . . . and if you choose to take a pen you may make notes of what I am going to say." McClellan faced mounting criticism for his inactivity, in the *Tribune* and among Radicals in Congress. "Mr. Bennett has stood by me in the hour of the bitterest anxiety of my whole life. . . . He and he alone has upheld me, cheered me, and encouraged me."

[4] Margaret Leech: *Reveille in Washington* (New York: 1941), Garden City Publishing Co. edition (1945), 125.

Thereupon, with Ives taking full notes, McClellan described the military situation in every theater. He outlined his plans in each of them. Buell, he said, would advance through Bowling Green and take Nashville within a month, supported by a powerful flotilla of gunboats on the Cumberland. Burnside would attack Roanoke Island, off North Carolina, then go to New Bern and send a detachment to occupy Beaufort. The Army of the Potomac would go into action in the spring, and so on.

After the interview Ives filed a dispatch at the telegraph office: "General McClellan confides his plans to none. . . . Within the last few days, those who are admitted to even a partial confidence . . . are elated at the prospect presented." Ives said Lincoln thanked him for this dispatch the next day, when Ives wrote Bennett and Hudson the whole story. Fred Hudson exultantly wired congratulations. Walking with McClellan to the Capitol that morning as the General went to face his inquisitors in Congress, Ives was invited "to come in *every* evening at his home, and . . . he would always tell me all he knew."

Ives began to feel a little apprehensive. Wikoff, "a notorious chatterbox," met him the following morning and detailed, "paragraph by paragraph," another secret letter that Ives had written. Wikoff said Bennett had read it to him. "I felt *sorry*, to say the least," Ives confided to Hudson. "I would only say that if the knowledge of any such letter as I wrote yesterday should transpire—or even of the existence of such a letter—it would be an irreparable calamity."

McClellan, bent on securing the *Herald's* support, apparently had no misgivings whatever. The same morning, Ives wrote, "a darkey came up and requested me to go to the Commander-in-Chief's house." McClellan had fresh news for him from General Halleck. McClellan "is as guileless and innocent as a child, and we must be careful not to injure him, even to promote *Herald* interests. . . . I asked him, today, how often I should disturb him, and he replied:—'*Every day*.' " [5]

Hudson covered up for Ives in an editorial January 17 containing speculations based on the letters: "We do not belong to the military profession, nor do we boast to have been entrusted with any special confidential information from headquarters. . . ." The mere idea of it sounded fantastic. The *Herald* continued to "puff" McClellan regularly.

This cozy arrangement continued for three weeks without a hitch, but time was running out for the serpentine "doctor." Ives's know-it-all air and mysterious role had roused the enmity of Simon Parker Hanscom, the onetime Massachusetts Abolitionist who was chief of the *Herald* Washington bureau. On January 28 Hanscom informed the War Department that Ives had no connection with the *Herald* except as a local reporter, was not authorized to get Washington news, and had come to town as a speculator. Ives heard from Wikoff and William B. Shaw of the bureau that Hanscom was "abusing me systematically." It probably wouldn't hurt him at the Department, and "my hold with McClellan I also think sure; but you know I am thin-skinned, and this abuse bothers me and makes me want to go home."

Ives did go home. But just then a fourth member of the bureau, L. A. Whiteley, committed what Bennett regarded as an inexcusable *faux pas* by criticizing Mrs. Lincoln's decision to restrict the guest list at the Union Ball. (Bennett and his wife had received invitations.) "For stupidity and presumption such as this, we have a remedy, and know how to apply it," the old man thundered right on the editorial page.[6] Holding Hanscom responsible, he sent Ives back to Washington to discharge him at once. Ives did so, and proceeded to take over himself. He instructed the telegraph office that nothing was to go to the *Herald* without his signature. At the Navy De-

[5] Ives to Bennett, Jan. 15, 1862, Ives to Hudson, Jan. 16, 1862. Bennett Papers. These letters, with several others from the Bennett collection, appear in the *American Historical Review*, Vol. 39, No. 2 (Jan. 1934), 284-97.
[6] *Herald*, Feb. 5, 1862.

partment he got Assistant Secretary Fox to promise "to have *everything* given to the *Herald*—as far as he dares exclusively." At the War Department he told Assistant Secretary Tucker, according to the Philadelphia *Inquirer*, that "he expected the *Herald* to be posted in advance of all other newspapers to secure its support." He would use his own judgment, he said, about what should be withheld.

Marching into the War Department the next day with a few drinks under his belt, Ives presented his pass, signed by McClellan and admitting him to the Department "at all times." He demanded to see Secretary Stanton. "The Secretary is engaged," said Assistant Secretary Peter H. Watson. Ives asserted that he had a perfect right, as special representative of the New York *Herald*, to see Stanton any time he chose. The Secretary, said Watson firmly, was busy with members of Congress. All right, then, Ives shouted, the *Herald* will fix your kite and the administration's, too. Stanton heard the fracas and opened his door. In strode Malcolm Ives.[7]

Times, and Secretary Stanton, had changed since he had obligingly arranged the interview with McClellan. Sam Wilkeson had reported in the *Tribune* a few days before: "Rumor grows into belief that Secretary of War Stanton will resume in fact, as he has commenced to do in form, the conduct of the war which usage and department law give him the right to do." Stanton was intent on doing exactly that: seizing the initiative from McClellan, whom he increasingly mistrusted. Now Ives, spouting platitudes about the amity between them and how the *Herald* backed their every move, thanks to their co-operation in giving him news, roused him to fury. Stanton had Ives thrown out as an intruder. The following night Ives was arrested in his suite at the Willard and carted off to Fort McHenry in Baltimore harbor. The order for his arrest charged that he was a spy.[8]

Such were the hazards of inside journalism. If Wilkeson,

[7] Philadelphia *Inquirer*, Feb. 12, 1862.
[8] *Herald, Tribune*, Feb. 11, 1862.

Wikoff, and Ives were its top practitioners in the capital, there were plenty of others. Abram S. Mitchell, born and brought up on the banks of the Cumberland, helped General Buell map his Cumberland campaign while gingerly corresponding for the *Times*.[9] Joseph Howard of the *Times* rivaled Wikoff as Mrs. Lincoln's confidant. Ed Stedman of the *World* got much of his inside information by serving as Attorney General Bates's pardon clerk. L. A. Whiteley of the *Herald* kept his ears open at his desk in the Treasury Department.

Generally speaking, all of them were as much concerned with furthering the editorial causes of the papers they represented as they were in getting news. Just as the *Herald* worked closely with McClellan, so the *Tribune* and its men in Washington cultivated the Radicals who hated him, foreseeing as early as February 1862 that he probably would be the Democratic candidate for president in 1864.

2. "The Quarter-deck Brute"

In their cramped offices on Fourteenth Street, opposite the Willard, newsmen sensed a change in climate which they quickly transmitted to the nation. "The red tape and barnacle business has had its day," the *World* said. The Philadelphia *Inquirer*, the *World*, the *Tribune*, and others ran a vignette of the new Secretary of War in action, crackling with orders to subordinates, snapping "Good day!" to favor-seekers, attacking mountains of official papers with a vigor that was wonderful to behold. For a time it seemed that Edwin M. Stanton would overshadow Lincoln himself as the dominant personality in the administration.

Stedman appraised him for *World* readers: "Force—undaunted Force—Stanton's indisputable characteristic—streamed from the eyes, hair, whiskers, and very garments of

[9] *Times*, Feb. 25, 1862, dispatch signed "York."

the new Secretary of War." Wilkeson thought him "able and prodigiously magnetic," and more: "I believe that he is terribly in earnest." A *Times* staffer depicted him as "a stout, thick-set man, about 5 feet 8 inches high . . . hair and beard very black, the latter worn very thick and long. . . . His face is round and solid in expression, with blunt features. . . . He has never studied the art of pleasing, and has not the gift of paying compliments in conversation." That was putting it mildly. Stanton would be known in time among newsmen as "the Quarter-deck brute," "the damned rascal Stanton," a man who could rage like a lion, curse with magnificent conviction, and put the fear of God into the hearts of reporters, "some of whom," Noah Brooks of the Sacramento *Union* observed, "appeared to regard him as a fiend incarnate."

At a railroad executives' convention that February he hailed Grant's victories in the West, pointedly omitting mention of McClellan. An Associated Press reporter, having failed to attend himself, heard of Stanton's speech from S. L. M. Barlow, a friend of McClellan's, and wrote: "Secretary Stanton paid a high compliment to the young and gallant friend at his side, Major General McClellan, in whom he had the utmost confidence, and the result of whose military schemes, gigantic and well-matured, were now exhibited to a rejoicing country." Stanton was beside himself. He thundered that the report was "an impudent forgery." He demanded a retraction. He wrote Dana that "agents of the A.P. and a gang around the federal capital appear to be organized for the purpose of magnifying their idol." [1] There was no longer any doubt among editors where Stanton stood on McClellan.

A question of far greater moment to the newspaper world was what Stanton would do about censorship. The chief censor at the time, one H. E. Thayer, was an erstwhile manufacturer of mathematical instruments with what a House investigating committee described as "a very meagre knowledge of

---

[1] *Tribune*, Feb. 22, 24, 27, 1862; Charles A. Dana: *Recollections of the Civil War* (New York: 1913), 10.

public affairs." Certainly his decisions were bizarre enough to prove it. He refused to permit a *World* reporter to wire his editor confirmation of a story that had already appeared in the *Herald*. Wilkeson got away with wiring inside information, but ran afoul of Thayer's pencil when he tried to deny a report that an Assistant Secretary of War had been arrested for treason. Under this haphazard regime, punctuated by occasional blackouts ordered by Seward (as after Ball's Bluff and the *Trent* affair) the censorship had become a mockery.

Stanton moved swiftly. On January 22 his friend and fellow Radical, "Bluff Ben" Wade of Ohio, introduced in the Senate a bill authorizing the President to take over the telegraph lines and the railroads in a wartime emergency. Stanton urged its passage. The bill became law on January 31, and on February 2 Lincoln placed all telegraph lines under military supervision. Editors were notified that telegrams on military matters not authorized by the Secretary of War or the general in command were forbidden, and that offending papers would lose the use of both the telegraph lines and the railroads for transporting papers. Stanton appointed Sanford, the American Telegraph Company president, to the new post of Military Supervisor of Telegraphs, and Sanford promptly required oaths of allegiance and secrecy of his operators.[2]

These moves caused scarcely a flutter in the press, for it seemed obvious that the government, lacking the personnel to scrutinize tens of thousands of words transmitted daily from scores of telegraph offices, could exercise only nominal control. Circumstances varied too widely to make it effective. Late on the night of the executive order, for example, a Chicago reporter standing on a wharf in Cairo chanced to see two gunboats load and move noiselessly up the Ohio. Piecing together other clues, he rushed to the telegraph office with a story that a great movement was afoot which would shortly

[2] James G. Randall: "The Newspaper Problem and Its Bearing upon Military Secrecy during the Civil War," *American Historical Review*, Vol. 23, No. 2 (Jan. 1918), 305.

electrify the country. Grant's censor had the idea that he should pass anything that was untrue in order to mislead the enemy. He let it go. It proved to be the first the world heard of the launching of Grant's "secret" movement on Fort Henry.[3]

But Stanton had not yet begun to fight. On February 25 he notified police chiefs in all major cities that "all newspaper editors and publishers have been forbidden to publish any intelligence received by telegraph or otherwise respecting military operations by U.S. forces. Please see this night that this order is observed. If violated by any paper issued tomorrow, seize the whole edition and give notice to this department that arrests may be ordered." [4] For twenty-four hours there was bedlam. In Chicago, police pushed into the press rooms and stopped the presses between three and five o'clock in the morning while they perused every word being printed. Rumors flew around newsless Cincinnati the next day: Manassas had been taken with forty thousand Confederate prisoners, Price had surrendered in Missouri, General Banks had been "cut to pieces" on the upper Potomac. All manner of wild speculations disturbed Philadelphia and New York. The New York *Evening Post* said that members of Congress were too agitated by rumors to conduct business.

The press bellowed defiance. "The thing is incredible," said the *World*. "It is not possible that this free government is thus prepared to adopt the first necessity of a military despotism. This is the people's war. . . . There must be freedom of information, and freedom of speech. And so there will be, even though it rains interdicts." The *Times* was outraged, urging the rest of the press not to surrender. The *Tribune*, though pro-Stanton, warned that the responsibility for withholding news "will be a fearful one, and *it will rest wholly on the Government.*" Only the *Herald* managed a shrug: "Secretary

[3] Albert D. Richardson: *Personal History of U. S. Grant* (Boston: 1868), edition of 1885, 209.
[4] *O.R.*, Ser. II, Vol. 2, 246.

Stanton writes his emphatic manifestoes slapdash and with great mental reservations." The next day Stanton, apparently satisfied that he had proved he meant business, revoked his order.

The furor had hardly died away before the Secretary was roused to action by an item in the Washington *Sunday Chronicle*. "You will immediately take possession of the printing office in which publication is made," he directed Brigadier General James Wadsworth, commanding in Washington, "arrest the printers and publishers of the paper, take possession of all papers that can be found and destroy them, and hold the parties in custody that they may be dealt with according to the Rules and Articles of War." Wadsworth ransacked the office and arrested the employees, but released them after the editor explained that the objectionable news had been put in inadvertently after he had gone to bed.[5]

Stanton was intractable, unpredictable, a martinet who came as close to throttling the press as any man in American history. But not even Stanton, with his table-pounding threats, arrests, and orders, could keep the Bohemians from reporting the war.

A thousand miles westward, the indefatigable Richardson dropped in to say good-by to General Grant before heading for the *Tribune* office with the story of the fall of Fort Henry. "You had better stay a day or two," the General said amiably, "because I am going over to capture Fort Donelson tomorrow." [6] As Grant's army moved overland to join Commodore A. H. Foote's gunboats in the assault, reporters scrambled to record the first great battle in the West from every possible vantage point.

In the pilothouse of the *St. Louis*, tough little "Mack" Mc-Cullagh of the Cincinnati *Gazette* squinted through the Commodore's field glasses as she closed in. Foote, nursing his rheumatism on a cot, ordered McCullagh to keep up a running

---

[5] *O.R.*, Ser. II, Vol. 2, 269; Leech, *Reveille*, 161.
[6] Richardson: *Secret Service*, 218.

commentary. The reporter had volunteered as Foote's private secretary, scarcely with this in mind. "We are getting awfully close, Commodore; through this glass I can almost put my hand on the fellows at the guns in the fort." "That's right," McCullagh remembered the old man saying. "Put on a little more steam, Mr. Pilot, and get as close as you can." Shots were crashing into the *St. Louis* so rapidly that "Mack" lost his reporting faculty. "Jeeesus!" Between concussions he heard the old man tut-tutting behind him. "Don't swear, men; it does no good." "Two hundred yards!" McCullagh and the pilot ducked involuntarily. Foote tut-tutted again. The next instant the pilothouse seemed to disintegrate: a shell crashed through the armor plating and exploded, smashing the wheel to match timber. The pilot, a huge splinter protruding from his chest, looked at McCullagh "with what seemed a wondering, questioning expression," sank to the floor, and died minutes later. The young reporter turned helplessly to Foote, saw that his leg was shattered, and yelled for the surgeon. Together they carried him down the ladder and along the gun deck to his cabin. The flagship drifted downstream. She had been hit sixty-five times.[7]

Meanwhile the reporters ashore were having troubles of their own. "The Bohemian Brigade, in order not to be too late for what, with exquisite irony, is termed 'the fun,'" a Cincinnati *Times* man explained, had left all blankets and provisions behind. In semi-frozen slush ankle-deep, and under a black sky, they wandered from camp to camp, wind piercing the marrow "like arrows of ice," Franc Wilkie wrote. Junius Browne of the *Tribune*, wounded in the eye by a bit of flying cartridge paper, groped along behind army wagons to pick up pieces of hard bread jolted from them. André Matteson of the Chicago *Morning Post* got lost and went without food for fifteen hours before Wilkie found him in a gully. They divvied up Wilkie's fried pork and hardtack, oblivious to the

[7] Walter B. Stevens: "Joseph McCullagh," *Missouri Historical Review*, Vol. 25, No. 1 (Oct. 1930), 8, 9.

shelling of Confederate twelve-pounders. Browne and William E. Webb of the *Missouri Republican*, concluding that they might as well die fighting, fell in with Birge's sharpshooters and borrowed a couple of Enfields. The little, baldpated *Tribune* correspondent, a patch over his eye, crouched and fired; he swore later that he got his man. In another part of the field, Wilkie tried it, too, but concluded, as enemy shots nicked the log in front of him, that his obligation to the *Times* came first. He retreated.[8]

George W. Beaman of the *Missouri Democrat* appears to have been the only correspondent to get news through to his paper while the siege was in progress. At 2:00 a.m. on February 17, the New York papers rolled off extras with the *Democrat's* dispatch, relayed by the Associated Press from St. Louis. That morning crowds gathered outside the newspaper offices on Park Row; "in ferryboats, omnibuses and cars, men earnestly discussed the position of our troops," the *Times* reported. At 11:00 a.m. the *Tribune* hit the streets with another extra: "FREEDOM! FORT DONELSON TAKEN!" For once Dana played it on page one, beneath a cut of the flag. Curiously, the news had come, not from the War Department or the Bohemians on the scene, but from Fortress Monroe in Chesapeake Bay, where the *Tribune* representative heard it from exchanged prisoners just out of Richmond.

Bohemians scoured the Confederate works, and went to work on prisoners with what Browne deplored as "ultraprofessional" abandon. Charles C. Coffin, the solemn correspondent of the Boston *Journal*, sprinted by Wilkie. "As far as I could see him he kept up the pace, up hill and down, over breastworks, parapets, rifle-pits, rocks, fallen trees . . . with his head down, like an animal which trails by scent." A Chicago correspondent locked up Major General Simon Bolivar Buckner, C.S.A., to make a sketch of him. Another found Confederate Brigadier General Bushrod Johnson reluctant to talk, whereupon the reporter blandly pretended to read:

[8] Browne: *Four Years*, 68–71; Wilkie: *Pen and Powder*, 111–13.

"Bushrod K. Johnson, a native of Massachusetts, formerly one of the editors of Lloyd Garrison's anti-slavery journal, but compelled to fly to Tennessee on account of being detected in a forgery of his father's name . . ." The General hastily relented. A third reporter begged a wounded Confederate for an interview before he died: "If you have any last words, they'll appear in my paper in the very best form." [9]

The newsmen sneaked aboard hospital boats to make the 180-mile trip back to Cairo, carrying water and holding lanterns for nurses and surgeons, later scribbling dispatches madly amid the groans of the wounded. By a prior arrangement with J. J. Wilson, superintendent of the telegraph lines at Cairo, the St. Louis, Chicago, and Cincinnati men got their stories on the wire first, but throughout the victory-starved North, editors ran every account that came to hand for days thereafter. If they painted a confusing picture of the bitter three-day siege, they nonetheless gave context to two sentences that thrilled millions and would go ringing down the corridors of history—Grant's response to Buckner's request for an armistice: "No terms except an unconditional and immediate surrender can be accepted. I propose to move immediately on your works."

3. GOOD-BY, MR. DANA

THESE were piping times for Charlie Dana. Pacing to and fro on the green carpet, now gazing out the window at the tents and temporary barracks that dotted City Hall Park, now whirling to bark an order into the editorial room, now cursing softly and sitting down to scrawl instructions to Browne in Cairo or shake up Charles Brigham at Fortress Monroe or soothe Sam Wilkeson in Washington, he worked in the grim realization that a newspaper which had always been dedicated to political and intellectual leadership was on

[9] Browne: *Four Years*, 84, 85.

the same footing now as "the Main Chance" *Herald*. The pushing, yelling crowd he could hear down on Nassau Street, reading *Tribune* bulletins and waiting for more, told its own story. The *Herald*, even with Ives and Wikoff in prison and nothing of its own to show on Fort Donelson, hit a new peak of 118,000 that February—and still Greeley wanted space to air pet projects. The *Tribune* ran thirty columns of documents in Frémont's defense one day in March, presumably for the enlightenment of the Committee on the Conduct of the War. It was for such purposes, rather than for news, that the paper occasionally sallied forth in twelve- and sixteen-page editions. The weekly, on which the Tribune Association had made most of its profits, continued to lose readers—more than thirty thousand in six months—and while the *Tribune* could still proclaim that the daily, semi-weekly, and weekly editions "are fully 50,000 above the aggregate of any newspaper in the world," the daily remained around 53,000, and Association stockholders, many of them staff members, were uneasy about it.[1]

One of the major stories of the war exploded that March at Hampton Roads, one which illustrated the contrast between *Herald* and *Tribune* coverage as well as any. Editors had had plenty of notice that the Southerners were rebuilding the *Merrimac*, a forty-gun frigate they salvaged after the Federals abandoned Norfolk. In the fall Hudson had purchased a sixteen-foot Hell Gate pilot boat for B. S. Osbon, the daredevil naval correspondent whom he had lured from the *World*. Osbon skimmed across Hampton Roads in her one night, oarlocks muffled with sheepskin. He examined the *Merrimac* at first hand and did a story on the monster for the *Herald*, and a sketch for *Harper's Weekly*. By March 5, 1862, when her reconstruction as an ironclad was completed, at least half a dozen reporters were on the lookout at Fortress Mon-

---

[1] *Tribune*, Apr. 10, 1862, gave the circulation of its weekly "at this time" as 150,750. This compares with 189,000 the previous October. In the same period, its semi-weekly dropped from 22,000 to 18,000.

roe, including Dana's old standby Charles D. Brigham, J. Robley Duglison of the Philadelphia *Inquirer*, and representatives of the *Herald* and the Baltimore *American*. Providentially, Ericsson's ironclad *Monitor*, launched amid much fanfare a month before, left New York harbor for Hampton Roads the next day.

On March 8, C. C. Fulton, editor of the Baltimore *American*, wired Assistant Secretary Fox word from his correspondent: "Steamer Merrimac was lying near Navy Yard yesterday morning with flag flying and crew on board. She draws twenty-three (23) feet of water and was described to me as looking like roof of sunken house with smoke-stack protruding from water." [2] Fox was already en route; Fulton's wire went instead to the anxious President. At the fort that morning, Brigham at last got his glass on her black smoke. Gradually she loomed into view, looking "terribly saucy," said the *Herald* man. The Navy's lookout boat in the Roads fired a warning as she steamed toward the *Cumberland*, the proud old frigate off Newport News. The reporters at Monroe wired George Cowlan, a telegrapher at Newport News, to report what he could see from his side of the point. The key began to click. "She's heading this way. . . . She's heading straight for the *Cumberland*. . . . The *Cumberland* gives her a broadside. She keels over. She seems to be sinking. No. She comes on again. There goes a shell through this shanty. . . . She has rammed the *Cumberland*. God! The *Cumberland* is sinking." [3] Brigham peered at the battle smoke, nearly eight miles away, as the telegraph chattered. "The masts of the *Cumberland* which could be seen over the point of land were seen listing and finally to go over," he noted. From this awesome triumph the *Merrimac* went on to the *Congress*, raked her murderously at point-blank until she struck her colors, then withdrew. At 5:00 p.m. Brigham completed his *Tribune*

[2] Robert T. Lincoln Collection.
[3] John Emmet O'Brien: *Telegraphing in Battle* (Scranton, Pennsylvania: 1910), 62–4. O'Brien was the operator at Fortress Monroe.

dispatch and put it on the Baltimore packet, and it was relayed directly to Lincoln, on War Department orders, by the Magnetic Telegraph Company in Baltimore the next morning, Sunday, March 9. Brigham's final sentence was a chiller: "It is represented that the shells that struck the *Merrimac* had no effect on her but glanced off like pebble-stones." [4] (The same day, Admiral Dahlgren anxiously wired the President on the advisability of blockading the Potomac with stone barges.)

It was a memorable Sunday, and not only because the weird-looking *Monitor* had arrived off Hampton Roads at ten o'clock the night before. A cable crossing Chesapeake Bay from Fortress Monroe to Cape Charles was completed after twenty-three days' work at 4:00 p.m.—in the nick of time to enable newsmen to report the thrilling battle between the ironclads. Transmitted directly, their dispatches arrived a matter of hours after the terrifying ones of the day before. "Washington was gloomy at noon," the *Herald* bureau reported. "This evening the wind sets in the other quarter." New York editors went to press Sunday night with accounts of both days' fighting; the panic that the *Merrimac* is supposed to have struck in the hearts of the North was limited to a few hours of agony after the first extras.

Presumably Dana was off that Sunday, as usual. The *Tribune* contented itself with Brigham's brief sentences about the stand-off struggle between the *Monitor* and the *Merrimac*, along with his longer dispatch of the eighth, on page five. But Hudson's news sense served him well. He devoted his entire front page to the two-day story—a beautifully integrated layout featuring a map of Hampton Roads, details on all the ships involved, the news and its effect on Washington, and a reprint of Osbon's story of the previous October predicting the *Merrimac's* assault. He followed this the next day with three and a half columns from his own man, crude woodcuts of

[4] Twenty-two page telegram to the *Tribune*, Robert T. Lincoln Collection.

both ships, and sketches of John Ericsson, J. L. Worden, the *Monitor's* skipper, and Chief Engineer Stimers. More eye-witness accounts appeared in the *Herald* the day after this, and on March 14 Hudson again gave the first battle between iron-clads his whole front page, with a four-column battle dia-gram. The *Tribune* did not get around to pulling the details together in a rewrite until six weeks later.

Incidentally, the phrase that endeared the *Monitor* to the North came from a Norfolk *Day Book* reporter, watching the little craft from the Confederate shore. The Baltimore *American* man picked it up, writing: "I am struck with the pertness of the Norfolk description of her as 'a Yankee cheesebox on a raft.' It gives a better idea of her appearance than any of the engravings or descriptions in the New York papers." In the absence of a fully developed press-association service, this continual reprinting of what was unusual or striking or simply "pert" by reporters and hawk-eyed editors reading their ex-changes formed a vital part of the tapestry of the news. In this case the New York *Times* reprinted the Baltimore *American's* dispatch, other editors picked it up from the *Times*, and the "cheesebox on a raft" became common currency.

Neither Dana nor Hudson permitted himself to forget the main event: McClellan was still in the saddle, and at last on March 11 word came that the Army of the Potomac had moved into Virginia. Hudson got off an extra before noon—"THE EVACUATION OF MANASSAS." The army, accompanied by a host of correspondents, had advanced to discover nothing but log Quaker guns and abandoned enemy trenches on the old Bull Run battlefield. Dana had sent one of the *Trib-une's* prima donnas, Bayard Taylor, the big, genial poet and world traveler whose descriptive work in California and with Perry's expedition to Japan had provided the paper with some of its most notable reporting, to follow the campaign. Taylor piled on the satire, datelining one dispatch "Camp Disap-pointment, near Centreville," and was only too happy to accept an offer a few days later to go to St. Petersburg as Secretary of the American legation. War correspondence, he confessed, was "a test of human endurance" for which he had no taste.

What next? Ed Stedman of the *World* sent Manton Marble, his editor, private dispatches that unfolded the whole story. Returning to Fairfax Court House on March 13, Stedman found a council of war pending, "went to General Fitz-John Porter's headquarters till it was over, was then cordially welcomed, and he at once took me to a private room and talked with me an hour. . . . McClellan's wish has been, from the *first*, (*so F.J.P. was allowed to tell me*), to send 75,000 men by transports to the region between the York, Rappahannock, and James Rivers—and take Richmond." Once again the press-conscious McClellan, through his closest friend in the army, was spilling secrets in exchange for badly needed editorial support. The Cabinet and anti-McClellan corps commanders, Stedman was told, "have continually thwarted and opposed this military plan," but "it will probably be carried out. The General today says it will be. . . . The soldiers in the camp idolize McClellan, and although chagrined to lose a fight, are enraged at the attacks made upon him. The rank and file have stopped buying the *Tribune*, so the army newsmen tell me." The *World* immediately published an editorial calling for confidence in McClellan.[5]

As McClellan's transports loaded and Richmond papers described the mighty expedition heading for the York Peninsula, Stanton determined that not a word about it should appear in the Northern press. The editors of the Boston *Journal*, the New York *Journal of Commerce*, and the New York *Sunday Mercury* were arrested and threatened with court-martial proceedings for hinting about the campaign. Stanton had Postmaster General Blair direct all postmasters to bar from the mails any paper that published "facts excluded from the telegraph," thus extending the censorship to cover both mail and express

[5] Stedman: *Letters*, 268–70; *World*, Mar. 15, 1862.

dispatches.[6] Then, on April 1, Stanton issued an order for-bidding correspondents to accompany the army.

In every instance, the gold-spectacled terror in the War Office let loose his thunderbolts only to retrieve them. The arrested editors were released after a perfunctory inquiry; the post-office order became a dead letter from the day it was issued, and the embargo on correspondents with the army proved to be aimed at one man. William Howard Russell, more unpopular than ever because it was believed that he had used early news to play the stock market, applied vainly to Stanton for a pass. When he secured one through McClellan that got him aboard a transport, Stanton found out about it, issued his order, and had Russell, horse, carriage, bag and baggage carted down the gangplank.[7] Bewildered corre-spondents learned the next day that the order applied only to Russell, yet got nowhere when they sought passes themselves. "I went four days in a row," George Salter of the *Times* wrote after his initiation into what would become a routine proce-dure, "and each time it was, 'Come again, we have not decided this important point.' " Meanwhile, many newsmen, by hook or by crook, had already sailed. On April 7, Stanton finally directed E. S. Sanford to issue passes after requiring each recipient to sign a parole of allegiance in which he swore not to write information of value to the enemy.[8]

The lull in military news only added to the hubbub over McClellan. "The *Tribune* and its ten million adherents are howling against the General," wrote Stedman. The Associated Press, always tagging close behind the *Herald's* line, reported that a House resolution urging McClellan's removal was abandoned, "it being but too evident that it could command only a very few votes." *Tribune* readers learned that "it was withdrawn by the mover after a debate which showed a unani-mous purpose to pass it," a fair sample of the contradictory

[6] *World*, Mar. 25, 1862.
[7] *Herald*, Apr. 3, *Tribune*, Apr. 5, 1862, Washington dispatches. Russell sailed for England a week later.
[8] *Times*, Apr. 14, 15, 1862.

reporting that anything relating to McClellan seemed to inspire. Anyone "praised by the *Herald*, abused by the *Tribune*," Charles Henry Webb quipped in the *Times*, "has a claim upon the public sympathy that no man can disregard." Almost alone among major papers, the *Tribune* kept up a relentless barrage against him, and it is evidence of its still powerful influence that, with the army and most of the press solidly behind the man, he was widely accounted the underdog.

Whatever Horace Greeley thought of McClellan, the editor's relationship with Dana suddenly reached the breaking-point. As Charles Congdon, Dana, and others sensed at the time, Greeley probably felt a twinge of jealousy, compounded by differences that went back to Bull Run and earlier; he felt Dana was running too much of the show.

In any event, Dana confided to a friend two weeks later:

> On Thursday, March 27, I was notified that Mr. Greeley had given the stockholders notice that I must leave or he would, and that they wanted me to leave accordingly. No cause of dissatisfaction being alleged . . . I sent a friend to him to ascertain if it was true. My friend came and reported that it was true. . . . On Friday, March 28, I resigned. . . . On Saturday . . . Greeley called another meeting, said . . . that it was a damned lie . . . and finally sent me a verbal message . . . to remain as a writer of editorials, but has never been near me since to meet the 'damned lie' in person.[9]

Dana, in truth, never went back to the office.

The news rocked Park Row. After fifteen years, the *Tribune* without Dana seemed as incongruous as Currier without Ives. The first man to hold the title of "managing editor" in journalism, and the only one of those mysterious people at all well known to the public, was through; every paper in town, and many out of town, ran an item about it. He had

[9] Rosebault: *Dana*, 62.

left in a dispute over Abolitionism, many said. Greeley issued a categorical denial. Further, he said tartly, "Mr. Dana was never principal Editor; he never professed to be. Horace Greeley is still Editor; he always has been."

The dress rehearsals were over now. The parades, the months of waiting while the Army of the Potomac girded itself, the complex maneuverings of McClellan and his foes in the struggle over strategy, the devious detective work of the inside operators, the bombastic opening moves of Mr. Stanton regarding censorship, the gay irresponsibilities of Bohemians who thought the war a lark—these things faded into the files when editors learned that at long last one hundred thousand soldiers had landed on the York Peninsula in the mighty campaign that was to end the war.

Dana was gone, and there was tomorrow's issue to get out at the Rookery.

CHAPTER V

The Education of Mr. Gay

1. MEET THE NEW M.E.

A SLIGHT, middle-aged gentleman, Roman-nosed, eyes set rather close together, whiskers well-groomed, sat hunched behind his *Tribune* aboard a Staten Island paddle-wheeler, glancing impatiently toward the mast-rimmed Manhattan shore. For five years now Sydney Howard Gay had been turning out editorials for the *Tribune*. Friends on board could tell at a glance who had written the day's leader (as the first editorial on the sacred page was called), less by the look of this scholarly figure than by the tilt of his wife's bonnet. On Greeley days, it was down; one said nothing. On others, it had a pert tilt, and animated were the exchanges of pleasantries. But on this day early in April 1862, with or without his transpicuous lady, Gay transferred as usual to the Nassau Street omnibus, got off at Spruce, trudged up the dark iron stairs, hung up his coat, and discovered that he was the managing editor. Gay's high-legged stool and table were moved into the sanctum sanctorum, and a new regime began on the most influential paper in the land.

The job would come close to killing Sydney Gay. Certainly there was little in his background to commend him for it. Following a sickly youth at Hingham, Massachusetts, he had entered Harvard at fifteen, left after two years because of illness, traveled as an agent for Perkins and Company, China merchants, toured the West "doing nothing more creditable than shooting and loafing," as he put it, and returned to study law at his father's office in Hingham. He gave up "from certain scruples of conscience"—since the Constitution condoned slavery, he would not take the lawyer's oath. Young Gay drifted into William Lloyd Garrison's circle in Boston. In 1842 he took the road as lecturer for the American Anti-Slavery Society, and a year later became editor of the *Anti-Slavery Standard* in New York. Here he hit his stride. Edward Everett Hale said Gay made the paper "a brilliant exception to the dullness, almost proverbial, of what are called 'organs.' "[1] Edmund Quincy, Maria Weston Chapman, and James Russell Lowell livened its pages; in it Gay first published most of Lowell's *Biglow Papers*. Greeley was quite taken with the sheet, and in 1857 he had finally lured its crusading editor to the *Tribune*. In the office Gay was quiet, witty but a little aloof from the Pfaff's crowd, conscientious to a fault, imbued with the intellectual fervor that gave the *Tribune* its special flavor. Beyond serving as make-up editor of the weekly for a stretch, he had had nothing whatever to do with the news side until now.

The Staten Island ferry knew him no longer. His wife was soon writing one of the children that "he stays in the city all week. . . . I almost hope he doesn't keep his new job." Gay took a room near the office and lived, breathed, talked, and dreamed the New York *Tribune* around the clock.

The beginning was hardly auspicious. The abominated *Herald* got out no less than four "Triple Sheets" in Gay's first week—and in one of them scored one of the great beats of the war. At 6:00 a.m. on Wednesday, April 9, Hudson's night man checked with the press room, found the forms still standing, and bounded up to the composing room with a dispatch:

[1] Edward Everett Hale: *James Russell Lowell and His Friends* (Boston: 1899), 172. Other details are from MS which Gay prepared for *White's Conspectus*, Gay Papers.

Pittsburg, via Fort Henry, April 9, 3:20 a.m.—One of the greatest and bloodiest battles of modern days has just closed, resulting in the complete rout of the enemy, who attacked us at daybreak Sunday morning.

The battle lasted without intermission during the entire day and was again renewed on Monday morning, and continued undecided until 4 o'clock in the afternoon, when the enemy commenced their retreat, and are still flying toward Corinth, pursued by a large force of our cavalry.

The slaughter on both sides is immense. . . .

This was the first anyone heard of the Battle of Shiloh. Since Associated Press rules made it available to those willing to share the telegraph tolls once the recipient got on the streets with it, the *Tribune* and others rushed forth with extras, but the *Herald* trumpeted its beat for days.[2] "It is now being read by the President," Whiteley wired that morning. It was read to the Senate; Speaker Colfax read it to the House, where "all hearts were stilled and the very breathing almost suppressed until the last word." Greeley threw a fit. Where in blazes was Richardson? What was the matter with Browne? Gay explained patiently that Dana had assigned them to cover operations against Island No. 10 on the Mississippi; both of them were aboard Foote's flagship. Well, then, where was Henry Villard? With Richardson's encouragement, Villard had been contributing to the *Tribune* at space rates from Buell's army. It was clear that Buell had arrived in time to reinforce Grant, yet not a word had come from Villard.

At Pittsburg Landing, "a contemptible, isolated little landing on the Tennessee River," as the *Herald* man had it, the bluffs were alive with men in blue when Henry Villard ar-

[2] For this A.P. rule, see George B. Prescott: *History, Theory and Practice of the Electric Telegraph* (Boston: 1860), 386, or Townsend: *Campaigns*, 214. Dispatches from Washington were exempt, making the capital the relay point for exclusive stories throughout the war.

rived late Sunday afternoon aboard a transport with Buell. He found himself among "an immense, panic-striken, uncontrollable mob." "We were surprised at breakfast by rebels four times as strong as ourselves," Villard heard; he could get nothing more coherent from anyone he met. Pouring rain set in, and the Bohemians, sloshing around looking for Grant's headquarters amid rumors thick as blackberries, tried to piece together the outline of what seemed stark disaster, a hundred miles from the nearest telegraph station at Fort Henry. Not many were left. Henry Bentley of the Philadelphia *Inquirer* was captured in his tent during the initial attack on Sherman's position. Young Irving Carson of the Chicago *Tribune*, standing within seven feet of Grant, was decapitated by a six-pound shot. Another Chicago *Tribune* man, having volunteered as an assistant surgeon, was himself badly wounded in the thigh. Frank W. Reilly of the Cincinnati *Times* was shot in the leg.

Arriving on the scene with Grant, Whitelaw Reid of the Cincinnati *Gazette* found that Albert Sidney Johnston's yelling recruits had burst upon the Union camps with murderous effect: "Some, particularly among our officers, were not yet out of bed. Others were dressing, others washing, others cooking. . . . The first wild cries of the pickets rushing in, and the few scattering shots that preceded their arrival, aroused the regiments to a sense of their peril; an instant afterward, shells were hurtling through the tents; while, before there was time for a thought of preparation, there came rushing through the woods, with lines of battle sweeping the whole fronts of the division camps and bending down on either flank, the fine, dashing compact columns of the enemy." The disorganized Federals had been driven back to the high ground near the river, where Grant contrived to form a defense line under cover of the gunboats. That night Reid slept on the bluff; a few miles away Villard stumbled into Nelson's brigade headquarters, taking shelter beneath a rubber poncho hung between trees near a big log fire. Washing down hardtack and cold bacon with some of the General's brandy, Villard found the staff tight-lipped with anxiety; salvos from the gunboats crashed into the woods beyond at ten-minute intervals all night. None of them slept.

In the morning the counterattack got underway as Buell moved into action. Villard followed Nelson's advance with the ambulances. Rain and smoke obscured his view. His opposition was near by. Colonel William Camm led his regiment of Illinoians into action toward noon: "As we passed through the woods between the road and the review ground," the Colonel noted in his diary, "a man on a gray horse and wearing citizen clothes was trying to hide behind a large tree from the Rebels in sight beyond the field. He claimed to be the correspondent of the N. Y. *Herald*, but I made him get out of the way of my men." [3] Near the Shiloh meetinghouse, now an improvised field hospital, Meissner of the Chicago *Times* and Reilly did what they could to help. "I hope my eyes may never again look upon such sights," Reilly wrote. "Men with their entrails protruding, others with bullets in their breasts or shoulders, and one poor wretch I found whose eyes had been shot entirely away. . . . The battle has now been over for at least ten hours, yet so accustomed have I become since yesterday to the rattle of musketry, that there is a constant 'crack, crack, crack' ringing through my ears as I sit down to write. . . . On either side the battle was fought with a desperation which I could not have believed to exist in the minds of men." [4]

Reilly and the *Herald* man wrote what they could and got their dispatches aboard the first boat leaving for Fort Henry; the *Herald's*, by favor or by chance, was the only one sent. Villard, "too exhausted for any brain work," remained a day longer with Reid and others to go over the field. It was "grim, shocking, and sickening." The dead remained unburied; piles

[3] Fritz Haskell, ed.: "Diary of Colonel William Camm," *Journal of the Illinois State Historical Society*, Vol. 18, No. 4 (Jan. 1926), 856.

[4] Quoted in the New York *Times*, Apr. 13, 1862. See also Villard, I, 243–53.

of amputated limbs marked field hospitals. That evening Villard caught a hospital boat for Cairo, ran into Reid, and exchanged notes during the long river journey. At Cairo, Franc Wilkie read the story of Shiloh in Reid's eyes: "His expression suggested an escape from some imminent and frightful danger. He was no coward, but there was a good deal of apparent awe in that face." [5] It echoed in the lead Reid had written on the boat:

> Fresh from the field of the great battle, with its pounding and roaring of artillery, and its keener-voiced rattle of musketry sounding in my ears; with all its visions of horror still seeming seared upon my eye-balls, while scenes of panic-stricken rout and brilliant charges, and obstinate defences, and succor, and intoxicating success are burned alike confusedly and indelibly upon my brain, I essay to write what I know of the battle of Pittsburg Landing.

He continued on the cars to Cincinnati that night: 19,500 words in all—one of the most celebrated and controversial dispatches of the war. Both the *Herald* and the *Tribune* reprinted it, the *Herald* remarking that "it is the only detailed account given to the public—all the other statements being a mere compilation of bits and scraps, without beginning and without end."

Gay waited, hoping to hear from Villard. But Villard had been betrayed by the mails; the *Tribune* had nothing from him until all the Bohemians in the area had converged on the battleground, including Richardson, whom Gay sent thinking Villard had been killed. The controversy over Shiloh raged for weeks in the press, and it would continue for years to come. Was it true, as Reid had said, that men were bayoneted in their tents, that Sherman failed to throw out pickets, that Grant was caught completely unawares and did not even ar-

[5] Wilkie: *Pen and Powder*, 154.

rive on the field until the enemy had almost carried it that Sunday morning? "In the camps, as in the newspapers," Villard wrote nearly three weeks later, "you find it difficult to winnow the truth from the bushel of falsehood. Here are the ordinary obstacles to learning the facts about a battle—the jealousies, the cliques, the inordinate ambitions, the untrustworthiness of eyes and ears during periods of great excitement. . . . Every journalist who has spent the last two weeks in riding from camp to camp in the fathomless mud to question witnesses, verify assertions, and sift the truth out of contradictions . . . has concluded that the deepest of all wells in which the truth was ever sought is the Battle of Pittsburg Landing." Grant's brief report and those of his subordinates only exacerbated matters; as the *Tribune* pointed out, "All that the people really know . . . they have learned from newspaper correspondents, who are quite commonly regarded and treated as barely tolerated (sometimes as intolerable) nuisances in the camps."

Greeley never forgave Villard for the *Herald's* beat,[6] but Gay scarcely had time to fret about it. On April 10 the *Tribune* at last blossomed forth with news on its front page. It was the paper's twenty-first anniversary, celebrated with a change that Gay boldly announced would be permanent. The *Times* and *Herald* had changed over before the war, the *World* on June 19, 1861, and the *Sun* followed in May 1862, leaving only the *Evening Post* and the old blanket sheets to continue the tradition of running major news opposite the editorials in the center spread.

McClellan's mighty campaign against Richmond from the York Peninsula compounded the turmoil over censorship. Stanton ordered telegraphic service to the Philadelphia *Inquirer* suspended for a dispatch from Fortress Monroe, though General Wool had approved it. John T. Quigg of the *World*, having captured and interviewed a stray Confederate, was

---

[6] Gay to Villard, Jan. 31, 1864, Villard Papers in possession of his grandson, Henry H. Villard, of Garden City, New York.

arrested at Monroe and detained in the guardhouse on un-specified charges. For the first time, mail was held up; all let-ters, private or otherwise, had to be initialed by DeWitt Clin-ton, a young aide on Wool's staff. Every available copy of *Harper's Weekly* containing a picture of the Confederate works before Yorktown was confiscated by the zealous cen-sors at Monroe. "There is no light to guide, no compass to di-rect," Wilkeson wrote from Washington. Gay was exasperated. "When will the censor of the press treat all journals alike?" he asked in the *Tribune*. "Yesterday at the instance of the tele-graphic agent, we suppressed news in relation to the *Galena* [an ironclad sloop at Hampton Roads] . . . only to find the dispatch conspicuously printed in the Washington *Star* and the New York *World* of this morning." The *Times* thundered at "the vexatious despotism of the War Department since Mr. Stanton became its chief." Its reporters had been "paroled as if they were traitors"; the censorship "has become to Press and people an intolerable grievance." Similar angry outbursts were to be found in almost every paper one picked up.

Nevertheless, by the end of the month the public began to get a dim idea of McClellan's tortuous inching toward York-town. Just after lunch on May 4 came an A.P. bulletin: the enemy had evacuated Yorktown. Gay, who so loved the éclat of an extra that he declared he preferred it to a beat in the regular edition, exulted that by "precisely 2 o'clock we had summoned our pressmen and compositors, raised steam to drive our immense printing engine, and thrown off an Extra Tribune with the glorious news." This was as nothing to his performance the next week, when McClellan defeated the re-treating foe at Williamsburg and Lincoln personally directed the Navy's capture of Norfolk. On Sunday, May 11, the *Trib-une* reeled off three successive extras between 11:45 a.m. and 1:00 p.m. The bulletins were skimpy, but Gay gave them plenty of leading, threw in a cut of a screaming eagle perched on the shield of the Union, and ran some blood-stirring Byron in ten-point italic:

Freedom's battle once begun,
  Though baffled oft, is ever won.
Yet Freedom! yet thy banner torn, but flying
  Streams like a thundercloud against the wind.

Such pyrotechnics did not escape the notice of Frederic Hudson. At nine that evening, the *Herald* sallied forth with a cut of the flag and an assortment of headlines that ran three quarters of the way down column one. Both editors thought that the war was almost over.

The Peninsular campaign afforded the first great challenge to the press to provide sustained coverage of war fought on an unparalleled scale deep in enemy country. It was Sydney Gay's introduction to the exigencies of war reporting. The situation required, as Hudson saw at once and Gay only belatedly, as many men as a paper could put in the field to hustle the news, a chief correspondent to integrate their work, messengers to carry dispatches back to field headquarters, and agents to bribe the pursers of the swiftest steamers and attend the needs of the staff. Hudson had all of them. He stationed sixteen men with the Army of the Potomac,[7] and forwarded wagons, tents, skiffs, remounts, cash, clothing, and every accouterment they could possibly need.

Gay relied on Thomas Butler Gunn, the Englishman who had served the paper well in Charleston before the war, D. J. Kinney, and a trio of hastily hired recruits, Millar, Colston, and Ingersoll, backed by the knowledgeable Charles D. Brigham at Fortress Monroe. It was not enough; the *Tribune* was beaten time and again. Anxiously the new m.e. tried to awaken Gunn:

> I pray you remember that the Tribune is a daily *news*-paper—or meant to be—and not a historical record of past events. Correspondence to be of any value must be prompt, fresh, and full of facts. I know how difficult it is, under the censorship, to write, but there must be facts

[7] Wilkeson to Gay, June 1, 1862, Gay Papers.

enough of general interest all about you to make a daily letter. . . . I should like you to write daily, if only $\frac{1}{2}$, $\frac{1}{4}$ column, so that the report of all you may tell be continuous. The curiosity and anxiety about Yorktown is feverish, and the public like the paper best that is always giving something. If there is absolutely *nothing* to write about, drop me a line and tell me that. The Herald is constantly ahead of us with Yorktown news. The battle of the 16th we were compelled to copy from it.

Alas for Gunn! He was scribbling notes on the back of this letter after the fall of Yorktown when he mislaid it, and the next thing Gay knew he read in the editorial columns of the *Herald*:

One of our correspondents—who see everything, hear everything, and find everything—fished this unique epistle out of a pile of rebel documents. . . . We do not know the name of the *Tribune* reporter to whom it is addressed, but his notes in pencil are on the back of the original letter.

The *Herald* ran it in full, chortling gleefully at the admission of copying from its columns. "Thank you, Mr. Gay. But why not acknowledge this openly in your editorial columns, and not clandestinely in letters to your reporters?" [8] There were moments, and this was one of them, when Sydney Gay yearned for the peace of Staten Island. "God knows how the *Herald* got hold of your letter to me," Gunn wrote in a fluster. "The *Herald* men here repudiate the thing, but many of them would pick pockets." Furthermore, the hapless correspondent lamented, someone had stolen his horse.

Gay rushed Sam Sinclair, the business manager of the paper, to the Peninsula to organize the men and speed the flow of copy. Then he ordered Sam Wilkeson to leave the Washington office in charge of an assistant and go to the front himself

[8] *Herald*, May 16, 1862.

as chief correspondent. Wilkeson arrived in time for the Battle of Williamsburg, but lack of co-ordinated effort among his aides appalled him; it was impossible to keep in touch with them. Worse, he promptly fell victim to that most common of Civil War maladies, dysentery, writing Gay: "For nearly three days I have maintained my anchorage under lee of a Privy— and have dieted on black tea and blasphemy." The *Tribune*, he said, should have gone into the campaign with a Sibley tent for headquarters, a two-horse wagon and team, "a decent cook with enough imagination and brains to be quartermaster," a mess chest, eight reporters and mounts for each. Wilkeson himself found accommodations with one of the four corps commanders, Major General S. P. Heintzelman, but "he won't have my reporters crowding his narrow quarters. . . . They must shift for themselves." Wilkeson alone had a horse. There was only one *Tribune* messenger. Sinclair was too busy rounding up vendors to sell the *Tribune* in the army to attend the news side.[9] Gay could only be thankful that Wilkeson, for one, developed into a first-class war correspondent.

McClellan's magnificently equipped army fought its way to within ten, eight, six miles of Richmond, soaked by the heaviest rains of a generation, floundering through thickly wooded swampland astride the Chickahominy. Suddenly Joe Johnston turned with calculated fury on the almost isolated left wing of the Federals at Fair Oaks. Sam Wilkeson was in the thick of it when General Heintzelman arrived on the field and made him a volunteer aide. Smiling Sam gloried in his role, riding through the woods bellowing encouragement, helping to check the retreat of Silas Casey's broken brigade, carrying orders to all parts of the command. Both Heintzelman and Brigadier General John J. Peck cited him in their official reports.[1] Wilkeson, sick at heart because his nephew was one of the dead, stayed up that night writing by candlelight until

9 Wilkeson to Gay, May 12, June 1, June 6, 1862; Adams Hill to Gay, "Tues., a.m." (June 17, 1862), Gay Papers.

1 *O.R.*, Ser. I, Vol. 11, Part 1, 816, 890.

3:00 a.m., his tent and all of his personal effects lost in the
day's struggle, writing in the bitter realization that he had
probably been beaten again. "I was alone to do the work of
the battle," he wrote Gay in desperation. "No one man can
see a battlefield which is covered by extensive woods, and is
a mile and a half deep, & two miles wide." The failure of the
others enraged him:

> Millar reported to me at 9 o'clock at night after the bat-
> tle. Where in hell he had been, pretending to hunt me for
> three days, I don't know. He had seen nothing of the
> fight, and could be used only to copy surgeon's lists. I
> don't know and I don't care where Colston was. Whining
> forever about his poor diet, and the hardships he under-
> goes . . . he is not worth a curse for this business.

Turbulent and filled with the smoke and confusion of battle,
Wilkeson's Fair Oaks far surpassed the *Herald's* accounts,
which treated what had been a bloody check as a great victory for McClellan. Equally notable was the work of twenty-
six-year-old William Conant Church ("Pierrepont"), of the
Times, who, though shot in the leg by a spent ball, produced
an account to make Charlie Pfaff proud of him. It filled the
entire front page of his paper on June 3.

Here, on this desolate countryside—marshes, thick woodland of live oak, scraggly pine, vine-choked ash, clearings
dotted by unpainted farmhouses and rickety outbuildings—
were focused the eyes of millions. Half a hundred artists and
writers from all over the North walked and rode along the
deep-rutted roads, through successive tented cities, among the
thousands of blue uniforms, talking, sketching, taking notes,
arranging for transmission through messengers to boats leaving constantly from McClellan's headquarters at White House.
On May 12, McClellan had prohibited them from going to
the front, or elsewhere "beyond General Headquarters." [2] Most

[2] *O.R.*, Ser. I, Vol. 11, Part 3, 167.

of them simply ignored the order.[3] Provost marshals escorted a few to the rear, locked some in the guardhouse, threatened others; the rest took their chances, "sleeping in fence corners and living on the inevitable hoe cake, bought of the female portion of the colored community." At one point a dozen lucky ones boarded at a planter's home where "the curious custom was maintained of sending up a julep to our rooms before we rose in the morning."

Yonder, scribbling on one knee with a plank for a desk, crouched Lorenzo L. Crounse, chief correspondent of the *World*, a smooth-cheeked gentleman with a pointed beard, black-ribboned glasses perched on a thin, sharp nose, ears protruding as if to catch the latest. Alert, immaculate little Henry J. Raymond had come down to join Church, Franc Wilkie, Whittemore, Travis, "Argus," and the rest of his *Times* crew. Uriah Painter, the Philadelphia *Inquirer*'s crack correspondent ("made of iron," Stedman said), rode with the advance guard, interviewed enemy prisoners, and tried in vain to convince General Marcy, McClellan's chief of staff, that intelligence reports grossly exaggerated enemy strength. Bulbous Henry Bentley, stripped of all but his pantaloons and boots before escaping the Confederates at Shiloh,[4] came East to reinforce Painter and win a name among the Bohemians as the most incessant babbler and braggart in the crowd—"the Water Spout Man," they called him.

Conspicuous among them was a gangling six-footer who had said he would give a year of his life to go to Bull Run the year before, but had lost out.[5] George Alfred Townsend was not yet of age, but he had already served as city editor of the Philadelphia *Press* and more recently as a correspondent on

[3] *Report of the Joint Committee on the Conduct of the War* (Washington: 1863), Part I, 291. Representative Covode: "Were you not violating those orders when you went to the front?" Uriah Painter, Philadelphia *Inquirer*: "Yes, sir, but unless we came across some surly officer they would not bother themselves about it. . . ."

[4] Philadelphia *Inquirer*, Apr. 14, 1862.

[5] G. B. P. Ringwault to John Russell Young, July 26, 1861, Young Papers.

the upper Potomac. There he had been fairly dazzled by a *Herald* reporter:

His saddle was a cushioned McClellan, with spangled breast-strap and plump saddle-bags, and his bridle was adorned with a bright curb bit and twilled reins. He wore a field glass belt about his body, and was plentifully provided with money to purchase items of news, if they were at any time difficult to obtain. I resolved . . . to seize the first opportunity of changing establishments.

Now, saddle-bags loaded with smoking tobacco, spirits, a meerschaum pipe, packages of sardines, a box of cigars, and a hundred dollars in greenbacks, with a pair of matched pistols dangling from new holsters, Townsend rode on air. He was a *Herald* reporter. To look at him, it hardly seemed that he would make the grade. Smooth-cheeked, weak-chinned, alternately coltish and bashful, "with only drifting convictions," as he confessed, he ambled shamefacedly among the troops in wide breeches and square-toed boots, like an overgrown drummer boy. This young Townsend, interviewing Southern prisoners, catching the flavor of camp dialects, making a balloon ascent with T. S. C. Lowe, taking in poignant hospital scenes as he compiled casualty lists, would be heard from.

Perched atop a barrel with a knot of kibitzers behind him, a balding, self-contained young man with heavy handlebar mustaches quietly sketched a typical camp scene—a couple of privates sharing a newspaper. At twenty-six, Winslow Homer of *Harper's Weekly* had a penchant for depicting camp life exactly as he found it. William Waud, E. S. Hall, and Frank H. Schell kept their pencils busy on army scenes for *Frank Leslie's Illustrated Newspaper*. In addition to Homer, *Harper's* had F. Meyer, Theodore R. Davis, and ebullient Alf Waud on hand. Arthur Lumley, a prolific artist with a flair for panorama (he did one beauty from a thousand feet up in Lowe's balloon), almost kept pace with them singlehandedly for the *New York Illustrated News*.

Mechanicsville, Hanover Court House, Fair Oaks, Oak Grove: millions of words, reams of sketches made obscure places familiar across the land as spring turned steaming summer on the Peninsula. Through it all, McClellan kept using the press to push his demand for reinforcements. McDowell's division, which had been promised him, was withheld by Lincoln when Stonewall Jackson's campaign in the Shenandoah Valley threatened Washington. Raymond, Stedman, the whole *Herald* staff, and, to the surprise of *Tribune* readers, even Wilkeson joined in the clamor. Gay, rather than risk losing his top man, gave him his head, explaining editorially at one point: "We never saw, nor wish to see, any deference in his letters to our policies." The *Tribune* itself finally joined the chorus. Although some forty thousand reinforcements were sent him over a period of months, McClellan was never satisfied.

The *Tribune* had a reinforcement problem of its own which Gay could no longer ignore. On June 21, Wilkeson drew up a camp stool at General Peck's brigade headquarters and wrote in words that fairly leaped from the page:

Dear Sydney,

Millar got sick, or tired or scared—and vamosed ten days ago, I am told.

Ingersoll, seized with a panic at hearing our pickets driven in, ran back to Fort Monroe and to Washington.

Colston came to me yesterday with his lifeless drawling whine about the impossibility of getting "accomodations" and buying forage for his horse.—Soon he asked me for money (I have furnished him $25 in all) and announced his purpose of going to the White House for a box of summer clothing and of comforts sent to him by his wife. The mention of the word "comforts" by a newspaper man in the field enraged me. He has no more right to them than private soldiers have. . . .

The work needs *first class men:* men of physical courage, intelligence, tact, patience, endurance, DEVOTION.

To enlarge on this—while my hand is in. I wear four shirts a week when I am at home. The flannel shirt I have on I have worn five weeks. It is abominable, certainly. But it is not unendurable. . . . Rails make my bed. . . . My jacknife [sic] is my spoon, knife, fork, and toothpick. . . . My horse (the Tribune's) don't starve & by God! he shan't starve. I have burst open a planter's store room, and taken the hominy corn hidden for his family's food, and shelled half a bushel of it with my fingers, and fed it to "Bayard" out of my pocket handkerchief—running the risk of the Provost Marshal. That pocket handkerchief—certainly, I have washed it ten times. Washing! It has not cost me 80 cents since I left Washington. He must be damned helpless who cant wash clothes.

But enough. No man who in *any way* talks about his living—*alludes to it* as a subject which rests on his mind, is fit to follow an army in an enemy's country. Reporters must be earnest and devoted. . . .

Gay sent John F. Cleveland, Greeley's brother-in-law and a long-time staff member, to help Wilkeson reorganize matters, and racked his brain to find recruits. Where to find men willing to risk dysentery, enemy bullets, starvation, the ire of commanders, the guardhouse, and possibly court-martial simply out of an inner compulsion to convey a sense of what was going on to those at home? First he authorized Wilkeson to hire Uriah Painter away from the Philadelphia *Inquirer*, but Wilkeson found him "loyal to his paper, as he ought to be, to be worth a damn." So with Crounse; yet Wilkeson advised against hiring new men—"the probability is they will become frightened or disgusted with the service . . . it takes a long time to learn."

But from Adams Hill in Washington, Gay learned of a clerk in the Fifth Auditor's office who was aching to go, "a cool, brisk, quick-eyed young man" named Charles Anderson Page. Page's sole experience had been editing the Mt. Vernon *News*, an Iowa weekly, but Gay dispatched him to the front with a bay horse and a prayer. Page went into action at 11:00 a.m. on June 27, 1862 near Mechanicsville, notebook in hand, Minié balls zinging around him. "The tornado swept right and left as if one current of electricity had discharged every man's musket," he wrote in his first dispatch. With ears newly attuned to battle, Page caught something others had missed: "There are cheers and yells, for our men *cheer*, while they . . . *yell*." And Page showed a nice eye for the grotesque. "During the stampede, for a moment the attention of hundreds was attracted to a horse galloping around carrying a man's leg in the stirrup—the left leg, booted and spurred. It was a splendid horse, gaily caparisoned." Page had that magic quality of "devotion," coupled with a talent for observation and an ear for English which moved Gay to bestow "C. A. P." on his dispatches, initials being an accolade the *Tribune* seldom granted. Even Wilkeson thought well of him —"wonderfully industrious—popular—*and brave*. He had just as lief go under fire as go into an oyster house."

Page had arrived in time for the most momentous battles thus far in the war, the Seven Days in which McClellan changed his base from White House, on the Pamunkey, to Harrison's Landing, on the James, reeling under hammer-blows from Lee. Every available ship was pressed into service to transfer stores and munitions as the army fought its way through the swamps. The telegraph from White House to Fortress Monroe was cut; and no word of McClellan's fate was received for forty-eight hours, by the War Department or anyone else. C. C. Fulton of the Baltimore *American* got back to his paper on June 29 to find a special train waiting to take him to see Lincoln. Back in Baltimore at 9:00 p.m. he offered fellow editors his story over the wires of the Associated Press, mentioning his interview, and concluding: "We have the greatest military triumph over the enemy, and Richmond must fall." Two hours later, while editors waited impatiently, the following was received:

> The Secretary of War decides that nothing can be telegraphed relating to our affairs on the Peninsula. Have tried our best to get it off. C. C. Fulton, Agent, Associated Press.

To editors accustomed to the ways of the War Department, this was the first intimation of disaster. They were not reassured when they learned that a few hours later Fulton had been locked up in Fort McHenry on Lincoln's order for having advertised his interview—"the point of the President being," as Adams Hill explained to Gay, "that what is sent over the wires gets a quasi-official sanction in the popular judgment." [6]

The Bohemians, meanwhile, were in a pretty plight. Crounse, horseless and footsore, trudged along for four days without food until his messenger got through to him with chickens. Townsend, in similar plight, heard firing behind him, but "I did not go back; battles were of no consequence to me." On the bluff facing White Oak Swamp he found five other correspondents, "and they all pooh-poohed the battle, as such an old story that it would be absurd to ride back to the field." Dazed and despondent, even resigned to capture, they settled down to drinking apple whisky. Masses of troops moved through the woods beyond, horses bathed in foam. The reporters, as sated with war as Carlyle's peasants in the French Revolution, continued to drink and to commiserate until they fell asleep. The next day Townsend ran into a colonel who miraculously offered him stewed beef, bread, butter, and coffee; he fell to with trembling fingers.[7] W. D. Bickham of the Cincinnati *Commercial* launched his account in the man-

[6] Hill to Gay, July 2, 1862 (third of three letters that day), Gay Papers. Hill said the arrest caused "a hell of a stink" in Baltimore.
[7] Townsend: *Campaigns*, 183–91.

ner of a man overwhelmed: "O Friends! Could you realize the afflictions of the past five days, you could almost shed tears of blood."

In New York the outcome of the struggle was anything but clear. An official wire from Stanton said that the government had no news, but "nothing has been received to warrant the belief of any serious disaster." Whiteley told Hudson that "not one word is allowed to go." From S. P. Hanscom, the former *Herald* man editing the *National Republican* in Washington, Gay got enough by special messenger to write a conjectural piece on the change of base on July 1, and on successive days the tragedy of McClellan's confused retreat gradually unfolded in an atmosphere of increasing gloom. Hill wrote privately of "the bluest days since Bull Run." There was no overt sign of it, but correspondents and editors knew well enough: the Peninsular campaign was over.

The *Tribune* noted dolefully that there were very few fireworks that Fourth of July.

2. A Little Man with Glasses

A HUB-OF-THE-UNIVERSE atmosphere pervaded the sights, the sounds, the very odors of the ancient Rookery, warm and close with newsprint and ink, dust and tobacco. Here in the flare of gas jets men in shirtsleeves worked as if the world could not go on until it had read the latest edition, a notion that soon infected the casual visitor. He heard the o'ohing of crowds outside as the bulletins were posted, the nervous scratch of pens across paper, the insistent ring of bells, the copy-box clattering up the chute to the composing room, the scuffling of messengers from the telegraph office, the high-pitched voice of Horace Greeley expostulating with someone, the hiss of escaping steam, the rattle of windows as a steady rumble came from the bowels of the earth, the unintelligible shouts of teamsters from below as they pitched bundles of papers into American News Company drays and rataplanned off to dealers and railroad stations, the cryptic dialogue of men working against white space: "Set it brevier, leaded two points." "Where's Gunn's?" "Gone up." "Have Rooker kill the second Colston." "Put 'em on bogus—no 'good night' from Washington yet." He saw men wading through a sea of exchanges—hundreds of dailies and weeklies sent by editors in hope that something would strike Mr. Greeley's fancy, and because they, in turn, must see the *Tribune*. He saw others bending close over proof sheets, trimming them to fit, checking in the files, leafing through piles of manuscripts looking for a misplaced sheet of foolscap, or gazing vacantly at the bust of Henry Clay through Gay's half-opened door, lost in composition.

In the midst of it all, from noon until three in the morning, moved Gay, a curious anomaly, a gentle man "of soft manners and heart," the friend of Lowell and Wendell Phillips, the reflective scholar transformed by the sheer pressure of events into a paragon of brisk decision.

The sailing was not always smooth. I. W. England, the veteran city editor, suppressed a growing grudge against Gay for throwing out local news. It would erupt finally, three years later, in a scorching letter that England wrote to Greeley: "Sometimes for months at a time no line of mine could get into the editorial columns. . . . Columns of matter—fresh city news, gathered by a greater force of reporters than that of any other first class paper, are daily killed, after getting into the evening edition—yet I have no instructions, beyond the general one of compression, which is carried almost to a ridiculous point." [8]

Gay had inherited all of Dana's authority, and more. Greeley might cavil and carp, but he knew well enough that his managing editor must command unless he himself were to give up his lecturing, his far-flung correspondence, and his leader-writing for a job for which he had very little taste or

[8] Dated Mar. 4, 1865. Greeley Papers, New York Public Library.

judgment. It was enough for him that Horace Greeley and the New York *Tribune* remain indistinguishable in the public mind. James R. Gilmore, calling on Greeley in the winter of 1863, was astonished to hear the editor say that he had relinquished control. Gilmore, a stronger administration-supporter than Greeley, declined to write for the paper for fear of Greeley's editing. "But I have resigned the blue pencil," Greeley told him. "You would not report to me but to Gay; and he is of your way of thinking." Gilmore turned to Gay in disbelief. "He is not jesting," Gay said. "He has agreed that I shall direct the policy of the paper." And so, as Gilmore and others testify, he did. Greeley was responsible only for his own editorials.[9]

Gay's troubles never ceased. Richardson and Villard were covering the campaign against Corinth, Mississippi, that May, when Major General Henry W. Halleck ordered all "unauthorized hangers-on" to leave. Did that mean newspapermen? The Bohemians, already stung by what several of them considered his "insolent manner," were told that it did. Halleck was described by the same *World* reporter who dubbed him "Old Brains" as resembling "an oleaginous Methodist parson dressed in regimentals." The general let it be known through his aides that he suspected some correspondents were spies, though the real reason for his order was said to be his distaste for the continuing recriminations in the press regarding Shiloh. Richardson, a passionate believer in the right to report, got up a formal petition: all the signers were there by the authority of the Secretary of War and had passes to prove it; expelling them would only leave the news to unauthorized reporters. Thirty of them, led by Richardson and the gentlemanly Whitelaw Reid, then waited on the General. He received them with a glassy eye—"his deportment was unmistakably rude and insulting," said Richardson. He "would *send* us news, if we would just remain outside the lines"—an offer they re-

[9] James R. Gilmore: *Personal Recollections of Abraham Lincoln and the Civil War* (Boston: 1898), 94.

jected with proper contempt. The Bohemians withdrew forthwith, though not without further contretemps. Curtis F. Gilbert of the Cincinnati *Gazette* landed in the guardhouse for asking Halleck's Provost Marshal General how an "unauthorized hanger-on" could pass through the lines without being arrested, and Franc Wilkie was also arrested for protesting too volubly to Halleck.[1]

"We have repeatedly made large outlays to no purpose, because of such orders as this of General Halleck," Gay lamented in the *Tribune*. But the Bohemians could circumvent Halleck as readily as they had McClellan. Although Thomas Knox, Peleg Tallman, and Frank Chapman, of the *Herald*, as well as the *Tribune's* Richardson, withdrew, both papers continued to run news from Halleck's army. Villard, whom Gay had had the good sense to hire as a regular *Tribune* correspondent in spite of Greeley, had not signed the petition. Richardson sent him back, and Villard remained on duty, nicely disguised in a blue uniform, until Beauregard withdrew from Corinth to end the campaign.

Richardson, a fighter by nature, was far from satisfied. He thought the whole press should force a showdown on the issue once and for all. Earnestly he wrote Gay from Cairo:

> Until it is clearly settled that an accredited Journalist, in the legitimate exercise of his calling, has just as much *right* in the army as the Commander himself, and is there on just as legitimate a mission, he *will* be considered by a large majority of Regular Army officers as an "unauthorized hanger on," and treated accordingly.

In time Richardson would have an opportunity to carry his fight to the President himself, over the head of a general far more fearsome than the oleaginous Halleck.

A more baffling problem of coverage arose when Stonewall

[1] Royal Cortissoz: *Life of Whitelaw Reid* (New York: 1921), I, 90; Wilkie: *Pen and Powder*, 178–80; Richardson: *Secret Service*, 372; *Tribune*, May 26, 1862.

Jackson staged his Shenandoah Valley campaign that month, routing Banks at Front Royal and Winchester, threatening Washington, and making good his escape while Union armies converged on him from three directions. Gay had an ineffectual Baltimorean named Hardenbrook with Banks. When Jackson struck, Hardenbrook was away from the army, the *World* correspondent was asleep in Winchester, and G. W. Clarke, a Britisher representing the *Herald*, was "musing over the dullness of the war" in the hotel at Front Royal. Volleys of gunfire woke him. Colonel John R. Kenly, commanding a detachment of nine hundred men there, dispatched Clarke to cut the rope ferry across the Shenandoah. Clarke won a citation in Kenly's report, but he was captured in the brisk skirmish that followed. He was introduced to the Confederate commander.

> Jackson reached his hand and caught mine, remarking he was glad to see anyone connected with the American Thunderer. "I am very glad to see you under the circumstances, General," I said, "and I hope you will be good enough to pass me out of your lines as soon as possible."
>
> At this the General's face changed slightly. He remarked that he had not time to attend to that just then, and rode off.

Clarke wrote to the General as a British subject to demand his release. At Winchester, Jackson granted him an interview.

> This time he wore a blue military overcoat. When I was introduced to him I could perceive that his hazel eye, peeping out from his full-bearded face, was eyeing me attentively. . . . Having shaken hands with me, Jackson said, "Be seated, sir; will you have a glass of water?" I accepted both, and after some commonplace civilities, observed:—
>
> "General, I suppose you will restore me my horse and clothes?"

120

"Oh," replied he, "it was taken in the camp and must be considered contraband of war."

"But . . . I stand as a neutral, and you know it to be the law of nations that a neutral flag covers neutral goods."

"Yes," returned the rebel chieftain; "but the Southern Confederacy is not recognized by neutral nations, and, consequently, cannot be bound by neutral laws." [2]

Clarke was released two weeks later at New Market—minus his goods. The other correspondents, for all their efforts to report Jackson's whirlwind campaign, might just as well have been captured too.

With Frémont, whom the President personally directed to trap Jackson from the west while Shields approached from the east, Gay had stationed George Smalley, a capable young graduate of Yale and the Harvard Law School recommended by Wendell Phillips. A devout Abolitionist, Smalley fell right in with Frémont's staff of Radicals, kept in close touch with headquarters, and wrote Gay voluminous private letters; but, except when Jackson beat the Federals at Cross Keys on June 8, Smalley had little worth reporting, and his adulation of Frémont betrayed him into representing Cross Keys as a victory. Charles Henry Webb of the *Times* far outshone him. Despite a talent for mischief Webb brought with him from Pfaff's, he was a competent reporter, among the first in the North to comprehend the genius of Thomas J. Jackson. "We may run the mountain fox to death yet," he wrote during the chase; but after the battle Webb administered a needed corrective:

> The correspondents of some papers claim it as a victory. . . . These gentlemen, whose feelings and sympathies so influence them that they cannot record faithfully, will have a long account to settle with history some day. . . . Will not truth and common sense satisfy the

[2] *Herald*, June 10, 1862.

popular craving, or is it always necessary to pander to the appetite that demands a victory in all cases, an assurance that the enemy lost at least one more than we? . . .

One thing is certain, Jackson is equally eminent as a strategist and tactician. He handles his army like a whip, making it crack in out of the way corners where you scarcely thought the lash would reach. This retreat of his, if retreat it can be called, has been conducted with marvelous skill. He has not much mercy on his men, but he gets extraordinary marches out of them on very short commons.[3]

Next to Jackson, the sensation of the campaign was Belle Boyd, the Confederate spy—a lady brazenly described by the *Herald* as "an accomplished prostitute." Nathaniel Paige, a *Tribune* reporter with General Shields's division, interviewed her at Front Royal. She admitted spying, he said, "but resents attacks on her virtue. . . . In personal appearance, without being beautiful, she is very attractive. Is quite tall, has a superb figure, an intellectual face, and dresses with much taste. . . . She can give you the name of almost every officer in the Rebel army. . . . Why she should be allowed to go at will through our camps, flirt with our officers, I am at a loss to know. . . . [She] wears a gold palmetto tree beneath her beautiful chin, a Rebel soldier's belt around her waist, and a velvet band across her forehead, with the seven stars of the Confederacy shedding their pale light therefrom." [4] Paige wrote Gay privately that General Shields was "closeted four hours" with her, but "I think she is not what camp gossip charges her with being." A Philadelphia *Inquirer* man completed the picture:

Belle has passed the first freshness of youth. She is a sharp-featured, black-eyed woman of 25, or care and intrigue have given her that appearance. [She was 19.] Last summer (with Patterson's army) she wore a revolver in

3 *Times*, June 16, 1862.
4 *Tribune*, June 12, 1862.

her belt, and was courted and flattered by every lieutenant and captain in the service who saw her. There was
a kind of . . . dash about her, a smart pertness, a quick-
ness of retort, an utter abandon of manner and bearing
which were attractive from their very unwontedness.
The father of this resolute black-eyed vixen is a paymaster in the Southern army. . . .

The *Inquirer* man considered that his collegues had violated
some canon of journalism by implying that she was "personally impure." "Reporters who thus attack a woman," he wrote
gallantly, "exceed the license which justice and fairness allot
even to outlaws." [5] When Belle was finally incarcerated in the
Old Capitol Prison that July (only to be released and recaptured later aboard a blockade-runner) reporters mourned the
passing of a lively source of copy.

Time and again these days, Sydney Gay had occasion to
thank his stars for the nervous, bespectacled little man who
held the fort for him in Washington. Adams Sherman Hill,
introverted, pathetically nearsighted, frail, awkward, had
scampered for dear life at Blackburn's Ford a year before. He
was no war correspondent. But when Sam Wilkeson left for
the Peninsula, the unlikely Hill took command of "this 'bureau,' as S. W. phrases it," and proceeded to run it with dispatch. Hill's high-pitched, excited voice might be heard at
almost any time of the day or night, among fellow boarders at
the Ebbitt House, at the Willard bar, in the small, paper-
littered *Tribune* office, in the corridors of the Departments,
in incessant quest of news. At times, he said, he hated it: "During the last 18 months I have accepted one dinner invitation
have been to not one evening party and made not one call
except directly for business purposes save on Saturday evenings. . . ." Hill not only filed a nightly news budget sufficient to keep the *Tribune* abreast of the *Herald*, often a jump
ahead of it; he also directed the assignment of war corre-

[5] Philadelphia *Inquirer*, July 19, 1862.

spondents with the various armies as Gay's assistant, kept track of them, sped their copy on its way, recruited new men, bought horses for them, and the while served as the *Tribune's* insider and Gay's confidential adviser. He was the son of a minister in Worcester, Massachusetts, and a graduate of Harvard College and Law School. After three years he gave up law-reporting to become night editor of the *Tribune* in 1858, moving to Washington as bureau assistant on the outbreak of the war.

Every night, after filing his copy, Hill hunched over his desk and in his crabbed hand scrawled a letter to his managing editor which he posted on the way home. Often he wrote two, three, four times a day, cramming his letters with news, gossip, speculations on government policy, evaluations of correspondents, hints of what to expect next, and wry observations on the state of the Union. Peering through his thick lenses like a wide-eyed child, Hill cultivated his sources assiduously, and they were legion. Fox in the Navy Department, Watson in War, Stoddard, the President's secretary, Secretary of the Treasury Chase, General Wadsworth, Senators Wilson, Grimes, and Sumner, Speaker of the House Colfax, Representatives Covode and Washburne confided in him regularly; Hill set aside the back room of the office "for secret copying [of documents] and for stolen interviews." [6] They came at such odd hours he finally gave up the Ebbitt House and lived above the office.

Perhaps better than any other correspondent, Adams Hill personified the new journalism in which speed, efficiency, and a nose for news supplanted the old emphasis on rhetoric, bombast and belles-lettres. On this score there was significant opposition to him in the home office. "Mr. Greeley's good opinion I am sorry not to possess," he wrote. [7] Hill did not produce particularly luminous prose, and he was incapable of the political commentary that Greeley expected of his Washington

6 Hill to Gay, Nov. 3, 1863, Gay Papers.
7 Hill to Gay, undated [Nov. or Dec. 1863], Gay Papers.

men. He did not consider that his province. "I think that the *Tribune* gains by giving all sides a hearing," he wrote characteristically after securing a document he knew Greeley would not like, "and it seems justice to all. And this is no side but an apparently impartial statement of facts. Above all, it is *news*."

Through Hill's steady stream of letters, Gay came to understand something of Lincoln's travail on the emancipation issue. On July 9, 1862 Hill wrote:

Mr. Sumner [Senator Charles Sumner, of Massachusetts] called upon the President twice on July 4th, to urge the reconsecration of the day by a decree of emancipation. The first time, Mr. Lincoln seemed not disinclined to do it for Eastern Virginia: objected to a general decree, as being "too big a lick." Stanton said we "wanted big licks now." Two hours later, the President said there were two objections: 1. That three more states would rise, Ky., Md., and Mo. He also suggested . . . that a decree would be a *brutum fulmen* [*i.e.*, a futile blast, doubtless Hill's phrase]. . . .

N.B.: Sumner told the above in *strict* confidence. . . .

When Radicals in Congress pushed through their Confiscation Act, by which the slaves of persons aiding the rebellion were declared free, Lincoln threatened to veto it. Some of its harsher provisions, including one which would have confiscated the offenders' property forever, had to be amended before he would sign the bill. "It surprises me that a President can live in such utter ignorance of popular feeling," Hill wrote to Gay, and many other letters came in the same tenor.

Acting on Hill's theory that the President was out of touch with the public, Gay addressed a letter to the White House on July 30:

Sir—

I take the liberty of sending you herewith a communication intended by the writer for publication in the Tribune. . . .

I am receiving daily many similar letters from all parts of the country for the paper, evincing a deep-seated anxiety on the part of the people.

I do not publish them because I know they would exercise a most serious influence on the public mind.

I cannot, however, justify it to myself that the public of the *Tribune* should at this moment be denied the privilege of being heard through its columns and the Government at the same time left in ignorance of that which so many thousands of people desire it should hear. Taking a middle course, therefore, I send you one letter as a specimen of all the rest. . . .[8]

The letter he enclosed said "the President . . . hangs back, hesitates, and leaves the country to drift." Surprisingly enough, Lincoln responded immediately. Weighing the emancipation issue in his mind and studying public opinion perhaps more closely than he had ever studied it, Lincoln during these weeks talked with all manner of people, sometimes arguing for emancipation with those who opposed it and against it with those in favor. He telegraphed Gay: "Please come and see me at once," asking that if possible he bring the author of the letter, one George Rathbun, of Auburn, New York, with him. Gay replied that a death in his family prevented his coming at once, but Lincoln did not forget. Nine days later he telegraphed: "When will you come?"[9] On August 10, without Rathbun (a Radical who told Gay: "It would be a mere waste of time and money"), the managing editor made his appearance at the White House.

Discreetly, Gay pressed the argument for emancipation, while Lincoln, one gathers from a reference to the meeting in one of Hill's letters, parried with anecdotes. Gay the Abolitionist shortly yielded to Gay the managing editor: Would the Army of the Potomac join Pope's in front of Washington

[8] Robert T. Lincoln Collection.

[9] Roy P. Basler, ed.: *The Collected Works of Abraham Lincoln* (New Brunswick, New Jersey: 1953), Vol. 5, 353, 364.

when it returned from the Peninsula? Was McClellan to remain in command? The President said nothing, turned to his desk, and for two or three minutes appeared to be trying to find the proper pigeonhole for a document in his hand. Then he said slowly, without turning his head: "I shouldn't wonder." According to a later account, Lincoln's tone was friendly, indicating that he was not simply turning the question, but trying to be helpful without volunteering any information himself. Gay phrased half a dozen such questions, which Lincoln answered the same way, and the editor returned to New York feeling like a navigator who has made observations during a sunny interval between storms.[1]

If Gay carried away a favorable impression of the gentle, angular man and his stories and quizzical replies, it also appears that he left a good one behind him. A White House caller bearing a letter of introduction from Gay a few weeks later said that Lincoln recognized the handwriting instantly and remarked: "I believe Mr. Gay is a truly good man, and a wise one." [2]

Yet from Lincoln's standpoint, the Gay interview proved a failure. He wanted the *Tribune* with him—having Greeley "firmly behind me," he wrote once, "will be as helpful to me as an army of one hundred thousand men"—yet Greeley still held aloof. James R. Gilmore, the shadowy intermediary between the *Tribune* and the White House, told Lincoln a week later that Greeley's impatience was mounting, and Lincoln reluctantly agreed to allow Gilmore to tell the editor that a proclamation would be issued in due course. Hill, too, learned on August 21 that "the President had an emancipation proclamation prepared three weeks ago and would have issued it, but for the opposition of Seward and Blair." But Hill, for once, was two days too late, and Gilmore, if one is to credit his story, arrived in New York with his assurances

[1] Clipping, Rossiter Johnson to the *Tribune*, Apr. 13, 1891, Gay Papers. This is the only account of the interview which has come to light. The paper said nothing of it at the time.

[2] H. L. Stevens [?] to Gay, Sept. 7, 1862, Gay Papers.

hours too late also. For on August 20 the *Tribune* blazed forth with Greeley's open letter to the President, "The Prayer of Twenty Millions." It demanded more imperiously than prayerfully that Lincoln enforce the Confiscation Act, asserting that "Slavery is everywhere the inciting cause and sustaining base of treason." Greeley's tone all but precluded an answer, yet Lincoln found words to answer "The Prayer" as only he was able: "If there be perceptible in it an impatient and dictatorial tone, I waive it in deference to an old friend whose heart I have always supposed to be right. . . ." There followed the famous "paramount object" letter, in which Lincoln asserted that "what I do about slavery and the colored race, I do because I believe it helps to save the Union; and what I forbear, I forbear because I do *not* believe it would help to save the Union."

Gay had argued that patience, persuasion, and kind words would bring the President around in time, and he continued to feel so. He wrote Lincoln that "your letter has infused new hope among us at the North who are anxiously awaiting that move on your part which they believe will end the rebellion by removing its cause." [3] How sharply this differed from the views of his old-time Abolitionist friends appeared when Gay heard from Wendell Phillips. Phillips thought Lincoln's letter "the most disgraceful document that ever came from the head of a free people. . . . I don't agree with you about A. L. He won't be flattered—he can only be bullied or frightened into the right policy. . . . If the proclamation of Emancipation is possible at any time from Lincoln (which I somewhat doubt) it will be wrung from him only by fear. He's a spaniel by nature—nothing broad, generous, or high-hearted about him." Phillips considered "The Prayer" "superb, terrific." "If I could rouse myself to envy anybody I could almost envy G. for the power to do it—no not the *power* but the *post*—none but he could have done it with any effect. Just the man. Just

[3] Undated, Robert T. Lincoln Collection.

the act." Gay could not have thought so; it was one of those times when his power to stay the hand of Greeley failed him.

While Gay and Greeley, each in his way, sought to force Lincoln's hand, a new figure had risen on the military horizon. Major General John Pope, brought East by Lincoln to organize Frémont's, Banks's, and McDowell's commands into the Army of Virginia, was described by Hill as "a small thick-set man, with black beard, bright thoughtful eye, ample forehead, large, full head." Nathaniel Paige, the Albany youth whom Gay assigned to the new army along with George Smalley, was unimpressed. "My opinion of the man," Paige wrote Gay after Pope's indecisive action against Jackson at Cedar Mountain, "is that he is a great humbug." Something of Pope's reputation for bluster had preceded him from the West, where a *World* man had set down the conqueror of Island No. 10 as "ambitious and vain" with "a snappish and positive manner, which is not innate, but rather put on with his uniform." From experience in the West, Richardson warned Gay to be wary of "Pope's lying," advice that Gay passed along to George Smalley at Pope's headquarters.

Pope used the press quite as assiduously as McClellan. Smalley quickly worked his way into favor at headquarters and reported to his chief after Cedar Mountain: "Pope personally corrects! the dispatches—is very good-natured, etc. but will have facts his own way." And again: "I have written this letter at Pope's request. . . . Pope was rather worried by the Times & World's attacks & asked me if I would send you for editorial use such points as he desired made." As was often the case, newspapers measured the General by his political beliefs; he found a ready champion in the *Tribune* because Hill had already discovered that "He is thoroughly with us (anti-slavery) men I think." The *Tribune* reaped the benefits. Hill heard it said at the War Department that Smalley's dispatches "betrayed an unusual intimacy with the General."

Smalley, Paige, and William A. Croffut, a shorthander who occasionally left his post in the Treasury Department to help the *Tribune*, began to beat the *Herald* consistently.

On August 19, Pope showed Smalley a telegram just received from "Old Brains," that nemesis of the Bohemian Brigade, who was now General-in-Chief in Washington:

> You will immediately remove from your army all newspaper reporters, and you will permit no telegrams to be sent over the telegraph lines out of your command except those sent by yourself. You will also suspend the transmission of any mail matter other than that of official communication. Halleck.[4]

Smalley begged to be allowed to remain, for a battle appeared imminent. "This is not an official interview," Pope said confidentially. "I imagine you needn't go till you get the order." [5] Smalley sent a special messenger to Washington with the news. Halleck was incensed; he telegraphed Pope the next day:

> I think your staff is decidedly leaky. The substance of my telegrams to you is immediately telegraphed back here to the press. . . . Clean out such characters from your headquarters.[6]

On the morning of August 21, Pope concluded reluctantly that he could delay no longer; the press must pack up and leave. Smalley retreated to the Willard and wired Gay for instructions. "Keep as near the army as possible and lose no opportunity of getting news at any expense of trouble or money," Gay replied, and told him to use his own discretion regarding the disposition of his men.[7]

4 *O.R.*, Ser. I, Vol. 12, Part 3, 602.
5 George W. Smalley: *Anglo-American Memories* (New York: 1911), 134, supported by Smalley to Gay, Aug. 22, 1862, Gay Papers.
6 *O.R.*, Ser. I, Vol. 12, Part 3, 602.
7 Quoted in Smalley to Gay, Aug. 22, 1862, second letter of that date, Gay Papers.

As was to be expected, Halleck's order only drove the Bohemians underground. L. W. Buckingham of the *Herald* told Smalley that he was going to defy the order and remain with Sigel's corps. Charles A. Page, fresh from the Peninsula, got himself into Pope's army as a hospital assistant. One reporter was arrested nine times before giving up. Smalley sent Nathaniel Paige and Croffut to Alexandria every day to pump officers returning from the army, and stationed Henry Thompson at Manassas Junction and H. O. Olcutt at Fredericksburg to glean what they could. He forwarded their copy to Gay by messenger, sometimes to Baltimore and thence by telegraph, sometimes all the way. These were the days when Jackson and Lee were closing in on Pope with desperate urgency, hoping to crush him before McClellan's army, returning from the Peninsula, could join him. Through Major Charles G. Halpine, a former newsman on Halleck's staff, Hill and Smalley constantly sought to have the ban on correspondents lifted, to no avail. But Smalley's makeshift arrangements worked surprisingly well. He hired new men, and under his brisk direction the augmented staff—"we have nine men at work, at Alexandria & in front," he boasted—kept the paper well posted and wrung from Gay one of his rare congratulatory letters.

It was not that the *Herald* crowd was asleep. L. A. Whiteley sniffed out Halleck's momentous decision to withdraw McClellan's army from the Peninsula on July 29 [8]—five days before McClellan received his orders—but most of the *Herald's* manpower appears to have been stranded with the Army of the Potomac. McClellan's withdrawal was one of the least publicized movements of the war, though the Confederates were perfectly aware of it, and reporters who had rejoined his army, most of whom had had to smuggle themselves in as clerks in the paymaster's office or as nurses or staff officers, had nothing to report when they got there.

Despite the *Tribune's* edge, no paper handled the Second

[8] Whiteley to Bennett, July 29, 1862, Bennett Papers.

Battle of Bull Run in a way that could be described as less
than chaotic. Pope himself did not know the whereabouts of
the main body of the enemy. Reporters banned from his army
discovered almost before Pope knew it himself that Jackson
had got in his rear at Manassas Junction. Editors so far forgot
themselves as to take Pope at his word when his triumphant
messages were released by the War Department. Then Jackson closed in, Longstreet's men sprang from concealed positions to envelop Pope's left, and there was a scene at the Stone
Bridge on the Centerville road almost like that of the year
before.

A Washington lady, her window thrown open that hot
Sunday, the last day of August, heard the blatant cry of a
newsboy: "General Jackson and 60,000 rebels taken!" She
entered it in her diary. "Later—The papers were rather premature. The latest news is that the Federals are falling back." [9]
This, too, was reminiscent of the year before.

As Pope's beaten, bewildered army straggled back toward
the capital, Adams Hill confided to Gay:

> For the first time, if I remember, I believe it possible
> . . . that Washington may be taken. . . . In the absence
> of instructions, I take my duty to be, being accredited
> near the Gov't., I stay while it stays and skedaddle when
> it skedaddles.

For all his anxiety about the state of the Union, Gay must
have smiled at literal-minded Adams Hill, debating with himself whether a conscientious Washington correspondent
should remain there even if the government departed.

Ironically enough from Gay's point of view, the worse the
news got, the more obvious became the *Tribune's* superiority
in reporting it. "We all dread the morrow," Hill wrote before
signing off that Sunday night, and then a postscript: "We have
seen and rejoiced in the Tribune's triumph. Tomorrow should

[9] Lindsay Lomax Wood, ed.: *Leaves from an Old Washington Diary*
(New York: 1943), 211.

be the greatest." Page was on his way to New York, full of
the battle, one of the few correspondents to have witnessed
it. Pope had proved a miserable failure, an emancipation proclamation seemed impossibly remote, and—worst of all, from
the *Tribune's* view—McClellan was about to resume command.
Miles of soldiers cheered him as they marched by his house in
Washington a few days later. Men spoke of him as a possible
dictator. It was preposterous, but it reflected the national state
of mind. "I look forward to a description of the Cabinet voyage downstream," Hill wrote sardonically. "Please let me be
the special correspondent for that."

Gay, writing to praise Hill, Page, and Smalley for their
extraordinary exertions, might have doubts as to the future of
the Republic, but he could console himself that at least he
had learned how to run a newspaper. He had found the men
who had what Wilkeson called "devotion," he had put them
to work, and, in his own quiet way, by encouragement, nee-
dling, silence, he had rallied the staff to tremendous exertions.
It surprised them, as it probably surprised him. "The *Tribune*
is coming up fast as a *news*paper under your management,"
wrote Page.

By September 10, astute Sam Wilkeson was ready with an
appraisal:

> Sufficient time has elapsed, since your Premiership
> commenced, to enable your friends to pronounce judg-
> ment upon your management of the *Tribune*. I say, that
> the New York *Tribune* is the best edited paper in Amer-
> ica—in all respects, the most carefully, ably, and inter-
> estingly edited.

Edmund Clarence Stedman, disgusted with the *World* now
that it was turning "Copperhead," wrote substantially the
same thing at the same time, and a few months later Charles
Congdon, the brilliant, bibulous editorial contributor, was
ready to forget Dana: "You must know that the Tribune in
my opinion never was a better paper. It is due to you to say

this." A more detached critic than any of these, Edward Dicey of the London *Spectator*, one of the most capable of the foreign reporters in America during the war, objected to the *Tribune's* "doctrinaire" editorial articles, but the paper as a whole under Gay's management he considered "better printed, more thoughtfully written, and more carefully got up than any of its cotemporaries." [1]

However bracing such comments may have been to Sydney Gay, he had little time now to reflect on the long road he had traveled since that spring when he had looked forward with dread to every issue of the *Herald*. The President, reacting to Pope's defeat, was reported in one of Hill's private letters to have remarked that he had heard of "knocking a person into the middle of next week," but "the Rebels have knocked us into the middle of last year." It was worse than that. The enemy was launched on a full-scale invasion of Maryland.

[1] Edward Dicey: *Six Months in the Federal States* (London: 1863), I, 42.

✵ CHAPTER VI ✵

A Man at Antietam

A FARMER careened down Pennsylvania Avenue on a lathered horse late on the afternoon of September 4, 1862, shouting to one and all that rebels "by the thousand" were crossing the Potomac at Edward's Ferry. All day similar reports winged through the capital. For twenty-four hours the War Department refused to credit them, as if invasion were too horrendous to be accorded official recognition; but by nightfall on September 5, editors were poring over their maps of the Potomac region in the certainty that a decisive battle loomed.

Defeat likely meant recognition of the Confederate States of America abroad and a negotiated peace, for with another enemy army under Braxton Bragg threatening Cincinnati, continuation of the war could only bring further humiliation on a cause that was apparently hopeless. "Are we going, as all Republics have gone?—to the military devil?" asked Adams Hill. McClellan's reappointment seemed to him the final blow: "*Abraham Lincoln has killed himself this week.*" [1]

If the Union was about to disintegrate, the walking file of the New York *Herald* must be the first to record it. Frederic Hudson, nettled by the resurgence of the *Tribune*, labored mightily to restore the *Herald's* leadership. He instructed

[1] Hill to Gay, Sept. 7, 1862, Gay Papers.

L. A. Whiteley that every dispatch to reach Washington from the *Herald* crew with the army must be telegraphed, regardless of length or importance. Under his eagle eye, Whiteley made elaborate preparations as the Army of the Potomac marched off to the northwest to meet Lee's challenge. He assigned Oscar G. Sawyer, competent and experienced, to McClellan's headquarters, J. P. Dunn to Burnside's command, Leonard A. Hendrick to Franklin's, Alfred B. Talcott to Hooker's, George W. Hosmer to Couch's, Ward to Mansfield's, sent Finley Anderson, an able and courageous reporter, to reconnoiter on the other side of the enemy, stationed James Nye Ashley, an experienced telegrapher, at Frederick, perhaps in the hope that his practiced fingers would find an untended key, and held S. M. Carpenter in reserve. In Baltimore, Henry M. Flint was alerted; Flint enjoyed excellent facilities for obtaining news through officials and train-dispatchers of the Baltimore & Ohio Railroad, and was first with Lee's proclamation inviting the citizens of Maryland to rally to the Confederate cause. Whiteley and Sawyer worked out a mysterious scheme for transmitting dispatches from McClellan's headquarters, so secret that they kept it from other members of their staff. By September 11, all the *Herald* men were at their posts, and Whiteley was in touch with them through a constant stream of couriers.[2]

Sydney Gay viewed with apprehension such of these preparations as were known to him. Once again the *Tribune* editor found himself going into a campaign outmanned. Worse, the *Tribune's* shining lights were out: Sam Wilkeson, at his farm in Canaan, New York, was only now recovering from his racking experiences on the Peninsula, eating potatoes stewed in cream ("Jove! what a dish. My wife shall be canonized for instituting it. She shall go into the Calendar of the Blessed, as Ste. Catherine de Pomme du Terre"); Charles A. Page remained in Washington to watch the troops there; William H. Kent, a bright prospect uncovered by Smalley, went to Har-

2 Whiteley to Hudson, Sept. 10, 1862, Bennett Papers.

per's Ferry and was shortly captured with its garrison. Hastily Gay telegraphed Albert Richardson, the able chief of his Western correspondents, to leave Cincinnati to its fate and report to George Smalley at McClellan's headquarters. In Washington, Hill recruited a Treasury Department clerk named John Evans, "a red-whiskered, ghost-like man" whose mere appearance aroused merriment wherever he went. (Alf Waud of *Harper's Weekly* caricatured him privately, beard streaming in the wind, and Homer Byington wrote later that "if the army can't get up a fight, it has no small amount of fun out of poor Evans.") Josiah Rhinehart Sypher, a young attorney and intimate of the redoubtable Thaddeus Stevens, had just returned to his home in Lancaster after corresponding for the *Tribune* on the Mississippi when he found Gay's orders: Go at once to Harrisburg. D. J. Kinney was posted at Frederick. In the army itself, along with Smalley and Evans, Gay had only Nathaniel Paige ("not good at battles," Hill had warned) and H. Thompson, a messenger.

Richardson pulled out of Cincinnati two hours after receiving Gay's telegram, arrived in Washington at ten on the morning of September 12, bought a horse and equipment, somehow secured an outdated pass signed by General Burnside, and, after a sixty-five-mile ride, reached the army at three on September 14, just as it was forcing passage of South Mountain on the way to strike Lee on the Antietam. Smalley, whom Gay had designated "chief of staff," had been jittery about lack of manpower, and greeted Richardson with relief. Trivialities divert the minds of men even as the earth trembles with events that shape their destinies. Not having met before, Smalley and Richardson were amused to discover that they had both been born in Franklin, Massachusetts, in 1833.

Smalley had been warned before leaving Washington that Halleck's ban on correspondents applied to McClellan's army as it had to Pope's; so he had given headquarters a wide berth. But during the fight that afternoon at South Mountain, he had found an officer at his side—McClellan. "What troops are those?" the General asked, watching dark-blue uniforms swarming up a distant slope. Smalley offered his field glasses. McClellan shook his head. He seemed detached, thought Smalley, "a General watching maneuvers." The reporter had never seen him before, but "I thought an air of indecision hung about him." [3] In any case, Smalley concluded, newsmen were safe. Richardson wrote Gay the next day that "I took tea last night & breakfast this morning, at a farmer's table, with Gen. Marcy, & several others of McClellan's staff. Marcy [chief of staff] said he should not order us out but was a good deal curious to know how we got in." Richardson told him it was a military secret. "I think McClellan's policy will be to treat correspondents courteously—at least for the present," he concluded. General Halleck's ban was never rescinded; it simply died of neglect.

The Army of the Potomac snaked through Turner's Gap, then went swinging south through lush farm country, among apple orchards, fields of ripe wheat and corn, its polished bayonets glinting in the sun. Early on September 16 the advance reached the sluggish, brown Antietam, ran into a spate of enemy fire from across the river near Sharpsburg, a little village nestling near the juncture of the Antietam with the Potomac, and came to a halt. From a low ridge, at four that afternoon, Richardson could see the graybacks clearly, moving here and there in the undulating country beyond. McClellan cautiously set about deploying his eighty-seven thousand, going over the ground all the rest of the day.

Smalley got wind of a flanking movement to be led by Hooker's corps against the rebel left, and at the same hour that Richardson rose in his stirrups to get a better look through his glass at Lee's veterans, Smalley spurred off with members of Hooker's staff. None of them knew who he was, and none thought to ask. Hooker's men pushed north on the Boonsboro road, cut west, and went splashing across the Antietam's

[3] Smalley, 140.

upper fords. The enemy spotted them, and opened with artillery. Smalley may have remembered telling Nathaniel Paige to meet him in the morning near McClellan's headquarters at the Pry house, an appointment he obviously could not keep now. Still, Paige always bridled so at taking orders it was just as well; Richardson could handle the center, Evans, the red-bearded apparition, was downstream with Burnside on the left, and Thompson, sent off to New York with dispatches that morning, might be back in time to help, at the rate McClellan was moving. The rest was up to Smalley, and he knew it. Perhaps a vision of Phoebe Garnaut crossed his mind—a pretty, fragile girl, Wendell Phillips's adopted daughter, his fiancée. He wrote her every day, and kept a careful record to see how his letters fared in the army's undependable mails. She should see him now, coolly riding his charger with Hooker's staff, quite dashing in his new blue uniform. It was the uniform that had emboldened him; he had got it on the strength of a staff appointment from Brigadier General Carl Schurz, given with a wink and "indefinite leave on special duty."

Smalley had left Washington expecting to be gone a day or two, and for two weeks had had nothing with him of what were called "necessaries" but a toothbrush, a mackintosh, and his field glasses. George was a stolid, handsome man, not quite thirty, powerfully built. Ten years before, he had stroked the first Yale crew to race Harvard, on Lake Winnepesaukee. Intellectually inclined, an ardent devotee of the *Tribune*, he counted Phillips, Schurz, and Ralph Waldo Emerson among his friends. Other Bohemians regarded him as something of an aristocrat, with his law degree and his Boston inflection (his father was a Congregational minister in Worcester), if not a snob. Later, in the gentlemanly regime of Whitelaw Reid, this thickset, square-jawed, fastidious individual would seem perfectly placed as the *Tribune's* correspondent in London, living in liveried splendor on Chester Square, giving dinners for members of the court which outshone those at the American embassy, advocating court dress for American ministers, rousing E. L. Godkin to dub him "the Tory Squire." But those who had seen George Smalley in action at Antietam would forgive him.

Hooker got his men across the Hagerstown road, pushed south, and was developing his attack as dusk fell. "If they had let us start earlier," Smalley heard him mutter, "we might have finished tonight." Now the enemy would be ready, come morning. Reluctantly Hooker pulled his men back in the gloaming to a valley about a mile north of the little white Dunker church. Smalley bivouacked within sight of the headquarters tent. His bridle around one arm, he tossed fitfully under his mackintosh in sporadic, drizzling rain.

A heavy mist lay close to the ground when he awoke at dawn. Hooker was already in the saddle. "The old man would have liked to be with the pickets," a staff officer grumbled. Almost before Smalley could bolt his cold bacon and mount, the troops were on the move, pushing grimly forward with long Enfields and Springfields primed, through timber to a ridge, down the ridge toward the East Wood, the adjoining cornfield they would make famous, the Dunker church across the road. As the mist lifted, bayonets flashed in the sunlight amid the tall corn: Jackson lay in wait for them. Now there was again that dread sound that reminded men of a crackling canebreak as the East Wood and the fences of the field came to life. It was drowned out shortly by a tremendous artillery barrage from McClellan's rifled guns across the river. Richardson, standing near the Pry house, pulled out his watch and counted over sixty detonations to the minute. As it died away, Hooker resumed the advance. Smalley saw him, the nose prominent, the chin a little weak, the handsome face more flushed than ever, riding along the firing line. Hooker saw Smalley, too, "in advance of my whole staff, . . . gazing on the strife as . . . at a scene upon the stage." Hooker turned to an aide: "Order that man to the rear." A few moments later the General had dispatched his entire staff on missions. Hooker turned to look about him.

"Who are you?"

"Special correspondent of the New York *Tribune*, sir."

"Will you take an order for me?" He pointed to a thin line of troops wavering under enemy pressure. "Tell the colonel of that regiment to take his men to the front and keep them there."

Smalley spurred off to find the colonel. He delivered the order, but the colonel looked at his shoulders—no insignia.

"Who are you?"

"The order is General Hooker's."

"It must come to me from a staff officer or from my brigade commander."

"Very good," said George icily. "I shall report to General Hooker that you refuse to obey."

"Oh, for God's sake, don't do that!" the colonel yelled, suddenly convinced. "Orderly! . . ."

Smalley told Hooker about it when he returned. "Yes, I see," said "Fighting Joe," "but don't let the next man talk so much." [4] Off went the *Tribune* man on another mission, and yet another, taking a kind of grim pride in going the shortest route, transported by the dreadful music of battle. There is no accounting for the way men behave under such circumstances, calling upon resources deep within them never yet understood. Be they glandular or cerebral or spiritual, in George Smalley they produced a fatalistic calm that moved Hooker's aides to proclaim him "the bravest of the brave," and stirred Hooker himself to tell George Wilkes of the *Spirit of the Times* in his emphatic way later: "In all the experience I have had of war, I never saw the most experienced and veteran soldier exhibit more tranquil fortitude and unshaken valor than was exhibited by that young man." [5] Once the blue jacket was torn by flying shrapnel; twice his horse was hit.

[4] Smalley, 146; Hooker in *Wilkes' Spirit of the Times*, Feb. 7, 1863.
[5] *Wilkes' Spirit of the Times*, Feb. 7, 1863.

A Man at Antietam

In a letter the next day, Richardson, whose own reputation for risk-taking was considerable, would beg Gay to "give Mr. Smalley an earnest caution to be more prudent. It is wonderful to me that he came out of the battle alive."

Hooker, in his brassy uniform astride a big white charger, was a sitting duck for sharpshooters; Smalley tried to tell him so just before a bullet struck the General's foot. Hooker swayed in his saddle; aides caught him as he fell, and he was carried to the rear, cursing mightily as blood trickled from his boot. The assault had reached its zenith: the cornfield, windrows of bodies lying amid the trampled stalks, belonged to regiments pitifully decimated by Hood's Texans; across the road, powder-blackened survivors of George Greene's division of Mansfield's corps held the ground around the riddled clapboard church. But Mansfield was dead, Hooker was wounded, the two corps were disorganized, and two thousand of Sedgwick's men went down attempting to support them. Farther south, the sunken road near Lee's center had become Bloody Lane, and far to Lee's right, Burnside dallied fatally before the triple-arched stone bridge over which he might have delivered the decisive assault.

Smalley rode over to McClellan's headquarters toward noon to try to fit the holocaust he had witnessed into the main story. Lieutenant James H. Wilson, who had seen him earlier on a mission for Hooker, begged him now to try to persuade Hooker to resume command. Wilson sounded desperate, as if he had lost all faith in McClellan's capacity; Smalley understood him to mean that Hooker should take command of the whole army. He protested that it was not his place to deliver such a message, but when other staff officers said excitedly that the day depended on it, he spurred off. Smalley found Hooker in a little brick farmhouse, lying on a cot. How was it? "You can see for yourself," the General said faintly, and asked for news. Smalley told him McClellan was faltering, had not yet used his reserves; Lee would probably be able to withdraw across the Potomac unless— "You need not go on," Smalley remembered Hooker saying before he could finish. "I cannot move." [6]

That was that. Smalley reported it to Wilson, arranged for a rendezvous of *Tribune* men at nightfall, and set out on a tour of the lines. That night, in a narrow room of a farmhouse crowded with wounded, Paige, Evans, Smalley, and Richardson prepared their reports by the light of a single tallow candle. Paige had little to contribute beyond a list of killed and wounded he had collected behind the lines. Smalley looked at him in disgust. "Is that all that you have done?" he asked. "Haven't you been in the battle and under fire?" With the sounds of dying men in their ears and the world waiting, the two men came close to fisticuffs. That night Paige wrote Gay seven pages of complaint about Smalley, whose "manner of exercising his authority is unendurable to me." Paige recounted their farmhouse meeting:

> I told him that part of the day I had been exposed to severe cannonading but that I had not been under musketry fire—that I did not consider it the duty of a correspondent to foolishly expose his life when there was nothing to be gained by it. . . . He differed with me and gave me to understand by his tone of voice that he considered me a coward. . . .
>
> It is my humble opinion that he could have been of more service to the Tribune if he had left the carrying of orders to staff officers of the army & attended to the staff of the Tribune.

While Richardson and Evans wrote accounts for incorporation into his narrative, Smalley worked out his lead:

Battlefield of Antietam,
Wednesday Evening, Sept. 17, 1862.
    Fierce and desperate battle between two hundred thousand men has raged since daylight, yet night closes on an

[6] Smalley, 148.

uncertain field. It is the greatest fight since Waterloo, all over the field contested with an obstinacy equal even to Waterloo. . . .

Around midnight the big fellow commandeered Richardson's horse and headed for Frederick, without food or sleep. Through Boonsboro, Turner's Gap, and Middletown he rode, composing in his head, now and then dozing in the saddle. At Frederick he found the telegraph office closed; no one knew where the operator lived. The man appeared at seven in the morning, and "after some demur" agreed to take a short message. Smalley sat on a log by the door, handing him sheet after sheet until he thought enough to fill a column was on its way to the *Tribune* via Baltimore. Then he tried to charter a special locomotive, but the station master said he would require a military warrant. As a forlorn hope, Smalley telegraphed the War Department. There was no answer. He waited, nervous and close to exhaustion, fearing to run into Sawyer or Talcott or someone else from the *Herald*, wondering if he should not have heeded Richardson and gone via Hagerstown. Hours later he got aboard a mixed train for Baltimore, still with no acknowledgment from New York of his dispatch.[7]

In Washington, the morning of September 18 was not a happy one, least of all in the War Department. At five o'clock the previous afternoon Halleck had received a message from McClellan that began: "We are in the midst of the most terrible battle of the war—perhaps of history." Nothing of substance had come since. Secretary Welles called and went away in a torment. Of McClellan, old Welles noted in his diary that day: "His dispatches are seldom full, clear, or satisfactory. 'Behaved splendidly,' 'performed handsomely,' but wherein or what was accomplished is never told. Our anxiety is intense. We have but few and foggy dispatches of any kind these troublesome days."[8] Over in State, Secretary Seward nursed

[7] Smalley, 150, 151, supplemented by letters in the Gay Papers.
[8] John T. Morse, ed.: *Diary of Gideon Welles* (Boston: 1911), I, 140.

his hopes as he penned a letter to John Bigelow, consul in Paris. News, he said, seemed "thus far favorable—but at the moment I write we are waiting anxiously for the report of yesterday's engagement." Part of the trouble was that in moving to the Antietam, McClellan for once had outrun the field telegraph service, the men who strung wire across the countryside at the rate of two miles an hour, and in consequence "Little Mac" had to send by courier to Hagerstown, whence messages were relayed circuitously by telegraph to Harrisburg, Baltimore, and Washington.

No one could have been more apprehensive than Lincoln. He had taken a solemn vow when Lee had reached Frederick a week before, that he would issue the proclamation he had withheld so long if the invasion were repelled. Today he had no heart for routine work.[9]

The Baltimore agent of the American Telegraph Company could surmise from such messages as he had seen that officials in Washington were still as much in the dark as the rest of the country. When a dispatch for the New York *Tribune* came in, he therefore relayed it to the War Department. So it was that around noon the first coherent account of the Battle of Antietam, a press dispatch signed Smalley, came to the hands of Abraham Lincoln.[1]

Beginning at half past one, the War Department sent it over a page at a time to Adams Hill at the *Tribune* bureau, as it was copied. To save time, Hill persuaded Sanford to order the Baltimore operator to send it to New York, "but the Baltimore man wilfully or stupidly mistook the direction, gave no answer, and it was only through Snyder at the Washington office who said it had not gone, that I learned about it," Hill lamented. Smalley seemed jinxed. Hill had not given up hope. At ten thirty that night he returned from the telegraph office to write Gay: "No dispatch has up to this hour come over

9 Basler: *Collected Works*, lists but two brief items.
1 Smalley, 151, supported by Adams Hill to Gay, Sept. 18, 1862, Gay Papers.

the wires directly from the battlefields for any other paper, at
least none worth speaking of. This is the only authority in
town tonight."

Ten minutes before the New York-bound express left Baltimore that night, a distraught man in a dusty, torn uniform
leaped from the boxcar on which he had ridden from Frederick, and got aboard. Standing beneath a dimly burning oil
lamp at one end of the car, George Smalley scribbled all
through the night, leaning against a partition, peering at his
pencilings in the uncertain light as the train lurched on, a
man reliving Antietam in a trance. There had been the shock
of the counterattack, on the heels of Hooker's early-morning
assault:

In ten minutes the fortunes of the day seemed to have
changed; it was the rebels now who were advancing,
pouring out of the woods in endless lines, sweeping
through the cornfield from which their comrades had just
fled. Hooker sent in his nearest brigade to meet them,
but it could not do the work. He called for another.
There was nothing close enough, unless he took it from
his right. His right might be in danger if it was weak-
ened, but his centre was already threatened with annihila-
tion. Not hesitating one moment, he sent to Doubleday:
"Give me your best brigade instantly."

The best brigade came down the hill on the right on
the run. . . .

Reaching Jersey City at daylight, Smalley continued aboard
the ferry, huddled on a bench, sunken eyes on the paper,
thoughts in Maryland:

Burnside hesitated for hours in front of the bridge
which should have been carried at once by a *coup de
main.* . . .

McClellan's glass for the last half hour has seldom been

turned away from the left. He sees clearly enough that Burnside is pressed—needs no messenger to tell him that. His face grows darker with anxious thought. Looking down into the valley where 15,000 troops are lying, he turns a half-questioning look on Fitz John Porter, who stands by his side, gravely scanning the field. They are Porter's troops below, are fresh and only impatient to share in the fight. But Porter slowly shakes his head, and one may believe that the same thought is passing through the mind of both generals: "They are the only reserves of the army; they cannot be spared." . . .

Aboard the cross-town omnibus now, he read it over, touched it up, oblivious to the stares of sleepy-eyed passengers.

At 152 Nassau Street, the compositors Sydney Gay had ordered to wait burst into cheers as he stumbled in; "at 6 a.m. the worst piece of manuscript the oldest hand had ever seen" was split up and deciphered in tremulous haste. "Somewhere near the uptown breakfast hour," as Smalley remembered, a *Tribune* extra hit the streets with six columns about the bloody Battle of Antietam. It was a thunderous beat; more— by Civil War standards, it was a masterpiece. No flatulent claims of "Glorious Victory" greeted those who swarmed around the newsboys; he had written graphically, but with restraint and with unmistakable conviction, explaining the battle plan, taking the reader over the whole field. He correctly appraised the trouble as poor co-ordination, and the result as a stalemate, but one which in all probability would force Lee back across the Potomac.

The New York *Times*, the *Evening Post*, the Philadelphia *Inquirer*, *Harper's Weekly*, *The Times* of London, and un- counted others reprinted it. To Bryant's paper, it was "a truly admirable account, which ranks for clearness, animation, and apparent accuracy with the best battle pieces in literature, and far excels anything written by Crimean Russell," a salute that, coming from a competitor, was almost without precedent.

Foreign ministers forwarded it to their governments,[2] and
John Hay told Hill that it surpassed any official report written
since the beginning of the war.[3] To thousands of readers, Antietam was a vivid experience etched on their minds by one
man who had proved once again Wilkeson's theory that the
only way to report battles lay in being *"so closely observant
of them as to be in danger of being killed."* [4] Richardson's full
story, printed September 22, was of almost the same caliber;
he, too, had been in the thick of it.

What had happened to the *Herald*? "It is difficult to manage correspondents after they get to the field," Whiteley had
written Hudson beforehand. "They become so much absorbed
with what they see that they forget to relate it." Surviving
manuscripts do not show what went awry, but Bennett sent
his son to the front immediately thereafter. Alexander Wilson,
managing editor of the *Times*, attributed his paper's failure
to a want of organization, and assigned J. M. Winchell to give
each correspondent written instructions thereafter.[5] Gay and
Hill, overjoyed that "we have beaten the *Herald* out of sight,"
had their own explanation. "I entirely agree with you," Hill
wrote, "that we have surely and completely beaten the other
papers in this as in previous campaigns, and that it is because
we have men devoted to their work." Smalley, after three
hours' sleep, was already on his way back to the army.

Luck had played no small part in Smalley's stunning beat,
but no one could say he had not earned it. The picture of a
special correspondent of the New York *Tribune* delivering
Hooker's orders on the bloodiest field of the war became part

[2] *Tribune*, Sept. 23, 1862, Washington dispatch. News of Antietam is
generally believed to have deterred the British from recognizing the Confederacy.
[3] Hill to Gay, Sept. 22, 1862, postscript, Gay Papers. Interestingly, Ken-
neth P. Williams: *Lincoln Finds a General* (New York: 1949), II, 456,
quotes from it as "a very remarkable dispatch," without identifying its
author.
[4] Wilkeson to Gay [July 5, 1862?], aboard "Steamer on the Bay," Gay
Papers. Italics, here as elsewhere, are those of the person quoted.
[5] J. M. Winchell to William Conant Church, Sept. 27, 1862, Church
Papers: MS Division, Library of Congress.

of the richly varied legacy that the Bohemian Brigade left to American journalism.

Just three days after Smalley's dispatch, newspapers carried one from Washington which said that after January 1, 1863, all slaves in any area still in rebellion would be declared free. "GOD BLESS ABRAHAM LINCOLN!" said the *Tribune*. Sydney Gay opened a letter from his friend Wendell Phillips, he who had called Lincoln a "spaniel," a "first-rate second-rate man," and perhaps Gay chuckled. "How decent Abe grows," said Wendell.

CHAPTER VII

"The President Says . . ."

1. FAREWELL TO LITTLE MAC

IN THE weeks following Antietam, Abraham Lincoln's or-
deal with the bafflingly irresolute commander of the Army of
the Potomac came to a climax long anticipated by reporters
in Washington. The public knew little of it. Considering the
volume of editorial praise and censure of McClellan over a
long period, the press was singularly discreet in dealing with
his relations with the President; reporters knew more than
their editors deemed wise to print.

As one element in a complicated equation, the press was
partly responsible for Lincoln's dilemma. However acute his
misgivings as to McClellan's capacities, exasperating as he
found McClellan's procrastinations, his cautious perfection-
ism, his constant carping, Lincoln was ever aware that "the
Young Napoleon" was idolized not only by the army but,
thanks to the early eagerness of the press to make him a hero,
by most of the country as well.

Lincoln had considered removing him from command as
early as May, when a visit to the Peninsula convinced the
President that the campaign was not going well. He "would
have done so in three days had not Lovejoy's unfortunate
resolution inspired by Forney, interposed," Adams Hill wrote

Gay as the disastrous end of that campaign was coming to light.[1] Lovejoy's motion, passed by the House on May 9, commended McClellan's "high military qualities which secure important results with but little sacrifice of human life," and apparently was just enough to stay the President's hand. Later, Lincoln frankly told Noah Brooks that he had tolerated McClellan largely from dread of the reaction to his dismissal.

When McClellan made his shocking suggestion during Second Bull Run, that "Pope be left to get out of his scrape," Hill, who did not know of these words, recorded that "the President was never so wrathful as last night against George." A month later the question of dismissal was again on the President's mind. Hill said that Lincoln, mindful that he had not won a majority of the popular vote in the four-sided presidential election of 1860, observed with wry humor that "he is a minority president, how can he dismiss McC., a 'Majority General?' "

Deeply troubled, the President visited the army near the Antietam field during the first days of October to persuade McClellan to press the advantage he had won there, and, upon returning to Washington, urged an immediate offensive against Lee in northern Virginia. George Smalley wrote Gay revealing letters on McClellan's reception of this advice. Smalley concluded from long talks with Colonel Thomas M. Key and others of McClellan's staff that the General's heart was still set on the Peninsula, and that he had no intention of launching the vigorous campaign Lincoln had in mind. Albert D. Richardson's soundings tallied exactly.

While the army dallied, Adams Hill learned from General Wadsworth in Washington on October 13 that this time the ax was likely to fall. "He had just come from the President who had read him a long letter to McClellan in which he urged

[1] Hill to Gay, July 8, 1862, Gay Papers. On page 7 of the same letter, Hill wrote: "I would add here that it was the President who on last Saturday [July 5] stated that had it not been for Lovejoy's resolution he would have removed McClellan." This does not appear to have come to light before.

and urged an immediate advance," Hill wrote Gay that evening. "In conversation he [Lincoln] seemed to doubt that George would move after all. Said he'd got tired of his excuses, said *he'd remove him at once but for the election.*"

At last the reluctant General did move, but too late. On November 5, 1862, less than twenty-four hours after the polls had closed in the congressional elections, Lincoln administered the *coup de grâce.*

The army said farewell to Little Mac with many displays of emotion. On the day of his final review, three of his staff officers set out to beat up Richardson, as the representative of the paper that had relentlessly campaigned against their chief, but they were dissuaded. "I would have given my left arm for a weapon," Richardson wrote Gay. "The next morning I buckled on a navy revolver, & went among them for an hour; but they did not renew the demonstration." Like the staff officers, the army soon resigned itself to the loss, and correspondents wrote with more hope than conviction of brighter days ahead.

2. LINCOLN AND THE REPORTERS

As ADAMS HILL's letters on the Lincoln-McClellan problem suggest, newspapermen in Washington, by talking with those who had just seen the President and by direct interview as well, were opening a window in the White House which had never been so accessible to them before. The relationship between Lincoln and the working press—war correspondents as well as Washington reporters—was freighted with consequence for the news revolution.

From the beginning of political parties in the United States, successive administrations had used pet newspapers as organs for the release of news and quasi-official expressions of policy. Lincoln upset this precedent: from the outset, he would have no organ.[2] The collection of news in Washington became the free-for-all it has remained ever since.

There is no explicit evidence as to why Lincoln adopted this policy, but it fitted his constant purpose of marshaling support from all quarters, whereas an organ tended to accentuate party lines. At least two editors hoped to get Lincoln to return to the old practice. Simon P. Hanscom, the amiable former chief of the *Herald* bureau, became editor of the Washington *National Republican* after Bennett discharged him, and for a time ran a column of "official intelligence" containing many exclusive tidbits Lincoln gave him; but the paper never won a large following, and its pretensions to officialism were taken so lightly that Hanscom finally dropped them. Then there was what Lincoln wrote of to Stanton as "my paper as you jokingly call it," the Washington *Chronicle*. Lincoln himself persuaded John W. Forney, his most ardent editorial supporter, to convert the *Sunday Chronicle* into a daily in 1862, attended the dedication of its building, and favored it with government advertising and printing. But so far as news was concerned, Forney complained: "When I go to see him he asks me what is the last good joke I have heard." [3]

Almost all reporters were well received at the White House. William O. Stoddard, the young secretary, saw some of them every day, waiting outside Lincoln's office. "The President likes to have them come, and meets them cordially." [4] Nor was it difficult to get there. The two doorkeepers were not vigilant after office hours, William A. Croffut of the *Tribune* remembered, "and I often walked into the White House and went straight up to the private secretaries' room adjoining his own, without seeing any person whatever." Gideon Welles thought it deplorable. "It is an infirmity of the President," he

2 *Tribune* editorial, Nov. 21, 1860.

3 Tyler Dennett, ed.: *Lincoln and the Civil War in the Diaries and Letters of John Hay* (New York: 1939), 146.

4 William O. Stoddard: *Inside the White House in War Times* (New York: 1890), 134.

noted in his diary, "that he permits the little newsmongers to come around him and be intimate. . . . He has great inquisitiveness. Likes to hear all the political gossip as much as Seward."

Once they were in his presence, Lincoln put the reporters at ease, usually lounging in his chair and asking them almost as many questions as he answered. Ben: Perley Poore of the Boston *Journal* headed a delegation that called to complain about certain vagaries of the censorship. "I don't know much about this censorship," Lincoln said innocently, "but come downstairs and I will show you the origin of one of the pet phrases of you newspaper fellows." He led them to the basement, where a huge sheep carcass dangled from the ceiling. Gesturing toward it with a merry twinkle, he said: "There, now you know what *revenons à nos moutons* means!" [5]

It was tacitly understood that Lincoln's remarks on such occasions were not to be attributed to him in print. "The President holds no conversations intended for publication," the *Herald* said in reproving a *Tribune* reporter for quoting him.[6] But the homely figures of speech and anecdotes that larded these informal interviews might be heard in hotel lobbies and department corridors almost from the moment his callers departed: Abe had said sending reinforcements to McClellan was like "shovelin' flies across a barnyard," he had described Admiral DuPont's elaborate preparations for the attack on Charleston, ending in a futile bombardment, as "a very long grace for a thin plate of soup," or he had compared Meade's feeble pursuit of Lee after Gettysburg to "an old woman shooing her geese across the creek." [7]

At times the gaunt man spoke of army affairs with what W. H. Kent of the *Tribune* aptly described as "as kind of cheerful melancholy." At others, Lincoln's melancholy was

[5] Allen Thorndike Rice, ed.: *Reminiscences of Abraham Lincoln by Distinguished Men of His Time* (New York: 1886), 226.

[6] Issue of Jan. 22, 1862.

[7] The "soup" quotation is in Adams Hill to Gay, Apr. 14, 1863, Gay Papers. The others are more familiar.

unrelieved, and the man was too ingenuous to conceal it. Reporters' letters are studded with such instances. "President blue and cross this morning," Hill noted at the time of Pope's bewilderment at Second Bull Run; "better this afternoon, and said wasn't so bad as thought earlier." November 29, 1862: Lincoln returned from an interview with Burnside at Aquia Creek, "greatly discouraged," Hill reported. March 31, 1863: "The President, night before last, was dismal in conversation with Senator Trumbull." April 15, 1863: Senator Sumner told Hill he had just seen Lincoln on the *Peterhoff* affair (a diplomatic tangle regarding the disposal of mails captured aboard a British blockade-runner) and found him "gloomy." May 6, 1863: Sumner commented to Hill on the President's "low frame of mind" after Chancellorsville.

L. A. Gobright dropped in one night to find the President deeply concerned about the Vicksburg campaign. "I can't sleep tonight without hearing something," he said, and invited the Associated Press man to walk over to the War Department with him. On the way, a messenger stopped him with a telegram, which he read beneath a street lamp. "Bad news, bad news," he said slowly; then, in an admonitory tone: "Don't say anything about this—don't mention it." Gobright read it and ventured that the report was probably untrue. He thought the deeply lined face looked relieved, but Lincoln repeated: "Don't say anything about this." [8]

When the news looked good, on the other hand, Lincoln could co-operate with almost boyish enthusiasm. Joseph A. Ware of Forney's *Chronicle* called on him one evening later in the same campaign, and was greeted heartily. "Here are two dispatches," said Lincoln, "one from Rawlins and one from Hurlbut. Don't stop to read them, but I'll copy the short one while you copy the long one, as you can write faster than I." Thereupon the President and the reporter sat down to transcribe them in time for the morning *Chronicle*.[9]

[8] Gobright, 336, 337.
[9] Richardson: *Grant*, 336.

When Lincoln was too busy to see them, reporters sometimes sent in their calling cards with questions on them. He would scrawl a few words on the reverse side. In this, as in other ways, his attitude toward them contrasted with that of his cabinet and of most other public officials. Croffut of the *Tribune* asked if he might be present when the state governors conferred with the President. "Certainly," said Lincoln. "You can, as far as I am concerned." When the session began, Governor Yates of Illinois looked at Croffut and asked if all present were state executives. "I am an exception," said the reporter, and started for the door when Lincoln explained that he had consented to Croffut's presence. "We shall not say or do anything today that is secret, in any sense, and our only chance is to take the American people frankly into our confidence. However, it is for you gentlemen to say." But Croffut saw so many scowls that he slipped out.[1]

The War Department usually forbade mention of Lincoln's numerous quick trips to the army until he was back in Washington, and, except for Noah Brooks, reporters never went along on them. But when Lincoln went up to West Point to confer with General Scott on June 24, 1862, a *World* man reported that "Mr. Lincoln was especially cordial in allowing reporters to proceed with him, remarking that he was not as afraid of reporters as some people are, and illustrating the fact by telling an appropriate and pertinent story." Joseph Howard, Jr., the *Times* man present, said the story was "about a shark who swallowed a red-hot harpoon," but none of them reported it. Conway, the *Herald* man on the trip, had never met Lincoln. This was how it went:

"Reporter for the *Herald*, eh? Well, I'm not afraid of you. Walk right in and sit down."

"Mr. President, . . . I was sent up here by the acting editor of the *Herald* to ascertain, if possible, the motive

[1] He got a full account of the meeting anyway: *Tribune*, Sept. 29, 1862.

of your sudden visit to this place. Perhaps you will consider it impertinent of me to inquire into the subject."

"No sir, I do not consider it in any way an impertinence. At worst it might be thought an imprudence. . . . You gentlemen of the press seem to be pretty much like soldiers, who have to go wherever sent."

Lincoln went on to remark that Bennett was a great editor, according to this reminiscence: "the greatest in the country, perhaps, if my good friend Horace Greeley will allow me to say so. Now there . . . is an illustration of what I mean by trusting gentlemen of the press. If I made it to some of your profession they would instantly use it in their papers, and get me into hotter water with my friend Horace."

Conway asked if the purpose of the trip was to see Scott, as Frederic Hudson had surmised. For answer, Lincoln pointed to the Parrott gun factory across the river, remarking that he was ever investigating new inventions in firearms. "Is that why you came, you would have me believe?" Lincoln smiled at him. "I would have you consider whether one theory is not as good as the other." He acknowledged that he had seen Scott. "I was glad of the chance to talk with him about the situation of the country. Now I don't think I could say more were we to talk until bedtime." [2] In showing his friendly manner, his willingness to talk freely in confidence, his easy parrying of a question he knew was on the record, and his firm but gentle manner of closing, this interview may be taken as typical of many Lincoln gave.

For all his friendliness with reporters, Lincoln never gave his full confidence to any of them, thought L. A. Gobright; but certainly one member of the Washington press corps was as close to Lincoln as any of his wartime friends—Noah Brooks. Brooks often breakfasted with Lincoln, accompanied him on trips to the army, went to the theater with him, was

[2] Emmanuel Hertz, ed.: *Lincoln Talks* (New York: 1939), 272, from an undated *Herald* clipping.

accepted by Mrs. Lincoln almost as a member of the family, and was to have been John Nicolay's successor in 1865 as Lincoln's senior secretary. A genial, intelligent widower in his early thirties, Brooks represented the most widely circulated newspaper on the West Coast, the Sacramento *Union*. Lincoln gave him a strength return from the Army of the Potomac once, saying: "You can send that to California, by and by. It can't get back here in time to do any harm. But don't ever let on that I gave you those figures. They'd hang me for giving information to the enemy." [3] Lincoln, said Brooks, thought Stanton went too far in administering the censorship.

The President's ceaseless quest for news was familiar to the reporters who saw him striding back from the War Department, often after midnight, and sometimes they would bring him news at odd hours when they had reason to believe it would be new to him. Toward two in the morning once, John Russell Young and a fellow editor of the Washington *Chronicle* persuaded the night watchman that the President should be roused at once. Presently Lincoln came down to the magnificent Blue Room, "hair tousled over a sleepy face, in slippers and night gown. Curling up on the lounge, eyes half closed, he listened to the news." The fall of Charleston was reported in a Southern paper, fresh from the hands of a picket. The President, "slowly nursing his knees," interrupted the reader: "What is the date of that paper?" Young said it was July 20. "July 20th. Well, I have news from Charleston July 22nd, and then the bombardment was going on vigorously." Crestfallen, Young and his friend stammered apologies. The President was "so gentle over our regrets, so courteous, so much obliged for our coming—for did we not see it might have been news— . . . that we came from his presence as if dowered, and not as unseemly visitors who had robbed him of his peace." [4]

[3] Sandburg, II, 86.
[4] Young: *Memories*, 57, 58. Young chose a month at random in recalling the incident, here changed from December to July (1863), when such a report came.

Lincoln recognized the news revolution for what it was, for it impinged on his own life in many ways. Further, he wanted, knew he needed, all the editorial support he could muster; a liberal policy toward a press hot in pursuit of news served this end. Thus we find him writing Bennett to explain why a reporter had been refused a pass, concluding: "I write this to assure you that the administration will not discriminate against the *Herald*." [5] He wrote a memorandum, presumably to Seward: "It is important to humor the *Herald*. Is there any objection to Hanscoms telegraphing the proclamation?" [6] He sent a note to Stanton: "I am appealed to by the proprietors of papers here, because they have to get telegraphed back to them from New-York, matter which goes from the War Department. Might not this be avoided without harm or inconvenience to any?" [7] He consented to a remarkable arrangement for the relaying of inside information to the *Tribune* through James R. Gilmore and Robert J. Walker in exchange for Greeley's support. [8] (The scheme bore little fruit for either party, and existed only briefly.)

Then there was the matter of passes. Theodore C. Wilson of the *Herald* went through fantastic convolutions to get one that would enable him to join the army on the Peninsula in July 1862, writing Hudson that for two days he had shuttled between Baltimore and Washington, trying staff officers, provost marshals, General Wool, Stanton, Welles, Sanford, even the Surgeon General. At the War Department at last, success: "met President Lincoln in the hall; stopped him; briefly stated my case; finally induced him to tell assist. sec'y war to do all he could for me, as long as it was not inconsistent with the public service," and promptly got passage on a transport. [9] Charles A. Page related a similar instance of Lincoln

[5] Basler: *Collected Works*, IV, 539.
[6] *Ibid.*, VI, 120.
[7] *Ibid.*, VII, 546.
[8] Sandburg, I, 559.
[9] Undated, headed "Aboard U.S. Dispatch Steamer *Metamora*," Bennett Papers.

giving passes to half a dozen reporters later, and, inevitably, "he told us an apropos story." [1] E. A. Paul of the *Times* turned to Lincoln to extricate him from another War Department entanglement on passes, and when Stanton insisted on citing regulations, Lincoln had John Nicolay arm Paul with a special pass to circumvent them. [2] Later the President occasionally gave reporters special "red letter" passes, bearing his signature in red ink on heavy cardboard, which were good anywhere. [3]

In these small ways the overburdened man in the White House ameliorated life for his friends in the Bohemian Brigade. He was on friendlier terms with many of then than with the general run of Washington reporters. From the beginning of the war, when "Jasper" of the *Times* called to give him a firsthand account of the bombardment of Fort Sumter, [4] Lincoln welcomed them, asked questions, drew them out, and frequently invited them to come to see him again whenever they returned from the fronts. At army headquarters at various times, he recognized Charles C. Coffin of the Boston *Journal*, B. S. Osbon and Sylvanus Cadwallader of the *Herald*, and Henry E. Wing of the *Tribune*, and on each occasion paused to chat with them. Coffin remembered his surprise when the familiar angular figure emerged from a momentous conference at City Point in March 1865, followed by Grant, Sherman, Meade, Ord, and others, "saw and recognized me, extended his hand, and said smilingly, 'What news have you?'" [5] It was Lincoln's favorite question.

The President particularly liked to sound out army reporters about officers, for, young and impressionable as these Bohemians were, they enjoyed better opportunities for observa-

[1] Charles A. Page: *Letters of a War Correspondent* (Boston: 1899), 314.
[2] Robert T. Lincoln Collection, May 23–5, 1864, and Henry J. Raymond to Nicolay, May 30, 1864, John G. Nicolay Papers, MS Division, Library of Congress.
[3] George Forrester Williams in *The Independent*, Vol. 53 (Oct. 10, 1901), 2400.
[4] *Times*, Apr. 17, 1861.
[5] Rice, ed.: *Reminiscences of Abraham Lincoln*, 176.

tion than most of his informants, and they were less likely to have axes to grind. Henry Villard called on him late in November 1862 after nearly eight months with Buell's Army of the Cumberland. "He asked my opinion of the principal commanders under Buell, which I expressed with entire frankness," said Villard, adding that the President listened attentively and invited him to return.[6] Henry Wing, a mere stripling, found himself being led on one night in June of 1864 regarding Grant. He appraised Grant as a reticent, introspective commander who had overcome his drinking habit and won the almost unlimited confidence of his men, while Lincoln listened with "almost painful interest," if one may credit a reminiscence written nearly half a century later. Conscious of having done most of the talking, Wing rose in some embarrassment to take his leave. Lincoln gestured to him, palm down, to stay. "My boy, you have told me just what I wanted to hear." Wing saw the President privately perhaps half a dozen times, for at the close of his first call Lincoln had given him the usual invitation to return—"It is an order," he said.[7]

Williams of the *Times* received a similar "order" after recounting details of Sheridan's victory at Winchester to Lincoln in September 1864, "but being very young I supposed the President's invitation was merely a compliment." Having returned to the capital from Sheridan's army a month later, Williams was greeted by John Hay: "Mr. Lincoln saw you on the Avenue today. He is surprised that you have not come to see him." The reporter hastened to the White House.

Lincoln explained that "I am always seeking information, and you newspaper men are so often behind the scenes at the front I am frequently able to get ideas from you which no one else can give." After a few pleasantries on the adventurous life of correspondents, Lincoln suddenly asked: "What do you

[6] Villard, I, 340.

[7] Henry E. Wing: "Stories of a War Correspondent," *The Christian Advocate*, Feb. 6, 1913.

think of General Sheridan as an army commander?" When Williams had given his opinion, Lincoln mused, as if he had forgotten Williams's presence: "General Grant does seem able to pick out the right man for the right place at the right time. He is like that trip hammer I saw the other day . . . always certain in his movements, and always the same." [8]

The lonely man in the White House sometimes unburdened himself to trusted reporters when he was worried about the military situation, talking with remarkable candor—perhaps, as Williams suggested, more to himself than to them. "Last Thursday and again yesterday," wrote Simon Hanscom to Gay on July 6, 1862, "I had two interviews with the President." Lincoln had gone into one problem at considerable length: should he bring Halleck and some of his troops East to reinforce the hard-pressed McClellan, in the face of Halleck's opposition to such a move? "President puzzled as to know what to do." Albert D. Richardson, writing Gay on March 20, 1863, threw light upon the kind of anxieties that plagued Lincoln almost unremittingly:

I have just returned from spending an hour with the President. . . . He is not sanguine about Vicksburg. He thinks all these *side* expeditions through the country dangerous. . . . He says that his only hope about the matter is that the military commanders there, on the ground, know prospects and possibilities better than he can.

About Charleston he is equally dubious. [Admiral] DuPont *said* he should be ready by the 8th, but after all the conditions he required had been compiled with, and the President expected the attack had begun, he [DuPont] seemed to have quite forgotten his promise and sent a messenger up here for three more ironclads. . . . He sent word back to DuPont, "I fear neither you nor your officers appreciate the supreme importance of *time;* the more you prepare, the more the enemy will be prepared."

[8] *The Independent*, Vol. 53, 2398 ff.

The reporters who knew this lean man saw no mythological being, saw not the lights and shadows, the deeper implications of word and action, the sense of history leavened by a sense of humor, the pragmatic approach informed by a constant higher purpose, that would appear in retrospect. Much eluded them in the strictures of time and place; and yet these young men knew the timbre of his voice, the homely warmth of his smile, the depth of his anxiety, and the man himself, as reporters have seldom known a President.

Lincoln's manner of dealing with men widely characterized as "newsmongers," "shameless liars," "unauthorized hangers-on," inevitably had subtle and far-reaching effects in the departments, in the armies, on the public mind, on reporters themselves, and on his successors.

3. FREDERICKSBURG

FEW correspondents had the staying power to follow the armies throughout the war. If bullets, illness, or ennui did not get them, they were expelled, captured, drafted, or simply worn out. Editors had to reorganize their staffs after every campaign.

With McClellan gone and immediate action in prospect, Sydney Gay had to do some quick juggling. George Smalley succumbed to "camp fever," and was recalled to serve as an editorial assistant. That left Richardson in charge, but A. D. R. was chaffing for time off, having seen his wife and children for a total of four days in a year. Gay summoned Henry Villard to come East to relieve him.

After McClellan's remote and mystical ways, Richardson found the new commander of the Army of the Potomac, thick-chested, magnificently bewhiskered Ambrose E. Burnside, "very obliging and approachable." Burnside had a naïve and easygoing way with correspondents, having observed philosophically once that newspapers would not make or break him, and the previous summer had offered to lend a *Tribune* correspondent his horse. Richardson judged well when he wrote Gay: "I am very sure of one thing: Whenever he gets a positive order to Go, he will Go if it breaks his neck." [9]

It was some time before the amiable commander had the opportunity. The army marched down to the Rappahannock, only to wait weeks for the pontoons on which to cross it for a mighty assault upon Lee at Fredericksburg. Villard, after an interminable delay in getting a pass, arrived in camp from Washington on December 6, and Richardson took his leave. The big Bavarian set to work at once, assiduously cultivating old and new acquaintances; General E. V. Sumner, commanding one of Burnside's three "Grand Divisions," greeted him heartily, summoned an aide-de-camp, and ordered that Villard be tented and provided for. Villard had his problems: against the *Herald's* nine-man crew and seven representing the *Times*, he had but three: J. Warren Newcomb, who, said A. D. R., "lacks energy and *snap* to an almost fatal degree"; the same Nathaniel Paige who had enraged Smalley at Antietam; and R. D. Francis, a stout Englishman discharged by the *Herald* on Whiteley's representation that he was "useless." But by this time Henry Villard knew his way around a battlefield—he had covered Bull Run, Shiloh, and lately had come from the corpse-littered field at Perryville, Kentucky, where he was one of the few to report competently Buell's repulse of the Confederates under Braxton Bragg. General Burnside showed him "a prepossessing *bon-homie* that made one feel at home with him at once." [1]

Came the morning of December 12, 1862, ushered in by a Federal artillery barrage so deafening that Burnside's telegrapher complained that he could not hear his instrument. As a heavy mist lifted, five long lines of men in blue made their

[9] Undated (c. Dec. 5, 1862), Gay Papers.
[1] Villard, I, 350.

way across on the swaying pontoons; to Villard "they seemed to be stepping on the water itself." The next morning the assault was launched, on a foe perfectly positioned on the heights beyond Fredericksburg. Villard rode with the staff of Brigadier General W. H. French on the Federal right, dismounted, and lay on his stomach on the first crest. Division after division sought to storm Marye's Heights, to be mowed down in what amounted to massacre. After three hours he heard French say the position could not be taken frontally, and at half past three, sick from what he had seen, Villard headed for the rear to avoid being trapped. Back in Fredericksburg, he found the streets packed with cowering fugitives; he reconnoitered further and, at six, returned to Burnside's headquarters across the river to await Paige and Newcomb, who had been covering the left and center. They appeared in due course—Paige "mulish and intractable," Newcomb so drunk he was stupefied.[2]

Villard labored until after midnight, closely interviewing officers of the divisions he had not seen in action as they came to headquarters. He was convinced now that the defeat was irretrievable: Shiloh had been a fight; this was sheer carnage. Burnside had suddenly clamped down on both mail and telegraph. His staff tried to tell Villard the action had been nothing more than a prelude, but the reporter knew better. He decided to make a run for it.

After a couple of hours' sleep, Villard set out at three in the morning in pitch blackness for Aquia Creek, moving like a thief in the night. He was thrown when his horse stumbled; upon remounting, he lost his sense of direction. He gave the horse his head. At dawn the sight of debris along the supply line reassured him, and after covering less than twelve miles in six hours Villard presented himself at the tent of the quartermaster in charge at Aquia. No one had arrived ahead of him; but the quartermaster said he had orders to grant no trans-

[2] Richardson quoting Villard, to Gay, Dec. 16, 1862, Gay Papers.

portation without a special permit from headquarters. All Henry got from him was breakfast, which he was eating when Charles C. Coffin of the Boston *Journal* appeared.

Villard paced the pier, pondering how to cope with both the quartermaster and Coffin. He spied two Negroes fishing from a boat, lured them in by offering a dollar apiece for the use of their rods, then said he wanted them to take him fishing way out—out in the Potomac steamship channel. Once beyond the hearing of those on shore, he produced a couple of five-dollar bills—theirs if they'd help him catch the first steamer north! In about an hour, along came a government-chartered freighter. Villard signaled, and the captain came to the rail. "He asked whether I had a transportation order. . . . As he slowed down, I got hold of a rope hanging from the side . . . pulled the boat up to an opening in the guard railing, jumped aboard, tossed the greenbacks to the oarsmen, and told them to make off as fast as possible, which they did with a vengeance." The captain was "wrathy." Villard mollified him by flourishing an army pass, wrote his account during the forty-mile voyage, caught some sleep, gave the captain fifty dollars for services rendered, hopped in a carriage at the capital, and made for the *Tribune* rooms.[3]

Villard pushed through the crowded office at nine-thirty that rumor-mad Sunday night. Sam Wilkeson, back on the job now, locked him up in the back room with a shorthander and a messenger: "Telegraph a four-column dispatch. . . ." He began dictating, stating "as strongly as possible that the Army of the Potomac had suffered another great, general defeat; that an inexcusable blunder had been made in attempting to overcome the enemy by direct attack." It was not a happy beat; Greeley refused to let the *Tribune* assume sole responsibility for the dreadful news and insisted that Gay modify Villard's judgments with liberal editing, but Monday morning's *Tribune* would carry the first authentic details of the most terrible repulse of the war.

[3] Villard, I, 363–89.

Heading across the street to the Willard for supper when he was done, Villard was hailed by Senator Henry Wilson: "What's the news?" Villard told him Burnside was in such a plight the Senator should tell Lincoln about it; the army must be ordered back across the river before it was annihilated. Villard had returned to the *Tribune* office after his supper when Wilson came in to say that the President wanted to see him at once.

So, late that Sunday night, a correspondent with the mud of Falmouth still on his campaign clothes met the President in the second-floor reception room of the White House. Lincoln shook his hand. "I am very much obliged to you for coming. We are very anxious and have heard very little." In the guttural inflections with which Lincoln was already familiar, Henry Villard told him the worst, sparing nothing as scenes at Marye's Heights and along the sunken road came before him. Lincoln questioned him for half an hour. Every general officer he had spoken to, Villard concluded, held that the army must be withdrawn; but Burnside, up to the previous night anyway, had no such intention. The President should order the withdrawal. Lincoln looked at him with a sad smile. "I hope it is not as bad as all that," he said, and thanked him again for coming.[4]

Defeat has ugly consequences in the minds of men, a fact never more apparent than after Burnside's beaten army recrossed the Rappahannock. Congress must have a scapegoat; Senators called on the President to ask that Secretary Seward resign; others talked of compelling the overthrow of the entire Cabinet. "Lincoln said yesterday," wrote Sam Wilkeson to Gay on December 19, "that if there was any worse Hell than he had been in for two days, he would like to know it. He is awfully shaken."

Wilkeson heard—and was certain it was true—that Stanton and General Halleck had been on the verge of fisticuffs; and

[4] *Ibid.*, 389-91.

it appeared to Sam that Stanton, more pre-emptory than ever, was taking it out on correspondents:

> Stanton has refused to let Richardson, Villard, & Thomson have passes to go to the Army!! The quarter-deck brute gets more violent and stupid every day. . . . I shall have to smuggle these reporters to the front.

For that matter, "the co-ordinate branch of the government," as Wilkeson playfully referred to himself, was not in good fettle either. Villard presented him with an expense account that included the fifty dollars paid the ship captain. Wilkeson, in his cups, exploded with the wrath of an indignant stockholder, which he was. Villard resented his "insolence." Wilkeson struck him, whereupon, according to Richardson, "Villard knocked him down two or three times." Gay, shocked by reports of such behavior, wrote Sam for heaven's sake to be more circumspect. Wilkeson made the amende honorable.

Another curious manifestation of shattered nerves and general demoralization appeared in the sudden vogue for spiritualism, charlatans of every description appearing to work fresh miracles daily on a half-demented populace. Richardson touched on an amusing phase of it in writing Gay from Washington:

> Yesterday I dined with Brady, the photographer. He seems to know you very well. At his place I met John Pierpont, who . . . is very much interested in some "spirit photographs" which a Boston female artist is taking. You sit or stand for your picture. You see no one in the room. You get a good, strong, clear portrait, by the ordinary process. But lo—sitting or standing beside you on the plate is the white, shadowy form of somebody—whom you may or may not recognize—with features clearly distinguishable. That's the spirit. If you *get* a spirit with your photograph (like Glendower's, they

won't always come when you do call for them) the artist charges you $5. Mr. Pierpont firmly believes in their
veritableness. Brady says they are a humbug; that he can
produce the same thing without supernatural assistance.[5]

In New York, morale in the Rookery took a sharp turn
for the worse. Sydney Gay, a stouter supporter of the war
than ever since Lincoln had made his decision on emancipation, fell ill. ("If you were made of the best Sheffield cast
steel, you would break down under the labor I saw you per-
forming," said Sam Wilkeson.) With Gay out of the office,
Greeley began to talk earnestly of foreign mediation. Fredericksburg had horrified him, as it had horrified the Union.

Scapegoats, spirits, fisticuffs, talk of mediation: these and
a myriad other evidences of despondency testified to the
mercurial temper of a people bound together by telegraph
wires with Bohemians on one end of them and editors on the
other, as time mercifully ran out on 1862.

[5] Dec. 24, 1862, Gay Papers.

☼ CHAPTER VIII ☼

Sherman, Hell, and Fighting Joe

1. Cats in Hell without Claws

In October 1861 a reporter for the Cincinnati *Commercial*, a quiet, intuitive, well-mannered soul named Florus B. Plimpton, introduced himself to Brigadier General William Tecumseh Sherman at the railroad station at Muldraugh's Hill, Kentucky. Plimpton had been sent especially to interview Sherman, and came armed with a letter from Thomas Ewing, Jr., the General's brother-in-law. Sherman glanced at it. Then, pacing up and down the platform, he burst into violent discourse on the iniquities of journalism, spitting a fresh oath at Plimpton each time he passed. At length Sherman stopped in front of him, took out his watch, and said: "It's eleven o'clock; the next train for Louisville goes at half past one. Take that train! Be sure you take it; don't let me see you around here after it's gone!"

"But, General, the people are anxious. I'm only after the truth."

"We don't want the truth told about things here—that's what we *don't* want! Truth, eh? No, sir! We don't want the enemy any better informed than he is! Make no mistake about that train." He resumed his pacing, then wheeled. "If you want to get a real good dinner, the very best that can be had

Printing House Square, 1864. The view is toward the south with City Hall Park's foliage just visible to the right. (*Courtesy New-York Historical Society.*)

PLATE I

The Press Room of the New York *Tribune*, as illustrated in
a woodcut in *Frank Leslie's Illustrated Newspaper,* 1861. The
smallest of the three presses, a six-cylinder Hoe, is shown.

War News at Home.
From Frederic Hud-
son's scrapbook.
(*Courtesy Mrs.
Wesley P. Wilmot.*)

THE HERALD EXTRA
Latest War News

PLATE 19

"The Press on the Field." By Thomas Nast in *Harper's Weekly*, April 30, 1864.

PLATE III

Herald Headquarters, Army of the Potomac. Reporters relaxing at Bealton, Virginia, on a warm day in August 1863. Photograph by Mathew Brady. (*National Archives.*)

PLATE IV

Army Studio. Sketch by Edwin Forbes of his headquarters at Rappahannock Station, March 1864. (*Library of Congress.*)

PLATE V

War News in the Army. Billy Yank in characteristic repose, sketched by Edwin Forbes at Culpeper, September 30, 1863. (*Library of Congress.*)

PLATE VI

Newspapers in Camp. A familiar scene in the Army of the Potomac, sketched by Edwin Forbes at Rappahannock Station, September 18, 1863.

PLATE VII

Shiloh: A Battle Artist's Sketch. This original, drawn by Henry Lovie on the Federal center not long after the Confederates' initial assault, carries his instructions to the engravers. The circles identify guns and (center background) "ravine full of Rebel Infantry." On the ambulance in the foreground Lovie has written: "Road to Landing Immense confusion of wounded, fug'tives, waggons and ambulances, etc. can't exaggerate."

PLATE VIII

Shiloh: Frank Leslie's Woodcut. Lovie's drawing as it was reproduced in a double-page spread, May 17, 1862.

PLATE IX

Alfred R. Waud of *Harper's Weekly*, photographed by
Mathew Brady at Gettysburg. (*Library of Congress.*)

PLATE X

Samuel Wilkeson. (ABOVE LEFT) Portrait by Mathew Brady's Washington Studio, 1863. (*National Archives.*)

Frederic Hudson. (ABOVE RIGHT) A study by Mathew Brady during or shortly after the war. (*Courtesy Mrs. Wesley P. Wilmot.*)

Edmund Clarence Stedman. (RIGHT) (*Meserve Collection.*)

PLATE XI

Whitelaw Reid.
(*Meserve Collection.*)

Sydney Howard Gay.
(*Meserve Collection.*)

George Alfred Townsend, Mark Twain, and Joseph McCullagh, shortly
after the war. Photograph by Mathew Brady. (*National Archives.*)

PLATE XII

anywhere around here, just step over to that house which you
see yonder. But be damned sure you take that first train back
to Louisville!" [1]

Sherman was implacable, the most relentless enemy the Bohemians ever knew. Redheaded, grizzled, with fire flaming in
his eye, and "an utterance so rapid at times as to be almost
incoherent," as Franc Wilkie wrote, he had "a mood that
shifted like a barometer on a tropic sea." When reporters
approached, it pointed to "Storm." During Cameron's visit to
Louisville, one of them applied to Sherman for a pass, and
after being summarily turned down, said he would appeal to
the Secretary of War. "You have two hours to get out of
this Department, or I'll hang you as a spy!" said Sherman. A
Cincinnati *Commercial* man tried getting along without a pass;
Sherman put him in jail. William F. G. Shanks of the *Herald*
applied for one as an old acquaintance. No pass for you, Sherman said, adding gratuitously: "You see, I have as much as I
can do to feed my *soldiers*." [2]

Not long after Plimpton's visit an artist for *Frank Leslie's
Illustrated Newspaper* approached Sherman with a letter of
introduction from General Banks, the result being recorded
as follows:

General Sherman: "Well, sir I am glad General Banks
reports being so well satisfied with your conduct. I have
steadily refused to admit reporters of any kind within
my lines."

"But, General, I am no reporter or correspondent, not
writing more than a brief description of my sketches."

"You fellows make the best paid spies that can be
bought. Jeff Davis owes more to you newspaper men
than to his army."

"Well, General, I have come all the way from the
East. . . . The people of the East feel such an anxiety

[1] Whitelaw Reid: *Ohio in the War* (Cincinnati: 1868), II, 428.
[2] William F. G. Shanks: *Personal Recollections of Distinguished Generals* (New York: 1866), 22, 33.

toward your department that anything from here will be of peculiar interest."

"The people of New York feel such an interest that they sit by their fires, not knowing or caring about the wants of their soldiers. I wish no more discussion, sir. I have given my decision. If I allow you, I must allow all." [3]

The home-folks-are-anxious argument simply infuriated Sherman. An Associated Press man tried it on his adjutant general to get permission to send a brief telegram, but that individual had learned from the master: "No, sir! What the hell do we care about the country? You should go to Washington for news. This is no place to come looking for it!" [4]

So it was to the end. "A cat in hell without claws," wrote Elias Smith of the *Tribune* to Gay on April 20, 1865, "is nothing to a reporter in Gen. Sherman's army." The Bohemians never gave up; even the march through Georgia was fully reported despite Sherman's blistering excoriation, before setting forth, of "that class of men who will not take a musket and fight, but who follow an army to pick up news for sale, . . . and who are more used to bolster idle and worthless officers than to notice the hard-working and meritorious." [5]

Richardson, Shanks, and Joseph McCullagh considered that Sherman's attitude was largely affectation. "He liked nothing better than being talked about in the newspapers," thought McCullagh; his rabid denunciations were simply a means of getting attention. If that is true, perversity knows no bounds.

Richardson tried for an interview after Shiloh, suavely introducing himself as the *Tribune* correspondent. "The general's manner changed from Indian summer to a Texas norther." A reporter was supposed to know better than to

---

[3] *Frank Leslie's Ilustrated Newspaper*, Vol. 13, 34 (Dec. 7, 1861).

[4] David P. Conyngham: *Sherman's March Through the South* (New York: 1865), 75.

[5] *Ibid.*, 74–5.

approach him. "Have you not come to the wrong place, sir?" Richardson said no, he wanted to learn about the battle from Sherman's lips, and he got in a little speech of his own:

"You complain that journalists misrepresent you. How can they avoid it, when you refuse to give them information?" Some officers were drunkards and charlatans; would he denounce them all on that account? Wasn't it equally unjust to carry on about newspapermen in such a vein?

"Perhaps it is," said Sherman. "Sit down. Will you have a cigar? The trouble is, that you of the press have no responsibilities. Some worthless fellow . . . may send falsehoods about me to thousands of people who can never hear them refuted." [6] That was the real source of his animus.

Certainly there was solid ground for complaint: instances of grossly unfair reporting abounded; and an inefficient censorship let facts slip to the enemy. But a nation cannot sustain its armies in the field or its war effort at home over a period of months running into years in total ignorance of the course of events. There is no evidence that Sherman ever considered that argument. Instead of imposing stricter censorship, he proposed to outlaw the press. Commenting on his "perfect monomania on the subject of journalism," the Cincinnati *Commercial* reported that "his favorite often proclaimed plan for the successful management of the war is the suppression of every newspaper in the country. . . . He considers the press alone responsible for all the defeats of the Federal armies, inclusive of Bull Run." He told Shanks that it would pay the government to buy up all the printing presses in the country at the price of diamonds, and destroy them. [7]

Reporters generally responded in kind. The story that he was insane, picked up from the Cincinnati *Commercial* by the *Herald* and other papers, was a long time in dying. "IS SHERMAN INSANE?" ran a subhead in the Cincinnati *Times* after Shiloh, followed by its reporter's answer: "The general im-

[6] Richardson: *Secret Service*, 247.
[7] Shanks, 50.

pression here is, that he is demented." [8] A Philadelphia *Inquirer* man at Cairo noted a convenient way to distinguish him from General T. W. ("Port Royal") Sherman: he was "Crazy Sherman, as they call him here." His manners, one reporter wrote, were those of a Pawnee Indian; and when Sherman demanded an apology, the reporter apologized in print—to the Pawnees.[9]

For all his raving at the press as "a shame and a reproach to a civilized people," and at "these damned newspaper mongrels," there were reporters who admired him, and said so. The *Times* correspondent at Louisville in 1861 recognized "a man of marked ability" who "knows no motivation but devotion to the service." The same man watched him during a review,

> . . . absorbed in thought and giving no heed to the vain
> parade. . . . As Gen. Sherman passed full in front of me,
> and I looked at his severe and careworn face, every linea-
> ment stamped with character, every feature speaking an
> able mind, I felt more forcibly than ever the evil meas-
> ure of sending him away from Kentucky.[1]

Villard wrote glowingly of him as the hero of Shiloh. The *Tribune's* John E. Hayes, with him on the march through Georgia, wrote Gay that "General Sherman is an earnest, honest, and truly loyal man, and the more I see and hear of him the stronger grows my attachment and admiration for the man." Kent reacted similarly. "I like his grit," he confessed.[2]

It was all but inevitable that, sooner or later, Sherman's views on the right to report would collide with Lincoln's.

Correspondents in the Western theater hastened to Memphis in mid-December 1862 when they got word of Sherman's

[8] Issue of May 2, 1862.
[9] Shanks, 38.
[1] *Times*, Nov. 15, Dec. 3, 1861.
[2] Hayes to Gay, Dec. 15, 1864; Kent to Gay, Jan. 22, 1865, Gay Papers.

impending expedition against Vicksburg. The General had anticipated their appearance:

IV— . . . No citizen, male or female, will be allowed to accompany it, unless employed as part of the crew, or as servants to the transports.

V—Should any citizen accompany the expedition below Helena, in violation of these orders, any colonel of a regiment, or captain of a battery, will conscript him into the service of the United States. . . . If he show a refractory spirit, unfitting him for a soldier, the commanding officer present will turn him over to the captain of a boat as a deck-hand, and compel him to work in that capacity, without wages, until the boat returns to Memphis.

VI—Any person whatever, whether in the service of the United States or transports, found making reports for publication which might reach the enemy, giving them information, aid and comfort, will be arrested and treated as spies.[3]

Sherman seemed to have taken every possibility into account. Half a dozen intrepid Bohemians weighed their chances. Some had passes signed by Grant, the Department commander, which they hoped would prove superior to Sherman's order; others had friends among the officers. Sylvanus Cadwallader of the Chicago *Times*, Franc Wilkie of the New York *Times*, Richard Colburn of the *World*, Thomas W. Knox of the *Herald*, and men from the leading St. Louis papers, the *Missouri Democrat* and the *Missouri Republican*, slipped aboard the transports.

The plan called for landing the troops at Chickasaw Bayou, on the Yazoo River about six miles from Vicksburg, and assailing that formidable city on its flank and rear. Heavy rains beat down on the steep bluffs as the men debarked. They lost their footing and slithered to a gory defeat against a foe too

[3] S. M. Bowman and R. B. Irwin: *Sherman and His Campaigns* (New York: 1865), 81.

strongly posted. In two days, December 28 and 29, 1862, Sherman lost seventeen hundred men, the Confederates barely two hundred. The blame, however, rested more on Grant and the weather than on Sherman, for it had been Grant's plan, carried out by Sherman probably as skillfully as circumstances allowed. The correspondents, wet and miserable in defeat and as much concerned with keeping clear of Sherman and his staff as of the enemy, had to write surreptitiously of an affair they had meager opportunities to witness. They addressed their reports to blinds in Memphis and Cairo for forwarding, and slipped them into the mail aboard the headquarters boat. Colonel A. H. Markland, U.S. Postal Agent, thereupon fished these suspiciously fat envelopes out of the bags, opened them, and turned them over to Sherman. Tom Knox learned of it the next day. The *Herald's* chief of correspondents in the West had no esteem for Sherman—he had written Bennett earlier in the year: "Sherman threatens to arrest all journalists who make criticisms," and again: "Sherman is making an ass of himself" [4]—but his dispatch had treated Sherman's generalship rather tenderly. Now he rewrote it:

> . . . General Sherman had issued no order appointing a certain time for the assault upon the batteries, and there was no common understanding among the various generals of divisions and brigades. . . .
>
> By some criminal oversight, there had been little preparation for battle on the part of Sherman's medical director, and the hospital boats were but poorly supplied with many needed stores. Since the battle, Gen. Sherman has persistently refused to allow a hospital boat to go above, though their detention in this region is daily fatal to many lives. The only known reason for his refusal is his fear that knowledge of his mismanagement will reach the Northern press.

[4] Dated July 25, Aug. 19, 1862, Bennett Papers.

This was as nothing to the revised account of "D.," the *Missouri Democrat* man, who described the expedition as "a stupid blunder" with confusion at the beginning, drunkenness on the way, and a debarking upon which "all hell broke loose." For his connivance in opening the mails, said "D.," Sherman deserved a penitentiary sentence. Taking no chances, this time reporters steamed upstream as bearers of their own dispatches.

Although the *Democrat* account was worse, it was the *Herald* of January 18, 1863, containing Knox's work, that caused the explosion. Fairly quivering with rage, Sherman had Knox placed under arrest and brought before him. He ordered a staff officer to read the dispatch aloud. He interrupted after every assertion to demand Knox's source. He ordered his staff to procure and read battle orders, plans, and reports to refute what Knox had written. "The Elephant," as the amiable Knox was known among Bohemians, apologized and promised corrections, but pointed out that his facilities for obtaining information had been limited by Sherman's policy toward correspondents.

Sherman was in no mood for explanations or apologies. He wrote Brigadier General Frank Blair, questioning him on twenty-two counts, "because Knox quotes you all through." Blair, a political general favorably disposed toward reporters, admitted showing Knox his official report and supplying information, but most of his specific answers did not square with what Knox had written. Blair implied that it was about time Sherman forgot his mania—only recently Sherman had falsely accused him of harboring a *Missouri Republican* reporter in his brigade—and concluded: "I hope to receive no more letters of the same character from you and shall not answer them if I do." [5]

Sherman had Knox brought before him for another long session. "Of course, General Sherman, I had no feeling against

[5] *O.R.*, Ser. I, Vol. 17, Part 2, 580–90.

you personally," Knox said with more candor than judgment,
"but you are regarded the enemy of our set, and we must in
self-defense write you down." To Blair, Sherman wrote that
night: "I could hardly believe that a white man could be so
false as this fellow Knox . . . and am glad that your letter
enables me to put the fellow where he really belongs, as a
spy and an infamous dog." The day would come, he said,
when "every officer will demand the execution of this class
of spies, and without hesitation I declare that if I am forced
to look to the New York Herald for my lord and master instead of the constituted authorities of the United States my
military career is at an end."

Admiral David D. Porter, whom Sherman also asked specific questions "and generally whether I acted the part of an
intelligent officer or an insane fool," tried to quiet him: "As
. . . you have no political aspirations, you can well afford to
pass without notice what is said by the press. . . ." But by
February 4, Sherman had made up his mind: the case of the
General versus the Bohemian Brigade must be a fight to the
finish. He announced his decision to Porter:

> I am going to have the correspondent of the N.Y.
> Herald tried by a court martial as a spy, not that I want
> the fellow shot, but because I want to establish the prin-
> ciple that such people cannot attend our armies, in viola-
> tion of orders, and defy us, publishing their garbled
> statements and defaming officers who are doing their
> best. . . . This should not be, and must not be, and, as
> someone must begin the attack, I must assume the un-
> gracious task.[6]

As the court convened the next day at Young's Point in
traditional sashes and full-dress regalia, the Bohemians recognized the challenge for what it was. "The worst phase of
the matter," T. A. Post of the *Tribune* wrote Gay, "is the
precedent which the conviction of Knox would establish. If

[6] *O.R.*, Ser. I, Vol. 17, Part 2, 889.

convicted, then the whole Northern press is gagged. . . . No one can send intelligence of matters connected with the army, and especially no one can criticize the conduct of Generals in the field without subjecting himself to a similar charge."

Knox faced not one charge but three: he had published information of value to the enemy; he was a spy, on the ground that he had violated Sherman's order specifying that anyone accompanying the expedition and making reports should be so treated; and he had violated the Fifty-seventh Article of War by failing to submit his account to the commanding officer before publication. After fifteen days the court found Knox guilty only of violating Sherman's specific orders, but attached "no criminality" thereto. Brigadier General J. M. Thayer, president of the court, read the sentence: Knox was to be "sent without the lines of the army, and not to return under penalty of imprisonment." [7]

Both sides appealed. Sherman, bitterly disappointed by the qualified verdict, wrote Grant that the case "involves certain principles that I think should be settled by the highest authority of our Government, and I beg most respectfully their reference, through the Judge Advocate-General, to the Commander-in-Chief." [8] Apparently Grant did not forward Sherman's appeal; the records show no further action on it.

The newspaper fraternity was no less aroused. Colburn, Wilkie, and others left the army for fear of similar action. The *Missouri Republican* revived the charge that Sherman was insane. In Washington, Albert D. Richardson, that fervent champion of the right to report, got busy circulating a petition, with the help of John W. Forney, urging that the President set aside the verdict. General Thayer said that the court considered Knox's guilt to rest on a technicality, and Sherman's rival, Major General John A. McClernand, added that in his opinion banishment was too harsh a fate for the reporter.

[7] *Ibid.*, 890–2.
[8] *Ibid.*, 892, 893 (Feb. 23, 1863).

On the evening of March 20, Richardson, accompanied by James M. Winchell of the *Times*, called on Lincoln to present the petition. Would the President stand by his general or would he uphold the right to report? The personable Richardson turned on all his fluency and charm. Lincoln listened, said Winchell, "with patient interest" as Richardson argued that Knox had been wronged, the sanctity of the mails violated, the principle of a free press desecrated by drumhead court-martial, and a precedent set which would hang like Damocles' sword over the head of every reporter in the armies. "The discussion was long and animated," said Winchell, and it obviously put Lincoln in a ticklish position. He could not have known that Sherman had written his wife that "I will never again command an army in America if we must carry along paid spies," and that "I shall notify Mr. Lincoln of this if he attempts to interfere with the sentence of any court ordered by me"—but from what he knew of Sherman, he might have guessed as much.

Lincoln suggested that a recommendation to Grant that he remit the sentence might smooth matters, but Richardson argued that unless the President revoked it himself, Grant was certain to stand by Sherman. Winchell said little, listening while Lincoln and Richardson talked it out. He recorded the scene later:

> Mr. Lincoln's manner was all consideration and kindness and sympathy, but these concealed a firmness that seemed immovable.
>
> At length, while walking about the room . . . he exclaimed, "Well, you want me to make an order setting aside the action of the court. I wish to do what is right, and what you ask, for it seems to me . . . our newspaper friend has been a little too severely dealt with. Still, I am not on the spot to judge of all the circumstances, and General Grant is; and I do not see how I can properly grant your request without being sustained

by his consent. But let us see what we can do. I will write something to put our ideas into shape." With a pleasant laugh he began at once to search for paper and pen. He was aided in this effort by little "Tad," who was present —and I must say, somewhat troublesome. . . . He found a piece of paper with some difficulty on the table (littered with documents lying in complete disorder), and a very poor pen, with which he at once set to work. . . .

We were delighted with the document, and of course said so.

"But," said the President, "I had better make this conditional on the approval of General Grant. . . . I will just add a few words," and he did so, making the order close as follows:

"Now, therefore, said order is hereby revoked so far as to allow Mr. Knox to return to Gen. Grant's headquarters, and to remain if Gen. Grant shall give his express consent, and again to leave the department if Gen. Grant shall refuse such assent. A. Lincoln."

"There," he remarked, "I think that will be about right, and I have no doubt Gen. Grant will assent." [9]

"And he did so," Winchell added—but here memory played him false.

Knox sent the document to Grant on April 6. It was as Richardson had feared. "Whilst I would conform to the slightest wish of the President, where it is formed upon a representation of both sides of any question, my respect for General Sherman is such that in this case I must decline, unless General Sherman first gives his assent to your remaining," Grant wrote. Knox, brave fellow, went back to his bête noire. Sherman remained immovable, acidly commenting on Thayer's and McClernand's view that the offense was technical, and adding: "Notwithstanding the President's endorsement of that

[9] James M. Winchell: "Three Interviews with President Lincoln," *The Galaxy*, Vol. 16, 34–7 (July 1873); Richardson: *Secret Service*, 319.

conclusion, I cannot so regard it." He closed with a characteristic flourish: "Come with sword or musket in your hand . . . and I will welcome you as an associate; but come as you do now, expecting me to ally the reputation and honor of my country and my fellow-soldiers with you, as the representative of the press, which you yourself say makes no slight difference between truth and falsehood, and my answer is, Never." [1]

Sherman had won his battle with Knox, but the Bohemians had won the war. Lincoln's action effectually quashed Sherman's campaign to rid the army of reporters. The General wrote Grant in disgust: "Mr. Lincoln, of course, fears to incur the enmity of the Herald, but he must rule the Herald or the Herald will rule him; he can take his choice." Write what he would, there was no denying that his precedent-setting case had boomeranged. In setting aside the verdict and referring the case to Grant, Lincoln had tacitly supported the right of reporters to attend the army. In response to the anxious pleas of his brother John, the Senator, and of his wife, William Tecumseh Sherman decided to give up his newspaper war. [2] He still averred that a war could not be won if the press remained free, still cursed those "infamous lying dogs" who somehow told lies of value to the enemy; but he knew that his cause had been lost.

2. "Out of the Jaws of Death . . ."

The war was fought on a scale of such magnitude that Sydney Gay saw the futility of attempting to assign his men and evaluate their reports, even with the steady flow of behind-the-scenes information from Hill and Wilkeson in Washington, without regional assistants. In the single uneventful month of January 1863, engagements worthy of report flared at Galveston, Texas, at Springfield, Missouri, at Fort Hindman,

[1] *O.R.*, Ser. I, Vol. 17, Part 2, 894, 895.
[2] Lloyd Lewis: *Sherman: Fighting Prophet* (New York: 1932), 267.

Arkansas, at Bayou Teche, Louisiana, at Woodbury, Tennessee, at Suffolk, Virginia, and at Charleston, South Carolina. The Eastern theater, and more particularly the Army of the Potomac, remained Gay's chief concern, but with the maturing of Grant's Vicksburg plans the *Tribune* could no longer leave the West to the whim of second-raters and five-dollars-a-letter men as it had since Richardson's recall. Richardson was needed, and on March 26 Richardson was sent.

A. D. R. was delighted to get back to his base at the rickety hotel in Cairo. He had passes on most of the western railroads, was widely known both in person and by reputation, and found as ever that the West stirred his yen for adventure. He put in nearly a month finding and instructing new correspondents in Missouri, Arkansas, Kentucky, and Tennessee. Gay was anxious that he needle W. D. Bickham, a Cincinnati *Commercial* man serving the *Tribune* on the side, into sending more news from the Army of the Cumberland, especially since Buell had been succeeded by Major General William Starke Rosecrans, whom many thought "the coming man." A. D. R. went to Murfreesboro to see Bickham and appraise Rosecrans himself. "As representative of the *Tribune*, I have never been so warmly received at any Army headquarters," he wrote. "I hope I have sense enough not to *puff* anybody on that account," he added, but the army was in "splendid condition." Rosecrans professed to have heard much of Richardson, and invited him to dinner. A. D. R., a free-thinker, wrote confidentially:

> Like Hooker, "Old Rosey" has salient weak points. He is blunt, though he don't blurt out such imprudent speeches as Hooker; does not show such vanity as Hooker; but *his* streak is his Catholic faith. He believes in some of the most staggering claims of his Church; sends requests to have certain sisters pray for him; thinks Gareschi (his old chief of staff) helped to buy the Stone River victory by a religious sacrifice of himself, *per con-*

tract with the Almighty, etc. Of course I learn these
things from men about Rosecrans, not from himself, but
fanatic or no fanatic, it is wonderful how enthusiastically
everybody believes in him. . . . And he impresses me
as a pure, earnest, strong man.

What really stirred Richardson's blood was the daring raid
on railroads which Colonel A. D. Streight planned to under-
take with fifteen hundred picked men—all the way to Atlanta.
"Won't it make a sensation down in Dixie, if fortune smiles
on it! . . . Not half a dozen men, all told, know of it." He
had a mind to go himself, "but fear I must go to Vicksburg." [3]
The correspondent he assigned to the Streight expedition
failed to appear in time; but Richardson was to see Streight and
his men again.

On May 1, 1863 Richardson stepped aboard a steamer at
Memphis for the run downstream on his way to cover Grant's
renewed attempt at Vicksburg. A messenger caught him with
two letters of instructions from Gay, which he acknowledged
hastily in pencil:

Your suggestions about more of the Romance & picturesqueness of the war, & less of the common place will
be of great service to me. I will endeavor to have them
acted upon by all our correspondents.

Perhaps it was with these instructions in mind that Richardson made his fateful decision when the steamer deposited him
at Milliken's Bend. There he learned that active operations
were already under way at Grand Gulf, where the *Tribune*
had only one man, T. A. Post, whom Richardson regarded as
slow. To reach Grant's army there, fifty-five miles below
Vicksburg, he could either take a three-day overland trek, or
slip past the Confederate batteries by water and get there in
eight hours. Thus far, ten of fifteen boats attempting to run
the batteries had made it; time was of the essence, and the
water route was unquestionably the richer in romance and

[3] Richardson to Gay, Apr. 11, 1863, Gay Papers.

picturesqueness. Richardson, bald little Junius Browne, who was to assist him in the campaign, and Richard H. Colburn, an imperturbable *World* reporter, boarded a barge at ten o'clock on the night of May 3 with the Mississippi shimmering in the light of a full moon.

Browne reflected that in heaven he would recall his last assignment with pleasure, if this was it. The tug chugged along reassuringly, towing two barges at seven miles an hour; the Bohemians lolled comfortably on bales of hay, smoking cigars and sampling an officer's Catawba; fellow passengers, some thirty officers and deckhands, in all, chatted pleasantly, if a little uneasily, on the beauties of river travel by moonlight. At 1:00 a.m. a rocket shot up from the Mississippi shore, signaling their approach to Confederate gunners who commanded the river for nearly seven miles around the big bend at Vicksburg. Ten minutes later, the shore batteries opened. A shell exploded in one of the barges, but the tug kept steadily on amid gunfire that reached a crescendo as they glided by Vicksburg itself. Browne stood watching the batteries spout tongues of flame; Richardson and Colburn, hiding behind bales, yelled that he was crazy. All but two miles of the gantlet was run when a shot crashed into the tug. Her boiler exploded, and amid the screams of scalded men, she went down like a plummet. Shells and flying debris ignited the hay bales on the barges. An eerie yell of triumph came across the water.

"I suppose we'll have to surrender," said a passenger. "Surrender, the devil!" yelled Colburn, struggling to push blazing bales overboard. "I suppose we'll have to fight them!" As Richardson pointed out, "the facilities just then were somewhat limited." One by one, roasting men plunged into the river. The Bohemians floated downstream, planning to strike for the Louisiana shore as soon as they were out of danger. The sound of oarlocks dispelled that notion, and presently, said Browne, "we were hauled in like catfish." [4]

[4] Browne: *Four Years*, 231-8; Richardson: *Secret Service*, 337-45.

When news of the affair reached the army the same morning, all three of the correspondents were reported killed. It was then that Sherman purportedly said: "Good! Now we'll have news from hell before breakfast." [5]

Three soaking Bohemians were marched barefoot through the streets of Vicksburg in the moonlight, interviewed by the Confederate provost marshal, and locked up in the city jail. Before noon on May 4 they were paroled by the exchange agent and assured that they would be sent North by the first flag-of-truce boat from Richmond. Confederate officers interrogated them: How long did the people of the North expect the war to last? What did they propose to do with all the Negroes? Transferred to the dome of the courthouse, the three Yankee reporters were, as Browne observed in some surprise, "rather lionized than otherwise." Officers and editors visited them; the Vicksburg papers hailed their bravado in attempting to run the batteries. Crowds gathered to gape and question them at stations all along the way to Richmond, said Browne. Confederate rolling stock being what it was, their train "crawled along like a tow-boat on the Erie Canal." Counting a two-day stopover in Jackson, Mississippi, with stops along the way for meals, the trip took eleven days.

At 5:00 a.m. on May 16, A. D. R., Brown, and Colburn were marched into Libby Prison. Eight hours later, who should appear but Colonel Streight and one hundred of his officers, captured by Nathan Bedford Forrest near Rome, Georgia. Richardson greeted Streight with melancholy humor, then sat down to pencil a note to Gay. The three newsmen had paroles, he said, "but we have no information when we are to be sent North." Manton Marble, editor of the *World*, wrote to ask for Colburn's release, and, as Richardson wrote later, it was "obeyed as promptly as if it had been an order from Jeff Davis. . . . It was simply his good luck being on the *World*: for personally he is a radical Republican." [6]

[5] Browne: *Four Years*, 238.
[6] Richardson to Gay, Feb. 1, 1864, Gay Papers.

Colburn's reappearance without Richardson and Browne greatly disturbed Sydney Gay, who had often dreaded the consequences should the Confederates get hold of anyone from the *Tribune*. Gay wrote to Lincoln at once. The President promptly telegraphed:

June 1, 1863

Col. Ludlow, Fort-Monroe.

Richardson & Browne, correspondents of the Tribune captured at Vicksburg, are detained at Richmond. Please ascertain why they are detained, & get them off if you can.[7]

The next day Ludlow wrote Robert Ould, Confederate Commissioner of Exchange, to ask their release, pointing out that the practice had been to treat newspaper correspondents as noncombatants and free them. Ould wrote a sizzling reply:

I have been struggling for nearly twelve months to establish just such a rule as to non-combatants without success. . . . What peculiar immunity should the correspondents of the Tribune have over . . . delicate and noble-souled women who are either languishing in your prisons or "released" to the rigors . . . of the wilderness?

It seems to me that if any exception be made as to any non-combatants it should be against such men as the Tribune correspondents who have had more share than even your soldiery in bringing rapine, pillage, and desolation to our homes. . . . You ask me why I will not release them. 'Tis because they are the worst and most obnoxious of all non-combatants. . . .[8]

Ludlow promptly renewed his demand. He wrote Gay that he would continue until they were released, but the problem of noncombatants "has given me more trouble than all military exchanges." The case of the *Tribune* men would top them all.

[7] Basler: *Collected Works*, VI, 241.
[8] *O.R.*, Ser. II, Vol. 5, 746.

187

Secretary Stanton, on June 29, telegraphed Ludlow to "exert yourself—Browne's health is said to be failing. If they are held as hostages or for any other reason, ascertain and report it." Ludlow replied: "They are held in retaliation for citizens arrested and held by us. That is the assigned reason. The real reason I believe to be that they are connected with the Tribune and are held to annoy." [9] Ould remained adamant.

In Washington, Whitelaw Reid of the Cincinnati *Gazette* asked that "some specific retaliatory measure be adopted." Major General E. A. Hitchcock endorsed the idea, recommending to Stanton that "two rebel prisoners of the rank of captain be placed in solitary confinement and so kept until the two . . . shall be released by the rebel authorities, notice of the fact being sent through to Mr. Ould." Stanton referred it to Halleck, who approved; but the plan was dropped.[1]

Brigadier General S. A. Meredith, who had replaced Ludlow as Commissioner of Exchange, wrote Ould on August 27: "I would again earnestly call your attention to the case of the Messrs. Richardson and Browne. . . . When Vicksburg was captured the editors of the Whig and Citizen fell into our hands and were immediately paroled and sent away." This had no force, the unshaken Ould replied. "They were paroled by the terms of the surrender and not by any special grace of your authorities. . . . Richardson and Browne will be released just as soon as you agree to discharge non-combatants." [2] But a general exchange cartel such as Ould wanted, Union authorities considered out of the question, as it would embody recognition of the Confederacy.

On September 3, Richardson and Browne were transferred to Castle Thunder to relieve the crush in Libby, an old tobacco warehouse where five hundred and fifty Union officers were then incarcerated. Richardson rather regretted leaving them. "Classes are organized in Greek, Latin, French, Ger-

[9] *O.R.*, Ser. II, Vol. 6, 59.
[1] *Ibid.*, 183, 184.
[2] *Ibid.*, 232, 238.

man, Spanish, Mathematics, & Phonography, while there are plenty of surgeons and chaplains to encourage amateurs in Physiology and zealots in Dialectics. The 'Libby Lyceum' meets twice a week, with spirited debates, & there is a MS newspaper styled The *Libby Chronicle.* Then there are many excellent singers to while away the evenings." [3]

At Castle Thunder the unhappy pair soon welcomed Leonard A. Hendrick and Solomon T. Bulkley of the *Herald,* captured by Mosby's guerrillas. George H. Hart of the *Herald,* another of Mosby's captives, joined them presently, and a certain Bohemian camaraderie pervaded the filthy room in which they were confined. The commandant would point them out to visitors, said Browne, as if they were polar bears in a zoo. Hendrick, something of a wag, told a wide-eyed Virginian that he was really there because in testing his fabulous new "Hendrick gun" in Richmond, he had accidentally sunk a blockade-runner in Wilmington harbor. When alone, they played whist and talked of little but escape. Bulkley plotted with one of the guards, but unwittingly slipped him a roll of dollar bills in the dark instead of the fives he had promised, with the result that the newsmen were clapped into a cell with the toughest rogues in the prison. Hart and Hendrick were exchanged after two months for a couple of Richmond *Enquirer* men who had been captured on an expedition in Chesapeake Bay; Bulkley was released in another special exchange February 26, 1864. [4] But Richardson and Browne remained.

The *Tribune* men, curiously, were permitted to hire an attorney, a privilege denied political prisoners in the North. They engaged Humphrey Marshall, a prominent Kentuckian soon to become a member of the Confederate Congress, but Ould denied Marshall's petition for their parole. Marshall told his clients that, while no parole had ever been repudiated be-

[3] Richardson to Gay, Gay Papers.
[4] Abby Sage Richardson, ed.: *Garnered Sheaves: From the Writings of Albert D. Richardson* (Hartford: 1871), 66.

fore, he could do nothing for them: they were *Tribune* men. They petitioned Confederate Secretary of War James A. Seddon, as A. D. R. wrote Gay from prison on February 1, 1864, "enclosing one of the Paroles for his examination, and requesting him to return it. He *kept* the Parole; made no reply to our memorial; but issued an order that we be held as hostages for Citizen-Prisoners now in the North. Not for any designated prisoners, one for each of us, as usual in the holding of hostages—but for them *all*, as it seems!" By now their case had become celebrated, North and South: documents relating to it were published in a pamphlet by order of the Confederate Congress.

On February 4, 1864, Richardson and Browne were transferred to the penitentiary at Salisbury, North Carolina, a prison that came to rival Andersonville as the most notorious in the Confederacy. In this enclosure of tents and rude huts surrounding an old cotton factory, they found one man in ten down with smallpox. "What with the perpetual smoke in which we are compelled to live, the penetrating cold, our scanty fare and the total absence of anything to read," wrote Browne on February 19, "the time drags more heavily than ever before. However, as we have more to endure, we have more strength to endure it. . . . Both of us are in excellent health and spirits."[5]

It was brave talk, but a month later Richardson's desolation became complete: he learned that Louise, his wife, who had been living at his father's place in Franklin with the four children, had contracted measles and on March 4 had died of "congestion of the brain." A few weeks later one of his daughters had died.

Another attempt to release him, this time in exchange for James P. Hambleton, editor of the *Southern Confederacy* of Atlanta (a sheet which had declared, incidentally, that the *Tribune* prisoners should be hanged), came to naught when Ould refused Major General Benjamin F. Butler's offer. Ould

[5] Gay Papers.

was under pressure to secure Hambleton's release; "I have urged and urged the enemy to release him," he explained to General Bragg, "but . . . Richardson always turns up as his price. I shall be happy to carry out any instructions the President may give on the matter." [6] Jefferson Davis evidently approved Ould's course; the *Tribune* men were not to be surrendered for anyone.

Though Ould wrote that "I have had dozens of offers of the enemy to exchange Richardson" and Governor Brough of Ohio and others were actively at work for Browne, the two men at Salisbury knew little of these efforts; none of Gay's letters reached them, and they concluded bitterly that they had been forgotten. William E. Davis, a Cincinnati *Gazette* correspondent with Sherman's army, was captured in Georgia and joined them in June. Night after night the three men burrowed in the earth to tunnel their way out. They squirmed through one night and breathlessly pushed up to the surface to make a heartbreaking discovery. They were two feet short of the enclosure. The tunnel was discovered at daylight when an officer fell into it. [7]

By the fall of 1864, over ten thousand Union prisoners languished within the Salisbury stockades, and between twenty and fifty of them were dying daily. The three reporters were assigned to the hospital detail, Davis as general superintendent, Browne to supply medicine to outdoor patients, and Richardson to look after the records. Though they were seriously debilitated, on the whole their health held up remarkably well.

On December 18, 1864 the five hundred and ninety-third day of his imprisonment, Browne got outside the first enclosure on a hospital pass. Behind him, Richardson, without a pass, chatted with the adjutant of the garrison with a coolness that disarmed suspicion, then ambled by the sentry unchallenged, presumably on hospital duty. The two hid in an out-

[6] *O.R.*, Ser. II, Vol. 6, 1035; Vol. 7, 1299.
[7] Browne: *Four Years*, 337.

house until after dark, when Davis joined them and they went through the outer gate, hid in a barn so close to the enclosure that their pursuers overlooked it, and, traveling by night with the aid of Negroes who fed them in hideouts along the way, made good their escape. Close to prostration, the three stumbled through the woodland of western North Carolina, waded streams up to their waists in icy water, trudged through snow a foot deep in the Blue Ridge, fell in with Dan Ellis, a famous Union scout in East Tennessee, and after hairbreadth escapes from enemy patrols on an odyssey of three hundred and forty miles, arrived safely in Knoxville. From there Richardson sent a telegram that thrilled *Tribune* readers: "Out of the jaws of death, out of the gates of Hell . . ."

Salisbury prison scenes so haunted Richardson that he went to Washington to testify before a committee of Congress, then set out on an extensive speaking tour to bring pressure on the administration for a more liberal exchange of prisoners. Thousands heard the *Tribune* reporter's moving recital of the horrors of Salisbury; his efforts, with those of Walt Whitman and others, were instrumental in bringing General Grant to relax restrictions on exchanges in the closing months of the war.

The Confederates were slow to admit that their prized *Tribune* captives—the most important prisoners in the garrison, according to the Salisbury *Daily Watchman*—had escaped. It would have afforded Richardson a laugh had he known that on the day of his arrival in Knoxville, Robert Ould sat in his office in Richmond writing a letter to Edward A. Pollard, associate editor of the Richmond *Examiner* and prominent Confederate historian, a prisoner whom Grant had ordered held until Richardson was released. "I am compelled by a sense of duty to decline the exchange," wrote Ould. "I have already refused to exchange Richardson for half a dozen different named parties. . . ."[8]

· · ·

[8] *O.R.*, Ser. II, Vol. 8, 88.

At least thirty-one artists and correspondents fell into the hands of the Confederates at one time or another during the war, though none of them, and few other prisoners of any kind, were held so long as Richardson and Browne.

The runner-up among reporters taken prisoner, probably, was Finley Anderson of the *Herald,* who wrote Hudson on February 10, 1863, aboard the ram *Queen of the West* that he was going up the Red River with Colonel Ellet. "One of the principal considerations which induced me to accompany the colonel is an opportunity to test my own personal courage. . . . I have been in several battles, and sometimes under pretty heavy fire. But that is not enough. I want to see, just for my own gratification, what kind of stuff I am made of." [9] Anderson had ample opportunity to find out. Four days later the *Queen of the West* ran aground, he was taken prisoner, thrown into "an iron dungeon" in Texas for ten days, and incarcerated in sundry other places for a total of eleven months. [1]

3. FIGHTING JOE

MAJOR GENERAL JOSEPH HOOKER owed no small part of his fame to the press. He was indebted especially to the Associated Press copyist who happened to tag a series of takes, "Fighting—Joe Hooker" one night during the Seven Days. It was intended simply as a guide-line; more than one editor (in one instance a typesetter) removed the dash and set it as a subhead: "Fighting Joe Hooker." [2] By that unaccountable process familiar to newsmen, the name stuck, and Hooker, much to his distaste, was "Fighting Joe" ever after. Hooker disapproved because he thought that it made him sound impetuous, which in fact he was. Antietam, and particularly Smalley's widely read account of it, further enhanced Hook-

[9] Bennett Papers.
[1] *O.R.,* Ser. II, Vol. 6, 822.
[2] Shanks, 189; John Bigelow, Jr.: *The Campaign of Chancellorsville* (New Haven: 1910), 6.

er's fame; Fighting Joe, pale-eyed, ruddy, curly-headed, martial-looking, became a popular idol.

Hooker not only fought impetuously, he talked that way, and to reporters. Charles A. Page listened to him bluster for two hours one night after Antietam. "McClellan knows *I* am a better general than he ever dared hope to be," Hooker said. As to Fitz John Porter, McClellan's favorite, "So help me God, I will never go into another battle where Porter commands the reserve." Page added: "He also told me that he had talked fully as plain to Lincoln & Stanton." [3] Hooker told S. M. Carpenter of the *Herald* that Burnside was a "fool," McClellan a "secessionist." [4]

After Burnside's dismal "mud march" in January, Hooker not only advised William Swinton of the *Times* that the commanding general was "incompetent," as Swinton told Henry J. Raymond, but denounced "the President and the Government at Washington as imbecile and 'played out.' Nothing would go right until we had a dictator and the sooner the better." [5] At a White House levee Raymond confided that alarming comment to Lincoln. The President "put his hand on my shoulder and said in my ear, as if desirous of not being overheard, 'Hooker does talk badly; but the trouble is, he is stronger with the country today than any other man.' " [6] Two days later, on January 26, 1863, Joe Hooker supplanted Burnside as commander of the army, bearing in his pocket a fatherly letter from the President that said: "I have heard, in such a way as to believe it, of your recently saying that both the Army and the Government needed a Dictator. Of course, it was not *for* this, but in spite of it, that I have given you the command. Only those generals who gain successes, can set up dictators. What I now ask of you is military success, and I will risk the dictatorship. . . ."

[3] Page to Gay, Sept. 24, 1862, Gay Papers.
[4] Carpenter to Hudson, Feb. 3, 1863, Bennett Papers.
[5] Henry W. Raymond, ed.: "Extracts from the Journal of Henry J. Raymond," *Scribner's Monthly*, Vol. 19, 422 (Jan. 1880).
[6] Francis Brown: *Raymond of the Times* (New York: 1951), 224.

A volatile, engaging personality for all his tall talk, Hooker dealt cordially with reporters as he set about reorganizing his troops into what he termed "the finest army on the planet." He took the time to initiate an important reform in army correspondence: just before launching his Chancellorsville campaign, he directed that all news dispatches from the army must be signed. Later he formalized it in a characteristic order distributed to editors through the Associated Press. After enjoining them not to give the location of units or publish official reports without sanction, he concluded:

> After any fight the reporters can open their fire as loudly as they please, but avoid, unless it is a general battle, giving the designation of forces engaged. Require all reporters' signatures to their published letters. These rules being observed, every facility possible will be given to reporters and newspapers in this army, including the license to abuse or criticise me to their heart's content.[7]

Hitherto only the pen names or initials of a few outstanding reporters appeared; many editors, like Bennett, insisted on complete anonymity. Sam Wilkeson had expressed the prevailing view when he wrote Gay: "The anonymous greatly favors freedom and boldness in newspaper correspondence. I would not allow *any* letter writer to attach his initials to his communications, unless he was a widely known & influential man like Greeley or Bayard Talyor. . . . Besides the responsibility it fastens on a correspondent, the signature inevitably detracts from the powerful impersonality of a journal."

Hooker's order had a mixed reception among the Bohemians. "I do not desire the ostentation," wrote Thomas M. Newbould of the *Tribune*, and left word at headquarters that he was "N." (The *Tribune* nonetheless printed his full name.) L. W. Buckingham of the *Herald* wrote in the midst of the battle at Chancellorsville that "it is discouraging for corre-

[7] *O.R.*, Ser. I, Vol. 27, Part 3, 192 (June 18, 1863).

spondents to have their names paraded before the public as authors of carefully written letters; for sometimes the letters are written on horseback or in woods, and often with shells screaming to us to 'hurry up!'" Lorenzo Crounse thought it a sensible rule; George Alfred Townsend, who had quit the *Herald* partly out of disgust with Hudson's insistence on anonymity, said a byline put a reporter on his mettle and made him "exert extraordinary means to achieve success." Unquestionably it made for more responsible reporting, and though Hooker boisterously disclaimed the purpose of diminishing criticism, it had its effect there, too. Editors set the reporter's name in small caps at the end of his dispatch; some, notably the *Herald*, occasionally used it also in the last deck of the headlines. After Hooker passed from command, names tended to shrink to initials or disappear, but enough of them remained to establish for Fighting Joe a fair claim to having given the byline to American journalism. For the first time, some reporters became familiar by name to readers throughout the Union.

Despite his cordiality, Hooker proved early in his regime that the Bohemians would be held responsible for security violations. He arrested Edwin F. De Nyse of the *Herald* for writing inadvisably of a reconnaissance, placed him in irons, and convened a court-martial, which sentenced De Nyse to six months' hard labor. Hooker commuted it to transportation out of the army, with orders never to return.[8] The Philadelphia *Inquirer* also roused his ire. Sypher of the *Tribune* wrote, however, that "I do not apprehend any trouble as Hooker is *right with us*."[9] With Villard covering Admiral DuPont's assault on Charleston, Richardson in the West, Smalley editing in the office, and Sam Wilkeson working for the *Times* in Washington after quitting the *Tribune* in a rage over Greeley's persistent talk about mediation, it was Sypher, the young Lancaster lawyer commended by Richardson, to

[8] L. L. Crounse to Adams Hill, Mar. 22, 1863, Gay Papers.
[9] Sypher to Gay, Mar. 20, 1863, Gay Papers.

whom Gay was forced to turn as his chief in the Army of the Potomac.

Intelligent, active, and headstrong, Sypher was not a reporter to take to being herded about. He wrote Gay on April 9:

Yesterday while riding in the calvacade during the review the officer of the day ordered back all civilians privates & clerks, whereupon all report[er]s but myself fell back to the middle of the column. The officer repeated the order to me. I told him to give my compliments to Gen. Hooker and inquire of him whether he desired the Correspondent of the Tribune to report the doings of the orderlies or of the General officers, whereupon he allowed me to keep my place. . . . The other reporters were cursing the Tribune for having the inside track.

Warned by Hooker that he would stop all newspaper dispatches three days before he moved, Sypher devised a code, which he sent to Hill in Washington and Gay in New York, complete with examples and translations. "Draft" meant movement; "note," battle; "interest," victory; "send copy to Philadelphia Press" indicated the army was crossing the Rappahannock below Fredericksburg, "to Lancaster Express," above it.[1] Sypher and Hill added refinements as the great hour approached. Under him, Sypher had Thomas M. Newbould, a recruit from the Philadelphia *Press* whom General Dix had expelled from Fortress Monroe on February 28 as "a sensationalist,"[2] Nathaniel G. Shepherd, a poet described by a colleague as "dignified and doleful," and Francis, the fat messenger. A fourth man, James B. Hammond, had been hired as a shorthander at Hooker's headquarters, where he secretly copied and forwarded official documents to the *Tribune* until told that he must drop his newspaper work. Even without

1 Sypher to Gay, Apr. 7, 1863, Gay Papers.
2 *O.R.*, Ser. I, Vol. 18, 545.

Hammond, Sypher was confident. "I am now all right," he wrote Gay when Shepherd arrived. "Won't need further reinforcements to take Richmond."

In the last days of April, Hooker sent the main body of his army on a nicely screened movement to the northwest to cross the Rappahannock and Rapidan rivers far upstream while Sedgwick, with twenty thousand, demonstrated on Lee's front. The complicated maneuver was superbly executed, and Hooker thought he had his foe in a trap. The army was "bouyant with hope and overflowing with ecstasy," Sypher's *Tribune* dispatch said. Lee wheeled, alert to his peril, and on May 2 sent Jackson's hard-marching veterans by remote roads halfway around Hooker's army for the surprise assault that crippled the Federal right, cost Jackson his life, and so demoralized Hooker that he was never able to regain the initiative. It was a confusing struggle, fought in the heavy undergrowth later famous as the Wilderness, and fought at the same time by Sedgwick on the Fredericksburg field of the previous December, some ten miles east. With only nine thousand of the enemy to oppose him, Sedgwick carried the heights that had been denied to Burnside, and reporters who were with him smelled victory in the offing. But thanks to Hooker's hesitation, Lee was able to overwhelm Sedgwick before Sedgwick could form a juncture with the main body of the Federals for a decisive assault.

Sypher worked from Hooker's headquarters. Instead of making observations from a single vantage point, he rode madly to and fro wherever there was firing, barking orders at Shepherd like a wild man. Writing Gay from Chancellorsville on May 5, he had little idea what was going on. "We have had a terrible siege. Three days fighting and more yet to come. Shepherd is utterly worn out with fatigue. We have both been in the saddle from 12 to 18 hours for the last 8 days after sleeping on the ground without blankets or shelter & having but three or four hours of that poor comfort." The main battle, thought Sypher, was yet to come; so he trusted his dispatches to Francis, who was to deliver them to the agent on the Baltimore train, rather than go in to the office himself as Gay had directed.

William Swinton of the *Times* departed immediately after Jackson's assault—"so badly scared," wrote Hill in Washington, "that a telegram was sent after him from the office here, requesting that care be used in printing his account as he gave it." The *Times* withheld it entirely; but the next day Crounse (who had switched from the *World* because of its change of politics) came through to confirm what Swinton had written, and the two reporters, both competent men, scored heavily for their paper.

For days it was difficult for readers to determine whether Chancellorsville had been a victory, a crushing defeat, or another drawn battle like Antietam. "We have had about two hundred and fifty rumors good and bad," wrote George Templeton Strong on the evening of May 4, "all of them 'authentic.'" Another diarist wrote: "It would seem that Hooker has beaten Lee, and that Lee has beaten Hooker; that we have taken Fredericksburg, and that the rebels have taken it also; that we have 4500 prisoners, and the rebels 5400; that Hooker has cut off Lee's retreat, and Lee cut off Sedgwick's retreat, and Sedgwick has cut off everybody's retreat generally, but has retreated himself although his retreat was cut off. . . . In short, all is utter confusion."

Consternation reigned in the *Tribune* office. Newbould had sent one dispatch early in the battle which was good for an extra; thereafter the *Tribune* men fell silent. In a frenzy, Sydney Gay wired Hill: "Are you all dead?" [3] Finally Hill got a code message from Sypher and relayed it through the rigid censorship: "SEND COPY TO LANCASTER EXPRESS." With that, Gay printed news that removed all doubt about Chancellorsville—Hooker's beaten army had recrossed the Rappahannock. Sypher, arriving at last at the office, brought in an account so critical of Hooker that Gay disclaimed it as repre-

[3] Quoted in Hill to Gay, May 5, 1863, second letter of date, Gay Papers.

sentative of the *Tribune's* opinion, though stoutly refusing to doctor it.[4] Fighting Joe had not yet decided that reporters might criticize him to their hearts' content; he ordered Sypher's arrest, and Shepherd was told by his staff that criticism would have consequences ugly for the critic.[5] Sypher dared not return to the army until Hooker was removed seven weeks later.

After the nerve-racking experience of Chancellorsville, Gay roundly berated Sypher, and as for Shepherd, the m.e. informed him that "you betray a want of energy, celerity, aptness to comprehend military movements and ability to report them." About the only note of comic relief in the Rookery came from a suggestion by Hill: "Why not have carrier pigeons?" To learn the truth about the army, Gay considered that the one man available upon whom he could rely was George Smalley. He sent Smalley down to the Rappahannock to interview officers, pull together the whole story of the campaign, and find out what the army thought of Hooker.

Smalley returned after extensive talks with Sedgwick, Meade, Hooker, and others. The commander had been perfectly cordial. "If I am to be investigated, it might as well be by you as anybody," Hooker had said. But the reporter found Hooker "the mere wreck of what he was last fall . . . played out by wine and women."[6] The army appeared to him to be shockingly demoralized, and for Hooker there was apparently no logical successor.

Gay, listening to this somber report, perhaps sensed something of what Lincoln had felt when news had come to him of Hooker's withdrawal. Noah Brooks had seen Lincoln on that occasion, and would never forget how Lincoln had handed him the telegram and said, in a voice trembling with

4 *Tribune* editorial, May 8, 1863.
5 Shepherd to Gay, May 15, 1863.
6 Smalley is thus quoted privately in *War Letters 1862–1865 of John C. Gray and John Codman Ropes* (Boston: 1927), 117. In his *Anglo-American Memories* (1911), Smalley makes a great show of mystery about "what I learned in that month of May, 1863, on the banks of the Rappahannock."

emotion: "Read it—news from the army." The President had walked the floor, hands behind his back, crying: "My God! My God! What will the country say! What will the country say!" Now Smalley wanted to know what kind of piece he should write. Gay shook his head sadly. "Write an editorial," he said, "keep to generalities, and forget most of what you have told me." [7]

[7] Smalley: *Memories*, 160.

✳ CHAPTER IX ✳

Gettysburg

1. "Who Is Byington?"

JUNE brushed the cheek of the city blithely, as if there had been no Fredericksburg, no Chancellorsville, as if there were no war at all. It set the poplars to rustling full-blown leaves to the plashing music of the Egyptian iron water-lily fountain in City Hall Park, the open-air horsecars to rumbling on Broadway, and pickaninnies to hitching rides behind them in blissful ignorance of "No Colored People Allowed On This Car" signs. Lord & Taylor's sported new green-striped awnings (how summer brought out the awnings!); Tiffany's sold more and more wedding bands, and a long line of gleaming barouches with their tops down waited outside A. T. Stewart's as horses patiently stamped off the summer flies. June set visitors to climbing Trinity steeple to survey the teeming multitudes on the main thoroughfare of America, and swishing maidens in hoopskirts to twirling their parasols on promenade by the Astor House. In the Rookery across the park, the inchoate shouts of men vending lemonade and flavored ices came drifting through the open windows the way they always had, come June, and looking up from the park you could see white paper caps bobbing in the top row of windows as compositors worked at their type cases beneath the skylight.

People had accustomed themselves to living with the war now, and a great many of them seemed too busy to concern themselves overmuch. Newspaper circulation, still fantastically inflated by prewar standards, had leveled off. There were fewer extras, though during and after major battles they were still snatched up faster than the newsies could make change. The peak had been reached in 1862, and it remained unsurpassed until the closing days of the war.

At his paper-cluttered desk, Sydney Gay scanned dispatches, letters, maps, rival papers, oblivious to the pleasures of the season. Where was Lee? During the first week of June the enemy had withdrawn from his old diggings around Fredericksburg, but Stuart's cavalry screened the movements of the Army of Northern Virginia so effectively that for nearly two weeks the mystery remained. On the 14th came word that enemy patrols were prowling on the outskirts of Harrisburg, that a Federal detachment under Brigadier General R. H. Milroy had been routed from Winchester, in the Shenandoah Valley. There was a touch of panic in Washington— men spoke of barricading the streets, and the planks were taken up on the Chain Bridge. Reports of brushes with enemy detachments, of great clouds of dust rising as from troops on the march, came from every direction. Reporters scurried about, asking anxious questions. "Fox & Harrington each say, and I hear quite directly from the chief of Hooker's detectives that the whereabouts of Lee are absolutely unknown," Adams Hill reported to Gay on the 17th. "The detective said he'd ridden 150 ms. without learning anything." Rumors and reports pointed to one conclusion as certain. Lee was moving north.

Clearly, a crisis was in the offing, an invasion more formidable than that of the year before, and the *Tribune's* facilities for reporting it caused Gay misgivings as severe as the threat itself. "I hope that your men with the army are of the right

203

stuff," wrote Hill, "but I fear." [1] Charles A. Page could not obtain leave from his Treasury Department job, Smalley was needed in the office, Richardson was in Libby, Villard with Rosecrans, Sypher banned by Hooker. On June 20, Nathaniel Shepherd was arrested on Hooker's order for what Shepherd thought "a very innocent letter," and ordered out of the army. [2] That left Thomas Newbould, whom Smalley wrote off as "a cipher," and T. C. Grey, an untried correspondent who had joined the *Tribune* force after Chancellorsville, to cover the whole invasion.

Casting about, Gay enlisted A. Homer Byington, editor and publisher of the Norwalk (Connecticut) *Gazette*, a frequent contributor to the *Tribune* while in Washington, to fill in. Byington was no great shakes as a writer, but he had boundless energy and he loved the *Tribune* as if it were his own. He had been in newspaper work since he was fourteen years old. Byington, said Hill, "understands what a newspaper requires." Remarking that he was "very industrious and shrewd," Wilkeson wrote once that "Byington would get rich in Andersonville prison." F. H. Bellew, artist for the *New York Illustrated News*, agreed to help (unfortunately he had saddle boils and was of small use) along with Kent and a couple of others Hill designated "second-raters," M. D. Landon, and one Lewis. Gay was convinced by now that manpower was less important than one perceptive correspondent who had "devotion," but there was no telling who had it except under fire.

The confusion over Lee's whereabouts came from the fact that his army advanced in three widely separated corps. Ewell was already in Pennsylvania before Hill and Longstreet had crossed the Potomac. Ewell's gaunt men in butternut sent shudders of apprehension through the North. His advance went clear to the banks of the Susquehanna at Wrightsville, a scant seventy miles from Philadelphia. "Men of the North!"

[1] June 10, 1863, Gay Papers.
[2] Hill to Gay, June 21, 1863, Gay Papers.

the *Tribune* shouted on June 26, "Pennsylvanians, Jerseymen, New Yorkers, New Englanders! the foe is at your doors! Are you true men or traitors? If you are patriots deserving to be free, prove it by universal rallying, arming, and marching to meet the Rebel foe! Prove it NOW!" The Philadelphia *Inquirer* pulled out the blackest type in the shop: **To Arms! Citizens of Pennsylvania! The Rebels Are Upon Us!** Emergency calls went out from editorial offices: on June 28, Hudson, with a swarm of *Herald* men already following the invasion, telegraphed Tom Knox in St. Louis to report to Harrisburg "at the earliest possible moment"; on the same day the Cincinnati *Gazette* wired Whitelaw Reid to leave his post in Washington and "join Hooker's army in time for the fighting."

That day reporters learned that it was Hooker's army no longer. Mercifully, Fighting Joe resigned in a huff when Halleck refused to sanction his plan for incorporating the Harper's Ferry garrison within his own command. In his place Lincoln appointed a man already known to *Herald* readers as "tall and spare in form, slightly stoop-shouldered and wearing spectacles, who looks more like a scholar than a soldier," better known to the troops as "that damned old goggle-eyed snapping turtle," George Gordon Meade. "The relieving of Hooker is received with a kind of apathetic indifference by the army," T. C. Grey wrote his managing editor the next day, "although many are loud in denouncing the act *at this particular moment*." What a moment it was! Lee's entire army deep in Pennsylvania, Meade's from thirty to sixty miles south of it in Maryland, and Jeb Stuart molesting him.

The news looked so ominous Gay deliberately subdued his headlines on June 29 to minimize the scare, but there was no tempering the dispatches. From Harrisburg came word that "the enemy is within four miles of our works, advancing," and from Lancaster: "The excitement here amounts to panic. Everything is leaving." York, Carlisle, Chambersburg were in the hands of the invaders. Federal troops burned the million-dollar bridge across the Susquehanna at Wrightsville. Martial law was declared in Baltimore; tar barrels and sugar hogsheads barricaded the streets. Mayor Alexander Henry of Philadelphia exhorted the populace: "Close your manufactories, work-shops and stores before the stern necessity of common safety makes it obligatory. Assemble yourselves forthwith for organization and drill." Third Street, the city's press row, was thronged as never before. At Harrisburg, men drilled in the streets with brooms and boards in lieu of guns.

That day Staurt's flying squadrons ripped out telegraph lines and disrupted the army's rail communications with Washington and Baltimore. Correspondents in Washington made frantic attempts to get to the army. Reid, Uriah Painter of the Philadelphia *Inquirer*, Sam Wilkeson of the *Times*, Kent of the *Tribune*, and others left for Baltimore at eleven in the morning, only to be told on arrival that the special train they requested was out of the question. They returned to Washington, learned the next day that the line had already been repaired as far as Frederick, turned around and went back to Baltimore. They reached Frederick on the evening of June 30. Here Reid pushed on alone, the others having decided to go back to Baltimore to try what they thought would prove a quicker approach to Meade's army by way of the Western Maryland Railroad to Westminster.

Reid rode all night by moonlight, aware now that time was running out. The papers reported Lee concentrating, Meade marching to meet him. Reid found Meade's headquarters at Taneytown, Maryland, four miles south of the state line, early the morning of July 1, and set about scraping up what news he could. "A horseman gallops up and dismounts. It is a familiar face—L. L. Crounse, the well-known chief correspondent of 'the New York *Times*, with the Army of the Potomac. As we exchange hurried salutations, he tells us that he has just returned from a little post village in Southern Pennsylvania, ten or fifteen miles away; that a fight, of what magnitude he cannot say, is now going on near Gettysburg, between the First Corps and some unknown force of the enemy; that Major General Reynolds is already killed, and that there are rumors of more bad news." [3]

Crounse ("a wonderfully smart fellow in the field," said Sam Wilkeson) had lost his bearings that morning and run into one of the Confederate columns advancing on the town. He fled, found Reynolds, and gave that impetuous officer, according to Crounse's later account, the information that led Reynolds to precipitate the Battle of Gettysburg.[4] Now he sat down on the porch of a tavern in Taneytown and in terse sentences wrote the first words the world would read of the battle, words that stopped the presses of the *Times* for a hasty "Postscript" early the next morning:

> Near Gettysburg, July 1—A heavy engagement has been going on since nine o'clock this A.M. between the rebel forces of Longstreet and Hill and the First and Eleventh corps, under Gens. Reynolds and Meade.
>
> The locality of the fight is beyond Gettysburg, on the Chambersburg Pike.
>
> Portions of the fight have been very severe, and attended with heavy loss.
>
> Thus far the onset of the enemy has been successfully resisted by the two corps mentioned, *and the Third and Twelfth are now coming up.*
>
> I regret to say that Major Gen. Reynolds was mortally wounded, and has since died.

A *World* correspondent disposed of Reynolds in better style, relating how he had been struck in the neck, and continuing: "Crying out, with a voice that thrilled the hearts of his soldiers, 'Forward, for God's sake, forward!' he turned for an instant, beheld the order obeyed by a line of shouting infantry, and falling into the arms of Captain Wilcox, his

[3] From Reid's dispatch, Frank Moore, ed.: *The Rebellion Record* (New York: 1861-9), Vol. 7, Document Section, 87.
[4] George Forrester Williams: "Important Services Rendered by War Correspondents," *The Independent*, Vol. 54, 212 (Jan. 23, 1902).

aide, who rode beside him, his life went out with the words: 'Good God, Wilcox, I am killed.' "

Crounse dispatched his copy by messenger to Frederick, then spurred off with Reid for the front. The roads were choked with troops and wagon trains, so they detoured through the countryside, Reid having supplied himself with maps. "Across the hills to the left," he wrote, "we could see the white-covered wagons slowly winding in and out through the forests, and the masses of blue drab toiling forward." At Two Taverns, five miles south of Gettysburg, they caught a few hours' sleep that night before pressing on early on the morning of July 2.

Homer Byington, the bustling editor from the Nutmeg State, now in the *Tribune's* service, had gone to Harper's Ferry on June 28 to find the Quartermaster of the Seventeenth Connecticut, who had his horse. "General Bob Tyler, of the Connecticut brigade, was there, and he took my map and marked a red ring . . . on it across the Pennsylvania line and said, 'In a few days there will be within that circle one of the biggest fights the world ever saw. Go round to Baltimore and head off Lee at York.' " Byington forgot about his horse and entrained for Baltimore. He got there the same day as the other reporters, but on learning that the Northern Central tracks were torn up, he took the unimpaired Philadelphia, Wilmington, and Baltimore line to Philadelphia, whence he was able to go west by rail as far as Lancaster. Here he found Sypher at home on the night of the 29th and urged him to get to work—with Hooker displaced, Sypher could forget about being banned.

From Lancaster, Byington telegraphed every scrap he could pick up, "not because the news is so very important," as he wrote Gay the next morning, "but because Herald has at least half a dozen men here picking up everything and telegraphing *ad libatum*. They are the most *drunken*, irresponsible crew that ever squandered a newspapers money." Drunk or sober, the *Herald* men had established a horse relay system to speed news from the army to the Lancaster telegraph office or, if necessary, all the way to New York. But Homer was not one to let the doings of the opposition distract him. After writing his chief, he awaited the Philadelphia papers for clues on the location of Lee, then hitched a ride to Columbia. The Columbia-Wrightsville bridge was out. Byington hired a boatman to stand by and ferry *Tribune* men (and no others) across the Susquehanna. Using Wrightsville as a base, he hoped to establish a horse relay of his own from there to the battlefield. He rode into York the evening of June 30 in a country preacher's buggy, having established relay posts at intervals along the way.

"Now and then I heard a gun go off to the southwest," Byington wrote later. "I ransacked the town, but Stuart had got all the horses. Finally I found one solitary horse and buggy, and gave the owner an order on the *Tribune* for the rig. I drove in the direction of the cannonading ten or twelve miles, and evaded some Rebel cavalry on the way, and got to Hanover." There we leave him, for the moment, on the morning of July 1.

Byington's pilgrimage, on a route which described three quarters of a circle from Harper's Ferry to Hanover, was exceeded only by that of Charles C. Coffin of the Boston *Journal*. "Carleton" went from Harrisburg to Washington to Baltimore to Washington to Baltimore to Frederick to Westminster and thence to the field, covering over three hundred miles before seeing the smoke of battle on the morning of July 2. Others never saw it: Thomas Nast of *Harper's Weekly* got no closer than Carlisle, thirty miles to the north, where he sketched the shelling of New York militia by a detachment of Confederates with a single battery. Then Nast was locked up in Harrisburg when it was learned that he was related by marriage to a lady who had been seen wearing a Confederate flag around town. Knox, after his long ride from St. Louis, was also stranded in Harrisburg along with others immobilized by order of Major General Darius Couch. Still more newsmen were marooned in Baltimore. George Law of *Frank Leslie's* and Bill Young of the *Herald* were captured by Confederate cavalry.

Yet, as Meade's forces took up positions they would make historic—Culp's Hill, Cemetery Ridge, Round Top—that beautiful second day of July, there were plenty of Bohemians on hand to record it. The Boston *Journal's* Coffin; Reid of the Cincinnati *Gazette*; the *Tribune* men, Sypher, Grey, Newbould, Bellew, Shepherd, and Byington; E. A. Paul, Frank Henry, Wilkeson, and Crounse of the *Times*; a "Bonaparte" of the *World*; hard-riding Alf Waud of *Harper's Weekly*; T. Barnard of the Associated Press; Edwin Forbes of *Frank Leslie's*; George W. Hosmer, Charles H. Graffan, George H. Hart, L. A. Hendrick, Thomas N. Cook, Galen H. Osborne, J. H. Vosburgh, Nathaniel Davidson, and heaven knows how many others from the *Herald*; Uriah Painter and J. H. Taggart of the Philadelphia *Inquirer*; J. F. McDevitt and a couple of others representing the Philadelphia *Press*; a Philadelphia *Age* man; another from the Pittsburgh *Gazette*; and others lost beyond recall found vantage points among the rocks and crags. Peering from Seminary Ridge across the way was one of the few professional correspondents in all the Confederacy, Francis Lawley of *The Times* of London.

It was a maze for them to solve: not two armies facing each other in neat battle array along a three-mile fishhook line of low hills and ridges, as we tend to visualize them today, but a tumult of wagons, ambulances, caissons, infantry, orderlies, stragglers, staff officers, going now this way, now that, through intermittent clouds of smoke which obscured a blazing sun. Through most of the day the armies remained relatively quiet while the last brigades came up, sporadic artillery practice mingling with the rat-a-tat-tat of the sharpshooters. Toward evening Lee launched assaults on both wings of Meade's army. A dreadful, redundant "Boom! crack-crack-crack-crack, boom! crack-crack-crack" all but drowned out shouted commands, high-voiced and tense, whinnies of frightened horses, the banter of boys trying to ease the tension with wisecracks, hideous gurgles in the throats of those who had been hit, cries for water, frantic questions, curses, cheers. Not a man among them could take it all in.

Those on the Federal left, looking down on Sickles's men in the Peach Orchard, saw that corps all but decimated and finally driven back by a relentless foe. Reid, shading his eyes in the setting sun, saw Sickles himself carried off on a litter, one leg a mass of blood, his hat pulled over his eyes and a cigar clenched between his teeth. At Culp's Hill on the other end of the line, Grey jotted notes on his saddle pommel with a sense of history upon him as Ewell hurled two divisions against the Federal position, Grey praying to God that the line would hold. It seemed to buckle for a moment, then stiffened. The Southerners were repulsed.

After a fitful night's sleep, Grey completed his dispatch early the morning of July 3. Then in his round, firm hand, he penciled a matter-of-fact note to his chief:

> Hd. Qrs. Army of Potomac,
> Friday, July 3, 1863.
> Seven o'clock A.M.

Mr. S. H. Gay, Esq.,
      Dear Sir:
                I am unable to forward you anything in addition to the enclosed letter but shall send just as often as possible. I have not seen Mr. Newbould since July 1 when we were at Taneytown, Md., and he thought of going with the cavalry. *I know of no other Tribune correspondents here except myself* and consequently feel my inability to send you full particulars of the battle at all points. I am first on the right and then on the left and gather all information possible.
                The battle is again raging furiously at intervals and another general engagement will take place today.

I am so much in haste to send this off by Francis by way of West Minster that I am unable to correct my letters.

Very respectfully,

T. C. Grey

Waiting for Francis, Grey jotted a postcript on the back: "Matters do not look particularly encouraging here. The rebels seem to be on all sides." He drew a crude diagram of the Federal position, which he conceived to be in the shape of a crescent. And a final afterthought: "At present I am under a knoll writing this with a perfect shower of rifle balls and shells passing over."

Grey and all the others, miraculously, passed through it unscathed. Lorenzo Crounse had his horse shot under him. Sam Wilkeson, arriving late on the 2nd after bumping along the rickety Western Maryland to Westminster, learned that his eldest son, Bayard, a nineteen-year-old artillery lieutenant, had had his leg blown off on the first day and was either a prisoner or a corpse in the hands of the enemy. Sam lived up to the finest traditions of journalism. Later, sitting beside the boy's freshly dug grave, he wrote the *Times* one of the great dispatches of the war.

Shortly after noon on the 3rd, Wilkeson, Reid, Frank Henry, and other reporters lay on the grass outside the little white farmhouse where Meade had his headquarters, trading information, shouting into one another's ears amid a storm of missiles. "Close by our heads went one," wrote Reid, "that was evidently some kind of small arm that had an unfamiliar sound. 'That,' said Wilkeson, aesthetic always, or nothing, 'that is a muffled howl: that's the exact phrase to describe it.' We discussed the question." Possibly it was one of the tenpenny nails some Confederate units were reduced to shooting. Then began what was probably the most earth-shattering artillery bombardment of the war. "Bonaparte" wrote in the *World*:

The boards of fences, scattered by explosions, flew in splinters through the air. The earth, torn up in clouds, blinded the eyes of hurrying men. . . . As, with hundreds of others, I groped through this tempest of death for the shelter of a bluff, an old man, a private in a company belonging to the 24th Michigan, was struck scarcely ten feet away by a cannon-ball, which tore through him, extorting such a low, intense cry of mortal pain as I pray God I may never hear again.

Wilkeson remembered hearing a bird sing just before the storm, the reporters listening to this eerie anomaly with a momentary sense of the inscrutable ways of man and animal. "In the midst of its warbling, a shell screamed over the house, instantly followed by another and another," wrote Wilkeson, "and in a moment the air was full of the most complete artillery prelude to an infantry battle that was ever exhibited. Every size and form of shell known to British and American gunnery, shrieked, whirred, moaned and whistled and wrathfully fluttered over our ground. As many as six a second, constantly two a second, bursting and screaming over headquarters, made a very hell of fire that amazed the oldest officers. They burst in the yard—burst next to the fence on both sides, garnished as usual with the hitched horses of aides and orderlies. The fastened animals reared and plunged with terror. Then one fell, then another—sixteen lay dead and mangled before the fire ceased, still fastened by their halters, which gave the expression of being wickedly tied up to die painfully. These brute victims of a cruel war touched all hearts. Through the midst of the storm of screaming and exploding shells, an ambulance driven by its frenzied conductor at full speed, presented to all of us the marvelous spectacle of a horse going rapidly on three legs. A hinder one had been shot off at the hock. A shell tore up the little step at the headquarters cottage, and ripped bags of oats as if with a knife. Another soon carried off one of its two pillars. Soon a spherical case burst opposite the open door—another ripped through the low garret. The remaining pillar went almost immediately to the howl of a fixed shot that Whitworth must have made. . . . Forty minutes,—fifty minutes—counted watches that ran, oh! so languidly! Shells through the two lower rooms. A shell into the chimney, that daringly did not explode. Shells in the yard. The air thicker and fuller and more deafening with the howling and whirring of these infernal missiles. . . . And the time measured on the sluggish watches was one hour and forty minutes."

Meade had been compelled to move his staff, but the Bohemians calmly stuck it out. In mid-afternoon came a lull. Then, as the smoke drifted from the valley, an audible "Oh-h-h" rose along the Federal line. "Here they come!" From a little more than a mile away across open country they came: row on row of men in gray, moving in near-perfect order. Forty-five regiments, banners flying, moved down the gentle slopes of Seminary Ridge, crossed the Emmitsburg road in full view of the waiting Yankees, and came on now amid devastating bursts of grape and canister which cut lanes through them. They converged on the Union center. Reporters held their breath, watching from behind whatever protection they could find: Hancock's men in blue, crouched behind stone walls and trees, blazing away, the butternuts moving up the slope relentlessly, by the thousand. Some reached the Federal line, cheering, madly swinging rifle butts; Brigadier General Lewis A. Armistead, hat raised aloft on the point of his sword, demanded the surrender of a Federal gun and was killed the next instant; others came in with their hands up. Wave after wave now they were receding in the face of fire no troops could endure, whole companies reduced to a few stumbling, crawling men. Dazed Bohemians were to grope numbly for language that would convey the grandeur and pathos of Pickett's charge.

Scarcely less anomalous than the bird twittering in the peach tree or the galloping three-legged horse that afternoon was the figure of Cullen B. Aubrey, a youngster known as "Doc," riding among the troops selling papers. For the first time, soldiers were able to read of a battle even as they fought it. Aubrey had met the Baltimore train at Westminster, strapped piles of unfolded Philadelphia *Inquirers* fore and aft on his saddle, and trotted back to the field to sell the troops an edition containing Painter's account of the first day's struggle before that of July 3 was over. "They went like gingerbread at a state fair," he remembered.[5]

Evening came, and with it a measure of peace. Meade appeared; a band struck up "Hail to the Chief." "Ah, General Meade," said Sam Wilkeson, never able to forget politics for long, "you're in very grave danger of being President of the United States." Meade, an omnivorous reader of newspapers and extremely sensitive to what they said of him, rarely spoke to reporters and pretended not to hear.[6]

An epochal victory had been won, of which the world knew nothing. Lee still had an army, but its offensive power had been smashed, perhaps for all time. Hosmer of the *Herald* had left at the end of the second day and gone all the way to the office with news, but it was apparent from his piece, printed in the paper July 4, that the outcome still hung in the balance. Crounse of the *Times* rode off at 3:00 a.m. on July 3 after learning the result of Meade's council of war, reporting rather ominously from Baltimore that "It was the determination of our Generals to fight to the bitter end." With seven dispatches to his credit in two days, the redoubtable Crounse had outdone himself. He and Hosmer were among the few to leave while the battle was in progress. Meade had decided against having the field telegraph strung to his headquarters, and the War Department had so little faith in the Western Maryland Railroad that the Adams Express Company was persuaded to run seven-mile relays of horses between Balti-

---

[5] Cullen B. Aubrey: *Reflections of a Newsboy in the Army of the Potomac* (Milwaukee: 1904), 138.

[6] Reid's dispatch, *op. cit.*

more and Westminster, where its messengers met Meade's
couriers, day and night. Even so, some of Meade's dispatches
to the War Department went astray; others were unaccountably delayed.

Grey left the field the night of July 3 for Westminster,
where he had to wait until eleven the next morning for a train.
By that time Reid, with one of the finest battle accounts of the
war jelling in his head, and Coffin had come up through a
drenching rain; but because of a traffic tie-up on the Western
Maryland, the three did not reach Baltimore until twenty-
three hours later. Shepherd, as completely out of touch with
the other *Tribune* men as Grey, and like him convinced that
the paper was hopelessly beaten, had no horse and remained
on the field.

Homer Byington was left in Hanover, twelve miles east of
Gettysburg, as the battle opened. Jeb Stuart and Kilpatrick
had staged a cavalry fight there the day before, and the reporter found the streets littered with arms and accouter-
ments. He stopped at the hotel to ask the proprietor if there
was a telegraph operator in town. "There he is over yonder,"
the man said, pointing to a little hunchback asleep on a bench
near the door.

Byington went over and shook him. "Where is your battery?"

Daniel E. Trone opened his eyes and looked up at him
blankly. "Home under my bed. The wires are all cut everywhere—no use trying to telegraph."

Byington introduced himself. History was being made that
very moment, he said. Trone must go home and get that battery. Trone went. Thereupon Byington proceeded to round
up a crew of repair men, rented a handcar from the president
of the railroad after signing a personal bond for it, and went
humping down the track to string up the wire. It appeared
that only a five-mile stretch of it was down. The men caught
Byington's enthusiasm, working to the distant thunder of

guns. Hours later, Trone hitched up his battery, and on the way back Byington saw the bent little operator wildly swinging his hat. "We've got Baltimore!" Byington and a Philadelphia *Press* reporter who had helped thereupon extracted a solemn oath from Trone: it was to be their wire, exclusively, for the next two days. Their papers would pay him well. Byington shuddered at all the money he had spent on this and the horse relays and the boatman at Columbia-Wrightsville; give him one solid beat, and the *Tribune* would forget about the cost. Excitedly he arranged a relay to run between Hanover and the field.

Byington mounted and was off in the direction of the firing. Meeting Major General O. O. Howard on the way, he secured details of the first day's fight from him, and found Sypher on the field. The night of July 2, Byington and Sypher got off by their private wire an account of the first two days' fighting. Nothing else of consequence got through that night: Hosmer of the *Herald* was still on the train for New York. At nine thirty, as Byington remembered later, the *Tribune* sallied forth with an extra, and something like sixty-five thousand copies were sold in the streets before the presses had to be stopped to prepare for the next morning's run. Sydney Gay was so jubilant he went home to Staten Island with a bundle of fireworks under his arm for his son Martin, and for once remained there the whole week-end. "It was a real celebration," he wrote his daughter. Perchance among the salutes he set off were some for the editor of the Norwalk *Gazette*.

Meanwhile, Trone, the country operator hunched over his key behind locked doors at Hanover, heard a strange signal: "dash-dot-dash; dot-dot . . . dash-dot-dash; dot-dot."

"That's K I," said Trone. "What the dickens does 'K I' mean? I'm afraid the rebels have tapped our wire."

Presently a message came. Trone spelled it out and looked up at Byington in amazement. "It's the War Department," he said. "The President wants to know, 'Who is Byington?'"

"Tell 'em, 'Ask Uncle Gideon,'" said Byington. The old
Secretary of the Navy knew every editor in Connecticut. So
it came to pass that, thinking the original message had been intended for him, "Uncle Gideon" wrote in his diary with
some relish:

> I was called at midnight precisely by a messenger with
> a telegram from Byington, dated at Hanover Station,
> stating that the most terrific battle of the war was being
> fought at or near Gettysburg, that he left the field at half
> past six p.m. with tidings, and that everything looked
> hopeful. . . . I had remained at the War Department for
> news until about 11. Some half an hour later the dispatch
> from Byington to me came over the wires, but nothing
> from anyone to Stanton or Halleck. The operator at the
> War Department gave the dispatch to the President, who
> remained. He asked, "Who is Byington?" None in the
> department knew anything of him, and the President
> telegraphed to Hanover Station. . . . I informed the
> President the telegram was reliable. Byington is the editor
> and proprietor of a weekly paper in Norwalk, Conn.,
> active and stirring, is sometimes employed by the New
> York Tribune, and is doubtless so employed now.
>
> The information this morning and dispatches from
> Gen. Meade confirm Byington's telegram.[7]

Back at the War Department, Stanton had forgotten his
aversion for reporters so far as to telegraph: "We've got Byington's first dispatch. Send along more. We are listening."
Byington did so, and he also told the War Department something else it didn't know: the Northern Central Railroad was
now intact from Baltimore to within six miles of the battlefield; trains should be sent for the wounded. The reply came
that a train would be sent at once, signed "A. Lincoln." [8]

[7] *Welles Diary*, I, 357. Entry of July 4, 1863.
[8] *Tribune* editorial, July 7, 1863. For the details of Byington's story, the
essentials of which are confirmed in this editorial, in the Welles diary, and
in Byington's letters of the time, I have followed his reminiscences in Crof-

More than two weeks later, when Byington went to call on Welles, the Secretary greeted him like visiting royalty. "He *thanked* me for getting the *first news* (in my dispatch to the Tribune) of the Gettysburg fight to them," wrote Byington to Gay. "Says Mr. Lincoln had a long talk about it, with him next morning, &c." [9] That was the morning Lincoln formally announced to the country that a great victory had been won at Gettysburg.

Once again, as in the case of the *Merrimac*, of Shiloh, Antietam, and Fredericksburg, the President had momentous news from a member of the Bohemian Brigade before official word could reach him. Byington's remarkable feat of rigging "a telegraph literally of my own construction," as he proudly termed it in writing his managing editor July 5, exemplified the practical ingenuity of a country editor who wouldn't be beaten: so far as available records show, he was the only Civil War correspondent to turn the trick.

2. "DOWN WITH THE 'TRIBUNE'!"

HARDLY had the Gettysburg victory been confirmed in some of the most stirring dispatches of the war—Sypher came into the *Tribune* office July 6 with an excellent account, Wilkeson's shone in the *Times*, Whitelaw Reid brought the fullest of all to the Cincinnati *Gazette*, Coffin was serenaded by thousands in Boston—when tremendous celebrations were set off by word of the fall of Vicksburg. All through June the *Tribune* had played Grant's siege on page one, column one; and if accounts of the grim proceedings were sometimes tedious, a full complement of Bohemians was on hand to write them. Any doubt that Easterners failed to grasp the importance of the great fortress city on the Mississippi vanished

---

fut's *American Procession*, 98–101, and in the *Official Program of the Centennial of Incorporation of the Borough of Hanover* (1915).

   [9] July 19, 1863, Gay Papers.

when Admiral David Porter informed Welles of its surrender. Church bells tolled throughout the East, one-hundred-gun salutes boomed in Albany, Syracuse, Utica, Bridgeport, New Haven, Newburyport, Portland, and in Boston a correspond-ent reported "more joyous excitement than in any previous event of the war."[1]

Victory flags were still waving in New York when the city plunged into turmoil.

Congress had passed a conscription law in March, providing that a draftee might hire a substitute or excuse himself by pay-ment of three hundred dollars to the government. Democrats attacked the law as unjust to the poor and challenged the government's right to exercise compulsion. On Saturday, July 11, the drawing of names began in New York at the provost marshal's office, Third Avenue and Forty-sixth Street. A crowd milled outside. George Templeton Strong reflected the prevailing apprehension in his diary: "Demos take it good-naturedly thus far, but we shall have trouble before we are through."[2]

It was bruited about that officials had stuffed the lottery wheels with the names of Democrats. Copperhead sheets spoke bitterly of "a rich man's war but a poor man's fight." On Sunday inflamed factory workers, day laborers, and team-sters met in shacks and car sheds on the east side. They had more to aggrieve them than the draft. Freed slaves were drift-ing into the city from the South, working for next to nothing; some had been employed as strikebreakers. The city's down-trodden immigrants hated the Negroes as only underdogs can hate underdogs, cursing emancipation, the war, and the draft law.

On Monday morning, July 13, a mob stormed the Third Avenue enrollment office, smashed the lottery machinery, and set fire to the building. A squad of police and later a de-

---

[1] *Tribune*, July 8, 1863.
[2] Allan Nevins and Milton Halsey Thomas, eds.: *The Diary of George Templeton Strong* (New York: 1952), III, 333.

tachment of invalid soldiers broke and fled for their lives amid a hail of brickbats and paving-stones. Two soldiers were beaten to death with their own muskets. Five adjacent buildings went up in flames while the mob drove off the Fire Department. John A. Kennedy, Superintendent of Police, was beaten within an inch of his life and hurled into an excavation filled with water.

The word spread with lightning rapidity. Thousands left their jobs to roam the streets in armed bands, raiding saloons, looting stores, burning warehouses, chasing Negroes. Policemen were clubbed to death. Men and women were attacked and plundered in broad daylight. A frenzied throng attacked the Colored Orphan Asylum on upper Fifth Avenue and burned it to the ground. Downtown another enrollment office went up in flames, and with it an entire block. Brooks Brothers was sacked. The charred bodies of Negroes dangled from lamp posts. Edward Mitchell looked out his window to see a swarm of tatterdemalions led down the street by "a hag with straggling grey hair, howling and brandishing a pitchfork." Horsecar and omnibus service came to a standstill. Frightened proprietors boarded up their shops. "Stalwart young vixens and withered old hags were swarming everywhere," wrote Strong, "all cursing 'the bloody draft' and egging on their men to mischief." Their men wrecked telegraph lines, ripped up rails, pitched rocks into private homes, raided a rifle factory on Second Avenue, routed the guards, and seized all the arms they could carry.

"*Tribune* office to be burned tonight!" Strong heard it; so did James Parton. Rioters surged down Fourteenth Street singing: "We'll hang Horace Greeley to a sour apple tree!" Down at the Rookery, Isaac England, the city editor who grieved that city news seldom got proper display, was having his innings, directing the entire staff under Gay's watchful eye. Shortly after noon, E. H. Jenny, at the front desk on the ground floor, sent up a warning that people were congregating on Nassau Street. A man in a light-colored coat and Panama hat, standing in front of about five hundred men and boys with stones and clubs in their hands, shook his fist at the *Times* building across the way, and yelled: "That's got to come down, and then the *Tribune!*" "Down with the *Tribune!*" the mob chanted. England heard the leader call for "Three cheers for George B. McClellan," and then "Three groans for Horace Greeley," which were "emphatically given." Greeley was "the nigger's friend." Lynch him!

The leader turned toward the *Tribune* building and yelled: "Come out of there, you God-damned black-hearted Abolitionist!" The crowd hooted. "Hang the damned son of a bitch!" Franklin J. Ottarson, Gay's first lieutenant, ran downstairs to get a policeman to arrest the man. The officer he found promptly vanished. The mob moved off, only to return in greater numbers twenty minutes later. Daniel Godwin, in the second-floor counting-room, heard a gravel voice exhorting: "What's de matter, you cowards or afraid? Down wit' de *Tribune!*" [3]

All hands remained at their posts. Gay went to warn Greeley, and found him busy talking with Theodore Tilton of the *Independent.* Gay said that the place must be armed: "This is not a riot, but a revolution!" Greeley agreed, "but I want no arms brought into the building," he said. Gay begged him to slip out the back way and get out of town. No, said Greeley, he and Tilton were going out to eat. "If I can't eat my dinner when I'm hungry, my life isn't worth anything to me." Greeley lumbered out the front entrance with Tilton and headed for Windust's Restaurant on Ann Street while Gay watched from a window. Not a hand was laid on him. [4]

At seven that night more than two thousand were milling around outside the Rookery when the paving-stones began to fly. Windows and doors were smashed. With a yell, the mob

[3] *Tribune*, Aug. 13, 1863; transcript of testimony, Grand Jury investigation.
[4] Hale: *Greeley*, 273.

burst into the counting-room, smashed desks and chairs to splinters, and set fire to papers on the floor. *Tribune* hands fought to put it out. A rioter called for a man with camphene to come in and gut the place. In the press vault, Tom Rooker and the engineer were getting ready to puncture the boilers and shoot steam and scalding water on the wild men. Rows of club-swinging policemen marched up Nassau Street, one hundred and ten strong. "There have been beautiful sights in the heavens above, and on the earth beneath," wrote a witness, "but to none of that small garrison . . . was anything ever more beautiful than that charge." There was a skull-cracking battle: some rioters were killed. The mob was driven out. Gay helped clean up the wreckage and succor the wounded until the ambulances arrived. Feeling like a Parisian during the Terror, he saw the *Tribune* to press, on schedule. It described the first day of the most violent civic disturbance in American history.

The second day, July 14, was worse. Armed gangs fought troops and police in the avenues. Gay had remained at the *Tribune* office all night, and had ordered reams of wet newsprint piled along the walls to reduce the fire hazard. Editors went right on editing, reporters reporting. James Gilmore arrived with a wagonload of old muskets requisitioned from army headquarters at Governor's Island. From the commandant of the Brooklyn Navy Yard he secured a howitzer and a consignment of bombs. The place was an arsenal when Greeley arrived.

"Take 'em away! Take 'em away! I don't want to kill anybody, and besides they're a lot more likely to go off and kill us." Greeley had gone home before the desperate fight of the night before, or he might have thought differently. Gay ignored him. The rioters were congregating outside again, yelling raucous threats. "The nigger-loving *Tribune*! Down with it!" Gay took time out to jot a brief note to his gentle Quaker wife, in the style he always used with her:

Gettysburg

My dear Lizzy—

I am very glad thou didn't know of our danger last night. We are barricaded and armed now and fear nothing. . . . . Don't thou be in the least alarmed. We have an escape over the roof, over the whole block.

A colonel home on leave volunteered his services. Gay took him up to the composing room and asked Tom Rooker to put him in charge of the defenses. The colonel at once discovered that the cartridges on hand were the wrong caliber for the guns. They decided not to tell the compositors.

A second note to Lizzie betrayed Gay's state of mind. "All is as quiet as possible here," he began, asked that some clothes be sent him, and signed off: "Yrs, etc. S. H. Gay." There was a hasty postscript: "I am talking while I write and wasn't thinking of what I was about in that stereotyped signature." (He had no idea that her life was in danger, too. A friendly tavern-keeper in West Brighton had warned her, and Mrs. Gay sat up all night, two pearl-handled pistols in her lap, listening to the footsteps of rioters on the boardwalk.)

At the *Times* office, two Gatling guns, one manned by Raymond himself, poked out the front entrance, commanding Park Row to the north. The rioters kept their distance, but that night they assaulted the *Tribune* again. This time the defenders were ready. Four typographers barred the composing-room door, ready to pitch composing sticks and fifty-pound turtles down the stairs. Five troughs, each ten feet long, projected from the editorial-floor windows, with reporters standing ready to roll thirty-pound shells down on the rioters' heads. There was a great show of guns from all windows. The rioters went away. For two more days terror gripped the city before thirteen regiments from Meade's army arrived to restore order. Several hundred persons (some said as many as a thousand) had lost their lives.

Gay, like many others, was convinced that the disturbance was part of a widespread Copperhead plot. Brigadier General

Henry Bustee told him on July 16 that "this riot was planned and set afoot by Gov. Horatio Seymour, Fernando Wood, and a small coterie of leaders of their stripe to inaugurate a revolution at the North and overturn the present Government," words which James Gilmore also heard and promptly sent to Lincoln. Bustee said that he had been a member of that coterie himself, but grew appalled at the lengths to which they were willing to go. Relating this to the President, Gilmore said he set no great store in Bustee, "but circumstances confirm what he says." [5] Governor Seymour had made inflammatory remarks beforehand. On July 4 he had told a mass meeting: "Remember this: that the bloody, treasonable and revolutionary doctrine of public necessity can be proclaimed by a mob as well as by a government." He had left town while the riot was brewing and voiced sympathy with the rioters while it was going on.

Homer Byington wrote Gay of a German acquaintance who had been in New York on a visit during which he was initiated into the Golden Circle Club, which had lodges in thirty or more parts of the city. The rioters, Byington said this friend informed him, originally planned to join hands with the Confederates during Lee's invasion and hurl Lincoln from power preparatory to establishing peace. Their first step was to restore McClellan to command, and Byington's informant had related other details that the reporter found convincing.[6]

Gay was sufficiently impressed by these and similar revelations to write Lincoln on July 26, warning that "Virginia was not in greater danger of revolution in the winter of 1861 than New York is today." [7] Only gradually was he convinced that the back of the conspiracy had been broken. Few doubted that conspiracy it was, organized and directed by cunning men: the police telegraph system, about which the ruffians

[5] July 17, 1863, Robert T. Lincoln Collection.
[6] July 19, 1863, Gay Papers.
[7] Robert T. Lincoln Collection.

knew nothing, had been disrupted almost at once; Superintendent Kennedy, though out of uniform, had been singled out for assault; barricades of horsecars and heavy wagons had been lashed with telegraph wire and thrown across the streets; and well-organized attempts had been made to isolate the city by burning ferry piers and ripping up rails.

A Federal investigation failed to identify the conspirators or even to prove a conspiracy. Among the few brought to book was James H. Whitter, a barber, the man in the Panama hat who had led the mob on the *Tribune*. He was fined two hundred and fifty dollars, and sentenced to a year in the penitentiary.

3. "Four Score and Seven . . ."

There was a sequel to Gettysburg of quite another kind. Tireless Adams Hill scribbled one of his nightly notes to Gay on November 15, 1863:

> I hope you'll send Smalley or some first-class man to describe the Gettysburg. 'Twill be a great pageant & it needs a man accustomed to study battlefields as well as to describe. C. A. P. [Page] I should think not up to the first-class description required. He suggested going himself yesterday: I said yes unless you sent somebody from N.Y.
>
> I suppose Everett can be had in advance.

The dedication of the National Cemetery was certainly an occasion calling for the very best hand available, but Gay decided against sending Smalley. Edward Everett's speech, as Hill had guessed, was already in type, but the President's dedicatory remarks would not be until he spoke them. Gay chose John I. Davenport for the assignment, possibly because Davenport knew shorthand.

By carriage, in special trains, in farm wagons, on horseback, and afoot, people streamed into the sleepy community that Lee and Meade had roused a little over four months before. The night of November 18, Gettysburg had quadrupled its population. Crowds and bands serenaded the President, Secretary Seward, and other dignitaries. John Hay, John W. Forney, and his bright *Press* editor, John Russell Young, sampled a little whisky in Forney's rooms, went out to listen, then came back for more. Forney, increasingly loquacious, finally responded to a serenade himself. He upbraided the crowd for not cheering Lincoln more heartily, as Hay wrote in his diary, and went on with a long eulogy of "that great wonderful mysterious inexplicable man who holds in his single hands the reins of the republic. . . ." Young joked that that was one speech he need not report—the boss "will see further about it when he gets sober." They went back to their whisky; boisterous renditions of *John Brown's Body* echoed far into the night.[8]

If the other reporters embarked on similar sprees, and they were not notably abstemious, it is understandable that their perceptions were not particularly acute the next morning. They saw the procession form on Baltimore Street and move somewhat raggedly toward the Emmitsburg Road, where white pine coffins were piled and rotting carcasses of horses lay where they had fallen. Young and others waited outside David Wills's house, where the President was staying. Men were shouting: "Three cheers for Old Abe." Young remembered how "the President came to the door, a fine flush and smile coming over his face at the rude welcome."[9] The reporters hurried ahead to the plank speakers' platform, to occupy wooden benches provided for them on one side.

Senators, governors, generals, and sundry notables filled the other side. In contrast, the reporters suggested a group of honor students awaiting awards at commencement. Slender, delicate-faced Joseph Becker, who had sketched the battle for

[8] Dennett: *Hay Diaries*, 120, 121.
[9] Young: *Memories*, 63 ff.

Frank Leslie's, was twenty-one; Charles Hale, on hand for the Boston *Advertiser*, was still a student at Harvard; Young was all of twenty-three; Davenport and Joseph L. Gilbert of the Associated Press were probably about the same age. Isaac J. Allen of the *Ohio State Journal* at Columbus, men from the Philadelphia *Inquirer*, the Cincinnati *Gazette*, the Cincinnati *Commercial*, the Chicago *Tribune*, the Chicago *Times*, and most of the New York papers took in the scene as Everett launched his oration.

Young was impatient for it to be over. He had a date to go over the battlefield with Forney and an officer who had been in the fight. Young and the others dreaded the prospect of a long speech from the President. They had badgered Hay and John Nicolay for an advance, but Lincoln's secretaries knew no more about it than the reporters. Young recalled the scene many years later:

> When Everett ceased, exhausted, excited, the two-hours' talk telling on him, there was a moment of rustle, hands extended in congratulation, the President and Secretary of State among the first. . . . The music ran on a bit and then the President arose. Deliberate, hesitating, awkward, "like a telescope drawing out," as I heard someone say, the large bundled up figure untwisting and adjusting itself into reasonable conditions . . . stood an instant waiting for the cheers to cease and the music to exhaust its echoes, slowly adjusted his glasses, and took from his pocket what seemed to be a page of ordinary foolscap paper, quietly unfolded it, looked for the place, and began to read.

The sight of the single sheet did not comfort Young—apparently Lincoln would speak extemporaneously from notes. That meant taking every word down as it was spoken. His boss, Forney, relentless perfectionist and devoted Lincoln supporter, was right there; Young knew he could not afford to botch his report. Fortunately he was an excellent "phonographer," as shorthanders were known, and Lincoln spoke slowly, in a voice that was high-pitched but, from where Young was sitting, perfectly distinct.

What did Lincoln say? The words that have since become known as the Gettysburg Address are not precisely the ones Lincoln delivered. The standard version (the Bliss copy) is his final and most careful revision, written in his own hand for reproduction in *Autograph Leaves of Our Country's Authors* about four months later.

It is no surprise that the reporters fell short of perfection in transcribing. They were cold. They had been sitting on the wooden benches for two and a half hours, looking on a little enviously, no doubt, while knots of people on the periphery of the crowd of fifteen thousand wandered off to explore Devil's Den and Little Round Top. Few of those wielding pencils were trained in the mysteries of Isaac Pitman's science. Like the crowd, they were distracted by a photographer who had set up his camera a few yards in front of Mr. Lincoln and kept fooling with a black cloth, adjusting his lens, and dodging this way and that for a glimpse of the President's face.

After the speech, Joseph L. Gilbert, the Associated Press man, succeeded in securing Lincoln's manuscript, whereupon the New York men discarded their notes: the A.P. would take care of it in plenty of time for them, and in official form. Unfortunately, Gilbert rather bungled the job, following his imperfect notes of what Lincoln had said (*e.g.*, "the refinished work that they have thus far so nobly carried on," "Governments of the people, by the people, and for the people") in some places, and the manuscript in others.[1]

Reporters from other cities, aware of the cavalier and unpredictable ways of the Associated Press in serving what Craig called "outside" papers, wrote their own reports. Most of them were worse than Gilbert's. The Philadelphia *Inquirer* had Lincoln say: "The world will little know and nothing

[1] Basler: *Collected Works*, VII, 19, 20, text and notes.

remember what we see here. . . . We owe this offering to our dead. We imbibe increased devotion to that cause. . . . We here might resolve that they shall not have died in vain." The newspaper version widely regarded as the most accurate, that by Hale, the young Harvard student, has several discrepancies, including: "The world can never forbid what they did here." [2]

What of Young, the expert shorthander? "I did not write the report which appeared in the *Press*," he wrote in recalling that day nearly thirty years later, "as the manuscript had been given to the Associated Press." It is barely possible that thirty years played tricks on him. The speech that the *Press* printed on November 20, 1863, when all the others first appeared, is not the New York Associated Press version. It is the best contemporary account that has come to light. [3]

All of the reporters inserted "[Applause]" at various points, a convention of the time which did not necessarily mean that there was any; the consensus of others who were there is that there was little or none until the end. The occasion did not call for it; neither did the beautiful words Lincoln was speaking. Young got the impression that the crowd was indifferent to them, but that was far from universal. Standing beside Allen of the *Ohio State Journal* was a captain, one sleeve of his uniform limp, biting his lip, eyes brimming. When Lincoln said: "The world will little note nor long remember what we say here, but it can never forget what they did here," the captain unashamedly broke and buried his face in his handkerchief. [4] He was not alone.

By following the Philadelphia *Press* version and Hale's in

[2] James G. Randall: *Lincoln the President*, II, photostat facing 312.

[3] The Philadelphia *Press* account contains only one error worth noting: "We are met on a general battlefield" instead of "great battlefield"; it includes the word "poor" in "our poor power to add or detract," an insertion which Lincoln made in his manuscript and which Gilbert, transcribing for the Associated Press, missed. There are other variations between this and Gilbert's work which establish it as by another hand.

[4] Robert S. Harper: *Lincoln and the Press* (New York: 1951) quotes Allen's dispatch, 288.

the Boston *Advertiser* where they agree in departing from Lincoln's manuscript, and by accepting the one that most closely adheres to it where the two accounts differ, we come as close as it is possible to come to the actual address. These, as nearly as they can be recaptured, are the words Lincoln spoke:

Four score and seven years ago our fathers brought forth upon this continent a new nation, conceived in Liberty and dedicated to the proposition that all men are created equal.

Now we are engaged in a great civil war, testing whether that nation, or any nation so conceived and so dedicated, can long endure. We are met on a great battlefield of that war. We are met to dedicate a portion of it as a final resting place of those who here gave their lives that that nation might live. It is altogether fitting and proper that we should do this.

But in a larger sense we cannot dedicate—we cannot consecrate—we cannot hallow this ground. The brave men, living and dead, who struggled here, have consecrated it far above our poor power to add or detract. The world will little note nor long remember what we say here; but it can never forget what they did here. It is for us, the living, rather to be dedicated here to the unfinished work that they have thus far so nobly carried on. It is rather for us to be here dedicated to the great task remaining before us—that from these honored dead we take increased devotion to that cause for which they here gave the last full measure of devotion—that we here highly resolve that these dead shall not have died in vain—that the nation shall, under God, have a new birth of freedom—and that government of the people, by the people, and for the people, shall not perish from the earth.

☼ CHAPTER X ☼

Artists and Writers

1. "GET THE NEWS—AND GET IT FIRST!"

THE ENERGY, enterprise, and lavish expenditure of money by the representatives of the press with the army, for the . . . single object of getting the news, and *getting it first*, too, would astonish people, were even only half told," Lorenzo Crounse wrote in *Harper's Monthly* of October 1863. While it may be doubted that readers were capable of astonishment at anything the Bohemians did by that time, few who read their dispatches realized the lengths to which the newsmen went to get them into type. "Probably in no business in existence is the competition so sharp as between the leading newspapers of New York," said Crounse. "When I say that cases have occurred where $500 would be a very small price to pay for a half hour's time, I state a common fact."

Competition ruled the Bohemians ruthlessly, like an unseen hand at the scruff of the neck. If it inspired some of their finest work, it also drove them to bribery, subterfuge, plagiarism, and outright fakery. It fueled the whole news revolution. It left a residue of anecdote and legend which enriched the lore of American journalism. Largely because of it, newsmen of the next generation were schooled to exalt the beat above all. Pfaff's and Windust's, the Astor House bar and city rooms, resounded to tales of Bohemians who had risked life and limb for a ten-minute advantage, hoaxed the opposition, or filched a rival's copy.

The *Herald*, under the smooth direction of Frederic Hudson, pushed its men harder than any other newspaper in the country. Each correspondent was told in a printed circular, wrote Shanks, "that there was no particular merit in being 'up' with his rivals; dismissal was to be expected if he fell behind them." Hudson lopped names off the payroll as casually as he killed dated copy. Shanks noted another technique: "The successful correspondent did as he pleased; his wishes were consulted, his advice asked, his requests granted, his accounts unquestioned, his salary advanced unsolicited." A reporter who drew a query on his expense account, on the other hand, could almost hear the ax being honed, and mighty were his exertions thereafter.[1]

Albert Richardson got his hands on one *Herald* circular (no mean achievement in itself, since the directive admonished: "You will reveal its contents to no one—not even to anybody claiming to be a Herald correspondent") and sent it to Gay. Fifteen hundred words of instructions as to forwarding maps, plans, Southern papers, biographical sketches of generals, and "contraband" information for the editor's eye alone were interspersed with urgent reminders:

> In no instance, and under no circumstances, must you be beaten. . . . You will have energetic and watchful men to compete with. Eternal industry is the price of success. You must be active—very active. To be beaten is to be open to great censure. . . .
>
> Remember that your correspondence is seen by half a million persons daily and that the readers of the Herald *must* have the earliest news. . . .
>
> Again bear in mind that *the Herald must never be beaten.*[2]

[1] William F. G. Shanks in *Harper's Monthly*, Vol. 34, 519 (May 1867).
[2] Richardson to Gay, Apr. 11, 1863, enclosure. Gay Papers.

The paper's expenditures astounded competitors. "The *Herald* is fooling away money here at the rate of $3000 per month," Byington wrote Gay from Washington. "Have 13 men. 19 horses. Have taken a *House* keeps open &c., furnish toddy *ad libitum* to teamsters, loafers, etc." [3] After the relatively minor battle of Mine Run, Frank Chapman, chief of *Herald* correspondents with the Army of the Potomac, offered five hundred dollars to a sutler's clerk to carry dispatches through guerrilla-ridden country to Washington. Lavish bonuses rewarded men who scored beats. The paper regularly paid from five to fifty dollars to Washington tipsters for items.[4] In all, Hudson estimated that he spent half a million dollars in excess of the *Herald's* normal editorial budget on the war.

All manner of devious methods came into use to improve transmission. William H. Stiner, *Herald* agent at Fortress Monroe, wrote Hudson that "the reason of our getting letters to New York ahead of the other papers was that when Sawyer did write, I had the clerks at the post office rake out our envelopes from the mail arriving from the front after the mail was closed and then sent them forward by special messenger to Baltimore to be mailed there." [5] This, of course, was for routine news. For anything better, Stiner, like any other *Herald* man, would not have hesitated to charter a locomotive.

The competition between this formidable organization and the *Tribune* under Gay's alert management heightened a rivalry that was already nationally famous. The relative merits of Greeley and Bennett, the chief antagonists so far as the public was concerned, were debated in the army camps.[6] When Brigadier General Lew Wallace ordered Richardson and Knox to supervise publication of the Memphis *Argus* after the fall of that city, the idea of a *Tribune* man and a *Herald* man serving as co-editors was so novel that the story

[3] Sept. 24, 1863, Gay Papers.
[4] Byington to Gay (May 1865), *ibid.*
[5] May 30, 1864, Bennett Papers.
[6] Oliver Willcox Norton: *Army Letters 1861–1865* (Chicago: 1903), 146.

went all over the country. A running fire of persiflage, insult, and calumny let no reader forget, even at the height of the war, that the two papers were mortal enemies, most of it coming from Bennett's corner. When the *Tribune* offered subscription premiums, a characteristic bit of Heraldry aimed at "poor, ragged Greeley" ran:

> We have printed his lottery advertisement at half price; but our charity goes farther. We will give our old clothes, hats, and boots to Greeley, if he will call for them. We used to give these articles to the niggers he loved so well; but how much more appropriately can they be given to this nigger-worshipper in distress. Also—we sigh to write it—our slops, crumbs, and bones are at his service, if he is really hungry. Ah, our abolition Lazarus shall find us no niggardly Dives.[7]

This sort of thing, which Bennett relished and his editorial men excelled in writing, led George William Curtis of *Harper's Weekly* to suggest privately that Gay issue "an edict that the existence of the Herald shall never be recognized in or by the Tribune in any way." Curtis proposed to "let the worthy old Scot lie and rave as much as he likes. . . . There are some animals that . . . cannot be touched or fought, for even if you hit and kill them they make you smell dreadfully." It was sound advice, but Gay could not always persuade Greeley to ignore a *Herald* thrust, and he could never ignore Hudson's battalions in the fierce struggle for news. On several occasions *Tribune* men at the front organized pools of money and manpower with rivals for the sole purpose of shutting out the *Herald*. If the *Times* or the *World* or the *Evening Post* scored, that was too bad; if the *Herald* was first, it was calamitous.

Any ruse was fair if it foiled the foe. One day in August 1862, one of the stories in Pfaff's Cave ran later, Frank Long

[7] Issue of Dec. 4, 1861.

of the *Tribune* left General Banks's headquarters on the Rapidan with a budget of routine news. His horse broke down, and he had to swim the Rappahannock to hop the train for Washington. Aboard it a passenger asked a little too inquisitively what in the world had happened to him. Long, still wet and panting, pretended to be a sutler's clerk fleeing for his life: Banks had been stampeded, he said, and all hell had broken loose. The stranger bounded across the aisle, hand extended—Nathaniel Davidson of the New York *Herald*. Had the young man told anyone? No? Fifty dollars, then, to tell him the story, exclusively for the *Herald*. Fifty more to be locked in a room on reaching Washington for one hour, to give the *Herald* people a chance to get it into their evening edition. Long graciously accepted, gave Davidson a lurid description of the disaster, and happily pocketed the greenbacks as the hoax was consummated.

Davidson was victimized by the predatory competitive system more than once. Henry Wing of the *Tribune* boarded a transport with him at White House, Virginia, at the end of May 1864 during an interlude when the severance of the telegraph made it necessary to relay dispatches by packet. Davidson obligingly got Wing a stateroom and said he was going ashore to hustle last-minute news. Moments later Wing happened to see his treacherous rival duck behind the pilothouse of an adjoining boat just as it was casting off. The *Tribune* man jumped ashore, commandeered a fisherman's skiff, grabbed one of the lines of the departing ship as it passed, and hoisted himself aboard. Davidson greeted him with a show of innocent surprise; but Wing sauntered over to an officer. "Do you know that disreputable-looking individual?" he asked out of the corner of his mouth. "He claims to be a correspondent. Officer, take my advice—that man should be put under surveillance, not to have intercourse with anyone or leave the boat until identified and vouched for." Davidson was promptly escorted below. He managed to prove his identity hours after

Wing had consigned his news to the Baltimore mail packet at Yorktown and returned to the front.[8]

Another yarn of the same twist has a reporter entering the provost marshal's office in Lisbon, Maryland, during the confusion attending Lee's invasion on September 13, 1862, for a special pass that would get him through the picket lines after the countersign was out. The man in semi-military garb at the table said regretfully that he lacked the authority to issue passes; however, he would be happy to write a note to the provost marshal at Ellicott's Mills. Thereupon he wrote, sealed, and handed over the following:

> Provost Marshal, Ellicott's Mills:
>
> The bearer represents himself as a reporter and messenger for the New York ——. From certain suspicious circumstances, I am strongly of the opinion that he is nothing but a Baltimore secessionist spy. He wants a pass, and I have referred him to you; but I think it will be well enough to detain him until he can satisfactorily identify himself.
>
> Yours, etc.,
Timothy Jones
Captain and provost marshal

The victim delivered this document and was held in custody for twenty hours while "Captain Jones" of the opposition caught up with his correspondence.[9]

Heading for the Nashville telegraph office after the battles at Chattanooga, Shanks of the *Herald* got to Bridgeport, Tennessee, by steamboat, and there bribed the engineer of a locomotive to take him the rest of the way without allowing anyone else on board. A hundred dollars convinced the engineer,

---

[8] Henry E. Wing in the *Christian Advocate*, Apr. 2, 1914.

[9] Lorenzo L. Crounse: "The Army Correspondent," *Harper's Monthly*, Vol. 27, 632 (Oct. 1863).

but just as they pulled off, Shanks saw a man in filthy civilian clothes swing carelessly aboard the tender. Shanks clambered back to talk with him a couple of hours later, only to discover that the tramp enjoying the railroad facilities of the *Herald* was Woodward of the Cincinnati *Times*. Shanks ordered the engine stopped. Woodward said that if they threw him off, he would report the engineer for taking a bribe. They proceeded to Nashville.

Going up a Nashville street on the run, Shanks bumped into Sylvanus Cadwallader, also of the *Herald*, coming out of Donnegama's Restaurant. Cadwallader had beaten him there, and said he had already filed a story but the lines were tied up. Shanks warned him of Woodward and departed to write further details. When Woodward came along, Cadwallader greeted him warmly, took him into the restaurant, "and ordered an elaborate supper for two, composed of such dishes as would consume the most time in preparation." By the time they were done, Woodward found army headquarters closed. His dispatch could not be sent without Major General Gordon Granger's approval, and Granger indignantly refused to read it when Woodward accosted him in a theater. There was nothing to do but go to bed. Woodward left word at the St. Cloud desk that he was to be called in time for the early-morning train. Shanks, lurking in the lobby, slipped the Negro porter five dollars to erase Woodward's name from the call list.

At the telegraph office, meanwhile, the sly Cadwallader had a hot supper sent up to every employee. That got his story as far as Louisville. The operator there reported that he had too much government business to handle it. Cadwallader replied with a deposit of ten dollars at the Nashville office to keep him on duty until 4:00 a.m. Half an hour later the story was on its way, and by 3:30 the operator reported that he had finished.

That, as Cadwallader recalled it years later, was the story of the machinations behind one beat. He added that Woodward, alas, overslept, was compelled to remain another day in Nashville, and lost his job.[1]

No Bohemian could afford to ignore the multiple uses of liquor. "Mr. Merriam of the Herald goes on General Ames' boat," J. B. Chadwick of the *Tribune* informed Gay in some distress, "with his messenger and servant as well as *five gallons of whiskey*." Greeley snorted at the expense accounts Charlie Page turned in, and finally told him he was "the most expensive man the *Tribune* has ever employed." Page's answer was to the point:

> Early news is expensive news, Mr. Greeley. If I have watermelons and whiskey ready when officers come along from a fight, I get the news without asking questions.[2]

George Bowerem of the *Tribune* once explained his dismal performance to Gay. "I am unable to cultivate the intimacy of many officers of Gen. Gillmore's staff by my extreme repugnance to whiskey." In the Bohemian Brigade, that at least had the virtue of novelty.

The New York *Times*, normally very well served, suffered a humiliating defeat on the fall of Vicksburg; nothing came through until the story was too old to print. It developed that Franc Wilkie had been away from the army for a few days, leaving two assistants with full instructions. The one carrying the vital dispatches boasted to a couple of competitors at a hotel in Indianapolis between trains that he could drink either of them under the table. They took him on, exercised a little sleight of hand with their own drinks, and at train time left him in the charge of the chambermaid.[3]

Funerals—events dear to newspaper readers in the sentimental Sixties—stirred the Bohemians on occasion to heroic

[1] S. Cadwallader: *Four Years with Grant* MS, Illinois State Historical Library, Springfield, 354–6.

[2] Page: *Letters*, Introduction, v.

[3] Frazer Kirkland: *Reminiscences of the Blue and the Gray* (Chicago: 1895), 480, and Wilkie: *Pen and Powder*, 350.

labors. The Cincinnati *Times* reported that at Brigadier General Edward Baker's rites, reporters were barred, and seemingly exhausted their repertory of ruses to gain admittance to the private home where the services were held. Finally one of them bribed the janitor to shoot him down the scuttle-hole, sneaked through the larder and up to the lobby, crept behind the parson during a prayer, stole the manuscript of the funeral oration, and made a clean gataway.[4]

At the burial of Brigadier General Phil Kearney, reporters were told that they could not accompany the cortege from the church. Then they noticed that Joseph Howard, Jr., of the *Times* was missing. When the procession returned, they recognized him, solemnly draped in a regulation surplice, holding in his hands a copy of the burial service.[5]

Nothing was sacred to the New York *Herald* save the name of Mrs. Lincoln. Here Bennett's social ambitions were involved. With a thorough appreciation of this situation, Sam Wilkeson pondered the fact, as he wrote Gay, that "the amiable and accomplished wife of the President of the United States consulted the spirits about the renomination." How would it do to print this—not in the *Tribune*, of course: in the *Herald*! "Some malicious person endeavored to enrich the Herald's telegraphic columns with this item last night. Seek and ye shall find,—but keep shady."

Fortunately, this competitive stiletto did not find its mark, but there were others that did. The Chicago *Tribune*, in May 1862, startled the North with a proclamation purportedly issued by Jefferson Davis predicting the downfall of the Confederacy within three months unless the people rallied to the cause. The Chicago *Times* gleefully announced the next day that it had been perpetrated by one of its reporters.[6]

The lusty struggle between Chicago's two leading papers stirred almost as much commotion as the *Herald*-versus-*Trib-*

[4] Issue of Jan. 1, 1862.
[5] Kenward Philp: "Joseph Howard, Junior," *Brooklyn Monthly*, I, 313 (July 1869).
[6] *World*, May 16, 1862.

une feud in New York. A nine-column, four-page blanket sheet, widely known as "the Little *Tribune*" to distinguish it from Greeley's paper, Joseph Medill's fighting journal won wide readership in the Western armies and boasted the West's largest string of war correspondents: J. A. Austen; bluff, rotund A. H. Bodman ("his principle strength is in the legs," said Richardson); Irving Carson, killed at Shiloh; Llewellyn Curry; big Joseph J. K. Forrest, a passionate partisan often embroiled with the brass; Richard J. Hinton; Ralph Kaw; H. M. Smith; George P. Upton; Joseph A. Ware; and T. Herbert Whipple among them. Such a crew, plus Medill's trenchant editorials, made what was widely accounted the most influential paper west of the Atlantic cities, but, for all his vigor, Medill never eclipsed his hated rival, Wilbur F. Storey of the *Times*.

Tall and sprightly, with thick white hair, long beard, and foghorn voice, Storey met the *Tribune's* righteous Republicanism with a sheet that was savagely Copperhead, peppered with a sensationalism in the news columns which rivaled Bennett's. (It was Storey's paper a decade later which ran the famous headline over the hanging of four pentitent murderers: "JERKED TO JESUS.") "I want news," he would bellow at his correspondents, "and when there is no news, send rumors!" [7] The *Times* claimed the largest circulation in the West, a following that explains the sensation caused in June 1863 by Burnside's famous order suppressing the paper. When Lincoln revoked the order three days later, such was Medill's hatred for Storey that he quite forgot his devotion to the First Amendment, and bitterly denounced the President. Like all Copperhead sheets, the Chicago *Times* magnified Federal defeats and tended to belittle victories.

A fight scarcely less bitter developed between William W. Harding's Philadelphia *Inquirer* and Forney's *Press*, though both were administration supporters. They employed the

---

[7] Franc B. Wilkie: *Thirty-Five Years in Journalism* (Chicago: 1891), 114.

largest staffs outside of New York, about equal in size. It was
Harding's ambition "to relieve this city of its dependence on
New York for news," [8] and he did it with a lively eight-page
sheet not much larger than today's tabloid in page size, packed
with special correspondence and more war maps than any but
the New York *Herald*. In the field of illustration, the *Inquirer*
was in a class by itself; woodcuts of generals, admirals, and
political figures ran several times a week, and on rare occasions there were even spot news pictures.[9] "In times of great
excitement" the circulation came close to seventy thousand,
a goodly portion of it in the Army of the Potomac. Though
professing independence, the *Inquirer* was known among politicians as a paper that could be bought. Ben Truman, one of
its reporters, said that "it was offered $28,000 to go for Wood-
ward [for governor] in the last election in Pennsylvania but
held out too long for $30,000." [1]

Against the wily Harding and his three brothers, John W.
Forney pitted everything he had. Restless, dynamic, a fabulous
drinker and storyteller celebrated for his oyster suppers in
Washington, Forney had made his reputation in Pennsylvania
when his paper boldly broke with the Buchanan administration and attracted thousands of devout followers in the year
before the war. He was easily that state's most influential
editor, but with the outbreak of war Forney saw that that was
not enough. The metamorphosis he achieved strikingly illustrates the impact of the news revolution.

"There has been a marked change I think in the specials
from Washington," one of his editors wrote John Russell
Young in October 1861, "but we are yet far behind the *Inquirer*. That paper is sweeping ahead terribly. . . ." Forney
hired more men and kept after his editors relentlessly as *Press*
circulation boomed. "It is my only ambition to make it indeed
a great paper," he told Young, and there was no doubt in his

[8] Philadelphia *Inquirer*, Apr. 2, 1863.
[9] *E.g.*, issue of Mar. 31, 1862.
[1] W. F. G. Shanks (quoting Truman) to Hudson, Dec. 18, 1863, Bennett Papers.

mind as to what made a paper great. Put more news in, he ordered, "not sensation inventions, but real news," and again: "We must be behind no longer." Though he was secretary of the Senate and wrote, as "Occasional," a political column that was compulsory reading for most of official Washington, his letters to Young seldom mentioned political matters any longer: it was news, news, news:

> Someone ought to go to the departments regularly every day and evening. . . . Stanton says nobody from our office now goes near him. This ought to be corrected at once.

> I have been treated shamefully by Gobright. The other papers here pay him $15 a week for telegraphic dispatches—and I pay him $80! and yet we get very little more from him tho' pledged.

> Your whole force should be thrown into the news. . . . With our immense force we can make a much better newspaper than any other in Philadelphia. Look at the St. Louis Democrat, the Chicago Tribune, and Pittsburgh Commercial and remember that except for the Tribune none of these papers have the advantages we have—assuredly not the talent. What we need is some one person who will see to the display heads and someone who will stay at the office and take care that important matter is not omitted. I do not know when I have felt more despondent than in viewing all these things within the last few days.

> Why, in God's name, can we not have this space filled up with *news*? [2]

The *Press* was a beautifully printed four-page folio, and, though one would not suspect it from reading Forney's com-

[2] Selected letters, 1861–4, John Russell Young Papers.

plaints, well-edited and freighted with enough news to discomfort the saucy *Inquirer*.

Competition flared high in Cincinnati, where the *Gazette* fought the *Commercial* for dominance; in St. Louis, where it was the *Missouri Democrat* versus the *Missouri Republican*; in Boston, Washington, and Baltimore. In all these cities, papers of only slightly less circulation and influence vied with the leaders, notably the Chicago *Post* and *Evening Journal*, the Philadelphia *North American* and *Bulletin*, the Cincinnati *Press*, *Times* and *Enquirer*, the St. Louis *Union* and *Journal*, each with special correspondents of its own in the armies. These "provincial" papers, the decline of the weekly editions of the New York papers as well as their own increasing press runs testified, were coming into their own.

So great was the pressure to be first that correspondents repeatedly tripped on false reports, rumors, and misunderstandings. Vicksburg surrendered three times in the papers before yielding to Grant, and Richmond at least as often. At various times it was reported that Lee had quit, that Jefferson Davis was dead, or that peace negotiations were under way, all ascribable to what the *Tribune* piously deplored as "the criminal anxiety to feed the public with news in advance of other journals."

"Never believe the first narrative of a battle," a well-seasoned *World* reporter counseled his readers. Villard said he never credited early reports "until occurrence substantiates what they represent as facts," for in battle "overexcited imagination is always so prominently developed" they could not be trusted. Reid blamed the public for "its hot haste" in "devouring the news before it is born," but there were always plenty of Bohemians dishing it out. " 'He lies like a newspaper' has become a proverb within the last twelve months," the Cincinnati *Times* complained in 1862. Although any fair-minded critic would own that the reporters were reasonably accurate a good part of the time, the percentage was not high enough to check the spread of skepticism among readers.

"Get the News—and Get It First!"

Walt Whitman wrote his mother from Washington during the Wilderness campaign of 1864: "The fighting has been hard enough, but the papers make lots of additional items, and a good deal they just entirely make up. There are from 600 to 1000 wounded coming up here—not 6 to 8000 as the papers have it. . . . (They, the papers, are determined to make up just anything.)"[3] John Bigelow complained to Seward from Paris that "Not a steamer arrives, but furnishes a pretext for covering the Continent with lies of the most pernicious character. . . . Half of Europe never read anything about our war except the telegraphic dispatches."

In the armies, everyone from privates to generals condemned the newspapers—and read them as avidly as the folks at home. "We have learned not to swallow anything whole that we see in the papers," Sergeant Lawrence Van Alstyne noted in his diary. "If half the victories we read of were true the Rebellion wouldn't have a leg to stand on." Lieutenant Samuel E. Nichols warned his sister that "the newspaper medium through which you get your news is so elevated at a little good news that he exaggerates enormously. . . ." Captain William Lyon wrote his wife: "My dear, put not your trust in newspapers!" Major Abner Small recalled that "we would read with amazement accounts of what our own troops were supposed to have done. The fact was that a battle had been reasonably expected, and the correspondents had it all written up in advance." From Meade's headquarters, Colonel Theodore Lyman wrote his wife in May 1864: "The newspapers would be comic in their comments, were not the whole thing so tragic. More absurd statements could not be. Lee is *not* retreating: he is a brave and skillful soldier and he will fight while he has a division or a day's rations left." In another letter he dismissed the "rout" of Lee with: "Such things exist only in the N. Y. Herald." Meade himself wrote his wife a few days later: "Do not be deceived about the situation of

[3] *The Wound Dresser: Walt Whitman's Letters to His Mother . . .* (New York: 1949), 176. In this instance, Whitman was mistaken.

affairs by the foolish dispatches in the papers. Be not over-elated by reported successes, nor over-depressed by exaggerated rumors of failures."

The tendency of every skirmish to bloom in headlines as "GLORIOUS VICTORY," especially in the early months of the war, became a bitter joke in the armies. Alfred Castleman, surgeon on the Peninsula, remarked: "Even the newsboys are being infected, though I heard one this morning, wittily burlesquing the reporters by crying, 'Morning Republica-a-an. Great battle in Missouri! Federals victorious. Their troops *retreating in good order*!' Wonder if it will not awaken the reporters to a sense of their ridiculous statements." [4]

Not all of these sins were attributable to regulars in the Bohemian Brigade. "This vexation at the slam-bang, going-off-half-cocked style of reporting . . . will continue . . . until the correspondence of the press is confined to accredited pens," a *World* reporter in Nashville observed in March 1862. "As it is, the number of those who go by the title of correspondents, and who claim the courtesies and bore for the facilities of such, is quite too large to be believable. 'Their name is legion.' I have yet to fall in with a civilian, aide, or chaplain who does not 'represent' a newspaper. The consequence is— well, everybody of sense knows what the consequence is."

Reams of misinformation came from the omnipresent "reliable gentlemen," or, even more suspect, "a reliable contraband," a former slave who had wandered within the army lines only to be pumped by eager reporters about the state of affairs in Richmond and other matters beyond his conception. In April 1862, *Vanity Fair* counted nine false reports attributed to "intelligent contrabands" in the *Tribune* alone "within the past month or so."

In a toast written for a New York Press Club dinner in 1869, Mark Twain proposed that all hands raise their glasses

[4] Alfred L. Castleman: *The Army of the Potomac: Behind the Scenes, A Diary of Unwritten History* (Milwaukee: 1863), 127.

to "the journalist's truest friend—the late 'Reliable Contraband,' one whose fervent fancy wrought its miracles solely for our enrichment and renown."

> . . . When armies fled in panic . . . and the great cause seemed lost beyond all hope of succor, who was it that turned the tide of war and gave victory to the vanquished? The Reliable Contraband. . . . Who took Richmond the first time? The Reliable Contraband. Who took it *every* time until the last? The Reliable Contraband. When we needed a bloodless victory, to whom did we look to win it? The Reliable Contraband. . . . Thunder and lightning never stopped him; annihilated railroads never delayed him; the telegraph never overtook him; military secrecy never crippled his knowledge. . . .
>
> No journalist among us can lay his hand on his heart and say he ever lied with such pathos, such unction, such exquisite symmetry, such sublimity of conception and such fidelity of execution, as when he did it through and by the inspiration of this regally gifted marvel of mendacity, the lamented Reliable Contraband. Peace to his ashes! [5]

Deliberate faking was not limited to conjuring up a reliable contraband. Bohemians reported entire battles they had neither seen nor heard about from witnesses, a feat notably performed by Junius Browne of the *Tribune*, on his own admission, when he heard rumors of the Battle of Pea Ridge. It was impossible for him to reach the field in time, and, knowing that the *Herald* would score otherwise, Browne simply concocted a dispatch, with ample references to the "gallantry" of one officer he believed to have been present, the weather, of which he was reasonably sure, and charges to and fro amid the usual clap-bang—a masterpiece of sheer rhetoric sufficient to fill a

[5] *Packard's Monthly*, I, 220 (July 1869). Clemens himself was not a war correspondent.

column. Delighted Bohemians learned later that a British newspaper had reprinted it with the comment that it was a model of what war correspondence should be.[6]

"Confessions of a Reporter," a bit of humor in *Vanity Fair*, suggested that the practice was not uncommon on local staffs either. The reporter's dying words were:

> I remember having written about thirty-six columns, minion solid, of Skating Carnivals, Ice Frolics, and Scenes at Central Park without ever going nearer to 59th Street than Crook & Duff's. I have also jerked about forty columns of scenes and incidents during processions . . . without any data whatever, beyond that furnished by a welch rabbit, a Toby of half and half, and a pencil and scrap of paper.[7]

The slanting of news to conform with editorial policy accounted for a good deal more fakery on many papers, though some editors, like Sydney Gay, did make a point of insisting that their reporters had no other obligation than to tell the truth and express their own opinions honestly. ("Keep to the sober truth," he wrote, "telling facts only that you *know* to be true . . . and do not try to make your letters sensational.") As neat proof of distorting as one could find was cited by young Stephen M. Weld, a lieutenant with McClellan's army, in a letter to his father:

> I copied a report for Hendricks [Leonard A. Hendrick] of the New York Herald this afternoon which you will probably see in tomorrow morning's N.Y.H. It was amusing to hear him "get off" the usual stereotyped phrases about the enthusiasm, alacrity, etc., of the soldiers, and then hear him say "big lie," etc., to each phrase. For instance, when he wrote about there being very few stragglers, I said I didn't agree with him as I thought there were a good many. "Oh, I know it," said he, "still

[6] Wilkie: *Pen and Powder*, 126–9.
[7] Issue of Jan. 4, 1862.

I must write it so." That is just the way these newspaper
reporters do. All the stories about fine drill, discipline,
etc., we know to be untrue half the time.[8]

One custom that greatly increased the reporters' reputation
for inaccuracy, yet also served to check it, was that of constant correction at the hands of competitors. There was not
much professional camaraderie among the Bohemians on this
score. "If ever the *Herald* correspondent makes his appearance in this division again," a *Times* man on the Peninsula
wrote his paper, "he will stand in great personal risk of being gently accelerated outside the lines with a first-class application of shoe-leather. His report of the battle of Hanover
is merely a tissue of absurdities . . . and as he left that same
evening for New York, he must have written it . . . from
hearsay." Instances of this sort abounded, usually with specific
refutations.

The news revolution burst upon journalism so suddenly
that conceptions of accuracy, completeness, and objectivity
remained largely unformulated in the editorial mind. In addition, unsophisticated readers in the early years of the war
were only beginning to learn how to evaluate reports even
when they were designated as rumors or as coming from "a
reliable gentleman just from the front." Here editors became
increasingly aware of their responsibilities as the war went on,
toning down headlines to convey more of the sense of the dispatches they accompanied, interpolating remarks to correct
or clear up dubious points, and suppressing those that were
suspect. The New York *Times* led the way in this, frequently
inserting such remarks as "It is well to say that this information needs confirmation," or "This comes from the Baltimore
Exchange, which is a rebel paper and likely to be accurately
informed of rebel movements," or "This undoubtedly means"
such and such "but beyond that the dispatch does not carry

[8] *War Diary and Letters of Stephen Minot Weld* (privately printed:
1912), 71, Mar. 10, 1862. The *Herald* was passionately pro-McClellan at the
time.

us," signed, "ED., TIMES." Most major papers, under a heading at the top of the editorial page titled "The War" or "The Situation," sought to correlate and appraise all important reports received within the preceding twenty-four hours in one cogent summary—a valuable feature often drawing on the private letters of reporters and other information not printed elsewhere.

Aside from the exigencies of competition, to which Villard and others assigned the blame for inaccurate reporting, the fact is that the work paid too little to prove attractive to many able men after the glamour of war correspondence began to wane. Reporters received from fifteen to thirty-five dollars a week at a time when a good compositor could make fifty. Gay lured Sam Wilkeson back to the *Tribune* for $57.50 a week, but that was exceptional, and at that the cost of living went up so rapidly that Sam barely made expenses: "Sixteen dollars a ton for coal, $13 a cord for wood, and seventy-two cents a pound for butter, are awful facts in the domestic life of a Tribune employee, father of a grown-up daughter, of a son in college, and of a starved son in the army." Twenty-five, plus expenses, was standard for a topnotch New York reporter in the field; the "provincial" men drew less. Stedman despaired of the profession. "*It does not pay,*" he wrote his brother. "It is better to be a tradesman." Junius Browne observed that a newspaper writer could be hired "for less than you would pay a good copyist." David G. Croly, managing editor of the *World*, complained that low pay "gets the employees in the habit of trying to make up their salaries by working for weekly and other journals." Cadwallader noted another result. Some correspondents, he said, would regularly make favorable mention of officers for a price.

Miserable as salaries were, the skyrocketing cost of newsprint made it impossible for publishers to increase them. The *Tribune* made a handsome profit in 1863, but an increase of $115,000 in newsprint costs cut its earnings in 1864 to one and a half per cent of gross income.

Under the circumstances, Bohemians were inclined to submit remarkable expense accounts. Their equipment became marvelously elaborate, and servants indispensable. "No man can write and be his own hostler &c. in a campaign," W. D. Bickham explained in forwarding his account to Gay. Expense accounts often exceeded salaries. Sam Sinclair, the penny-pinching business manager of the *Tribune*, took to challenging items on reporters' accounts even after Gay had approved them. "I have had quite enough of this—quite enough," wrote James Redpath after one such incident. He had not charged "a dime . . . that is not right. I know that this is not the custom of correspondents."

An idea of the actual expenses of a conscientious reporter can be gained from an account submitted by Henry Villard:

To salary from April 14th to July 21st [1863] (since which time I have been off duty): fourteen weeks and one day	$350.00
To one ream of paper, stamps, and stamped envelopes bought in New York	5.75
Expenses to and at Pittsburgh	18.50
To Cincinnati	13.00
At " (hotel four days)	10.50
Telegrams to Bickham and reply	3.75
To Louisville via Lexington and Frankfort	7.50
At " (2½ days)	6.50
Telegram to provost marshal-General for pass and reply	3.25
Field mattress, pillow and blanket	13.00
Saddle, bridle, halter, saddle-blanket, etc.	28.00
To Nashville (RR)	8.50
At " (3 days)	7.00
To Murfreesboro	1.50
Horse	105.00
Box of wire for large topographical map sent to office	12.00

Gratuity to telegraph operators at Murfrees-
boro for Sunday service   5.00
Mess expenses from May 22 to time I left Tul-
lahoma   74.00
Forage for horse ($8.00 per mo. to QM)   14.00
Servant's wages   20.00
To Nashville from Tullahoma   3.00
At Nashville (hotel)   7.00
To Louisville   8.50

Total Credit up to July 21st $725.25
" Debit [i.e., his drafts]   545.00
Balance due $180.25[9]

If the reporters with the armies acquired a reputation for
mendacity which perhaps exceeded their just deserts, the artists of the illustrated weeklies shared it with them. McClellan,
when asked whether their pictures of field works might not be
of value to the rebels, said that they were as likely to con-
found them.[1] "The exaggerated pictures of the illustrated
papers," said an Indianapolis *Journal* writer at Vicksburg,
"usually provoke our merriment." Some, like "The Charge of
Sickles Men at Fair Oaks" in *Harper's Weekly* of June 21,
1862, showing men going into the fight at shoulder arms while
those immediately in front of them desperately wield bayonets and musket butts, roused shouts of derision in the army
camps. Only in *Harper's* was a cavalry officer able to run his
saber clean through the back of a victim so that a foot of it
protruded from his chest. *Frank Leslie's*, *Harper's*, and the
New York Illustrated News accused one another of drawing
battle scenes in their offices. The woodcutter's awl and chisel,
the artist's impressionistic pencil, tended to clothe the war in
romantic pageantry. "The uniform of the Confederate army,
as Lady Montague would say, is 'multiform,'" a Cincinnati
Gazette man observed. "Those who draw their conceptions of

[9] Henry Villard Papers.
[1] Moore: *Rebellion Record*, Vol. 3, Incident Section, 11.

the appearance of the rebel soldiery from Harper's Weekly would hardy recognize one on sight." The New-York Historical Society's executive committee soberly reported in 1864 that "the testimony of parties engaged shows that these representations, when they are not taken from photographs, are not always reliable." But the work of such men as Alf Waud, Edwin Forbes, and Henri Lovie, abundant evidence in their originals and in contemporary letters shows, was usually done on the spot.[2]

The artists were an engaging lot. Less numerous than the reporters and even younger as a group, they made common cause with them, and delighted in the conception of the Bohemian Brigade. Often reciprocity prevailed: reporters furnished descriptions for the artists' drawings; they in turn helped the newspaper boys with maps, diagrams, and information. Misrepresentation in pictures being less offensive than in words, they had fewer scrapes with officers, and were generally welcomed everywhere. Brigadier General Quincy A. Gillmore put W. T. Crane of *Leslie's* to work depicting Fort Sumter in various stages of demolition during his bombardment of it in 1863, and sent Crane's excellent work to the War Department to illustrate his official report.[3] Theodore R. Davis of *Harper's* lived with Sherman's staff during the march through Georgia, winning the admiration of Major Henry Hitchcock as "a regular Bohemian." Major General John A. Logan said after the war that Davis probably saw more of it than any other single person. Among Davis's Bohemian eccentricities, according to Franc Wilkie, was his habit of changing clothes with a dead Confederate, "in full view of the combatants, and not infrequently when under fire . . . simply for the novelty of the change."

[2] Lovie's battle drawing, Plate VIII herein—sufficiently detailed to enable Leslie's engravers to follow it more closely than many—is a case in point. See David Donald, *et al: Divided We Fought*, or the collections of original drawings in the Library of Congress, the New York Public Library, and the New-York Historical Society.

[3] *O.R.*, Ser. I, Vol. 28, Part 1, 597, 601, 603.

Artists moved about more than the reporters, not only going from theater to theater, East and West, but roaming the camps everywhere in search of material. In 1861 Henri Lovie estimated that in three months he had ridden a thousand miles on horseback. Lovie, a tall, slender Cincinnatian of rapid pencil and brush, wrote *Leslie's* after Shiloh: "Riding from 10 to 15 miles daily, through mud and underbrush, and then working until midnight by the dim light of an attenuated tallow 'dip,' are among the least of my désagrémens and sorrows. . . . I am nearly 'played out' and as soon as Pittsburg [Landing] is worked up, and Corinth settled, I must beg a furlough for rest and repairs. I am deranged about the stomach, ragged, unkempt and unshorn, and need the co-joined skill and services of the apothecary, the tailor and the barber, and above all the attentions of home. . . ." [4]

A few artists wrote as well as they drew, especially Alfred R. Waud. He was the only Bohemian on one of Custer's raids in 1864, and did *Harper's* an admirable report of it. Another piece by Waud, "A Day in Camp," reveals the same eye for detail and feeling for mood found in the best of his wash drawings. [5] To many a pair of eyes in the Army of the Potomac, this remarkably American Englishman must have seemed Bohemia incarnate, in the words of George Augustus Sala of the London *Daily Telegraph*, "blue-eyed, fair-bearded, strapping and stalwart, full of loud cheery laughs and comic songs, armed to the teeth, jack-booted, gauntleted, slouch-hatted"—a man for whom the job was, no less than for George Alfred Townsend, "my elysium, my heart."

Financially, artists were no better off than correspondents. Winslow Homer commanded the top rate from *Harper's*, sixty dollars for a double-page spread. [6] Those on space rates

---

[4] *Frank Leslie's Illustrated Newspaper*, Vol. 14, 66 (May 17, 1862).
[5] *New York Illustrated News*, Vol. 4, 387 (Oct. 21, 1861). Waud went to *Harper's Weekly* the next year.
[6] William Howe Downes: *The Life and Works of Winslow Homer* (New York: 1911), 47. Homer worked at the front intermittently for about eight months.

found life particularly precarious, since there were many weeks when an artist had nothing reproduced, and there were unfortunates like F. C. H. Bonwill of *Leslie's*, whose portfolio of the Red River campaign fell into the hands of the Confederates when Banks's army was beaten at Sabine Cross Roads, Louisiana. Salaried artists at *Leslie's* could not have felt too secure either. On one occasion before the war, the art department went unpaid for three weeks. The treasurer explained that Mr. Leslie had bought a yacht.[7]

2. THE MUSIC OF THE NEWS

LIKE virtually every British observer of record during the war, George Alfred Lawrence of the London *Morning Herald* was appalled at the blatant irresponsibility of the Union press, the strident headlines, the virulent controversies. But Lawrence, a Confederate sympathizer, could not help marvel at the volume of reporting. "Every morning the latest intelligence streams forth—fresh, strong, and rather coarsely flavoured—like new whiskey from a still."[8]

Whatever else one says about them, the Bohemians, in the course of distilling one hundred million words or so, imparted a refreshing spontaneity to their work. They were prolix, uninhibited, inclined to hyperbole, and often disarmingly personal.

Dispatches characteristically show little evidence of organization. The standard who-what-where-when lead was still at least a generation away; Bohemians pressed for time and writing under circumstances seldom conducive to contemplation set down the first words that came to mind and went on from there. Some of the worst leads imaginable resulted. "I have nothing of particular interest to report," and variations thereof, greet the reader again and again. "I omitted to

[7] Albert Bigelow Paine: *Th. Nast: His Period and His Pictures* (New York: 1904), 23.

[8] George Alfred Lawrence: *Border and Bastille* (New York: 1863?), 188.

mention" something quite important might pop up in the fifth paragraph.

Murat Halstead, editor of the Cincinnati *Commercial*, opened his account of Fredericksburg with the sentence: "There was much difficulty in the early part of last week in procuring passes from Washington to the line of operations of the Army of the Potomac, but once procured, no one seemed interested in giving them a strict examination." This might be called the "So What?" lead, introducing a strictly chronological record of the campaign for anyone with the patience to read it. Often a sense of inadequacy overwhelms the writer at the outset, as in the lead C. C. Fulton of the Baltimore *American* wrote at the beginning of McClellan's momentous Seven Days on the Peninsula:

> White House, Saturday, June 28—The events transpiring at this point, and in the army before Richmond for the past four days, have been of such varied character and thrilling interest, that I scarcely know where to commence or end the record in order to make it understandable to the general reader.

More competent hands often were moved to effective leads after major battles. The magnificently cadenced sentence with which Whitelaw Reid introduced his account of Shiloh, though it would probably die on the rim of today's copy desk, surely is one of the greatest in all the literature of journalism. After Gettysburg, too, he was effective: "Two more days of such fighting as no Northern state ever witnessed before, and victory at last! Victory for a fated army, and salvation for the imperilled country!" Even more staccato was "Nemo's" opener to the New York *Times* at the culmination of a long siege: "Heaven be praised! Port Hudson is ours!" All the modern requirements were met by a Chicago *Times* man in this businesslike lead: "The greatest victory and hardest fought battle of the rebellion was consummated on Sunday morning by the unconditional surrender of the

it to saddle my slab-sided nag as quickly as possible,
while I bundled up in the best possible manner, took a
long swig of "Old Rye," and shortly after cantered down
the road from Poolesville to this point.

That is the sort of dispatch one feels inclined to peruse further. These men were groping, more or less blindly in the beginning, for an effective means of conveying a sense of what they saw and heard to people whose knowledge of war bore no more relation to the reality of 1861 than Sir Walter Scott's. Bohemians came to see that the informal first-person-singular narrative often served them better than the style of the official reports. Smalley wrote Gay after a few months' service: "I begin to think that if one could write for print just as he writes for private eyes his letters would be more fresh and to the point." Some of the most incisive reporting appeared in dispatches that gave the reader the happy illusion that he had come upon a confidential letter to the editor. As for the embarrassing predominance of "I's," Charles Henry Webb stated the case in writing the *Times* from the Peninsula:

> In a former essay, as historiographer of this campaign, I made a signal failure. I was too modest to chronicle personal observations and experiences. The consequence was that at the end of the demonstration I had nothing to write about. That mistake shall not occur again. After all, the experience of one man is that of thousands; chronicle this faithfully, and the record of any important event, from a too confiding experience with unripe melons to the storming of Sebastopol, is before the world.

As against relying upon the reliable contraband, that principle could scarcely be challenged.

The informality engendered by the personal-observation method was inhospitable to the flowery language, stock phrases, and phony heroics that plagued an age which thought of war as romantic. Many a Bohemian still wrote of "unparalleled gallantry," of "heroes fighting like tigers," of speeches like "Stand up for the Union, boys," and "Rally to the old flag!" uttered as the speaker "breathed his last on this earthly abode," but it was mainly the stringers and acknowledged hacks who did so. Even these tended to retreat under the withering ridicule of realists like Franc Wilkie, Webb, and Charles A. Page. "It is somewhat the habit," wrote Page, "to represent a body of troops . . . as 'eager for the fray,' 'burning to be led against the foe,' or, less elegantly, 'spoiling for a fight.' Writers who indulge the use of such phrases know nothing of armies, or do not state what they know, unless indeed they know it to be false. The soldiers themselves laugh at these expressions when they see them. They are not conscious of . . . any amorous inclination toward bullets. . . ."

The Bohemians' most persistent problems were related not to covering battles, but to finding copy when the armies languished in camp. Topics of interest all around them—the soldiers' games and recreations, their conversation, their routine, their food and equipment, everyday incidents of camp life—were too often taken for granted. So it was with the work of the Medical Corps, the Signal Corps, the engineers, the telegraph men, and other specialists, though all of them were dealt with in some degree. Usually dispatches during a lull related trifling maneuvers, parades and skirmishes, speculations on movements to come, and the designs of the enemy. The main event, understandably, was ever before them.

A delightful boisterousness pervades the work of the few Bohemians who tried their hand at humor. Alf Burnett brightened life successively for readers of the Cincinnati *Press*, *Times*, and *Commercial* with correspondence rich in incident from the Army of the Cumberland. As a typical instance, he wrote of a couple of boys who were absent without leave. They encountered General Nelson on the road without his insignia and pretended not to recognize him. He ordered them back to camp, but they said they guessed they'd go down the road a piece.

"Don't you know who I am, you scoundrels?"
"No, I don't," said one of the boys; and then, looking impudently and inquiringly into his face, said: "*Why, ain't you the wagonmaster of the 17th Indiana?*"

Burnett had served as a private before turning correspondent. He was so fat, he said, that "a near-sighted drill sergeant asked me what I was doing in the ranks with a bass drum." He professed to have overheard a spectator ask: "Do you drill that fat man all at once?" The sergeant: "No, I drill him by squads." Burnett: "I could have *drilled* him, if I had had a bayonet." When he first heard the command "Order arms!" said Burnett, "I dropped my musket and taking out my notebook, began drawing an order on the Government for what arms I needed. They say I ordered a Winans steam-gun with a pair of Dahlgren howitzers for side arms! Base fabrication! My ambition never extended beyond a rifled cannon, and they know it!"

Burnett's specialty, mimicking a backwoods preacher, made him a favorite entertainer in the ranks until a chaplain ordered him out of camp. Thereupon he gave a command performance for General Rosecrans and his staff. Burnett would slip a pair of spectacles on his nose, soberly introduce himself as "Reverend Ebenezer Slabsides," and expound on the "tex" found "somewhar between the second Chronikills and the last chapter of Timothy Titus, 'And they shall gnaw on a file, and flee unto the mountains of Hepsidam, whar the lion roareth and the whangdoodle mourneth for its first-born.' " But it was his correspondence, flavored with colloquialisms, backwoods humor, descriptions of cockfights and gambling in the army, and an exuberance all his own, that won Burnett a following as "The Fat Contributor." [9]

A gentler species of humor was dispensed by Samuel Fiske, a Massachusetts chaplain, as "Dunn Browne" in the Springfield *Republican*, and the provincial press nurtured many others.

Charles Henry Webb, later a close friend of Mark Twain, imparted a light touch to the correspondence of the New York *Times*. Webb delighted in unexpected twists in the

[9] See Alf Burnett: *Incidents of the War* (Cincinnati: 1863) for his dispatches.

midst of perfectly sensible recitals, ending one dispatch: "I hope to date my next letter from Richmond," a sentiment so trite as to be painful, adding, "—not from the tobacco factories, however." His work was crowded with bits of autobiography like the following:

> I was quartered for the night, or rather halved and sandwiched, between two Colonels, who neglected to take off their boots and spurs before retiring. . . . The Colonel on my right, events proved, was subject to nightmares, which led him to mistake me for a horse, and plunge his spurs violently into my flank—a flank movement which rather took me by surprise. I woke the Colonel and explained the mistake, whereupon he apologized, and amused himself the remainder of the night by spurring an orderly who lay crosswise in the tent.

Pushing across a stream too swollen for troops to negotiate in the spring of 1862, Webb barely escaped drowning. "It is said that at such critical moments all the inexcusable deeds of one's life pass . . . in rapid review," he wrote. "It did, indeed, occur to me, while whirling in the waters, that I wrote a paragraph complimentary to Secretary Stanton when he assumed office."

Unlike many of his fellows, Webb retained his perspective in writing of the enemy. "Of the horrors and atrocities that are related as having been practiced by the Confederate troops," he wrote, "I must confess I do not believe one. These men are our countrymen. . . . Are we to believe that the lapse of a year has transformed them to fiends?" This was the resolute fair-mindedness that prompted him to give Stonewall Jackson his due.

One topic the Bohemians treated with unfailing interest: the condition and state of mind of the slaves, about whom there was boundless curiosity in the North. William G. Crippen of the Cincinnati *Times*, who turned out excellent copy under the name "Invisible," illuminated the situation in

Virginia in 1862 in a dispatch representative of scores of
others:

> Early in the afternoon we reached the plantation of
> Hamilton Fletcher, Esq. . . . The residence is a very ex-
> tensive structure, so large I first mistook it for a hotel. His
> negro quarters are all neat little brick structures.
>   . . . The slaves of Mr. F., numbering between forty
> and fifty, seemed to be enjoying general holiday, and
> were gathered in large groups at the roadside. . . . I
> rode up to one of these groups, who had just been gossip-
> ing with some cavalry, and was saluted with—
>   "How is you, massa? We is mighty glad to see you,
> massa."
>   "Did any national troops encamp here last night?"
>   "Yes, massa."
>   "How many?"
>   "The Lor' only knows dey were so many."
>   "How did they conduct themselves?"
>   "Mity well, mity well, massa. Dey is the kind of sogers
> for ole Virginia."
>   "Did you know they were Yankees?"
>   "Guess um did," replied a fat old aunty, "and dey is
> gemmen ebry one ob dem. De white folks tell us dat
> when de Yankees come dey steal our close, un pull de
> wool out, un cut off de hans an de feet, an kill all de
> niggers."
>   At that they all burst into a hearty laugh, and one chap
> whose dress indicated he is a house servant, said—"An
> dey is gemmen 'long side dem dare nasty old Secesh,"
> and they all took another laugh. . . .
>   "Do you think the Secesh can whip the Yankees?" I
> asked.
>   At that they burst into a roar of laughter and one be-
> coming the spokesman for the party as the laugh sub-
> sided, said with a vigorous and comical shake of the head:

"Golly, nebber, master, nebber. When all dem Yankees gets down Souf, won't dem Secesh get out of dey way?" and then followed another merry shout.

This little incident illustrates all I have seen of the contraband business during the present visit to Virginia. The power of the master over the slave is temporarily lost, and may be lost forever.

Of the quality of Civil War correspondence, an honest appraisal must own that much of it is hackneyed, hastily conceived, turgidly written, deficient in clarity and perception. The judgment holds whether one goes by modern standards or accepts the prevailing view of the time. Writing in the *Nation* in 1865, Villard remarked that the war produced no great reporter, and that war correspondence had deteriorated steadily from 1862 on.[1] The editor of *The Galaxy* considered it one of "the woes of the rebellion." Anthony Trollope, writing in 1862, concluded that American newspapers were simply unreadable. Charles Nordhoff, the brilliant young managing editor of the *Evening Post*, penned an acid indictment in *Harper's Monthly* for June 1863, after visiting Port Royal:

How little—how very little, we who stay at home know of the war or of our soldiers! . . . The men who have written its history in the daily journals have been almost without exception . . . reporters in the lowest and poorest sense of the term, smart enough, perhaps, at hunting up "news," having, indeed, when in search of an "item," a nose as acute as the truffle dog's who smells out champignons in the oak forests of France; and like those wretched little curs they knew nothing, saw nothing, and smelt but one thing; their peculiar and abnormal training gave them only a nose for news. . . .

They are able to tell us—and the enemy—sometimes the

[1] "Army Correspondence: Its History," *The Nation*, I, 114, 116 (July 27, 1865).

general's plan before it is yet fully formed; they can write for us tedious columns of what we don't want to know; but as for giving us an idea of the war, of what qualities it has developed in American citizens, of what kind of men our soldiers are, how they bear their trials, what they think, what they talk of, what they aim to do, what they really do—scarcely one of them has done this, so far as I know.

Here, for instance, as I write, is this attack on Fort Sumter, one of the greatest events in the history of modern warfare. There have been some ambitious descriptions of it, but none satisfactory to the man who wants to know not only the facts, but the spirit of it. The *Tribune's* correspondent [Villard] wrote from on board the *Ironsides*, and his account is the only one worth reading. . . . It has the smoke of battle about it. . . . In other accounts I have seen you read only of smoke and clapbang, and lay the paper down as wise as when you took it up. . . . Even the *Tribune* writer, who clearly has the spirit and ability, is content with his one letter.

Walt Whitman expressed a similar feeling when he wrote that "the real war will never get in the books. . . . The actual soldier of 1861-5, North and South, with all his ways, his incredible dauntlessness, habits, practices, tastes, language, his fierce friendship, his appetite, rankness, his superb strength and animality, lawless gait, and a hundred unnamed lights and shades of camp, I say, will never be written." [2]

There is no denying that the competitive scramble, the perpetual search for a peg on which to hang the latest rumor, focused too much attention on headquarters. Hearing that General Rosecrans had left camp to visit Washington, a soldier in the Army of the Cumberland wrote in his diary: "If it be true, he has flanked the newspapermen by a wonderful burst of strategy. He must have gone through disguised as an old

[2] Walt Whitman: *Specimen Days in America* (London: 1906 edition), 122.

woman— . . . otherwise these newspaper pickets would have arrested and put him in the papers forthwith. They are more vigilant than the rebels and terribly intent upon finding some-body to talk about, to laud to the skies, or abuse in the most fearful manner, for they seldom do things by halves, unless it be telling the truth."

Such men seldom caught the sidelights of war, the little details that make the soldier come to life, the everyday oc-currences in camp, the behavior of individual Billy Yanks in battle, sidelights that might have gone to fill Nordhoff's large order, demonstrating "what kind of men our soldiers are." One can imagine, for example, what a reporter with a sense of pathos might have done with an incident that occurred not far from a *Herald* reporter at Shiloh. It lives only in a Colo-nel's diary:

After waiting for some time I was ordered to push for-ward to a certain point, and knowing a short route by an old road I led the regiment by the flank, the double files filling it. We soon met a wounded Buckeye, using a stout stick he had picked up in the woods for a crutch. He looked like an overgrown lad of 18, but he held one leg bent at the knee while the foot dangled about and dripped blood from his toes. Hobbling out of our way he leaned against a sapling, shifted a bloody sock to his left hand, and with his red hand gave me the military salute. It touched me as no courtesy has ever done, and I returned it with my sabre as though I was passing in the presence of a reviewing officer. "Throw that bloody sock away, comrade, the Surgeon will take that foot off and you won't need but one sock," I said. "Why, Colonel," he re-plied in a cheery tone, "it will fit the other foot." "Don't it hurt you?" I asked. "Not any worse than it ought to, Colonel," he replied. . . . The men gave him a volley of jocular compliments as they passed.[3]

[3] Camm diary, *op. cit.* (*Journal of the Illinois State Historical Society*, Vol. 18), 854, 855. Camm saw the *Herald* man a few moments later.

Having dealt with the Bohemians' deficiencies, one must enter a caveat. The men who sprang to the ramparts in the news revolution had no opportunity to prepare themselves, no precedents to guide them, no instructors; he who looks to them for literature might as reasonably expect statesmanship of the Jacobins. The strictures of their critics go too far.

If the journalism of a period, like its literature, be judged by the best of it rather than by total output, the Bohemian Brigade appears in quite another light. Certainly Whitelaw Reid, Lorenzo Crounse, Franc Wilkie, William Conant Church, Charles Carleton Coffin, Sam Wilkeson, George Smalley, Henry Villard, Charles Henry Webb, Edmund Clarence Stedman, Thomas W. Knox, Uriah Painter, Joseph B. McCullagh, William G. Crippen, W. S. Furay, Albert D. Richardson, and John Russell Young, among those already mentioned, together with John E. Hayes of the *Tribune*, George Ward Nichols of the *Evening Post*, Jerome B. Stillson of the *World*, Ben C. Truman of the *Times*, and, among the unidentified, "Keynote" of the *World*, were men of energy, style, and perception. If they lacked the magic touch, all of them wrote well enough to bring a sense of participation in the war to their readers, and at times they did it superbly. Through the reprint circuit the work of each, in varying degree, elevated standards of reporting the country over.

Three reporters deserve special mention. Hill may have thought Charles A. Page unequal to the ceremonies at Gettysburg, yet Page's *Tribune* work leaves a memorable impression. A small, rather handsome man of delicate features, keen eyes set deep, full eyebrows, mustache blending into a plumed beard, he mingled easily with officers and men in the ranks and developed a knack for turning out highly readable copy about anything from sutlers to the Sanitary Commission. He earned a solid reputation for accuracy. "If Page says that, it is so," was a remark of Greeley's which Dana simply paraphrased later, according to James Gilmore, in coining the motto: "If

you see it in the *Sun*, it is so." [4] Born in Lee County, Illinois,
the son of a farmer from New Hampshire, Page graduated
from Cornell College at Mt. Vernon, Iowa, worked a couple
of years on a country weekly, and came East for the first time
for Lincoln's inauguration. Page hoped to land the post-
mastership at Mt. Vernon; instead he got a $1,400-a-year
clerkship in the Treasury Department, where Adams Hill
discovered him for the *Tribune*.

"Read Page's '(C.A.P.)' letters to Tribune," Captain Oliver
Wendell Holmes, Jr., scribbled to his parents from Grant's
army in 1864, "—they are good—though he is a nasty toady-
ing snob—like most correspondents." [5] Others found Page personable enough; but whatever he was like in person (and
Holmes reflected the typical hostility of staff officers toward
correspondents), the man wrote in a quiet, offhand style,
taking the reader nonchalantly by the hand and showing him
the many facets of army life in a manner altogether charming. Few Bohemians were so closely attuned to their audience,
and none more consistently interesting.

Hardly gifted in understatement, but a straight narrator of
events, George Alfred Townsend returned from a year of
kicking about in Europe in 1864 to become perhaps the best-
known correspondent of all for the *World*. "Your G. A.
Townsend is a great correspondent," a reader wrote to Editor
Marble as evidence that some bylines were beginning to make
an impression. "His letters are the best out." [6] More impressive
was the compliment ascribed to Lincoln when he was asked if
he had visited a place. "No, it is not necessary for me to go
there," the President was reported to have said. "George Alfred Townsend has been there." [7]

"A beardless youth," as he described himself, "with that

[4] Page: *Letters*, Introduction, v.
[5] Mark de Wolfe Howe, ed.: *Touched With Fire: Civil War Letters
of Oliver Wendell Holmes, Jr.* (Cambridge, Massachusetts: 1946), 149.
[6] May 2, 1865, Marble Papers.
[7] Ellis Paxon Oberholtzer: *Jay Cooke: Financier of the Civil War*
(Philadelphia: 1907), II, 347.

unfortunate brownness of locks and lightness of eyes for which one is challenged at the polls as a minor up to his fortieth birthday," Townsend had read novels surreptitiously under his desk at the Philadelphia *Press* office and yearned for the Bohemian life almost from childhood. He worked best under pressure: his fast-moving account of the hunting down of John Wilkes Booth deserves its niche in *A Treasury of Great Reporting*. Thoroughness, clarity, and simplicity of narration were his fortes, yet he wrote rapidly. Townsend once turned out a column and a half of leaded nonpareil an hour, which was about as fast as the *World* composing room could set it.[8] Unlike some of his contemporaries, he cared nothing for his paper's politics; the world to him, as to a *Herald* agent he described, was a reporter's district.

Less noted, but perhaps more worthy of challenging Villard's assertion that the war produced no great reporter, was a Bohemian of poetic turn of mind, Benjamin Franklin Taylor of the Chicago *Evening Journal*. Probably few who saw him in the army camps around Chattanooga gave him a second look after he arrived there in the fall of 1863. Those who did saw a thickset, smooth-shaven gentleman of forty-four, of medium height and quiet manner. Taylor had been literary editor of the *Evening Journal* for more than a decade, prior to which he had taught school in Massachusetts and Michigan. Nothing about him suggested the bee-in-hollyhock brashness of an army reporter. Ben Taylor was excruciatingly shy. He had rather risk gunfire than ask questions; in the army he roamed far and wide and wrote absorbingly of what he learned, more as an essayist than in the topical style of the reporter.

Effusive at times, at others unabashedly sentimental, Taylor yet managed to write of the war with more power, more subtlety and depth of understanding than any of his colleagues, or, for that matter, than most who have tried it since. His battle dispatches, "dim and imperfect pictures taken by

[8] Ruthanna Hindes: *George Alfred Townsend* (Wilmington, Delaware: 1946), 21, quoting *World* of Nov. 6, 1899.

the flash of great guns," are as uneven as his figure suggests, and so with his essays on camp life. Taylor indulged in flights of fancy; the flag was ever streaming forth in his battle prose; many were his allusions to the deity, his tributes to "our brave lads." Yet there is implicit in all his work a personal sense of the terrible grandeur of the war, illuminated again and again by imagery. The poet in him kept the whole drama in mind. His Missionary Ridge and Lookout Mountain have a rolling majesty about them that honors the victories they describe. The very landscape seems to have inspired him, looking "as if the Titans had plowed and forgotten to harrow it."

The "print of War's fingers" appeared in Taylor's asides to his reader: "It may not seem so to you, but I have never felt so heavy a sense of loneliness as when I have seen broad forests of tall corn, the blackened stalks two years old, springing out of earth fairly tufted and matted over, the rusted plow careened in one corner, a wreck on a lee shore. . . ." Looking out the train window with him on the way to Chattanooga, you see "The woods begin to stand up, here and there, like people in a great congregation, as if the spurs of the Cumberland were thrust in the flanks of creation, and it was rising up to get out of the way of the rowels. . . . A tunnel, half a mile in length, yawns to swallow us with a throat black as a wolf's mouth. Above it towers the wooded crown, hundreds of feet; close at our right the world seems to make a mis-step and tumble into a deep ravine. . . . You run like a mouse along a narrow shelf high up the rocky wall, the bewildered Tennessee far beneath, winding this way and that to escape from the enchanted mountains. It flashes out upon you here, curved like a scimitar; it ties the hills up there with lovely knots of broad ribbon." And finally you come to Chattanooga, topographically "a town gone to pieces in a heavy sea." [9]

[9] Benjamin F. Taylor: *Mission Ridge and Lookout Mountain with Pictures of Life in Camp and Field* (New York: 1872), 17–25. Contains selections from Taylor's dispatches.

Here the Army of the Cumberland, stunned by Bragg at Chickamauga six weeks before, faced "the grim crescent of the enemy"—a foe apparently impregnable in ridges commanding the town. Taylor puts the reader there today:

> At 10 o'clock this morning, you were standing in front of Colonel Sherman's headquarters, and as you looked eastward you saw, without a glass, a column of the enemy moving slowly up the Ridge and a wagon-train creeping after it. You took a glass and held the fellows as if by the button-hole. Just then a roar from Fort Wood, close above you, and a long rushing, shivering cry . . . the shell crosses the intervals, strikes the Ridge at the heels of the lazy column, and its rate of motion is wonderfully accelerated. No steed was ever more obedient to the touch of the rowels. Again the Rodman speaks, and down comes the carriage of an angry gun for kindling wood. It can toss its compliments as lightly over to Mission Ridge as you can toss an apple over the orchard fence. . . . There goes Fort Wood again. Listen a few beats of the pulse, and yonder, well up the side of the Ridge, lies a fleece of smoke that was not there an instant ago, and here—*bomb*—comes the sound of the burning missile.

Taylor's subsequent account of how Bragg's "terrible arc of iron has been bent back upon itself and crushed like a buzzard's egg" carries a sense of the wrath of an army besieged for weeks, and its sudden, awesome venting: Hooker's men, clawing up Lookout's crags until hidden in clouds and mist; Thomas's, miraculously scaling Missionary Ridge without orders; Sherman's, driving Bragg with savage abandon, together scoring, under Grant, one of the few resounding victories of the war.

There were plenty of other reporters there and the Chicago *Journal* was not widely circulated, but the scissor syndicate brought Taylor a national audience soon after his Missionary

Ridge appeared. Nicolay and Hay, swamped with more papers than they could give a moment to, scanned the *Journal* for Taylor's work.[1] Nor did it escape Sam Wilkeson. "I have long had my eye on this man Taylor for the Tribune," he wrote Gay, forwarding a clipping. "In this vein, he is the best off-hand newspaper artist in the United States. You must some day get him." Taylor, alas, fell afoul of General Sherman in May 1864 for revealing that "our lines now extend from Nashville to Huntsville." Sherman ordered his arrest and trial as a spy.[2] Taylor departed, amid many tributes in the press, before Sherman could act. Later he distinguished himself reporting Early's whirlwind campaign against Washington.

In coming to flower relatively late in the war, the work of Page, Townsend, and Taylor (and of a fourth to be considered later) confirms the impression of one who has worked in the files that, Villard to the contrary, the quality of correspondence improved as it went along. The music of the news, discordant and hesitant at first, came singing over the wires more confidently now, the words tumbling after one another in a thousand times ten thousand staccato dots and dashes, now aimlessly, now importantly, and sometimes in those subtle sequences that move the hearts of men.

[1] Carpenter: *Six Months at the White House*, 154.
[2] *Rebellion Record*, Vol. 11, 29.

☼ CHAPTER XI ☼

Of U. S. Grant

1. RISING STAR

AFTER A comparatively dull winter, Washington's press row awoke to a buzz of anticipation on the morning of March 8, 1864. The hero of Fort Donelson, Shiloh, Vicksburg, and Chattanooga was coming to town to accept from the President the commission of lieutenant general, never before conferred as a permanent rank, and with it the supreme command. Simon P. Hanscom of the Washington *National Republican* hunted up that knowledgeable army correspondent, Lorenzo Crounse. Hanscom wanted to waylay General Grant at the station, but he did not know him by sight. Crounse was no help. Never having served in the West, he had no idea of Grant's appearance save that he was short, bearded, and wore a nondescript uniform. Hanscom and Crounse hurried over to Mathew Brady's studio. The quizzical little photographer shook his head; the only picture of Grant he could find showed the General with his hat hiding most of his face. The correspondents talked Brady into accompanying them to the station, where they found other reporters in the same dilemma. When the train arrived, Brady saved the day, recognizing Grant by the lines of his mouth. That was how the press identified the man of the hour.[1]

[1] Roy Meredith: *Mr. Lincoln's Camera Man* (New York: 1946), 162.

The Bohemian Brigade had certain preconceptions, rooted in their epoch, of what a military hero should be like. He might be a glamorous figure already well known to the public, like Frémont; a dashing young commander with a penchant for parades and a touch of the inscrutable about him, like McClellan; a man whose braided physique suggested heroics on a Napoleonic scale, like Hooker; a man of electric personality, like Sherman: these were images easily transmitted in the romantic tradition. Grant did not fit.

The reporters who met him at the station, however, probably were not disappointed: anyone who had followed Ulysses on his odyssey through the public prints knew just about what to expect.

Tom Knox, surveying the squat, quiet man gazing out the port of a river steamer more than two years before, could only tell *Herald* readers: "The General is decidedly unmartial in appearance, and would be the last man among the twenty occupants of the cabin who would be selected as the superior officer of all." The Philadelphia *Inquirer*, *Harper's Weekly*, *Frank Leslie's*, and the *New York Illustrated News* repeatedly confused him with a beef-contractor in a jaunty campaign hat named William Grant, whose picture represented the public's idea of Ulysses Grant for more than a year before the General or anyone else bothered to correct them.[2] At Chattanooga, a huckster did a lively business selling pictures of Grant at fifty cents apiece until a reporter pointed out that they were of someone else.[3] These things happened because the true Grant, as "Keynote" of the *World* had it, was "a man one would take for a country merchant or village lawyer," indistinguishable from ten thousand other midland soldiers. The Boston *Journal's* Coffin, the first time he met the General, mistook him for an orderly.[4]

---

[2] Philadelphia *Inquirer*, Mar. 1, 1862; *Harper's Weekly*, June 6, 1863, *New York Illustrated News*, Mar. 22, 1862, Apr. 26, 1862, June 7, 1863 (cover); *Frank Leslie's*, June 13, 1863.

[3] Cadwallader MS: *Four Years with Grant*, 346.

[4] Charles C. Coffin: *Four Years of Fighting* (Boston: 1866), 46.

"Grant," Junius Browne wrote briskly in introducing him to *Tribune* readers, "is about 45 years of age, sandy complexion, reddish beard, medium height, pleasant twinkling eyes, and he weighs about 170. He smokes continually." That was that: Browne moved on to more engrossing matters.

Some Bohemians found Grant's reticence overwhelming. A *World* reporter called him "The Unpronounceable Man." Franc Wilkie, assigned to headquarters at Cairo early in 1862, maneuvered an introduction: "Grant shook my hand heartily, pulled on the stump of an immense cigar, and said nothing." Wilkie remained with Grant nearly two years, picked up his mail at headquarters, saw the General every day. "He would always look at me with his bright brown eyes, but there was never a word." John Swinton, military editor of the *Times*, interviewed Grant in 1862 at the Astor House. Swinton elicited a few monosyllables on the war and the weather, tried other questions without avail, cleared his throat, shifted from foot to foot, and finally turned and fled.[5]

Yet hints of the man's personality, stubborn, forthright, unassuming, plain-spoken, imperturbable, emerged again and again from dispatches these men wrote with no inkling of his genius. Through them the public saw him at Fort Donelson, a chunky figure in dishabille, absently clenching a cigar which had gone out, writing Buckner the terms that seemed a summation of character. It heard him at Shiloh when a quartermaster warned that he could transport no more than ten thousand to safety across the river: "Well, if we are defeated, you will be able to carry all that are left." It glimpsed him at Vicksburg on the day of the big assault through the eyes of Joe McCullagh: Grant comfortably slouched in his saddle, whittling a piece of wood. When the attack failed, McCullagh heard him say: "We'll have to dig our way in," in the tone of a man announcing that it was bedtime.[6] Enough of plain U. S. Grant seeped

[5] John Swinton: "Two Remarkable Interviews," *The Independent*, Vol. 53, 1187 (May 23, 1901).

[6] *Missouri Historical Review, op. cit.,* Vol. 25, 247.

through in a thousand such sidelights to make people feel that they knew him, understood him, a man who would be right at home with any of them. From newspaper readers Grant received, in the days after Donelson, a total of ten thousand cigars.[7]

These stolid qualities lacked the stuff of which heroes were made, and the Bohemians, considering always that they had a solemn responsibility to judge military talent, thought their suspicions were confirmed at Shiloh. Grant was accused, with some justice, of having failed to entrench and post pickets adequately to avert surprise. Here was evidence that the ex-tanner from Galena was no more than he seemed. Murat Halstead, editor of the Cincinnati *Commercial*, exaggerated the prevailing opinion among newsmen when he wrote Secretary Chase that Grant was "a jackass in the original package," but not by much. Knox informed Bennett: "It would be a tragedy to the service (in my humble opinion) to have Grant entrusted with any great command as I think he has well demonstrated heretofore."[8] Abram Mitchell wrote the *Times* that Grant's "drunkenness or incompetency or both" had cost eight thousand Union lives at Shiloh. "Regarding Grant," reported a Boston *Traveller* man after such reports got around, "I find a universal dislike as a leader of men." "Keynote," reporting in the *World* that the soldiers were dubbing him Ulysses Surprise Grant, termed his report of Shiloh "an imbecility which has no parallel in this war," which was going some. Almost alone among them at the time, Henry Villard put his finger on one admirable quality: Grant, he wrote the *Tribune*, "is free of the wretched jealousies which so often disgrace the army, and never speaks ungenerously or unkindly of his brother officers."[9]

Grant was shaken by these newspaper assaults. Richardson and Knox were members of his mess while the criticism

[7] Horace Porter: *Campaigning with Grant* (New York: 1897), 381.
[8] Unsigned, July 22, 1862, Bennett Papers.
[9] Issue of May 5, 1862.

was at its height. He alluded to it only once, Richardson recalled; but then it was to blurt out that he had had "too much." He said he had a good mind to go to some remote outpost in New Mexico where the newspapers would leave him in peace.[1]

For all that, in his relations with reporters Grant showed such common sense as to make him almost unique. Unlike his friend Sherman, Grant launched no campaign against the Bohemians: reporters were simply to be accepted as concomitants of modern war, no matter if the professors at West Point and the administration in Washington had neglected to explain how to cope with them. "General Grant informs us correspondents that he will willingly facilitate us in obtaining all proper information," Junius Browne wrote Gay in 1862, adding dolefully that Grant was "not very communicative."[2]

On the problem of censorship, so hopelessly tortured by others, Grant said simply: "You yourself must determine what is proper to send. I trust your discretion and your honor to give no information of value to the enemy." With rare exceptions, it worked. At Cairo he once overheard that anxious mother hen who was his chief of staff, Colonel John A. Rawlins, cackling to a Chicago *Times* man that his story could not be sent. "Is the story true?" "Yes," said the reporter. "Very well, then," said Grant, "let it go."[3]

As to criticism, reporters might abuse him at will, though in one instance a Cincinnati man who had berated him up and down was summoned to his tent. "Your paper has been very unjust to me," Grant remarked, "but time will make it all right. I want to be judged only by my own acts." High-strung Meade, who winced at every barb, wrote his wife in 1864: "Grant is very phlegmatic, and holds in great contempt newspaper criticism, and thinks, as long as a man is sustained by

[1] Richardson: *Grant*, 253.
[2] Dated Nov. 25, 1862, Gay Papers.
[3] Richardson: *Grant*, 203.

his own conscience, his superiors, and the government, it is not worth his while to trouble himself about the newspapers." [4] Scarcely any of his contemporaries could have said that. It was an argument Grant used later to talk Meade out of resigning.

While he deprecated their importance, Grant read the newspapers assiduously. He called the *Herald*, ever trying to guess his next move, his "organ"—perhaps a wry reference to the fact that the paper launched a Grant-for-President boom in the fall of 1863. "Now, let me see what my organ has to say," he would remark with a kind of amiable sarcasm when it reached camp, "and then I can tell better what I'm going to do." [5] Finley Anderson was immensely flattered, following his release from imprisonment in Texas, to learn that Grant had read all about his tribulations in the *Herald*.[6] Grant thought so well of a piece George F. Williams of the *Times* had written on Sheridan's operations that he invited the reporter to supper.

Grant sustained subordinates who punished correspondents, but he seldom went beyond a reprimand on his own account— a record, considering the tactics of other commanders, that suggests remarkable forbearance. At one time or another, Bohemians roused the wrath of just about every officer with a star on his shoulder.

Major General Benjamin F. Butler went Sherman one better by ordering that Augustus Cazaran of the Boston *Traveller* be shackled with ball and chain and put to work in an exposed sector of the trenches for sixty days.[7] Butler clapped Henry Norman Hudson, chaplain, Shakespearean scholar, and *Evening Post* correspondent, into the bull pen with Confederate prisoners ("a most lousy, lewd, profane and ribald set," Hudson complained) for something he had written, and later

---

[4] *Meade Letters*, II, 238.
[5] Porter: *With Grant*, 168.
[6] Anderson to Hudson, Mar. 31, 1864, Bennett Papers.
[7] *Private and Official Correspondence of Gen. Benjamin F. Butler* (Norwich, Massachusetts: 1917), V, 702.

transferred him to a former horse enclosure which had not since been cleaned, holding him for fifty-three days without preferring charges.[8] Grant finally made Butler release him. Perhaps the most humiliating punishment of all was ordered by Meade when Edward Crapsey of the Philadelphia *Inquirer* hinted that Meade had favored a retreat after the Battle of the Wilderness. John R. Adams, chaplain of the Fifth Maine, wrote his wife of Crapsey's fate:

> He was placed on horseback, and an officer bearing a flag, a trumpeter, and six or eight orderlies rode with him through all the different corps; an occasional blast was given to attract attention, and lo! all eyes were turned to witness the spectacle. The correspondent was labelled, "Libeler of the Press." A sorry day for him.[9]

As Crapsey passed one sector of the line, Private Frank Wilkeson remembered, he was "howled at, and the wish to tear him limb from limb and strew him over the ground was fiercely expressed." Another recalled that the parading went on for hours, the victim "tied backwards to the sorriest mule available." Grant had been present when Meade wrote the order, remarking only that Crapsey came from a good family in Cincinnati. "Drumming out of camp" was a proceeding usually reserved for thieves. Meade assured his wife that it had roused "the delight of the whole army, for the race of newspaper correspondents is universally despised by the soldiers." But three months later the undaunted reporter applied to him for a pass, and Meade, his temper cooled, concluded to send him one without comment.[1]

Grant suffered greater provocation than was offered in any of these instances. On the night of May 5, 1864, when the Wilderness campaign hung in the balance, Meade and his

8 Henry N. Hudson: *General Butler's Campaign on the Hudson* (New York: 1864). Pamphlet, New York Public Library.

9 Emily Adams Bancroft, ed.: *Memorial and Letters of Rev. John Adams* (Cambridge, Massachusetts: 1890), 153.

1 *Meade Letters*, II, 203, 228.

staff came over to Grant's headquarters for consultation, gathering around a campfire a few yards in front of Grant's tent. Presently Colonel T. S. Bowers, of Grant's staff, thought he saw a shadow move behind a stump a few feet from them. Bowers whispered to Colonel W. R. Rowley. Rowley whirled and caught a tall, lank form crouching there listening: William Swinton of the New York *Times*. Brought before Grant, Swinton could only sputter crimson-faced excuses. Sherman would probably have shot the eavesdropper; Grant let him off with a reprimand.[2] A few weeks later Burnside, outraged at something Swinton wrote about his corps, asked Meade "that this man immediately receive the justice which was so justly meted out to another libeller of the press a day or two since, or that I be allowed to arrest and punish him myself." [3] Grant got the impression that Burnside intended to shoot the reporter, and immediately ordered Swinton's expulsion instead.

Warren P. Isham, brilliant, erratic correspondent of the Chicago *Times*, was the only newspaperman of record to suffer from Grant's personal displeasure. A few Copperhead reporters would stop at nothing, and Isham was one of them. Grant had cautioned him on his cock-and-bull yarns from Memphis, but Isham remembered Editor Storey's injunction, "If there is no news, send rumors!" He set the whole North to laughing, said Franc Wilkie, with a story that the Federal commander in Memphis had fled before Forrest's cavalry raiders "in but a single garment," with embellishments in kind. Then on August 8, 1862, Grant read a Chicago *Times* dispatch under the familiar Memphis dateline about a formidable fleet of rebel ironclads at Pensacola, a fabrication from beginning to end. Thereupon he directed Sherman to convene a court-martial, much to that officer's delight, and Isham landed in Alton Penitentiary "for the duration of the war." Grant let him off three months later.[4]

[2] *Personal Memoirs of U. S. Grant* (New York: 1885), II, 144, 145.
[3] *O.R.*, Ser. I, Vol. 36, Part 3, 751. The "libeller" was Crapsey.
[4] Wilkie: *Thirty-Five Years*, 95; Cadwallader MS, 24.

While the General was perfectly approachable, joked with correspondents, and now and again was a silent kibitzer at their whist games, few of them knew him well. But one reporter, the man whom Storey sent to plead for Isham's release, gradually cultivated a relationship with Grant which is unmatched in the annals of the Bohemian Brigade.

Sylvanus Cadwallader, former city editor of the Milwaukee *Daily News*, appeared to Franc Wilkie as "a slender man with dark mysterious eyes, a swarthy complexion, and a face somewhat wrinkled, who moved incessantly about in a nervous, uneasy manner." Others in camp looked at Cadwallader in disbelief when he arrived in August 1862. He wore a round-topped coonskin cap. As reticent as Grant himself, he "was not at all disposed to be companionable with the other newspaper men or anybody else." Wilkie thought him "furtive." [5] In time he would outdistance the best of them.

Galloping through enemy country to Memphis with news of Van Dorn's raid on Holly Springs, Mississippi, in December 1862, Cadwallader fell into the hands of a Confederate cavalry detachment, talked his way free after liberal applications of cigars and some whisky he produced from a canteen slung beneath his saddlebags, and pushed on to score a beat that Richardson, who disliked him, considered "a tall feather in his cap." Again, after witnessing Grant's initial repulse at Vicksburg, Cadwallader persuaded three Negroes to steal a skiff, took turns with them rowing seventy-five miles downstream without a stop, reached Eagle's Bend just as the mail boat was leaving, and racked up a two-day exclusive for the Chicago *Times*.[6]

Cadwallader feared that his first interview with Grant would prove his last. He had described in bitter terms the plundering carried on by Federal troops during an operation at La Grange in November 1862—just the story for a paper that deprecated

[5] Wilkie: *Pen and Powder*, 203.
[6] Richardson: *Grant*, 283, 289.

everything about the war. Passing Grant's tent one night, he was beckoned in. Grant silently leafed through a mass of papers on his table, found the Chicago *Times*, and asked him who wrote the piece.

"I did."

"Well—sit down," said Grant. "I simply want to say to you that if you always stick as close to the truth as you have here, we shall have no quarrel. The troops did behave shamefully."

Grant went on to expound his censorship policy. Somehow this lone wolf with the grotesque fur cap, this man who owned up to his story without apology, struck Grant's fancy. In January, when Grant established headquarters aboard the *Magnolia*, all civilians were excluded—except Cadwallader. A month later Major General S. A. Hurlbut suppressed circulation of the Chicago *Times* in Memphis; Cadwallader remonstrated, and Grant promptly revoked the order.

Silent Sylvanus, then, was already a favorite of Grant's when a series of incidents which, as both of them knew well enough, would have fairly rocked the country had they appeared in print in the midst of the Vicksburg campaign cemented their relationship for good. The question whether Grant was a drinker kept cropping up in the press; he was known to have drunk himself out of the army before the war, but now it was widely averred that he had sworn off. Colonel Rawlins, in fact, had exacted a pledge from him.

Cadwallader was sharing a tent with Colonel William Duff, a staff officer, on the night of May 12, 1863, when Grant came in at midnight to ask Duff for a drink. Duff produced his canteen. Grant was sitting on the edge of Duff's cot, pouring the whisky into a tin army cup, when he looked up in some surprise to see Cadwallader. No mention of it was made. Cadwallader did not need to be told that from then on he could have whatever he wanted. At Champion's Hill three days later, it was Cadwallader who told Grant that the enemy was driving back his advanced elements. "I guess not," said Grant.

The reporter insisted: "The men are pouring back pell-mell." "Did you see it?" "Yes." Grant hurried off a dispatch to Mc-Pherson, beginning: "Cadwallader says . . ."—tacit recognition of his standing. The Albany *Argus* noted in some surprise that for three weeks the whole country had been dependent on the Chicago *Times* for news of Grant's campaign. Cadwallader, it seems, was availing himself of Grant's official couriers.[7]

On June 6, 1863, Grant embarked aboard the U.S.S. *Diligence* for a reconnaissance up the Yazoo River to a place called Satartia in connection with the Vicksburg campaign. It was a memorable voyage. Cadwallader, in fact, remembered it for the rest of his life:

> I was not long in perceiving that Grant had been drinking heavily, and that he was still keeping it up. He made several trips to the barroom of the boat in a short time, and became stupid in speech and staggering in gait. . . . Lieutenant H. N. Towner of Chicago, acting A.D.C., was the only staff representative aboard. I tried to have Towner get Grant into his stateroom . . . but he was timid, and afraid the general would resent it. . . . I then went to Captain McDougall to have him refuse the general any more whiskey, in person, or on his order. This the Captain said he could not do—that General Grant was department commander. . . . Finding persuasions unavailing, I commenced on McDougall with imprecations and threats. I assured him that on my representations he would and should be sent out of the department in irons if I lived to get back to headquarters. He knew something of the vindictive feelings Rawlins had for those who supplied Grant with liquor, and finally closed the barroom, and conveniently lost the key in a safe place. . . . I then took the general in hand myself, enticed him into his stateroom, locked myself in the room with him (having

[7] Cadwallader MS, 123-81, *passim.*

the key in my pocket) and commenced throwing bottles of whiskey which stood on the table through the windows . . . into the river.

Grant ordered Cadwallader to get out. Cadwallader refused. Grant lurched to the door, tried to wrench it open, and shouted thickly that it must be unlocked at once. After much argument, Cadwallader persuaded him to lie down, and finally fanned him to sleep.[8]

It is not clear how far the Chicago *Times's* intrepid representative succeeded in deceiving a most important civilian aboard the *Diligence*. This passenger was none other than Charles A. Dana, now special agent for the War Department, sent specifically to appraise Grant and settle the drinking question once and for all. Dana's reminiscences note that "Grant was ill and went to bed soon after we started." Dana rapped on his door when the boat reached Satartia to report that the place was infested with guerrillas. Dana asked if they should not turn back. Grant "was too sick to decide," and said: " 'I will leave it with you.' " The *Diligence* turned back. It is a fair surmise that Grant's curious illness was no mystery to Dana. There is a perceptible tongue in his cheek when he turns to the next morning: "Grant came out to breakfast fresh as a rose, clean shirt and all, quite himself. 'Well, Mr. Dana,' he said, 'I suppose we are at Satartia now.' " [9]

They were at Haynes's Bluff. Cadwallader went ashore to hustle news. He was "thunderstruck" an hour later to find that Grant had got some whisky from on shore and "was quite as much intoxicated as on the day before." Cadwallader made some rapid calculations. The *Diligence* was to proceed to Chickasaw Bayou, where the party would leave her; at arrival time the landing would be alive with officers and men on commissary duty from all parts of the army. It would never do. Cadwallader went to Captain McDougall. "He was now

[8] *Ibid.*, 216–18.
[9] Dana: *Recollections*, 82.

very willing to take orders from me: First, not to start immediately, making the pretext of low fires, green wood, etc. Next, not to start until I assented." There ensued two hours of industrious procrastination. When Grant's patience threatened to burst all restraints, Cadwallader told McDougall to push off, "but to look out for a safe sandbar or beach to stick on for a while." The captain did this so well that the *Diligence* did not ease up to the landing until sundown.

Now all seemed well. But, alas, she tied up alongside the sutler's headquarters boat. Cadwallader at once hunted up "Wash" Graham, who kept open house aboard the craft, to warn him not to serve Grant. The reporter returned to find Grant's escort waiting, but no Grant. Nor was he aboard the *Diligence*. At length Cadwallader returned to Graham's craft. There, in the saloon adjoining the ladies' cabin, glass in hand among a crowd of officers and the spineless sutler, was U. S. Grant, gloriously drunk. Cadwallader cajoled him out. The grumbling commander made at once for Kangaroo, a large animal given to rearing and plunging off the moment he was mounted. Grant gave him the spurs as soon as he hit the saddle, and the horse shot away. Cadwallader thought that the game was up:

> Grant literally tore through and over everything in his way. The air was full of dust, ashes and embers from camp fires; and shouts and curses of those he rode down in his race. . . . I took after him as fast as I could go, but my horse was no match for Kangaroo. By the time the escort was mounted Grant was out of sight in the gloaming. After crossing the last bayou bridge three quarters of a mile from the landing, he abandoned his reckless gait, and when I caught up . . . was riding in a walk. I seized his bridle rein and urged the danger to himself and others in such racing. . . . He tried to snatch the rein from my hand, but in the scuffle I got the long-flowing double rein from over the horse's head and told him very firmly that

he should ride as I directed. . . . He became unsteady in the saddle. . . . Fearing discovery of his rank and situation, I turned obliquely to the left away from the road . . . in a thicket near the foot of the bluff. Here I helped him dismount, secured our horses . . . and induced the general to lay down on the grass with the saddle for a pillow. He was soon asleep.

Cadwallader hailed a member of the escort when it finally came up: tell Rawlins privately to send an ambulance. The escort went on, leaving the newspaper reporter standing guard over the man who less than a month later would be hailed as the conqueror of Vicksburg, prepared to cut off his shoulder straps at the first threat of discovery. Grant awoke an hour later; Cadwallader paced him to and fro until the ambulance arrived. "The general refused to get into it, and insisted on riding to camp on horseback. We compromised the question by my agreeing to ride in the ambulance also. . . . On the way he confessed that I had been right and he had been wrong throughout, and told me to consider myself a staff officer, and to give any orders that were necessary in his name.

"We reached headquarters about midnight, and found Rawlins and Colonel John Riggin waiting. . . . Grant shrugged his shoulders, pulled down his vest, 'shook himself together' as one just rising from a nap, . . . bid them good-night in a natural tone and manner, and started to his tent as steadily as he ever walked in his life." [1]

Grant's chief of staff, however, was not deceived. A letter from Rawlins the next morning began: "The great solicitude which I feel for the safety of this army leads me to mention what I hoped never again to do—the subject of your drinking. . . ." [2] Cadwallader entered into a pact with Rawlins and the staff to keep liquor from Grant thereafter. In spite of Lincoln's alleged remark about sending Grant's brand to other

[1] Cadwallader MS, 218–23.
[2] Written about an hour after Grant's return. See James H. Wilson: *The Life of John A. Rawlins* (New York: 1916), 128.

generals and his assertion that "I can't spare this man; he fights!" no one doubted that if news of such a carousal should become widely known, that would be the end of him. Dana saw Rawlins's letter and knew at least part of the truth; he concluded, wise fellow, to keep it from the War Department.[3]

Grant never made the most distant allusion to the Yazoo spree, but he had not forgotten: Cadwallader was treated as a full-fledged staff member, his tent pitched and struck for him by headquarters orderlies, his rations and feed for his horse provided, passes issued to him such as no newspaperman had known before. They were in the form of orders to "all guards and picket guards, in all the armies of the United States, to pass me at any hour of the day or night, with horses and vehicles; to all quartermasters . . . to furnish me transportation on demand for myself, horses and servants; to all commissaries . . . to furnish me subsistence on demand." Cadwallader was empowered, as he wrote, "to take possession of any vessel, from a tug to the largest government transport, allow no one but myself on board, and proceed wherever I pleased." Moreover, he had blank passes, signed by Grant, for anyone he cared to hire.[4] His special status is curiously substantiated in a letter that Colonel Theodore Lyman, of Meade's staff, wrote later, contrasting Meade's press relations with Grant's:

> The plain truth about Meade is, . . . that he, as a rule, will not even speak to any person connected with the press. They do not dare to address him. With other generals, how different: at Grant's headquarters, there is a fellow named Cadwalader, . . . and you see the Lieutenant General's staff officers calling, "Oh, Cad; come here a minute!" That is the style![5]

[3] Wilson: *Rawlins*, 128; James H. Wilson: *The Life of Charles A. Dana* (New York: 1907), 232.

[4] Cadwallader MS, 225, 226.

[5] George Agassiz, ed.: *Meade's Headquarters, 1863–1865: Letters of Colonel Theodore Lyman* (Boston: 1922), 359.

Frederic Hudson was too astute to let an opportunity to hire such a man slip by, and when De B. Randolph Keim wrote during Vicksburg that he could not get near Grant's headquarters, "Cad" was hired by the *Herald*. He continued to serve the Chicago *Times* for a time as well. The censor turned down his account of Lookout Mountain, the famous "Battle above the Clouds" at Chattanooga. Cadwallader, of course, went to Grant with it; Grant wrote "Send the within" on the back without a word or a glance at the manuscript.[6] Frederic Hudson could hardly ask for better service.

That March day on which Grant finally came to Washington provided dramatic evidence of one effect of the news revolution. Until reporting eclipsed commentary in the press, comparatively few leaders attained flesh-and-blood reality in the minds of the American people. Save to those who saw them on the hustings, Webster and Clay and Calhoun had been shadows rather than rounded personalities. In breathing life into the actors, in making their dress, diet, mannerisms, phobias, religious beliefs, offhand remarks, and private lives familiar in the remotest farmhouse, the press had permanently altered the relationship between leaders and the led. A sense of identification engendered by this new familiarity with leaders dramatized the war for the millions at home, attested by likenesses of Fighting Joe or Little Mac or Old Brains on mantels and kitchen walls and dressers no less than by the nicknames themselves. Described, puffed, criticized a thousand times over, hitherto obscure military figures evoked the prayers and peopled the dreams of those who had never seen them; the sense of oneness implicit in such songs as *We Are Coming, Father Abraham, Three Hundred Thousand More* welled up from a nation that knew its leaders as it knew its cause.

If Grant had been obscure, if he had been for a long time only dimly perceived, ignored because he lacked the super-

6 Cadwallader MS, 281, 349.

ficial trappings required of a hero, he had come now to seem the very apotheosis of the plain man, and as such the press exalted him and the country understood him. People did not know just what he looked like, but they knew him; they knew of his superb horsemanship, his blunt manner, his "hard scrabble" background, his dress, his deeds, and a lot of things also which were invented by reporters to fit the new Grant myth, such as a statement attributed to him that he preferred the plain pork-and-beans fare of the common soldier.

A *Tribune* reporter told what happened that day in Washington:

> At five o'clock this afternoon, an officer, leading a child by the hand, quietly and modestly entered the dining room at Willard's, and took a place at a table. A gentleman from New Orleans and his daughter recognized him, rose from their seats and shook hands with him cordially. In a flash, as by electric communication, the news that Gen. Grant was in the room spread through the immense hotel, and hundreds of guests, Senators, Representatives, Supreme Court Judges, women, officers, lawyers, and all the customary household of Willard's, sprang from their seats and cheered in the most tremendous manner, and crowded around the blushing and confused object of this sudden ovation, and overwhelmed him with their admiring interest. When his meal was concluded, . . . it was but a fall into another scene . . . in the lower hall. . . . The reception of General Grant at the President's levee in the evening was more furious than any scene that ever transpired in the East Room. He was literally lifted up for a while, and in obedience to a demand and to a necessity, so great was the desire to have a fair look at him, he was obliged to mount a sofa, under the auspices of Secretary Seward, who preceded him to that elevation. There has never

been such a coat-tearing, button-bursting jam in the White House as this soldier has occasioned.[7]

Noah Brooks of the *Sacramento Union* said: "It was the only real mob I ever saw in the White House." Crowds followed Grant in the street. And everyone who could read knew at last that with this man in the East, the final showdown in Virginia must be near at hand.

2. "THERE WILL BE NO TURNING BACK"

MORE than one associate in the *Tribune* office that winter noted that Sydney Gay was visibly aging from day to day. It was not the news treadmill alone. Like the copy on hooks in the composing room labeled "Must," "Should," and "Will Keep," the problems on which Gay was impaled were multifarious and of varying urgency.

The constant threat of Greeley's insisting again on plumping for a negotiated peace haunted him; scores of letters had come the year before, warning that it would wreck the paper if it did not, indeed, lose the war, but Gay knew Greeley. "I have no faith in wholesale bloodshed to *no definite end*," Greeley had written in a memorandum as early as August 22, 1861. "It is our duty to fight so long as we may with a rational hope of success—no longer." [8] Greeley lost rational hope periodically; by argument and by artifice, Gay struggled to counteract him. "About the only thing I have to show for four years' labor in keeping the *Tribune* a war paper while its editor in chief was a Copperhead and secessionist," he would write in bitter hyperbole in 1866, "is a chronic diarrhea." [9]

Securing a steady supply of Southern papers, the contents of which were devoured more eagerly in the North than

[7] Issue of Mar. 9, 1864.
[8] Greeley to Gay, Gay Papers.
[9] Gay to Edmund Quincy, Aug. 16, 1866, *ibid.*

where they were printed, provided an unremitting headache. The *Herald* blossomed regularly with long excerpts from the Richmond sheets, procured as if by magic. Gay tried everything, including the employment of professional spies. One was Dr. J. W. Palmer, a Baltimore & Ohio Railroad official known as "Altamount," who had many Richmond connections and appears actually to have gone there to secure papers. Unfortunately Palmer proved to be a hopeless alcoholic, and a secessionist to boot.[1] When Palmer failed him, Gay hired Charles E. Langley, an adventurer from Winchester, Virginia; Langley worked out an elaborate scheme for bootlegging the papers, but was apprehended in New Market before it was fairly under way. Regular correspondents on the Rappahannock, though dependent on the whims of Confederate pickets, remained the chief source.

Southern papers often yielded page-one news for the *Tribune* even in slow times, such as that provided in a startling piece from the Richmond *Whig* which Gay ran one day in January under the satiric head "WONDERFUL BIRD OF WAR." This was the petition of R. O. Davidson, a clerk in the Confederate quartermaster-general's office, "to the officers, soldiers and citizens of the Confederate States," relating that since 1839 he had been working on "a machine for aerial locomotion by man," that he had finally solved the problem, and that the engineering bureau of the War Department obstinately declined to heed him. "By the use of a considerable number of these machines all of the Yankee armies now upon our soil and their blockading fleets may be speedily driven off or destroyed," said Davidson; a thousand machines, carrying fifty pounds of explosives each, would drop them on the foe from a height beyond the range of artillery, return, reload, and "thus continuing the movement at the rate of 100 miles per hour," demolish an army in twelve hours. Five hundred dollars would build one "Artisavis, or Bird of Art," and Davidson wanted one-dollar contributions so that he could get down

[1] Hardenbrook to Gay, June 25, 1862, and others, Gay Papers.

to business.[2] *Tribune* readers enjoyed such excerpts as proof of the desperation of the foe, and no Northern newspaper could be without them.

Next to procuring these papers, Gay's most persistent troubles that winter involved personnel. Villard took umbrage at Greeley's criticism of his work at Chattanooga and resigned without bothering to explain that he had been ill. "The crotchets of Mr. Greeley never suited me," he wrote.[3] Adams Hill, the inexhaustible, quit for the same reason at the same time, in December 1863. "Despairing of being able . . . to keep color with Mr. Greeley's chamaleon policy," Hill wrote disgustedly to Gay in the last of his many letters, "I have undertaken to send you the news simply, supposing that in your absence some competent person would be present, with knowledge of the last editorial policy. . . ."

Villard and Hill, with Horace White of the Chicago *Tribune*, promptly set about meeting the provincial papers' growing needs by establishing the Independent News Room service in Washington, with the *Missouri Democrat*, the Rochester *Democrat*, the Springfield *Republican*, the Boston *Advertiser*, the Chicago *Tribune*, and the Cincinnati *Commercial* as their first subscribers.[4] Bitterly opposed by the Associated Press, they had some success for a time, but their operations were handicapped by the monopolistic contract between the A.P. and the American Telegraph Company, whose competitors were too weak and scattered to form an effective network.

Shortly after Villard and Hill left, Gay sustained another loss when Charles D. Brigham, the prewar correspondent in Charleston who had lately done yeoman service in the West, departed to become managing editor of the Pittsburgh *Commercial*.

But he did manage to lure Sam Wilkeson back to the fold.

2 *Tribune* Evening Edition, Jan. 19, 1864.
3 Villard to Frank J. Garrison, Apr. 5, 1864, Villard Papers.
4 Villard, II, 267.

(Of leaving the *Times*, Wilkeson wrote that Raymond had been "so kind, so generous, so respectful, so confiding, I had rather take a flogging than write that letter.") Effervescent as ever, Sam infused new life into the weary Washington bureau and brightened the daily round for Gay with effusions that contrasted strangely with Hill's earnest efforts.

"Please require the proof readers to read my proof from copy. *Typographical errors crucify me.* . . . I live like a dog here. . . . Cursing is medicinal. . . . I tell you he is a man to be taken by the throat. . . . Oh how well I knew the Barnard item would get you a scolding. . . . Would Mr. Greeley let me write with ripping pen a letter describing Stanton's Bastille here—the Capital Prison? . . . Oh! If you could get Crounse. . . . The most valuable article I have read in the Tribune for a year was the one in which it crowed over the beaten Herald. Ye paper which blows ye trumpet is ye paper which gets ye advertisements—my boy." And there was one that ended on a poignant note:

> Sydney, don't have a boy 16 years & 21 days old. He will go and enlist as a private soldier within a year after his older brother was killed in the front of battle. And he will hide in a city you don't know of—& will conceal the name and number of the Battery into which he has fled . . . and thence will write you letters upon the patriotic duty of letting sons of pith and vim fight for their bleeding country &c &c &c—
>
> And you will almost want to kill him.

Finally, there was for Gay a personal problem. His sensitive nature reacted less to the fearful pressure of the work itself than to the insecurity of his position. The Tribune Association, close as most of its members were to one another, on occasion became a hotbed of politicking. After years as "publisher" (*i.e.*, business manager), Sam Sinclair was maneuvered out of his job by a bloc of stockholders in the office, and Gay half suspected subordinates of angling for his own job—now England, now Ottarson, now Wilkeson.[5] He had not forgotten Dana's sudden end; and, for all its worries, managing the *Tribune* was life itself to him. Gay plugged away tenaciously, hoping that by keeping the news side bubbling he would forestall any move Greeley might have in mind to replace him with someone more tractable.

An atmosphere of grim expectation, unlike the hopeful, almost buoyant anticipation that had preceded earlier campaigns, was noted on every hand. George Templeton Strong reflected it in his diary when he discussed the rumors current in April, and concluded: "Well, this much is certain, that the struggle of the campaign now opening will be fearful and its results momentous. What if we fail? Has this people faith and virtue enough to persevere after another season of failure or even of *partial* success?" With Meade's futile Mine Run campaign of the previous fall piled on all the rest, people had schooled themselves by this spring of 1864 to expect victory only at terrible cost, if, indeed, they expected it at all. "Along with the rest of the country," wrote George Wilkes in the *Spirit of the Times*, "we hold our breath . . . hoping for the best, but silently gathering resolution to confront disaster."

Gay plunged into the details of planning for coverage, a task made doubly complex by Stanton's intransigence and Grant's success in keeping all plans to himself. "Stanton got his back up yesterday on the pass question," Homer Byington reported early in April. "Refused all comers and revoked the few he had permitted a few hours previously." That meant action, soon. As to Grant's plans, Gay knew only that, as Brigham had reported to him three months previously, Grant believed in moving all armies in concert. That made matters more complicated than ever. He telegraphed John E. Hayes,

[5] J. W. England to Greeley, Mar. 4, 1865, Greeley Papers, New York Public Library; Wilkeson to Gay, undated, Gay Papers. Wilkeson denied angling for the job, but apparently expected it. See Oberholtzer: *Cooke*, I, 480.

recuperating at St. Louis following General N. P. Banks's disastrous Red River expedition, to join Sherman's army in northwest Georgia, and sent Elias Smith along from Knoxville to help, leaving John L. McKenna to supervise all the stringers in the West. In the East, he named Homer Byington chief army correspondent, and trusted Byington to solve an incredible maze of rumor and report in deciding how to deploy his men among the armies of Butler, on the James, Sigel and Averell, in the Valley, Burnside, reported as moving almost everywhere in between, and Meade, who remained in immediate command of the Army of the Potomac near Culpeper.

There was a sudden tightening of the censorship. On April 24, Byington returned from Culpeper with four passes signed by Grant. On the 25th, Stanton repudiated them. On the 26th, Byington told T. C. Grey and a young messenger named Henry E. Wing to go ahead anyway, and they left, "bound to reach the front, or the Old Capital [prison], & as they have not returned, I presume they smuggled through somehow." All mail, to or from the army, was suspended. "In fine," Byington wrote his chief, "I've been more perplexed & concerned over these complications, the last two days, than a whole year's experience running my little Gazette up in Ct."

At the eleventh hour Stanton suddenly relented, probably because he discovered that Page and others were securing passes directly from Lincoln. Gay, in any event, was able to breathe more freely on May 1, for Page, Byington, and Grey, backed by two messengers, Wing and John Noyes, were ready to report an imminent offensive, James B. Hammond was with Burnside, and Villard had promised to help if need be. "Hope we shall *win*," wrote Byington, "but fear & tremble." He referred not to the mere life-and-death battle, of course, but to the mighty journalistic one. "Shall do our best." [6]

Stanton's embargo had disturbed the normally placid breast

[6] Byington to Gay, Apr. 22, 26, May 1, 1864, Gay Papers.

of Frederic Hudson more, perhaps, than it had Gay's. It trapped Frank Chapman, poker-playing chief of *Herald* army correspondents, in Washington when he was supposed to be at the front. Hudson knew the remedy. He wired Sylvanus Cadwallader, resting with his family in Milwaukee between assignments, to report to Nassau and Fulton streets forthwith. Cadwallader arrived April 27, in poor health and determined not to take the field. But Hudson had a way of making a man feel marvelously important, and no one was more important to him now than Cadwallader. Surely he wanted to witness the end of the war! He handed Cadwallader a letter from Finley Anderson, despairing of getting anywhere at Grant's headquarters and asking to be transferred. Cad must exercise his magic on Grant so that the world would know of his every act, said Hudson; no one else could do it. Hudson "proposed a larger weekly salary than I had ever received, and all my expenses paid in addition." Silent Sylvanus took the evening train for Washington. He bought a horse for two hundred and fifty dollars in gold, telegraphed Grant for a pass, and arrived at headquarters May 2.[7]

By now the *Herald*, it would seem, had enough others on hand: L. A. Hendrick, James C. Fitzpatrick, Nathaniel Davidson, Francis C. Long, John A. Brady, Anderson, Chapman, a special crew to collect casualties, and assorted messengers, with a chain of lock-boxes Chapman had built extending all the way to Washington, through which an elaborate relay system was contemplated.

Cadwallader learned more about the situation in a few hours than the others had been able to divine in weeks. Tersely he wrote Hudson on May 3:

> The army moves in the morning. Gen. Meade's H'd Qrs. break up at 5 o'clock—Gen. Grant's during the day. Our troops will force a passage of the Rapidan tomorrow. Immediate, and obstinate fighting is apprehended.

[7] Cadwallader MS, 362–4.

Burnside is in the rear as a reserve corps, and can be thrown to the right, left, or center, as demanded.

Mr. Chapman came as far as Meade's Hd Qrs. to-day. . . . Saw Mr. N. Davidson & Mr. Hendricks this evening. Both are prepared for any emergency. . . .

Grant expects Lee to attempt to cut the RR between here and Washington.

No private telegrams will be permitted to pass between here and Washington until further orders—which means, until 3 days after a battle. We shall all have to depend on mail and messengers.[8]

Cadwallader had already taken the communications problem into account. He had told Whiteley in Washington of a simple plan to beat the *Tribune*: he would send via Grant's private mailbag.[9] "We shall be wide awake, day and night," Whiteley assured the home office from his post at the *Herald* bureau.

At dawn May 4 and for hours thereafter, the Army of the Potomac tramped across the Rapidan on sturdy pontoon bridges, for the last time. Grant crossed at Germanna Ford shortly before noon, rode to an old farmhouse on a bluff overlooking the crossing, methodically dismounted, sat down on the porch steps, fished a cigar from his vest, and watched in silence as Sedgwick's corps made the passage. One of the omnipresent newsmen stepped up to ask: "General Grant, about how long will it take you to get to Richmond?" Grant looked at him with a twinkle of amusement. "I will agree to be there in about four days—that is, if General Lee becomes a party to the agreement; but if he objects, the trip will undoubtedly be prolonged." [1]

There was not a sign of opposition. The crossing made, the men pushed on a few miles to bivouac in a veritable jungle of scrub oak, chinkapin, pine, and thick undergrowth—ground

8 Bennett Papers.
9 Whiteley to Bennett, May 5, 1864, *ibid.*
1 Porter: *With Grant*, 43.

unpleasantly familiar to those who had fought under Hooker a few miles to the east precisely one year before.

Thursday, May 5, dawned hot and still. The army was to grope south through this well-named Wilderness, then turn Lee's right at Mine Run. Grant, placid as ever, lingered over his coffee in the big hospital tent he called headquarters, waiting to confer with Burnside. A half-starved member of the Bohemian Brigade slipped in, sat down uninvited, and helped himself to a complete breakfast while Colonel Horace Porter looked on in disbelief. Grant paid no more attention to this intrusion, wrote Porter, "than he would have . . . to the flight of a bird across his path." [2]

Presently enemy troops were reported advancing eastward on the Orange Plank road. Grant sent a division of Sedgwick's corps to check them. Hardly had this movement begun when Meade reported Ewell's corps moving to the attack on the Orange Turnpike, a parallel route a few miles north.

The Battle of the Wilderness was on, a battle fought blindly, savagely, by men scarcely able to discern one another in the tangled underbrush. The ground broke them up into small units, which surged ahead, buckled, reformed, and came stumbling on again, bullets flying so thick that tree trunks were severed, muskets became too hot to handle, woods only lately soaked by rain caught fire, and men could not avoid stepping on the dead and wounded.

Correspondents moved through the bedlam as in a dream. Finley Anderson was struck on the arm. Samuel Fiske of the Springfield *Republican* was mortally wounded. Coffin, pious soul, found his nerves so shattered that night that for the first time in his life he sampled some whisky. All of them knew that Grant's advance had been stopped dead; on the basis of past performance, the Army of the Potomac must withdraw. The grapevine had it, indeed, that Meade had urged withdrawal, but now the word went out that there was to be a general assault all along the line at five in the morning.

[2] *Ibid.*, 48.

The world knew nothing of what had happened in Virginia the last two days. Mosby's guerrillas were reported infesting the countryside between the army and Washington; the railroads had been cut. Homer Byington saw Frank Chapman of the *Herald* among a clump of Bohemians, "very ostentatiously offering $1,000 for a man to go through." Someone from the *World* went around offering the same amount. It was an unheard-of sum; but there were no takers.[3]

Late that night Byington summoned the *Tribune* men to a campfire near Grant's headquarters. Someone, he announced, looking at Grey, Page, and Wing in the flickering light, has got to go through. There was an awkward silence. Hammond was absent, checking the results of an attack that had been hurled against the Federal right at dusk. Grey and Page were experienced men, needed on the morrow. Wing was no longer a messenger; Byington, having no one with the VI Corps, had concluded just before the battle to "send Wing out there and put him on his mettle as a full-fledged reporter." [4] But Wing volunteered. The others looked grateful. Byington promised him a hundred dollars if he made it, and told him to leave at dawn.

This was Wing's first real assignment. A slender Connecticut youth of twenty-four, he had written army letters to the New Haven *Palladium* as a private, lost two fingers and was wounded in the leg at Fredericksburg, and on his release from service joined the Norwich *Bulletin*. He had won a minor job with the *Tribune's* Washington bureau on the strength of a leader Greeley liked in the *Bulletin*, and had come on to the army with stars in his eyes.

Emboldened by the prospect before him, Wing went to find Grant at headquarters. He told the General he was leaving in the morning. Was there any message for the country? "Well, yes," said Grant a little brusquely, preoccupied and perhaps still put out by Swinton's eavesdropping an hour or

[3] Byington to Gay, May 7, 1864, Gay Papers.
[4] To Gay, May 2, 1864, *ibid.*

so before. "You may tell the people that things are going swimmingly down here." Wing jotted down the words, smiling at their patent absurdity, thanked him, and turned away. But Grant had an afterthought. He followed Wing out of the hearing of others, and stopped him with a hand on the shoulder. "You expect to get through to Washington?" Grant paused a moment, then said slowly in a low voice: "Well, if you see the President, tell him for me that, whatever happens, there will be no turning back."

At 4:00 a.m. Wing set out for Ely's Ford, where he knew a Unionist lived. Finding him, Wing asked that he lead the way. The man said Mosby's guerrillas were rampant and he was too well known. The only way to get through, the man convinced him, was to go as a Southern sympathizer carrying news of a great victory for Lee's army to influential Confederate agents in Washington. Wing exchanged his buckskin jacket, corduroy trousers, calfskin boots, and natty kid gloves for a butternut suit, a pair of coarse brogans, and a dilapidated hat of quilted cotton. He carefully read and destroyed all of the *Tribune* correspondence.

In this new guise, Henry Wing pushed across the Rapidan and was making for the Rappahannock when he ran into a group of guerrillas near Richardsville. They cheered his story and gladly provided a two-man escort to Kelly's Ford. Kelly himself, a bitter one-armed secessionist standing on a bluff where he could hear the distant roar of battle, was not taken in. By the time Kelly convinced the guerrillas that they had escorted a Yankee, Wing was halfway across the river, swimming for dear life while bullets plashed around him. Man and horse got safely across, and Wing was opening up a fair lead on his two pursuers when he came upon a band of scavengers picking up abandoned army stores. Rather than risk apprehension here, he forsook his horse and hid in a clump of bushes until the guerrillas had galloped by.

Wing hobbled along for miles on foot, profoundly grateful at last to reach Manassas Junction toward dusk. But with no credentials to show, he was detained by the lieutenant in command. The guard was perfunctory, and Wing slipped off undetected in the dark, stumbled upon the tracks of the Orange and Alexandria, and began walking the ties. Unfortunately he ran afoul of a Federal picket on the Bull Run trestle and was sent under guard to post headquarters at Union Mills. Here an officer under whom he had served confirmed his identity, but that was small consolation. They laughed at him for trying to rent a handcar on a military railroad, he had no horse, and he was too exhausted to go farther on foot. Wing pondered his chances, certain that messengers for other papers would be along in the morning.

It had been a lovely day in Washington, albeit hotter than seasonable for so early in May. Trees were leafing out luxuriously in the President's Park; apple blossoms were at the height of their glory; everywhere the still air was full of little cottonlike pellets drifting lazily from the poplars. The town scarcely noticed. Business, here as in New York, was close to a standstill. Men gathered on street corners and in grog shops, as if to relieve their tensions by sharing them. Housewives leaned on open sills, chatting uneasily with one eye peeled for a newsboy. But there were no extras. Grant and Meade and a hundred and twenty-five thousand men had simply vanished from the face of the earth.

An anxious statesman called on the President to ask what was going on. "Well, I can't tell much about it," Lincoln was reported to have said. "You see, Grant has gone to the Wilderness, crawled in, drawn up the ladder, and pulled in the hole after him, and I guess we'll have to wait until he comes out before we know just what he is up to." Heavy circles under Lincoln's eyes told of his strain.

At the War Department that evening, members of the Sanitary Commission were conferring with Secretary Stanton toward ten o'clock when, as George Templeton Strong noted, "the long, lean, lank figure of Uncle Abraham suddenly appeared at the door. . . . Lincoln uttered no word, but beckoned to Stanton in a ghostly manner with one sepulchral forefinger, and they disappeared together for a few minutes, going into a side room and locking the door behind them." [5]

A fair surmise may be made as to why the President interrupted the honorable members of the committee to speak with Mr. Stanton. An hour earlier, a telegram had come through from Union Mills, Virginia, addressed to Charles A. Dana, who was absent attending a party. "I am just in from the front," it said. "Left Grant at 4 o'clock this morning." It was signed by one Henry E. Wing, and asked Dana's permission to send a message over the military telegraph to the New York *Tribune*.

Stanton had responded bluntly: "Where did you leave Grant?" Back came the cub reporter: let him send one hundred words to the *Tribune*, and he would tell all. Stanton peremptorily demanded an answer. Wing replied that his news belonged to the *Tribune*; his offer stood. There was a five-minute lull before the operator at Union Mills heard the "K I" signal again. This time the message was addressed to the post commander. The Secretary of War ordered that the reporter be arrested as a spy until he answered all questions. "Of course that settled it," Wing wrote years later. "I would not have told him one little word to save my life." Stanton stamped down the corridor to meet the Sanitary Commission men. At Union Mills, meanwhile, Wing was formally arrested by a friendly officer; he signed a parole and lay down on a bench to sleep.

Minutes passed, and the electric chatter began again. The operator turned around with a smile: "Mr. Lincoln wants to know if you will tell *him* where Grant is." Wing restated his proposition, doubtless more respectfully. The President accepted at once, "only suggesting that my statement to my

[5] *Strong Diary*, III, 442.

paper be so full as to disclose to the public the general situation," with the provision that the Associated Press should have a summary.

Standing beside the operator, Wing dictated the half-column dispatch that Gay emblazoned on the *Tribune's* front page the next day, datelined "Union Mills, Va., May 6, 9 P.M." It was that dispatch, perhaps, which "the sepulchral forefinger" summoned Stanton to read. It was the first word of Wilderness, official or unofficial.[6] Badly composed and fragmentary, it nevertheless temporarily cleared the atmosphere: Grant had fought a terrible battle; he had suffered no disaster; he was still confronting the foe. For the distraught President, however, it was far from enough. He must see Wing.

Lincoln had made up his mind to end the fearful drought of information at the War Department by sending Dana to the front, and the same special locomotive which bore Dana southward late that night returned, on Lincoln's order, with Henry E. Wing in the cab. A carriage met the disreputable-looking reporter at the station and whisked him to the White House at two o'clock in the morning. The President and several Cabinet members were waiting when the boy in butternut came in. Wing told all he knew, rising now and again as he described the action to point out the position of various corps on the big wall map. He lingered after the others had taken their leave.

"Mr. President, I have a message for you—a message from General Grant. . . ."

Lincoln looked at him in surprise. "Something from Grant to me?"

"Yes," blurted Henry a little self-consciously. "He told me I was to tell you, Mr. President, that there would be no turning back."

The long, seamed faced brightened, broke into a broad-wreathed smile, and on a sudden impulse he kissed the bearer

6 *Welles Diary*, II, 25, and Stanton bulletin, *infra.*

of this momentous message on the cheek. He made Wing relate the exact circumstances in which the message was given. Lincoln thanked him, told him to get some sleep and come to see him the next day.[7]

Wing went off to his room at the National, where three hours later he awoke to the sweet music of newsies on the Avenue: "News from the army! Grant found!" It was his own beat. He dressed and went over to the *Tribune* rooms. The entrance was choked with men asking excitedly: "Is it true?" "What is known?" He pushed in. There on a table stood Sam Wilkeson, shouting that the news was bogus—no one from the *Tribune* had come in yet. "Here I am, Mr. Wilkeson!" Sam looked dumfounded. The crowd cheered, and Wing was boosted onto a table to tell his story. He was king for a day; none of several newsmen who had left the army in the interim appeared. As for official information, Stanton released a bulletin at 7:10 p.m. "The report of the *Tribune* correspondent, published this morning and forwarded from here last night, is the substance of all that is known here at this hour."[8] The *Tribune* saluted Wing in an editorial. Wilkeson took up a purse for the boy who had defied Stanton, and another came from a delegation from Connecticut. His horse was recovered, and on Monday morning a little ceremony took place on the White House lawn when Wilkeson presented him with an elaborate saddle and bridle.

It is not hard to imagine how Lincoln felt when he heard Wing's news. Gilmore saw Lincoln ten days later, and quoted

---

[7] *Christian Advocate*, Vol. 88, No. 6 (Feb. 6, 1913), and Henry E. Wing: *When Lincoln Kissed Me: A Story of the Wilderness Campaign* (New York: 1913). Ida Tarbell accepted the story as Wing related it to her (Tarbell: *A Reporter for Lincoln*, New York: 1927), but a fifty-year reminiscence is rarely trustworthy. Some of Wing's recollections in the *Advocate* overstrain credulity. I accept this one because: salient details of his beat are supported in contemporary records; he recited the story to Miss Tarbell substantially as he had written it fifteen years before; Grant had told Lincoln nothing of his plans, and the message exactly fits the circumstances. We know, too, that Lincoln was up most of the night (*Welles Diary*, II, 25).

[8] *O.R.*, Ser. III, Vol. 4, 277.

him, in a letter written just afterward, as saying: "When my wife had her first baby, the doctor from time to time reported to me that everything was going on as well as could be expected under the circumstances. That satisfied me *he* was doing his best, but still I felt anxious to hear the first squall. It came at last, and I felt mightily relieved. I feel very much so about our army operations at this moment." [9]

The battle raged on. Witnessing a violent assault on Warren's corps the evening of May 6, even Sylvanus Cadwallader found his faith in Grant slipping. If the enemy could come on so after two days of it, what hope was there? Unable to sleep that night, Cadwallader wandered over to gaze at the embers of a campfire. In an army chair near by appeared a familiar figure, "hat . . . drawn down over his face, the high collar of an old blue army overcoat turned up above his ears, one leg crossed over the other knee, eyes on the ashes in front." Grant at length saw "Cad," greeted him casually, nodded when his friend urged the importance of sleep. The General got up and stretched. "Lee has been giving us sharp work for a couple of days," he said, and went to his tent. The sight of the man, the matter-of-fact manner, lifted Cadwallader "from the slough of despond, to the solid bedrock of unwavering faith." [1]

By noon of May 7, Cadwallader had rounded up everything the others had written, including the names of more than seven thousand of the killed and wounded. At 3:00 p.m. he set out, carrying two pouches of headquarters mail as well. Fitzpatrick of the *Herald* and Ed Crapsey of the Philadelphia *Inquirer* joined him. They were cantering along silently on a thick-dusted road toward the Rappahannock at nightfall when five men leaped from a thicket, muskets in hand. "Surrender," a suppressed voice ordered. "Speak and you die." The butt end of a musket cracked against Cadwallader's skull, and he toppled from his mount, unconscious. Mosby's men, con-

[9] Gilmore to Gay, May 18, 1864, Gay Papers.
[1] Cadwallader MS, 389.

vinced by his staff equipment and official dispatches that they had a special prize, kept close guard on him all night.

Next morning they encountered a small Union force near Fredericksburg. By the gift of his horse ("beyond doubt the most stylish horse in the Army of the Potomac," he had written Hudson proudly) and two hundred dollars in greenbacks, Sylvanus induced a sergeant left to guard him to look one way while he walked off in the other. The others got away during the melee and climbed trees; finally the Confederates rode away. Stripped of money and most of their clothing, the reporters had lost their dispatches as well: the *Herald's* casualty lists would appear in the Richmond papers. By 9:00 a.m. on Monday, May 9, the three had made their way to the lower Potomac and were floating on improvised rafts when a gunboat picked them up and took them to Washington.[2]

Whiteley said the country was still in a frenzy for news. Cadwallader locked himself in the back room of the office. "I have a dreamy consciousness of sitting for interminable hours," he recalled, ". . . of going to sleep, of waking nervously, seizing my pencil and scrawling a few more pages, of being told that it was four o'clock in the morning and that nothing further could be transmitted, of receiving a telegram . . . directing me to take the morning train for New York and report to the *Herald* office."

Hudson took him into his private office, gave up his desk to him, and ordered the colored janitor to stay within hearing of the call bell—Cadwallader was to have anything he could eat or drink so long as he remained at work. But "Cad" was at the end of his rope: "I was bordering on insanity for forty-eight hours." He was taken to the Astor House, where in nightmarish sleep he heard once again the ghastly cries of wounded men burning to death in the Wilderness.[3]

Back on the field a few hours after Cadwallader had left, Homer Byington penciled a note to Gay:

[2] *Ibid.*, 401–7; Philadelphia *Inquirer*, May 10, 1864.
[3] *Ibid.*, 408–12.

At Battle Field
"Old Wilderness, Va.
Saturday P.M. 7th May

My Dr. Mr. Gay—

We've had a most bitterly contested battle—really *worse* than Gettysburg inasmuch as the *bullet* has been more destructive than artillery. . . . Page goes in to-day with an escort of Cavalry. He was desirous of going & will write up the best account, probably that will be written, as he has seen much of it and will review all that Grey &c write. I hold John Noyes to dispatch next. It seems *necessary*, in order not to be beaten, yet it *costs fearfully*, & will involve the virtual loss of a horse each time. . . . The battle is not yet over—yet I believe and feel we must finally rout them. Hope success may attend our efforts for the Old Tribune. . . .

Page spurned extra compensation for the trip, left after dark with the cavalry to protect him for a few miles, and got through safely, though, as Byington predicted, he had to abandon his horse en route to take a train. It was worth it: the *Tribune* sold fifteen thousand extras on the strength of Page's account, and it was copied, Byington noted, "into every paper I put my hands on." [4] A *World* correspondent who had left at about the same time was captured.

From the Wilderness to Spotsylvania: fighting almost without interruption for eight days. "The world never heard of war before," the quartermaster general of the army tele-graphed. Sustained fighting posed further problems for the press, yet the Bohemian Brigade kept abreast of it, and re-ported more coherently and with more restraint than in pre-vious campaigns. To a certain degree, coverage was achieved as a co-operative venture. Byington agreed to let Hammond take out Boston *Journal* and Philadelphia *Inquirer* dispatches

[4] May 11, 1864, to Gay, Gay Papers. Page: *Letters*, Introduction, vi.

as well as the *Tribune's* on May 9, Hammond exacting a two-hundred-dollar fee from the three papers and making Byington sign a pledge that it would be paid his heirs in case of death.[5] (Hammond got through, but forgot to deliver the *Inquirer* dispatches.) The following day Byington himself came through via the new base at Aquia Creek with news of "the most terrific contest . . . of any day yet," after he had arranged with Coffin "to attend my interests at the front till I could get back & reciprocated by bringing *his* dispatches." The next day it was young Edmund Carleton, Coffin's nephew, who made the run, and the next, Villard, so that despite Mosby's men, the news kept flowing throughout the entire campaign.

The arrival of Dana at Grant's headquarters marked a significant departure in government news policy. The New York *Sun*, the *Express*, and other papers without special correspondents had urged at the beginning of the campaign that the War Department release daily bulletins. Whether the idea germinated from this or from Lincoln's demonstration of anxiety, in Wing's case, that the country be kept informed, Stanton suddenly began to issue them. They appeared in the form of brief telegrams to Major General John A. Dix in New York, Dix releasing them to the Associated Press.

Terse and authoritative as far as they went, they were based on Dana's reports to the War Department, and, of course, received conspicuous play in all papers. The most famous of the Stanton bulletins quoted the message Grant sent him May 11, ending in words that many editors set in italics or small caps: "*I propose to fight it out on this line if it takes all summer.*" The official bulletins continued intermittently to the end of the war, striking evidence at last that the government had come alive to the fact that the people must have news.

The brave work of the *Tribune* men elicited glowing let-

[5] James B. Hammond to Gay, May 19, 1864, Gay Papers.

ters to each of them from their managing editor. Byington, returning to the front on May 12, wrote one that must have delighted Gay in turn:

I received your dispatch just before leaving W. Am glad we have all been able to merit your approval. They tell me in W. that Bennett telegraphed Col. Whiteley (his W. office man) *five* times on Saturday [May 7] on account of Wing's despatch in the Tribune & the only way they could pacify the old Caledonian was by insisting it was a *canard*. Phila. Enquirer man told me & says Whiteley said to him he expected to be discharged, though not at all to blame & that Chapman, his army man had got to go sure. It hurt him bad enough to be beaten at Gettysburg but to be distanced *four times in succession since*, was more than he could bear! It does compensate some for one's army discomforts to beat the unconscionable old braggart.

It heartened Sydney Gay, too. Grey, Page, Wing, and Byington formed a team that made the *Tribune* the talk of Park Row, and the shabby old Rookery basked in new glory.

☼ CHAPTER XII ☼

The '64 Election

THE PROSPECT of the presidential election filled men with forebodings. Washington reporters sensed bewildering cross-currents in the thousand and one animosities, fears, and frustrations that the war had stirred. Both parties were split, the Republicans on the increasingly vexed issue of reconstruction, the Democrats on the war itself. Radical Republicans were split, some willing to go to any length to defeat Lincoln, others holding back only because they were afraid it could not be done. War Democrats were split, some forsaking their party to support the administration under its new National Union party banner, others denouncing Lincoln as a tyrant no less bitterly than the Radicals denounced him as a weakling.

Reporters bobbed and swirled in these troubled waters at the beginning of 1864, now reporting, now electioneering, and in some instances taking a hand in directing the course of events themselves. The new journalism was only beginning to develop a code as to their legitimate functions. Some held political sinecures; most knew intimately the politicos in their respective factions, and were ready enough to grant favor for favor. Until 1863, L. A. Whiteley held down a Treasury Department job while serving as chief of the *Herald* bureau. As to his newspaper work, he asked Secretary Chase to believe: "I have never allowed it to interfere with the performance of my official duty, but have devoted to it the rest of the 16 hours of each day not required in the auditor's office." Moreover, "It is not my intention that any of the correspondents under my charge shall make the correspondence a medium for the expression of sentiments obnoxious to the administration, and I have always been anxious to . . . render my efforts useful to its members." [1] When Chase finally discharged him, it was with the announcement that no newspaper correspondent could hold a Treasury Department job [2]—a declaration that would have been more convincing had it applied to Melville D. Landon, William A. Croffut, and Charles A. Page, of the *Tribune*.

In January 1864 it was not at all certain that Lincoln would run. No president had served two terms within the memory of most of the electorate—none since Andrew Jackson—and there were those who held that this was as it should be. James M. Winchell of the New York *Times* solved this particular puzzle early that month when a Senator arranged an interview for him at the White House. Lincoln spoke with Winchell for about an hour. To Winchell he seemed a little embarrassed, now and again throwing a leg over the arm of his chair. No, he was not yet a candidate, nor sure that he wanted to be, so oppressive had been the cares of office. Certainly he would not work to secure the nomination. Still, after all the nation had been through, he would have to own that it would be a very sweet satisfaction to know that he had won the approval of his fellow citizens. [3] That, as Winchell recalled it, was the substance of his remarks, and it shortly became "well understood" that Lincoln would accept renomination.

How did the reporters regard his candidacy? It is a mistake to assume that they always echoed the views of their employers; editorial discipline was no longer that rigid. Villard

[1] May 17, 1862, Salmon P. Chase Papers, MS Division, Library of Congress.

[2] *Tribune*, June 25, 1863.

[3] Winchell in *The Galaxy* (*op. cit.*), Vol. 16, 37 ff.

and Simon P. Hanscom, defending Lincoln in the *Herald* in 1860–1, when Bennett had little use for him; Wilkeson, defying *Tribune* policy by castigating the administration for its failure to reinforce McClellan; Josiah Sypher, bitterly critical of Hooker at a time when Fighting Joe could do no wrong in *Tribune* editorials; Winchell and Abram S. Mitchell, of the *Times*, boosting the Chase-for-President movement though their paper supported Lincoln; Richard C. Colburn and a Washington correspondent of the *World*, Republicans working for a paper that was emphatically Democratic—such instances suggest that the news revolution had endowed the reporter with a measure of independence. The Washington men, then, were not irrevocably committed to their editors' views of Lincoln, and one might suppose that these men who saw him often and knew him better than most editors rallied to his support. It was not so. A poll taken among them that January would have shown him a poor second to the man of the hour, Salmon P. Chase.

There were perhaps as many reasons for this as there were reporters, but a few may be surmised. Lincoln struck many as simply uncouth: the frontier stories he told, his habits of speech, his very ungainliness, counted against him with all but a few newsmen who, like Noah Brooks, did not let the popular stereotype deceive them. Some of the hilarious remarks attributed to Lincoln, as they made the rounds on Fourteenth Street, went beyond what a newspaper could print.[4]

Others, infected by the virus of the Radicals, considered Lincoln a trimmer more concerned with placating the border states than with punishing treason and stamping out the power of the slavocracy. Since the Emancipation Proclamation freed only those slaves beyond the reach of Federal authority, they did not believe he meant to go through with it. Further, to them it seemed that in offering amnesty to rebels who took an oath of allegiance and agreed to forswear slavery, Lincoln would throw away the victory when it was won. The Radi-

---

[4] Hill to Gay, Sept. 18, 1862, second letter of date, Gay Papers.

cals sought only a leader to give them voice, and to many a reporter among them the Secretary of the Treasury was the man.

Whitelaw Reid, Henry Villard, Edmund Clarence Stedman, James M. Winchell, Abram S. Mitchell, Sam Wilkeson, Homer Byington, and Charles G. Halpine climbed aboard with varying degrees of enthusiasm as the Chase bandwagon got rolling. The tall-domed Secretary had built a formidable reputation as governor of Ohio and in the Treasury Department; he had the backing of Jay Cooke and other wealthy capitalists; he had a free hand in dispensing patronage; he had a daughter, scintillating Kate Chase Sprague, who was an ornament of Washington society; and he had ambition.

But somehow Chase did not inspire much interest. "I fear the chances for making head against the Lincoln delusion are bad," wrote Whitelaw Reid to Greeley from the *Gazette* rooms in Washington on January 19, "but while there is life there is hope." [5] Byington, the next day, described the Chase forces as "a powerful combination," yet the most Senator Pomeroy, who "seems to be the nominal head here," could hope for at present was to keep the state legislatures from passing resolutions favoring Lincoln. "I do not propose to but [sic] my head against a rock," wrote Byington to Gay, "but should rejoice at the prospect of securing for our next President a man of the highest order of *brains*. I understand this to be Mr. Greeley's position and have no doubt you have some such longings." Greeley was for Chase in private, but would not say so in print. Caution and secrecy characterized the movement, since Chase was in the uncomfortable position of running against his chief.

Wilkeson heard that several Treasury clerks who had refused to contribute to a Chase-for-President fund feared for their jobs and had gone to Lincoln with "prayers for protection." Justice David Davis, of the Supreme Court, happened to be present, said Wilkeson, "and demanded of Old Abe

[5] Gay Papers.

what he would do if Chase turned out these non-conformist clerks. The aged [sic] replied with a grin—'the head I guess would have to go with the tail.' " [6]

By mid-February many state legislatures and Union party conventions had proclaimed for Lincoln. James M. Winchell's news sense told him that it was now or never. While serving the *Times*, Winchell was doubling as secretary of the Chase National Committee. He composed a document setting forth Chase's candidacy in lofty language, deploring Lincoln's "manifest tendency towards compromises and temporary expedients of policy," affirming the one-term principle, and asking for volunteers. The committee approved Winchell's composition, though none of them signed it, and copies were distributed all over the country. "Mr. Chase was informed of this proposed action and approved it fully," Winchell wrote later. With suitable caution, it was marked "confidential," and Chase took out a little additional insurance by writing a private letter in which he modestly declined to run.[7]

Suddenly there was what Byington described as "a comical explosion of the Chase movement." Ed Stedman and another innocent member of the committee inserted Winchell's "confidential" letter (known subsequently as the Pomeroy Circular) in the Washington *Constitutional Union*. Chase men ran for cover. Lincoln men thundered that Chase must go. Chase made his explanations to the President in a long and agonized letter, denying knowledge of the circular until it had appeared in print, offering to resign. Lincoln replied in his own good time that he had not read the circular "and I think I shall not," but that he had known of it several days before its publication in the press—a tactful way of puncturing Chase's pretense. "I know just as little of these things as my friends allow me to know," said Lincoln, and concluded that so far as the Treasury Department was concerned, "I do not perceive occasion for a change."

[6] Wilkeson to Gay, "Friday" (Feb. 18?, 1864), *ibid.*
[7] Winchell letter, New York *Times*, Sept. 15, 1874.

Henry Villard called on Chase to ask if this exchange might be published. He said Villard had better ask Lincoln. The President replied patiently to this inquiry that he would "prefer to avoid an unnecessary exhibition," but that Chase might do as he chose. The Secretary contented himself with giving Villard a summary,[8] and a few days later friends succeeded in persuading him that he had better withdraw from the race.

Some reporters, notably Sam Wilkeson, still were not resigned to Lincoln as a candidate. Wilkeson was reduced to daydreaming: "Five thousand Germans must irupt into Baltimore next June & storm through the city with a clamor that Frémont shall be nominated by them if the Convention dare to nominate Lincoln," he wrote Gay. But Frémont, once the Radicals' hero, stirred no more enthusiasm than Chase. At this stage of the campaign, the one indisputable fact that the Radicals were up against was that Lincoln had the support of the people. Byington, writing Gay on March 5, no longer doubted Lincoln's renomination, "although I think a decided majority of Republican *Leaders* are averse to him. Mr. G. [Greeley] hit it exactly—the People think of him by night & by day & *pray* for him & *their hearts* are where they have made so heavy investments." That being the case, "much as I should prefer a less amiable and slipshod man . . . I hope the Tribune will not affront its hosts of friends by any acrimonious discussion of his beauty or his merits."

The evidence came to Gay's desk from every section, and from men least disposed to accept it. Sypher, protégé of that bitterest of Radicals, Thaddeus Stevens, admitted that in Pennsylvania "the people go strong for Lincoln."[9] James R. Gilmore, that perambulating opportunist, made a swing through New England and reported: "Have talked with a great many people about 'who shall be next President?' and everybody & his neighbor says: 'Lincoln.'"[1] Brigadier Gen-

[8] Basler: *Collected Works*, VII, 222, 223.
[9] Mar. 4, 1864, Gay Papers.
[1] Feb. 4, 1864, *ibid.*

eral James A. Garfield, a Chase man, told W. H. Kent of the
Tribune after returning from the West: "The people are Lin-
coln-crazy." [2] Since it was obvious that the Democrats were
grooming McClellan for their nomination, reporters had little
political news to write until the conventions.

Joseph Howard, Jr., raucous, rosy-faced, known among
Bohemians for such exploits as telegraphing the genealogy of
Jesus while rivals waited for the wire, fabricating the story
that Lincoln had sneaked into Washington in disguise, covering General Kearney's burial in a surplice, and writing copy
that was saucy enough to win him one of the first regular bylines the New York *Times* ever bestowed,[3] sat contemplating
the low estate to which he had fallen at the city desk of the
Brooklyn *Eagle*. On May 3, 1864, Howard wrote Manton
Marble of the *World*:

> As you are aware I have long sought a connection with
> the *World*. I now desire it earnestly. I am doing well
> here, have entire control of inside matters and am pe-
> cuniarily satisfied. But—the Presidential excitement ap-
> proaches and this mill pond is excessively small. I would
> like exceedingly such a position as I formerly held on the
> *Times*. . . .
> May I be permitted to follow in your train of constant
> success? [4]

The answer was "No."

A reporter on the *Eagle* named Francis A. Mallison had
once been a copyist for the Associated Press. Howard persuaded Mallison to filch a pad of manifold paper and some
envelopes from its office. On the night of May 17, at the home
of a friend in Brooklyn, Howard dictated a proclamation,

[2] Kent to Gay, Feb. 25, 1864, *ibid.*
[3] "Joseph Howard, Jr.," *Brooklyn Monthly*, I, 315 (July 1869).
[4] Marble Papers, MS Vol. 7.

Mallison carefully recording it on the A.P. flimsies with a stylus stolen from the *Tribune*. The document made the startling announcement that Grant's Virginia campaign "has come to a virtual close," gloomily reviewed the military situation elsewhere, set aside "a day of fasting, humiliation, and prayer," and called for a draft of 400,000 men. By coincidence, Lincoln the same evening signed an order calling up 300,000 men, but did not issue it.

Mallison hoped to make a killing in the gold market, since the price of gold in terms of greenbacks was bound to soar on the adverse news. And for Howard, there was also the prospect of gaining revenge on editors who had turned him down, to say nothing of fresh notoriety.

At 11:30 p.m., Mallison affixed the names of Abraham Lincoln and William H. Seward, and, with a "good luck" from Howard, boarded the ferry for Manhattan. He got there too early. Mallison loitered nervously—he did not have enough envelopes to go around. Toward three o'clock in the morning he handed the sealed envelopes and the flimsies for which he had no envelope to a well-coached urchin.

Minutes later the night foreman of the *Herald* split the proclamation into takes and ordered a page form opened to make ready for a replate, an operation that late war news had made familiar long since. Two blocks north and one west, the same procedure began at the *World*. Three doors north on Park Row, the night clerk of the *Daily News* asked why there was no envelope. The boy darted out. Next door, a *Times* clerk sent the copy up to Lorenzo L. Crounse, the war correspondent lately turned night editor. Crounse was the only editorial man in town who was still on duty.[5] He thought it mildly curious that the A.P. had sent its "good night" fifteen minutes before, and was reading the copy when a message came from the *Daily News*. Had the *Times* received the President's proclamation? Reassured, Crounse replied that it was all

---

[5] Elmer Davis: *History of the New York Times* (New York: 1921), 58. The Copperhead *Daily News* has no relation to the modern tabloid.

right. He was marking it for type when he reflected that not only was the text a little peculiar, the handwriting was not familiar. Crounse queried the *Tribune*.

Mallison had quite forgotten that only the Spruce Street entrance of the *Tribune* was open at that hour; no one having responded at the Nassau Street door, the proclamation-bearer had moved on. Astonished now to hear that the *Tribune* had nothing, Crounse sent a runner to the Associated Press office over on Broadway, copy in hand. Back he came with a note: "It is false as hell." Crounse told the *Daily News*. But the Associated Press men, learning that the *Tribune* had no such dispatch, troubled themselves no further.

The *Herald* had run off twenty thousand copies when the night foreman heard that neither the *Times* nor the *Tribune* had a word about the news. He stopped the presses and investigated, got the bundles off the drays, and destroyed every copy. At the *World* the presses whirred on. Mallison's boy made his last stop at Wall and Water streets just as the *Journal of Commerce* compositors were leaving. The foreman summoned four of them and got the news into the last part of the run.

At 8:00 a.m. the day side at the A.P. put the proclamation they found in the *World* and the *Journal of Commerce* on the wires to all parts of the Union. General Agent D. H. Craig queried the Washington office: what was going on that they had missed it? Gobright dutifully trotted around to see Seward at about the time Major General John A. Dix, in New York, telegraphed the Secretary to verify the news. Seward quickly set them straight and hastened over to the War Department. Had the *World* and the *Journal of Commerce* been suppressed yet? Stanton said he had just learned of the hoax that instant. It was steamer day, said Seward—the thing would be all over Europe. Stanton bounded to a desk and wrote an order for Dix: take possession of the two offices, stop publication, and arrest the proprietors. It needed only Lincoln's signature.

In contrast to Seward and Stanton, Lincoln took the hoax in stride. "I had a two-hours' interview with Lincoln this morning," wrote James Gilmore to his friend Gay that day, "and in the course of it he told me that the announcement . . . was a fabrication: that he had decided to call for 300,000 in July, not before." That hardly sounds like indignation, but the President did yield to his agitated ministers. He signed the order.[6]

Meanwhile, Craig blanketed the country with Associated Press disclaimers, offering a thousand dollars for the perpetrators. The distraught editors of the *Journal of Commerce* and *World* added rewards of their own. Manton Marble got every copy off the *Scotia*, including the purser's. Gold had spurted eight points at the opening, but by 10:00 a.m. every newspaper bulletin in New York was proclaiming the proclamation a forgery.[7]

Stanton ordered investigation of the Independent Telegraph Company, and when its manager indignantly refused to surrender his records, the entire staff was carted to Old Capitol Prison. The New York, Philadelphia, Baltimore, Harrisburg, and Pittsburgh offices were seized and their employees arrested. Henry Villard, Horace White, and Adams Hill were taken into custody, and Villard was grilled for two days on the supposition that his news service had concocted the fraud to discredit the Associated Press.

Dix assumed that as the *World* and the *Journal of Commerce* were rabidly anti-Lincoln, they must have been privy to the plot. Long before his orders reached him, however, their proprietors had convinced him they were innocent. Dix, alas, had no choice.

To George Wakeman, a *World* editor working as usual that evening, it seemed that the hour of the police state had struck:

[6] In their history, Nicolay and Hay asserted that Lincoln's name was affixed by Stanton without the President's knowledge, but Basler, *Collected Works*, VII, 348, corrects them.

[7] *Strong Diary*, III, 449.

Half-past nine o'clock

Mr. Marble—

About nine o'clock a company of soldiers took posses-sion of the World office . . . with orders as the officer in charge stated them to Mr. Croly, that anyone would be allowed to leave the office but that no one would be permitted to enter it. So we did not see the object or meaning of that order. I went to Gen'l Dix's office to in-quire. Col. Van Buren said he could give no information and although Dix was there I was not allowed to see him or send a note to him. When I left Mr. Croly was going on to get up the paper not understanding that the order suppressed the paper. As no one, however, is allowed to enter the office I don't see how they are going to sell it. . . . I am going back to report what I have found out —which is nothing—to Mr. Croly if I can get word to him.[8]

One can imagine David G. Croly, angular, kindly, a fear-less and highly resourceful editor, blandly getting up the paper with the soldiers looking on, as if nothing on earth could stop him. But stop him they did.

Editorials thundered at the suppression order. Sydney Gay, Erastus Brooks of the *Express*, Moses Beach of the *Sun*, and Frederic Hudson of the *Herald* signed a long open letter to Lincoln explaining the circumstances and absolving the two papers, much as Gay detested them. Mallison, arrested within forty-eight hours, at once implicated Howard, who confessed readily. Lincoln promptly lifted the suppression order. (Im-prisoned in Fort Lafayette, Howard was released by Lin-coln's order after three months, Mallison after four.)

The hoax made a great stir in the press, largely because of the impending campaign. Gideon Welles noted that "the knowledge that it is a forgery has not quieted the public mind." The spectacle of bayonets in editorial rooms shocked

[8] Marble Papers, MS Vol. 7.

many administration supporters,[9] and Democrats seized upon it as evidence of Lincoln's contempt for the Bill of Rights, a tune to be played throughout the campaign.

The episode bears out Mencken's observation on the rutted ways of newspapers. There was no lobster trick; night editors remained only a few hours later than the rest. Operating procedure had yet to catch up to news around the clock. The hoax, the editors' letter to Lincoln said, "was very liable to have succeeded in any daily newspaper"; but Lincoln told them that editors are responsible for what their papers print. The news revolution was inculcating that lesson in terms of news, and the press had to learn it the hard way.

Neither the commotion over this incident nor news of Grant's heavy casualties in the Wilderness stemmed Lincoln sentiment; as most reporters had foreseen, the Baltimore convention renominated him with hardly a ripple of dissent. Sam Wilkeson, in the absence of the Germans he had hoped to hear shouting for Frémont, had to content himself with the observation that there was not much enthusiasm. The last-ditch Radicals had already dug themselves in by nominating Frémont in a convention of their own at Cleveland the week before, the idea being that he would withdraw if the National Union convention named someone besides Lincoln; but it was a forlorn hope which got no more than routine attention, even in the *Tribune*.[1]

Wilkeson did an outstanding job at Baltimore on the chief matter of interest, the struggle for the second spot on the ticket between supporters of Vice-President Hamlin, Daniel Dickinson, of New York, and Governor Andrew Johnson of Tennessee. Sam knew practically every politico worth knowing; as a member of the anti-Seward faction, he had a pipeline into the Dickinson camp, which hoped to rid the Cabinet of Seward by giving the vice-presidency to a man from the same

[9] *Strong Diary*, III, 449.
[1] June 1, 1864.

state; and at half-hour intervals Wilkeson kept the wires humming with bulletins to the *Tribune* on the course of the struggle in the hotel lobbies and on the convention floor. His old friend Simon Cameron played a decisive role in Johnson's victory, and Wilkeson's dispatches traced the machinations behind it about as well as historians have been able to do it since.[2]

As the top reporter in Washington, Wilkeson was a figure of some importance to Lincoln. Their relationship was a good deal less than satisfactory. The *Tribune* itself was partly responsible. Just prior to quitting in disgust with Greeley's peace editorials in 1863, Wilkeson had written Gay of the paper:

> In queer proof of its standing in the White House:— yesterday I took a powerful man to the President and made him ask *on his own account* for a personal favor to myself. "Why, Mr. Wilkeson has been constantly attacking the Administration," said Abe with a laugh. "We understand he has attacked or criticized or found fault with Cameron, Hooker, McClellan, Burnsides, and the way in which the war is carried on, and everything." The parlous gentleman does not read my telegraphic dispatches—but he does hear of Mr. Greeley's articles . . . and with a strange mental action, honest and natural however in its measure of feeling against the *Tribune*, attributed all to me, and made me responsible for it!! . . . Abraham refused my request. . . . Not strange! For the course of the *Tribune* has so constantly been made the theme of wonder and reproach in the White House that every editor connected with it, suffers with it.[3]

But Wilkeson's stint on the *Times* had not greatly improved his standing with Lincoln. On one occasion, to Lincoln's probable annoyance, Wilkeson brought his voluble

[2] *Tribune*, June 9–12, 1864.
[3] Mar. 7, 1863, Gay Papers, one of two Wilkeson letters of that date.

sister-in-law, Elizabeth Cady Stanton, around to the White House for an interview which the President, considering the lady's standing, could not well refuse. Wilkeson's frequent subtle twists in his dispatches did not help either. When Secretary Chase resigned after a patronage dispute on June 30, 1864, the *Tribune's* Washington correspondent blamed "the irritation caused by the quasi-Executive sanction of the warfare of the Blairs upon the purity of his departmental administration and his personal integrity. . . ." John Hay noted in his diary:

> This evening I referred to Wilkeson's blackguardly statement in today's *Tribune* and asked if I might not prepare a true statement of facts to counteract the effect of these falsehoods. He [Lincoln] answered, "Let 'em wriggle." [4]

Wilkeson's private opinion of "the border-state joking machine" eclipsed anything he dared print. "What a crime against their country was committed by the conspirators to elect McClellan," he wrote Gay after the election, "in that they compelled us to make Lincoln and his managers again our rulers for four years." True, he had worked hard for Lincoln's re-election, but "I never touched my pillow . . . without blushing at my business. . . . O' mornings and of evenings I washed my pen-hand excessively and penitentially." [5]

It seemed that Lincoln could afford to "let 'em wriggle" at the beginning of July, but that month and August brought a change of sentiment that left administration supporters stunned. The war correspondents had told of the tragic fiasco of the mine at Petersburg, in which a bungling of orders resulted in the butchery of Federals in the very crater they had hoped would crack Lee's lines. Sherman and Johnston, to judge from the dispatches, were engaged in a gigantic chess game in northwest Georgia. Confederates were on the ram-

---

[4] Sandburg: *War Years*, III, 333.
[5] Undated (Feb. 1865), Gay Papers.

page again in the Valley, and no one could forget that in mid-July Early had pushed to the very outskirts of Washington and sent McCausland to burn Chambersburg. Dispatches from Petersburg that hot, hot summer betrayed a sense of listless-ness and frustration which went all over the country. Always, before, people had been able to tell themselves the end was in sight—another campaign, another six months, another year at the outside. But the press and the people had conjured it too often; now, ironically, they could see no end.

Seward, the Pollyanna of the Cabinet, confessed on August 8 in a letter to the foreign corps that he was "not altogether able to dispel this popular gloom from . . . my own mind." Thurlow Weed, probably the ablest political manager of his time, Henry J. Raymond, chairman of the Republican National Committee, and Horace Greeley concluded that Lincoln could not be re-elected. So did Lincoln himself. Weed could find no one with "the slightest hope of success"; Raymond "heard but one report," that "the tide is setting strongly against us"; Greeley wrote privately: "Mr. Lincoln is already beaten"; and Lincoln regarded the prospect as so hopeless that he pondered what he could do to save the Union between the election and his successor's inauguration. *Wilkes' Spirit of the Times* called loudly for Lincoln's withdrawal, while Greeley, Whitelaw Reid, and others quietly launched a plan to call Republicans to a new convention to supplant him.

When the Democrats finally convened in Chicago on August 28, they had every reason to believe that they were nominating the next President. Reporters converged from all directions; the press section accommodated only one hundred, and scores of them overflowed into the galleries. Manton Marble headed the *World* contingent, which included George Adams, of the Washington bureau, and staffers from New York. Gay assigned Samuel R. Weed, his St. Louis man, to the proceedings, a poor choice. Weed reported that "each speaker seemed to try his best to out do the last in going to the furthest limits of treasonable speech." This was of a parcel with Republican reports generally. The Chicago *Tribune* had it that "treason to the government has for hours at a time cascaded over the balconies of the hotels, spouted and squirted, dribbled and pattered, and rained on out of door listeners and pedestrians." The "treason" charge, leveled at the Democrats throughout the campaign, rested on the slender fact that a minority openly opposed continuation of the war, but it was applied indiscriminately. No reporter appears to have got behind the scenes for the real story: the origin of the deal between the war and peace factions wherein a peace platform was adopted in exchange for nomination of General McClellan, candidate of the war men.

Marble, the leading Democratic editor, had written privately in March: "I believe any man who runs . . . on an open Peace Platform . . . is doomed to an utter rout at the polls. There ends all hope of Union and of the old form and spirit of Government." [6] Lincoln, in July, had demonstrated to the whole country, through the widely publicized Gilmore-Jaquess mission and others, that Jefferson Davis would settle for nothing short of Confederate independence, terms as unacceptable to most of the peacemongers as to everyone else. Yet, to capitalize on war-weariness and in the name of harmony, the majority at the Democratic convention agreed to accept a plank that denounced "four years of failure to restore the Union by the experiment of war," and called for immediate efforts toward peace and restoration of the Union. Many a Democrat must have shared George Adams's feeling, expressed in a letter to Croly in October: "The Chi. platform gave me a *chill* in the convention when it was read that I still feel." [7]

The campaign at once came to life. The *Tribune*, noting that the Democratic platform "in no manner condemns, even by implication, the gigantic Rebellion which has so long crimsoned our fields," announced plans to distribute one mil-

[6] Mar. 30, 1864, Marble Papers, MS Vol. 6.
[7] Oct. 26, 1864, *ibid.*, MS Vol. 9.

lion copies of it. McClellan waited a week to accept the nomination, then issued an equivocal repudiation of the "War
Failure" plank; but the Republicans clubbed him with it at
every opportunity. Both sides got in low blows. The *World*
trotted out a libel of long standing—credited to the Essex
Statesman, a paper which did not exist—about Lincoln's having
called for a lively song while touring the body-strewn field of
Antietam.[8] The *Tribune* asserted that McClellan had offered
to serve the Confederacy before turning to the Union, and that
at one point he had planned a *coup d'état*. Outright fabrications were in order. George Adams wrote from the *World's*
Washington bureau to ask Croly: "Why not start the story
that Montgomery Blair will declare for McClellan? He is
McC's *personal friend*." [9] Blair had just resigned as Postmaster-
General, but he stoutly supported Lincoln in the campaign.

For all that, editorial dirty work was less prevalent than in
previous elections. War news left less space for it; besides,
journalism was beginning to grow up. After three years of
tolerably factual reporting, readers could scarcely be expected to swallow the diatribes and fabrications of old, and
managing editors knew it. Croly fought to counteract the
World's reputation as a Democratic organ. "You see what a
terrible disadvantage we labor under as a party paper," he
wrote Marble during the campaign. "All our personal and
political affiliations compel silence on these topics which interest the public most, while the Herald subordinates everything to . . . its news columns. So long as this state of things
lasts we cannot hope to rival the Herald." [1] Forney, one of
the most partisan of editors, spoke for temperate campaign
journalism, writing John Russell Young: "In managing the
paper in Philadelphia I wish you to be cautious not to follow
in the wake of the N. Y. Tribune. . . . These personal assaults are malicious and belittle the campaign. McClellan in

[8] Harper: *Lincoln and the Press*, 306, 307.
[9] Marble Papers, Sept. 25, 1864.
[1] Undated (Sept. 1864), *ibid.*, MS Vol. 7.

my opinion is a weak candidate, and we must not make him strong by ridiculous prosecution." [2] Greeley had told John Nicolay: "I shall fight like a savage in this campaign. I hate McClellan." Yet the *Tribune* itself, under Gay's steadying hand, tempered its electioneering with a surprising amount of straight reporting. Along with Weed's account, it printed the full official report of the Democratic convention. Its front page detailed the hundred-gun salutes, fireworks, meetings, and sundry celebrations touched off by McClellan's nomination in seventeen Eastern cities. The private letters of its correspondents in this period scarcely mention the campaign; Byington, in Washington directing the flow of copy from Grant's army and helping Sam Wilkeson with the political news, was more concerned with the fact that correspondents had lost nine *Tribune* horses in three months.

The unremitting work of the Bohemian Brigade far eclipsed anything else in the papers, both in quantity and in significance to the campaign. Just as men were debating the shocking proposition that the war was a failure came Sherman's thrilling announcement, "Atlanta is ours and fairly won," followed by cascades of correspondence from reporters able at last to describe a triumphant achievement. Finding the telegraph restricted to government use and the railroads severed, stocky Elias Smith headed north with his dispatches on September 6. More than a week later, after trekking part of the way on foot, he delivered the first extensive account of the Atlanta campaign to the *Tribune*.[3] Ben C. Truman of the *Times*, David P. Conyngham of the *Herald*, George Ward Nichols of the *Evening Post*, John E. Hayes of the *Tribune*, A. J. Daugherty of the Cincinnati *Commercial*, and others who had braved Sherman's rages kept the story of his triumph on front pages for days thereafter, along with accounts of Admiral Farragut's final victory in Mobile Bay.

Lincoln sentiment picked up. Greeley threw to the winds

[2] Sept. 2, 1864, Young Papers.
[3] *Tribune*, Sept. 15, 1864.

the plan to nominate someone else, and on September 6 the *Tribune* proclaimed: "Henceforth, we fly the banner of ABRAHAM LINCOLN for our next President." McClellan men, however, were scarcely despondent. A monster rally of Democrats on Union Square the night of September 17 generated such enthusiasm among the great sea of people as to seem a sure portent of victory, and most of the polls taken aboard trains and steamboats in the New York area, a favorite diversion of the time, showed McClellan far in front. The *World* launched a series of articles headed "MISCEGENATION," a word that Managing Editor Croly is credited with coining,[4] to stimulate how would-you-like-your-daughter-to-marry-a-Negro sentiment. The hated draft continued, despite the pleas of Republican politicians that it would be their undoing.

Lincoln could not well have won but for events late in September. Frémont withdrew as a candidate, whereupon Lincoln eased Montgomery Blair out of the Cabinet to keep Frémonters, who hated Blair, from voting Democratic. Frémont, as it turned out, would have needed but 85,000 of the 1,051,-000 Lincoln votes cast in six states to give the victory to McClellan.[5] More dramatic, and of greater moment, were the developments that a handful of Bohemians in the Shenandoah Valley set before a restless electorate that month.

Jerome Bonaparte Stillson was a fragile boy of twenty-three from East Aurora, New York, who learned newspapering on the Buffalo *Courier*. Croly had hired him for the *World* that spring: "He has written some admirable military letters and knows just what we want." To the appraising eye of George Adams it seemed that "with a little experience, he will undoubtedly make a capital army correspondent." It soon appeared that Croly and Adams were mistaken. Stillson was beaten at every turn in the Wilderness campaign, wrote with his thumbs, and had no heart for his work. Croly had to send him back to the front practically at gun-point. "I feel quite

[4] "David Goodman Croly," *Dictionary of American Biography.*
[5] Computed from election figures in the *Tribune Almanac for 1865.*

ashamed of him," the managing editor wrote to Marble. ". . . I thought he would want to redeem himself, but he is a selfish fellow as I now see very clearly. He thought the expedition would be a fine frolic but there was more hard work than he bargained for." [6]

The elixir that transformed this sad specimen between May and September may be conjectured. On August 28 the War Department revived Hooker's old order that all dispatches must be signed,[7] and Croly, taking no chances with Stanton, saw to it that full names were used. A byline is a wonderful thing.

On September 19, Stillson and Richard L. Shelley of the Baltimore *American* apparently were the only men among those assigned to Sheridan's army who were with it when it struck. In Sheridan's slightly exaggerated language, he "completely defeated" the Confederates under Early: "We have just sent them whirling through Winchester and we are after them tomorrow," he telegraphed Grant. The War Department, out of what the *World* considered "petty spite," suppressed Stillson's first dispatches, whereupon Stillson applied himself to collecting material, raced to Harper's Ferry, entrained for his office, and in seven columns of lucid writing, helped to make Winchester one of the memorable battles of the war. Stillson relied less on his own eyes than on exhaustive, patient questioning of generals, prisoners, men in the ranks, and other witnesses, weaving a comprehensive narrative that enthralled his readers. Adams suggested to Manton Marble that "2,000 Worlds with Stillson's account of Sheridan's victory would be a magnificent thing for Sheridan's army." Marble promptly endorsed the idea to counteract the charge that the Democratic press disparaged Union victories.[8]

October brought state elections in Pennsylvania, Ohio, and Indiana which augured well for the Republicans. The race

[6] May 23, 1864, Marble Papers, MS Vol. 7.
[7] *Tribune*, Sept. 2, 1864.
[8] Sept. 27, 1864, with endorsement, "Can you do this? MM," Marble Papers, MS Vol. 8.

was obviously so close now that one resounding military victory—or one defeat—could determine the outcome of what seemed an election as fateful as any in history.

On October 19 disaster struck Sheridan's army at Cedar Creek.

The reporters at Cedar Creek with the Army of the Shenandoah—Charles H. Hannam and Charles Henry Farrell of the *Herald*, E. A. Paul of the *Times*, Elias Smith of the *Tribune*, Shelley, and Stillson—had been complaining that there was not much doing. Two defeats had deprived Early of offensive power, and Sheridan was conferring in Washington, so that there was no prospect of action. This situation was remedied by Lee, who forwarded Early reinforcements, and by Major General John B. Gordon, C.S.A. Gordon discovered a tortuous route along the slopes of Massanutten Mountain which would enable him to hurl his men on the unprotected left flank of the Federal army while Early assailed it in front.

This movement was executed to perfection, Gordon's men moving in single file by moonlight, stripped of cooking utensils and canteens so that no clanking would betray them. Gordon fell upon the sleeping camps of the Federals at dawn. Three hundred out of 340 pickets were captured. The Federal left crumbled before it had time to form; the center gave way to Early's yelling onslaught; the right, comprising the famous VI Corps, was remote enough from the initial impact to make a stand, but had to withdraw when the rest of the army fell apart. Sixteen hundred prisoners, twenty pieces of artillery, huge quantities of supplies were taken. The Federals were driven four miles, and fugitives were making for Winchester. Thousands of long yellow envelopes littered the abandoned camps, to be curiously examined by the Confederates—soldier ballots for the forthcoming election.[9] Early's army had only to overwhelm the VI Corps to consummate

[9] A reminiscence in the New York *Times*, Dec. 26, 1875.

the rout, but half-delirious rebs were looting tents and supply bins, heedless of orders.

Sheridan was still abed in Winchester when an aide knocked to report distant artillery fire. The General must have slept with the windows closed. It was probably Grover, he said, making a reconnaissance. He dozed a few minutes longer, then reluctantly got up and climbed into his clothes. A knock again. "The firing is still going on, sir."

"Does it sound like a battle?" The aide said no. Sheridan buttoned his tunic. Grover, banging away to find out what Early was up to . . . "Order the horses saddled."

"The hour of 10 o'clock had arrived," wrote E. A. Paul in the *Times*, "and Winchester, to outsiders, seemed to be the only halting place, when all of a sudden—no man present will ever forget the moment—cheers were heard to the rear! What was it? queried everyone; reinforcements? No. . . . Sheridan . . . mounted on a favorite horse, now almost jaded. . . . Such cheering, such wild enthusiasm, I never heard or had any conception of before." Here was drama no Bohemian could miss. Farrell saw the little Irishman ride by, "his horse in heavy perspiration, having come on a dead run for a distance of thirteen miles." Details were waiting for Thomas Buchanan Read in any paper he picked up. Hannam heard the General yell: "Turn about, boys! We're going to sleep in our old camp tonight!" and saw him raise his cap to thunderous cheers. Stillson heard a staff officer describe the army's plight as "awful." Sheridan snorted: "It's nothing of the sort. It's all right, or we'll fix it right!" Launcelot, thought Stillson, never knew a moment like this:

Galloping past the batteries to the extreme left of the line held by the cavalry, he rode to the front, took off his hat and waved it, while a cheer went up from the ranks. . . . Generals rode out to meet him, officers waved their swords, men threw up their hats in an extremity of glee. General Custer, discovering Sheridan at the moment he arrived, rode up to him, threw his arms around his neck, and kissed him on the cheek. Waiting for no other parley than simply to exchange greeting, and to say, "This retreat must be stopped, by God," Sheridan broke loose, and began galloping down the lines, along the whole front of the army. Everywhere the enthusiasm . . . was the same.

The army, in truth, already had recovered its equilibrium; it remained for Sheridan to organize the counterattack. Using the VI Corps as a nucleus, he got the army into position and had it rolling in less than five hours:

> The roar of the musketry now had a gleeful, dancing sound. The guns fired shotted salutes of victory. Custer and Merritt, charging in on right and left, doubled up the flanks of the foe, taking prisoners, slashing, killing, driving as they went. The march of the infantry was more terrible. The lines of the foe swayed and broke before it everywhere.

Early, in brief, was put to rout, the captured artillery recovered, the lost ground regained. Reporters could scarcely believe it. "The main army is encamped in precisely the same position it occupied this morning," wrote Stillson. Paragraph after paragraph communicated the exultation of the army to the people of the North—and what reading young Stillson made of it in the *World!*

> Headquarters tonight is wildly exciting. Scores of officers are here, talking the battle over. General Custer arrived about 9 o'clock. The first thing he did was to hug General Sheridan with all his might, lifting him in the air, whirling him around and around with the shout, "By J——s, we've cleaned them out and got the guns!" [1]

[1] *World*, Oct. 22, 1864.

No matter what the official dispatches said, Copperhead editors could always deprecate them. "Intelligent readers will doubtless analyze for themselves the series of ante-election victories which may now be expected by telegraph," smirked the Boston *Courier* when the first news came in. But when Stillson's account appeared in the *World*, supported by an editorial that ranked it with Stedman's Bull Run and Smalley's Antietam, there was no longer room even for innuendo. Considering how bitterly the *World* fought for McClellan and how universally it was recognized that victories would hurt his chances, the publication of Stillson's account of Cedar Creek—far and away the best account of it in any paper—was a resounding triumph for the principle of news above all.

"What a magnificent success Stillson has made," chortled George Adams in a letter to Croly. "Everybody here is talking about him and his account. Every paper here copied it. . . ." [2] The boy correctly identified every enemy division (a feat that was almost unique), denied the widely published report that Longstreet had superseded Early, correctly estimated relative losses, and correctly predicted that the battle would be the last in the Valley.

Cedar Creek, dramatized by the pulse-quickening cadences of Read's "Sheridan's Ride"—

> The terrible grumble, and rumble, and roar,
> Telling the battle was on once more,
> And Sheridan twenty miles away

—seemed a very microcosm of the war, the foe taking advantage of Federal negligence and ineptitude, new leadership at last coming forward, and the boys in blue rallying to save the Union.

The waves of oratory fell silent; the last paraders went home. An almost ominous stillness settled over the land on November 8. Federal troops were placed aboard ferryboats in

[2] Oct. 26, 1864, Marble Papers, MS Vol. 9.

New York harbor, inconspicuous but ready for trouble. It was the quietest election day men could remember. Long lines of men huddled under shop awnings and umbrellas in the rain, waiting their turn to vote. Down at the *Tribune*, Sydney Gay completed elaborate preparations for compiling the returns that his stringers would relay from the remotest upstate hamlets. The earliest were not reassuring: Lincoln was trailing in Westchester County; in the city itself, McClellan was piling up a two-to-one lead. Upstate was expected to offset that, but Buffalo, which had given Lincoln a majority in 1860, was running narrowly against him. Associated Press flimsies reported emphatic Lincoln majorities from all over New England, but New Jersey was going for the General. Pennsylvania looked as uncertain as New York. Storms cut off returns from the West, but at press time the *Tribune* and the *Times* claimed Lincoln's election.

At the White House, Noah Brooks had found the President uneasy, confessing that he was "very far from certain." Going to the War Department in the evening, Lincoln amused the company by reading some of Petroleum V. Nasby's amiable nonsense while the returns trickled in. Whitelaw Reid and other reporters came in to discuss them with him. By midnight there was no longer much doubt, and a jolly oyster supper brought the long months of tension to a close, the President himself, as Hay noted, "awkwardly and hospitably" serving the oysters.

The next day Gay went over the returns carefully and wired Whitelaw Reid, who was filling in for Wilkeson at the time, that Lincoln had carried the Empire State. Reid replied: "Your dispatch, & a later one from Mr. Greeley were, singularly enough, about the only satisfactory advices we have had from New York today. I put both in the hands of the President, who seemed quite gratified by the Tribune's attention." [3] Gay and Greeley were right. New York was Lincoln's, the final tabulations would show, by 6,749 out of nearly three

[3] Nov. 9, 1864, Gay Papers.

quarters of a million votes cast, leaving McClellan only New Jersey, Kentucky, and Delaware.

Lincoln's simple pleasure in the "attention" of a newspaper that had been a persistent source of vexation to him illuminates, in its small way, the familiar magnanimity of the man. Byington wrote Gay seven weeks later:

> Saw the President last night. He was delighted with yesterday's tabular editorial on increase of vote. He has that on the brain. . . . It pays us in getting news to strike a favorite hobby thus occasionally, & particularly with Mr. Lincoln—makes him *very communicative*.[4]

Lincoln then gave Byington a full summary of the situation on every front, a reminder of what news editors and Bohemians through thick and thin of the campaign had never let the public forget: there was a war yet to be won.

[4] Dec. 30, 1864, Gay Papers.

✸ CHAPTER XIII ✸

Appomattox, and After

1. "A Strange and Tender Exultation"

THE NEW journalism had endowed reporters with a world of their own, with its own news and gossip, its own terminology, its own heroes, villains, clowns, myths, behavior patterns, stories of failure and success. In Charlie Pfaff's Broadway cellar, where once the talk had been of artistic and literary aspiration, the visitor in the fourth winter of the war might have heard how Ben C. Truman of the *Times* beat the War Department by four days with news of the battle at Franklin, Tennessee; or of *Herald* reporter William J. Starks's astute deduction in the woods near Petersburg that hundreds of squirrels chattering in the treetops betrayed the recent passage of enemy troops, thereby saving Grant from capture during a reconnaissance; or of the fate of R. D. Francis, the fat, sputtering Englishman hired and discharged in turn by the *Herald*, *Tribune*, *World*, and *Times*, only to land in a Confederate prison; or of the wondrous Sylvanus Cadwallader, now chief *Herald* correspondent in the Army of the Potomac, establishing a tented headquarters, complete with a chef from Willard's, that rivaled Grant's, and from there directing a swarm of correspondents and messengers so efficiently that the army itself bought eleven thousand *Heralds* a day at ten cents each to find out what it had been up to.

It was a world that had grown unimaginably in four years. On February 12, 1865, a day of no special remark save to the Lincoln family, the telegraph lines carried 59,600 words of special correspondence from Washington to New York, much of it relayed from the field, in addition to the Associated Press budget—a total in excess of a week's business before the war.[1] From Grant's headquarters, Cadwallader wrote his wife that he was spending two thousand dollars a month on correspondence, exclusive of salaries.[2] At the *Tribune* office there was talk of the need for a machine that would set type faster than the boys upstairs could "sling 'em," and within a year the Alden Machine, first of a long line of experimental type-setters, would have a trial at the Rookery.[3] News syndicates sprouted: Whitelaw Reid was sending his Washington correspondence to a string of Western papers; Stanton, apparently abashed by his behavior during the false-proclamation excitement, showered favors on Villard's and Hill's Independent News service; B. S. Osbon established a Navy News Bureau. Viewing all this show of enterprise, the *Round Table* thought it time someone started a school of journalism.[4]

The war dragged. Sherman dropped out of sight as his army headed north from Savannah, and there was nothing to read but the interminable "all quiet" dispatches from Petersburg. Thomas had flared briefly in the headlines in December when his army crushed Hood at Nashville, Ben Truman again telling the world about it in a notable beat for the *Times*. From then until the end of March, aside from the closing of Wilmington, North Carolina, last haven of the blockade-runners,

[1] *The Telegrapher*: Journal of the National Telegraphic Union, Vol. 1, 60 (Feb. 27, 1865).

[2] Cadwallader MS, 495.

[3] Resolution of thanks from directors of the Alden Machine Co., Mar. 12, 1866, Gay Papers. Twenty years later the *Tribune* became the first daily to adopt the machine that Whitelaw Reid christened the Linotype.

[4] *The Round Table*, June 18, 1864. The first school of journalism was founded in 1908 at the University of Missouri.

and the fall of Charleston in February, the ennui went unrelieved; newspapers returned to conservative headlines, and editors who still had heart for prediction thought the end yet a year away.

On March 25, Lee made a bold sally at dawn, designed to break Grant's lines at an earthwork known as Fort Stedman. The attack was in hand by the time most correspondents were out of their beds; in this and in other operations at Petersburg, trench warfare concealed so much from witnesses that it was practically impossible to report. Privately, bored Bohemians were amused to hear that in the dim light a brigadier mistook Edward Crapsey of the Philadelphia *Inquirer* for a staff officer and ordered him to wheel a battery into action. Eager to erase his stigma as "Libeler of the Press," Crapsey sprang to arms and comported himself in a manner that wrung a tribute from the general in his official report—paid, unfortunately, to the staff officer.[5]

Like a bolt out of the blue there came from City Point on April 3 a dispatch from a new war correspondent:

> This morning Gen. Grant reports Petersburg evacuated; and he is confident Richmond also is. He is pushing forward to cut off if possible, the retreating army. I start to him in a few minutes.
>
> A. Lincoln.

Editor Stanton made a few emendations and released it immediately. More dispatches followed. Cannon boomed all over the North. Boys went whooping through streets waving extras with type that could be seen half a block off: "GLORY!!! HAIL COLUMBIA!!! HALLELUJAH!!! RICHMOND OURS!!!" Thus the Washington *Star*. Eight hundred salutes shook the capital. Noah Brooks wrote that to brimming eyes the Stars and Stripes "seemed to burn." In New York, the *Times* and the *Tribune* ran American eagles on their front pages which

[5] G. F. Williams in *The Independent*, Vol. 54, 211 (Jan. 23, 1902).

spanned four columns above the fold. Church bells tolled, bands played, business ceased. Broadway was a river of flags. Even in Wall Street, wrote George Templeton Strong, "men embraced and hugged each other, *kissed* each other, retreated in doorways to dry their eyes and came out again to flourish their hats and hurrah." [6] In City Hall Park, massive roars greeted every bulletin posted by the *Tribune*; *John Bown's Body* and *The Star-spangled Banner* welled up from thousands of throats as bareheaded crowds waited for more; the presses that had told of Bull Run and Seven Days, Fredericksburg and Chancellorsville, Gettysburg and the Wilderness, hummed their new song all day long, and that night circlets of gas jets flared brightly in the *Tribune's* windows to symbolize the saving of the Union.

What went on in Richmond? Where was Jeff Davis, and what of Lee's army? The Bohemian Brigade, rallying to meet an apparently insatiable demand for news, quite surpassed itself. Arthur Henry of the *Tribune* and William H. Merriam of the *Herald* were the first to reach the fallen capital, but those who went in with General Weitzel's troops were not enough. Reid, Page, Colburn, Coffin, Townsend, Stillson, Crounse, Williams, and many another veteran scrambled by means fair and foul to board transports for Richmond, there to record scenes as in a dream: Lincoln walking through the desolated streets, pausing to gaze at the grim walls of Libby; coal-black Thomas Morris Chester of the Philadelphia *Press*, writing to his paper from the speaker's desk in the Confederate House of Representatives; George Williams inquiring for the trunk he had left at the Spottswood House the night he had fled for his life four years before, now gravely informed by the clerk that it had been expropriated long since for the manufacture of artillery wheels.

The end, coming one week after Richmond's fall, evoked no such demonstrations. Stanton's official bulletin arrived in time for the morning editions on April 10. "The news is from

[6] *Strong Diary*, III, 575.

heaven," wrote James Russell Lowell. "I felt a strange and tender exultation. I wanted to laugh and I wanted to cry, and ended by holding my peace and feeling devoutly thankful. There is something magnificent in having a country to love."

With emotions not unlike Lowell's, Bohemians took up their pencils to write "Headquarters, Army of the Potomac—" for the last time. On April 14 the papers carried their detailed accounts of the campaign and the surrender, some beautifully, memorably executed.

Perhaps he who best caught the exultation, the pathos, the finality of the struggle with its moving conclusion in the McLean house was the young man who had served so well in the Valley, Jerome B. Stillson. Long of wind, now and again tedious in syntax, Stillson's account nonetheless thrilled with the organ tones of the *Battle Hymn of the Republic*. Stillson had been at pains to get abundant information from officers; he kept himself out of his narrative; and he wrote of Lee with notable compassion. With the more detailed accounts of troop movements elided, this is what greeted readers of the *World* on their front pages April 14, 1865:

HEADQUARTERS OF LIEUT.-GENERAL GRANT
Wednesday Morning, April 12.

On that morning of Monday which beheld the occupation of Petersburg and Richmond by Union troops, the two grand armies of the Potomac and the James began a pursuit which will be remembered as the swiftest, the most unrelenting, and the most successful in history.

Lifted and thrown, by the tremendous onsets of Saturday and Sunday, from the earthworks he had occupied for years, Lee, uniting his forces near Chesterfield Court House, westward and midway between the two cities he had deserted, pushed straight on for the Appomattox. Crossing the river at Devil's Bend, he struck the Richmond and Danville Railroad at Amelia Court House on Wednesday, and began to strain every sinew of his command to escape down that road via Burke's station to Danville, before Grant could head him off.

Grant was too quick for him. The flight of the Army of Northern Virginia had not begun before the hounds—swift legions with steel fangs and baying cannon—were on its track. . . .

Three days and nights, hurrying, hurrying, the two great armies, scarcely fifteen miles apart, thundered in through villages and valleys, over hills and streams, toward a common goal. That goal—the Richmond and Danville Railroad—which should strike it first? Should we come upon it to find that the prey had passed; . . . to sit ourselves down forthwith, thanking God and Grant that at least we had got Petersburg and Richmond? Or should we, *could* we, have the gladness of meeting the hunted thing face to face out of its dens, giving it a shot between its scared eyes, worrying it, torturing it into giving up its fearful ghost at last?

The last vindictive thought inspired the men not only to endurance, but to a kind of frenzy. They marched as victors should; they sang and cheered along the roads like demons. . . . Dark divisions that sank to slumber in some forest in the evening at ten, awoke with the drum at two, to eat a meal as hasty as a bird's, and then to start, with bands playing, flags waving, and shouts that might have roused the tardy sun, upon the roads again. All the hardships and inconveniences of other marches were turned to joys in these. Wading rivers became a joyous *divertissement*. The soldiers went into the water up to their waists, joking, laughing, and emerged shaking themselves and rolling upon the banks like a happy drove of Newfoundlands. Villagers, astonished and curious, asked what "you all" were going so fast for?

"We're the devil after Lee!" cried a soldier.

"O, we're after Lee,
infantree and cavalree,
and we're bound to smash him up before the morning."

After Lee! After Lee! General Grant, General Meade, General everybody who appeared in sight of the tugging columns, received an ovation.

"Hard work, General, but if you want us to go, we will go," said a red-faced soldier to General Grant, as he was riding by one afternoon near sunset.

"Keep going for a while yet, then, boys," said the General.

"We will! we will! if you'll promise us a sight of Lee," and the air rang with cheers.

. . . . . .

In the midst of disaster, Lee had not utterly despaired. He had not yet, it appears, given up hope of reaching Danville. It has been shown how, on this same Thursday, while the Second corps pressed upon his rear, and while Sheridan and the Sixth corps destroyed the flanking column under Ewell, the main body of his forces, pushing down at railroad speed between the Army of the Potomac and the Appomattox toward the Southside Railroad crossing at High Bridge, came upon the detachment of cavalry and infantry sent out in the morning by General Ord. This detachment, although fighting bravely, was completely used up by overwhelming numbers. . . . General Ord hastened up the Twenty-fourth corps too late to relieve his own unfortunate advance, but early enough to check Lee's in the vicinity of Rice's Station. Foster's division, which was first, found itself outflanked on the left. Turner's division thrown in on the left, and a detachment of cavalry still beyond, at last sufficed to cover the hostile front. . . . A series of brilliant charges toward nightfall . . . gave us nineteen pieces of artillery and two hundred wagons, and drove them still further into the strong fortifications which guard High Bridge.

During the night Lee was very busy. Crossing a portion of his troops over High Bridge, he prepared his trains and the remainder for the retreat to which, on the following morning, he was compelled by the charges of half an army. Setting fire to the High Bridge, and falling slowly back along the lower side of the Appomattox, he parked his trains and assumed a new position just beyond the pleasant village of Farmville. Here, until night, he held us at bay. From here he directed his last unavailing efforts to pierce our lines, to get around our left flank, to escape to Danville. The Army of the Potomac kept a front of steel before him, losing, in the contest, one of its noblest officers, General Thomas A. Smythe, of the Second Corps. The Army of the James, stealthily marching below, and possessing Prince Edward's Court House, shut off escape in that direction. Moving up from Prince Edward's Court House to the left, General Ord took position in conjunction with the Second Corps in the afternoon, effecting an almost complete surround of the devoted rebel army.

At night, General Grant, entering Farmville, sent his first note to General Lee, asking the surrender of his forces. On this day as before we had effected large captures of prisoners, stragglers, and *matériel*. The debris of the rebel retreat lay in every road and gully, and on the banks of every stream. The universal statement of prisoners was that the rebel army was falling to pieces from sheer exhaustion. General Grant, too prudent before to arrogate his right to a triumph not yet wholly won, and too generous to insult a great antagonist by a demand that would have been a boast so long as his foe had a chance of success, now chose to "shift from himself the responsibility of any further effusion of blood," by a request so firm and so chivalrous in its wording, that Lee himself was deeply touched by it.

Still hoping, still laboring with sleepless energy, and relying somewhat, perhaps, upon a possible relaxation of the pressure brought about him under the belief that he would comply with Grant's desire, General Lee may have endeavored to sustain the last impression by his dispatch, sent in reply:

"Though not entirely of the opinion you express of the hopelessness of further resistance on the part of the Army of Northern Virginia, I reciprocate your desire to avoid useless effusion of blood, and therefore, before considering your proposition, ask the terms you will offer, on condition of surrender."

He commenced Friday night, getting his trains and his army across the Appomattox, partially burning the bridges behind him. Such a movement did not escape the keen vigilance of Grant. Ere the dawn of Saturday, while the rebel commander, doubling again in his tracks, had begun a northwesterly march, striking the Petersburg and Lynchburg pike leading to Appomattox Court House, the Union armies were following close on his flank and rear. Meade, with the Second, Sixth and Fifth corps, pursued along the pike and along the south bank of the Appomattox. Sheridan marched straight for Appomattox Court House, in a line direct as possible, between the river and the Lynchburg railroad. Ord, with the Army of the James, still kept on like a wary hound below, making for Appomattox Court House via Pamplin's Station.

And now, again, the fury and the terror of the march.

All day long, plunging, stumbling, dropping its hundreds of stragglers and wagons and worn-out animals by the way; sore of foot, desperate at heart, but still held in some sort together by the stern, magnificent will of a single man, the hunted Army of Virginia kept up its superb retreat. . . .

That evening, Custer's division of cavalry, quickly followed by Merritt's, had succeeded in reaching Appomattox Court House, working around to the very front and advance-guard of the rebel army, which they engaged. A savage conflict, lasting about two hours, resulted in a victory that gave us a thousand prisoners, thirty-six colors, and twenty-two pieces of artillery. Lee's army, after this repulse, stood still, marshaled near Appomattox Court House.

The shadows of evening fall; the sounds of battle cease; a hundred thousand yellow camp-fires mock the stars. Not all their light combined is bright enough to show the watchful eyes of Lee what fate is gathering round him. He knows that Meade, with the Second and Sixth corps, is behind him and to the east of him. He knows—for he has been made to feel—that

Appomattox, and After

Sheridan is before him. But he does not know that the Fifth corps, after a terrible, swift march, has arrived to join Sheridan; that the Twenty-fourth and Twenty-fifth corps are coming up from below, and will be ready to co-operate before morning. He does not know, in fact, that while the night speeds on his army is surrounded!

. . . . .

This is hardly the time or the place in which to do justice to the character of Robert E. Lee. Yet one element of it was certainly indicated by what occurred next morning, if it had not been sufficiently shown before. Pride *might* have impelled Lee, on that morning, to make the last attempt which he did make to escape from the toils; but pride alone might have hestitated to assume the responsibility of sacrificing more lives in an effort so forlorn. It is not too much to say, after having become somewhat acquainted with his nature through those who know him best, that the strong allegiance to principle which alone impelled him to "take up arms amid a sea of troubles" in behalf of a faulty cause, alone impelled him to make a last, vain, bloody struggle against a sea of troubles at the end. It will not fail to be recorded that Robert E. Lee, before his surrender, ran a good race and fought a gallant fight.

He had some hope, it seems, of breaking through our lines. His resolve of the night before was to make the attempt against Sheridan in his front, who he imagined, from the fact that he had nothing but cavalry the night before, would have nothing but cavalry to oppose him in the morning. Burning his wagons, spiking and burying his artillery, sacrificing even his own private baggage to assist in lightening the burdens of his army, he made, early on Sunday morning, a tremendous dash down the Appomattox Court House road, against the sleepless "man of the sabers." The musketry of the Fifth corps, joining with the carbines of the cavalry in a hoarse and savage

344

reply that sent his men back like horses on their haunches, told him at last that "all was over and done."

.   .   .   .   .

Grant received his guest with the simple, soldierly frankness that is part of his nature. As Lee, calm, dignified, perfectly self-possessed, advanced into the room, the Lieutenant-General arose, and both clasped hands. The rebel chief sank into the proffered chair, and within a few minutes both were earnestly engaged discussing the terms of the capitulation.

General Lee desired to know distinctly what General Grant had to propose.

General Grant assured him that the language of his previous dispatch explained all his wishes. . . .

Being completely at the mercy of his conqueror, General Lee was evidently pleased with the liberality of these terms. He expressed no dissent to them whatever. After making particular inquiry as to the private baggage and horses of his officers, he requested to know whether General Grant would permit those among his men who owned private horses to retain them.

General Grant responded that although he disliked to put such a condition into the terms of surrender, he would instruct his officers who would have charge of such matters to see that General Lee's wish was complied with.

Whereat General Lee expressed himself satisfied.

Lee then remarked upon the extreme destitution of his troops. They had had no supplies of any consequence, he said, for the last two days. "Even the prisoners I have taken from you, General," he remarked, "have suffered from lack of food. I could not help it. My own men have been almost starving."

Grant promptly declared to Lee that he would divide with him. He fulfilled his promise before nightfall by ordering rations of beef and coffee for twenty-five thousand men to be sent to the rebel commissary.

Appomattox, and After

Sitting down at the little table, the Lieutenant-General then proceeded to write a dispatch addressed to General Lee, containing the terms on which he proposed to receive the surrender. General Lee, after reading it, drew his chair up to the table and wrote his acceptance. . . .

After a few minutes of private desultory conversation, General Lee took his departure, General Grant attending him to the door, and taking his hand at the threshold. The entire interview was conducted, on the part of General Lee, with the manly but conscious bearing of a soldier fairly beaten, but not cowed; on that of General Grant, with the generous spirit of a conqueror who could afford to admit the ability, the courage, and the deserts of a noble foe.

.   .   .   .   .

If ever troops had cause to be glad, they were the Army of Northern Virginia. That army, fleeing across sixty miles of open country, had sacrificed everything. Its wagons, more than half its artillery, baggage, cooking utensils and supplies had been wasted away. Nearly all the officers had attired themselves in their best clothes, in view of the certainty of losing everything else they had. Col. Marshall, Lee's adjutant-general, said that neither the general, nor himself, nor any member of the staff that he knew of, had undressed for seven days. It had been one long, ceaseless, sleepless march, from the labor and suffering of which every one was ready to be rid, even at the price of defeat.

.   .   .   .   .

The campaign has made General Grant what he never was before—a great general in the estimation of the whole army. It has elevated every corps commander into the pride of his command; it has given the Army of the Potomac that decisive victory for which it has heretofore striven in vain through four years of almost constant fighting; it has given the Union a fresh and final assurance that "it must and shall be preserved."

JEROME B. STILLSON

2. THE TURNING OF THE RULES

ON Saturday, April 15, 1865, Private Jenkin L. Jones, Sixth Wisconsin, was lazing in a field near the foot of Missionary Ridge with a detail sent to graze the cavalry horses. As he glanced back at the budding valley toward the defenses of Chattanooga, taking in the peaceful scene at about two o'clock that afternoon, Private Jones was astonished to see the American flag over Fort Creighton slowly descend to half-mast. Minutes later, as he wrote in his diary, "the news reached us as if by magic."

At 56 East Twenty-second Street in New York, Woodward Hudson, seven-year-old son of the managing editor of the New York *Herald*, got up that morning before his parents and was pestering the maid for breakfast when his unreading eyes caught heavy black lines on the front pages of the *Times* and the *Tribune*. "I ran upstairs and asked my father, who was shaving, what it meant," he remembered. Frederic Hudson had come home early the night before, exhausted by a week of extraordinary labor. The automaton of the *Herald* stared at his son in the mirror for a moment, put down his razor, and turned. "His hand shook and tears came to his eyes as he took the paper. I never saw him show such emotion before or since." [7]

Sydney Gay had stayed late at the *Tribune*. The galvanizing flash from the Associated Press came a few minutes before midnight. No sooner had he sent it up to be set in type than Tom Rooker came down with a long strip of proof, saying that he thought Gay had better see it before it went into the paper. Gay read it—a blistering excoriation of Lincoln which Greeley had written as the lead editorial before going home. "Tom, tie up the type, lock it in your cupboard, and don't say a word about it."

A memorandum came from the A.P.: "Our Washington

[7] Woodward Hudson: *Fragmentary Chronicles*, II (MS).

agent orders the dispatch about the President 'stopped.'
Nothing is said about the truth or falsity of the dispatch."
Gay knew that old Gobright was sometimes taken in by the
wild talk he heard in Washington; there was nothing to do
now but pray. Minutes later Byington, alone at the *Tribune*
bureau, wired that Abraham Lincoln was dying. From then
until morning the flow of copy was almost uninterrupted.
There were official bulletins from Stanton, dispatches from
Gobright's trembling fingers, and more details from Byington.
The President was still alive, but there was "not the slightest
hope."

Page one had been locked up before the first bulletin. Gay
ordered the column rules turned to dress it in mourning. He
threw out all of the editorials to clear page four for the fateful dispatches, and he ran every one of them, including the
A.P. memorandum and a false report of Lincoln's death which
Byington later contradicted, in the exact order received. The
staff worked quietly, grimly, replates with fresh bulletins
continuing up to 4:30 a.m. The flaring jets proclaiming victory from the windows downstairs were turned off. Crape
was draped on the *Tribune's* street bulletins.

"It seemed for a month as if the sun was blotted from the
sky," W. A. Croffut wrote.

Greeley, if one is to believe a later rendition of Gay's story,
was too angered by the fate of his editorial the next morning
to heed the news. Gay heard that "the old man" wanted to
see him.

"They tell me you ordered my leader out of this morning's paper. Is it your paper or mine? I should like to know
if I cannot print what I choose in my own paper."

"The paper is yours, Mr. Greeley. The article is in type
upstairs and you can use it when you choose," Sydney Gay
heard himself say, *"but if you run that editorial, there will
not be one brick left standing on another in the* Tribune
building."

348

Nothing more was heard of it. One day Tom Rooker quietly unlocked his cupboard and distributed the type.[8]

3. IN THE NAME OF THE NEWS

WHAT is to be said, in a final summation, of the Bohemians and their work? Does it really matter that Sam Wilkeson buried his health in the swamps of the Chickahominy to tell the world about the Peninsular campaign, that George Smalley rode through a storm of bullets to acquire firsthand knowledge of Antietam, that Henry J. Winser paddled more than fifty miles in a leaky dugout to get his account of Farragut's victory at New Orleans aboard a steamship for the New York *Times*, or that others among them developed what Wilkeson called "devotion" to their papers and their work? One may hazard that the war would have been won without them. The most common observation about them, in fact, is that they provided useful information to the enemy, and there is no doubt they did.

But there can be no doubt, either, of the enormous contribution that the steady flow of news made to Union morale. No people were ever more tightly bound by a sense of shared experience than the millions who read the dispatches. This underlying sense of solidarity prevailed over divisive factors, periods of black despair, peace sentiment, Copperheadism, because the day's news, however unsatisfactory, always whetted hope for the morrow. "That word *extra* has been a word of power all through these four years," George Templeton Strong mused. "How many scores or hundreds of times has the suspicion of its distant sound started me up from this

[8] Hale: *Lowell and His Friends*, 178. Gay often related the story orally, but the background is clouded. Why Greeley should have denounced Lincoln when the paper had just come around to Lincoln's view in editorials urging "magnanimity in triumph" is not clear. Lincoln's failure to make Greeley Postmaster General might account for it, but the promise of the post appears dubious.

very desk. . . ." [9] The people of the North lived for the next edition.

The new understanding of the meaning of nationality which welled up in Lowell when he heard of Lee's surrender, or in Edward Everett Hale in "The Man Without a Country," implicit in Stillson's Appomattox dispatch, in the deep-throated roars of the crowds outside newspaper offices, in the profound simplicity of Lincoln's phrases at Gettysburg, rested in part on the fact that for the first time in history an entire nation knew what it was about, knew its leaders, knew what had happened yesterday and what might be happening today, and a man could sense that his neighbor, his community knew. The very words and phrases of the dispatches became common currency in conversation: "contrabands," "skedaddle," "retrograde movement," "flank attack," "inside track," "parole," "military necessity," "all quiet on the Potomac," "On to Richmond," and so on ad infinitum. Lincoln began the last paragraph of what was to prove his last public utterance, "In the present *'situation'* as the phrase goes"—the word he italicized being one that the daily summaries of war news in the papers had made a colloquialism. These small signs of mass integration told their own story.

The idea that the people should look to the press for news of public affairs, and thereby make them their own affairs, as Frank Luther Mott has observed, is deeply embedded in the democratic tradition. In the crucible of the Civil War, that idea attained a shape and meaning it had never had before. Lincoln called it "a people's war." The Bohemians, reporting the war so voluminously and incessantly that it became an inescapable reality in every corner of the land, helped to make it just that. Driven by the tremendous pressures of the news revolution, they hurdled a succession of restrictions imposed by Scott, McClellan, Halleck, Hooker, Sherman, Stanton, and others; they beat the censors by rail, by mail, by messenger, by artifice, by cipher, and by enlisting superior

[9] *Strong Diary*, IV, 16.

authority; and in the end they established the right to report as one that was recognized, however grudgingly, as vital to the democratic process.

The whole emphasis of American journalism had changed. Only a decade before, James Parton had celebrated the virtues of Horace Greeley in one of the most popular biographies of the time. But in April 1866, Parton wrote in the *North American Review*:

> Our journalists already know that editorials neither make nor mar a daily paper, that they do not much influence the public mind, nor change many votes, and that the power and success of a newspaper depend wholly and absolutely on its success in getting and its skill in exhibiting the news. The word newspaper is the exact and complete description of the thing which the journalist aims to produce. The news is his work; editorials are his play. The news is the point of rivalry; it is that for which nineteen-twentieths of the people buy newspapers; it is that which determines the rank of every newspaper. . . .
>
> It is plain that journalism will henceforth and forever be an important and crowded profession in the United States. . . .
>
> All this is new, but it is also permanent. . . . An editorial essayist is a man addressing men; but the skilled and faithful journalist, recording with exactness and power the thing that has come to pass, is Providence addressing men.

If he did not feel quite like Providence addressing men, that most indigenous of American professionals, the newspaper reporter, no longer had cause to hang his head. He had a basic function to perform in American society, and now that society knew it. New ground had been broken by the brash young men who call themselves Bohemians, and defied censors, generals, the elements, and often their own common sense, in the name of the news.

A BIOGRAPHICAL SUPPLEMENT

CONCERNING THE LATER DAYS OF SOME PERSONS IN THE TEXT

SYLVANUS CADWALLADER continued briefly with the New York *Herald* as Washington bureau chief, living with his old friend Rawlins in Georgetown. In the 1880's, Wilkie referred to him as "a prosperous sheep rancher in the southwest," and in this period he wrote guardedly of his experiences with Grant in the Chicago *Times*. After Grant's death he undertook a full reminiscence, "Four Years with Grant," written in the mid-1890's. The manuscript, running to some seven hundred pages, remains unpublished and was all but forgotten until the late Lloyd Lewis came upon it in 1945. (Lewis planned to draw on it in his biography of Grant.) Cadwallader lived his last years at Fall River Mills, California.

CHARLES A. DANA (1819–97) resigned as second assistant Secretary of War in July 1865 to edit the new Chicago *Republican*, which he shortly quit. In 1868 he acquired an interest in a paper that had been of small consequence during the Civil War period, and infused it with what he called "human interest stories" and a terse, lively style that led Eugene Field to suggest, "You'll need no epitaph but this: 'Here sleeps the man who run/ that best and brightest paper, the Noo York *Sun*.'" His fun-poking support of his old chief, "the Woodchopper of Chappaqua," in the 1872 presidental campaign, and of Hancock, "a good man, weighing 240 lbs.," in 1880, were typical of Dana's marvelous perversity in politics. As the cynical, long-bearded, skullcapped editor of the *Sun* he attained a renown second only to Greeley's, less for editorial leadership than for his own acute news sense and that of his managing editor, Chester S. Lord.

SYDNEY HOWARD GAY (1814–88) was discharged as the *Tribune's* managing editor in June 1866, in the same roundabout way that

353

A Biographical Supplement

Greeley had deposed Dana. Like Dana, he refused an offer to continue as an editorial writer, sold his *Tribune* stock, and never forgave Greeley. E. B. Washburne, James Gilmore, Henry Wilson, and others credited Gay with having kept the *Tribune* a war paper in spite of Greeley. Broken in health, Gay did not resume editorial work until 1868, when he became managing editor of the Chicago *Tribune*. After the Chicago fire in 1871 the paper suffered a loss of revenue, and the managing editor was discharged as an economy measure. From 1872 to 1874 Gay wrote editorials for William Cullen Bryant's *Evening Post*, then devoted years to *Bryant's History of the United States*, a popular work to which the aged Bryant contributed only the preface. He completed a life of James Madison in 1884, and died four years later at his Staten Island home.

ADAMS SHERMAN HILL (1833–1910), the youth who fled from Blackburn's Ford and later emerged as the *Tribune's* energetic Washington man, continued in newspaper work until 1872. In that year he joined the Harvard faculty as assistant professor of Rhetoric, and in time he became chairman of the English department. James Ford Rhodes lived with the Hill family for some years during the writing of his celebrated *History of the United States*.

WINSLOW HOMER (1836–1910) and THOMAS NAST (1840–1902), among the artists' contingent of the Bohemian Brigade, attained the widest renown. Homer's moody genius in oils and water color made him the pre-eminent American seascapist. Nast was the volatile political cartoonist whose influence survives most obviously in the forms of the Democratic donkey, the Republican elephant, and the Tammany tiger, all of which he made famous in *Harper's Weekly*. Four other war artists of later note were EUGENE BENSON (1839–1908), a *Leslie's* man who lived chiefly in France and Italy and developed an impressionistic style that won him frequent exhibition in the Royal Academy; EDWIN FORBES (1839–95), who devoted most of his remaining years to reworking his huge sheaf of *Leslie's* drawings in vivid etchings of war scenes; HENRY MOSLER (1841–1920), a *Harper's* graduate whose genre work won him the cross of the Legion of Honor in France;

and lusty THEODORE R. DAVIS (1841–91), who hunted buffalo on
the plains and won fame as a portrayer of the Wild West. (Davis
also designed the White House porcelain service, in 1879.)

JOSEPH HOWARD, JR. (1833–1908), the perpetrator of American
journalism's most infamous hoax, enjoyed a surprisingly successful career after his release from Fort Lafayette. He worked for
a succession of New York papers, contributed to the Boston
Globe and the Chicago *Daily News*, and at one time was president of the New York Press Club. The Boston *Globe's* publisher
declared that Howard's letter in its Sunday issue, which he wrote
for twenty-one years, "was good for ten thousand subscribers in
New England." In 1886, "Howard's Column," breezy and nos-
talgic, was among the first such features to attain wide syndica-
tion. Howard lectured extensively on his bizarre experiences as
war correspondent, chronicler of presidential campaigns, and
hoaxer.

FREDERIC HUDSON (1819–75) retired from the *Herald* to care for
his invalid wife at his home in Concord, Massachusetts, in 1866.
His own health was shattered, but he soon recovered. In the next
decade, Hudson's private papers show, he refused a series of glitter-
ing offers from New York newspapers, largely out of his devotion to the Bennetts. His voluminous *History of Journalism*, published in 1873, was accurately described at the time as "a rag bag
of shreds and patches," but it was the first in the field and contains
considerable matter not found elsewhere, along with pæans for
its underwriter, Bennett. Hudson died of injuries sustained in a
railroad accident.

JOSEPH BURBRIDGE MCCULLAGH (1842–96), after four years in
Washington for the Cincinnati *Commercial* and the Associated
Press, managed the Cincinnati *Enquirer* and the Chicago *Republican* for brief interludes, then moved to St. Louis after the Chicago fire to edit the *Missouri Democrat*. He founded the *Morning
Globe* in 1872 and combined them as the St. Louis *Globe-Democrat*. The hardheaded Irish boy who had barely escaped death in
Foote's flagship became a rich and notably successful editor, biting of wit, confident of judgment. For the rest of his life the

Globe-Democrat dominated its area and gained a reputation as one of the country's better newspapers.

CHARLES A. PAGE (1838–73) was appointed United States consul in Zurich by the Johnson administration in 1865. He later entered the evaporated-milk business in Switzerland and died in London at the age of thirty-five.

WHITELAW REID (1837–1912), an occasional *Tribune* hand as early as 1864, succumbed to Greeley's blandishments in 1868 to become his first lieutenant. Made wealthy by his stock in the Cincinnati *Gazette*, Reid obtained financial control of the Tribune Association just before Greeley's death in 1872, and thereupon assumed the editorship. Genteel and orthodox, he guided the *Tribune* competently, retaining for it some of the magic imparted by Greeley's name. Reid was minister to France, 1889–92, Republican candidate for vice-president in 1892, and ambassador to England from 1905 until his death. In 1924, in the regime of his son and daughter-in-law, Ogden and Helen Rogers Reid, the *Tribune* purchased the remains of its old rival from Frank A. Munsey. Whitelaw Reid, grandson of the reporter who distinguished himself at Shiloh and Gettysburg, became editor of the *Herald Tribune* in 1947.

ALBERT DEANE RICHARDSON (1832–69) rebounded from his harrowing experiences in prison to describe them in a book, hiring as helper a boy later famous as Daniel Frohman, the theatrical manager, who would remember Richardson as "the finest man I ever knew." Richardson went on a tour of the Far West for the *Tribune* in 1865. *Beyond the Mississippi*, a book based on this trip, enjoyed an enormous sale. He followed this with *A Personal History of U. S. Grant*, still one of the better Grant biographies. Samuel Bowles, who accompanied him West, wrote of him as a young widower who "wears black broadcloth and 'biled shirts,' . . . drinks French brandy and Cincinnati Catawba, . . . and shines brilliantly among the ladies." Richardson fell in love with Abby Sage McFarland and announced his intention of marrying her as soon as her divorce from Daniel McFarland, a dissolute Tammany politician, became final. On November 25,

1869, McFarland shot Richardson right in the *Tribune* office. Henry Ward Beecher and Octavius Brooks Frothingham thereupon brought the sensational episode to a climax by marrying Richardson to Mrs. McFarland on his deathbed.

EDMUND CLARENCE STEDMAN (1833–1908), whose Bull Run was often cited as one of the most graphic of battle dispatches, quit the *World* as a "secession sheet" when it turned Democratic in the fall of 1862, and after a year of occasional correspondence for the *Times*, abandoned journalism in favor of stock-brokerage. "The Bard of Wall Street" for forty-five years, Stedman wrote tolerable poetry and excellent criticism. As the leader of the New York literary circle of his time, he was a paragon of gentility who, like his friend THOMAS BAILEY ALDRICH (1836–1907, briefly a *Tribune* war correspondent) looked back with incredulity at his Bohemian days at Pfaff's.

JEROME BONAPARTE STILLSON (1841–80) tried a stint as managing editor of the *World* after seven years as its Washington correspondent, succeeding David G. Croly in 1872. He preferred reporting, and in 1876 joined the *Herald* staff in time for the Sioux War. Unlike a colleague, who was killed, he missed Custer's Last Stand. Stillson's fourteen-column account of an exclusive interview with Sitting Bull, Custer's conqueror, telegraphed from Bismarck for two thousand dollars, was a celebrated feat. He died in Denver less than four years later.

WILLIAM SWINTON (1833–92), the sharp-featured *Times* man caught eavesdropping on Grant's council of war, was one Bohemian well grounded in military strategy and tactics. In 1863 and 1864 his unsigned résumés in the *Army and Navy Journal* (founded by another *Times* war correspondent, William Conant Church) were accounted models of their kind by professional soldiers. Swinton's *Campaigns of the Army of the Potomac* (1866) shocked Northerners by its dispassionate tone, particularly its use of "Confederate" for "rebel." It is still a valuable reference, since Swinton interviewed many officers and was at pains to submit proofs to Meade, Hooker, Franklin, Couch, Hancock, Lee, and Johnston. (He did not submit them to Grant or

Burnside, understandably, and the book fails to give Grant his due.) In 1869 he became professor of English at the new University of California; he quit after a ruckus with its president five years later. Millions of school children were exposed to the texts Swinton subsequently turned out on almost every grade-school subject. His brother John (1829–1901), managing editor of the *Times* for part of the war, was later a prominent Socialist editor and leader.

BENJAMIN FRANKLIN TAYLOR (1819–87) quit the Chicago *Evening Journal* in 1865 to free-lance, lecturing and writing. His poetry, though not particularly engaging today, enjoyed a vogue, and three travel books written in the 1870's show flashes of Taylor's peculiar genius for description. His papers are deposited in the library at Lowville, New York.

GEORGE ALFRED TOWNSEND (1841–1914) returned from reporting the Austro-Prussian War to embark on a long career of feature writing, chiefly from Washington, for the Chicago *Tribune*, the Cincinnati *Enquirer*, and ultimately a score of others. He wrote discerningly of the political scene, his social satires were gentle and in good humor, and as "Gath" (a well-considered perversion of his initials) he won nation-wide recognition. In 1896, looking back with nostalgia on his days in the field, Townsend culminated a fund-raising campaign with the erection of a sixty-foot stone arch and tower to the memory of the Civil War correspondents near Gapland, his home on South Mountain, Maryland. On its rose brick panels are the names of one hundred and fifty-seven artists and writers, including nine (chiefly staff officers who wrote as a sideline) from the Confederacy.

HENRY VILLARD (1835–1900) remained a reporter until 1868, when he was named secretary of the American Social Science Association. Interested in an Oregon railroad through a bondholders' committee, Villard turned to railroad finance. He gained control of the Northern Pacific in 1881, went bankrupt building it through the mountains, raised new capital, regained control, and in 1889 became board chairman. In 1890 the one-time Bohemian, who married the daughter of William Lloyd Garrison, engineered mergers from which he created the Edison General Electric Company, predecessor of General Electric. Villard did not entirely forsake journalism. In 1881 he gained control of the New York *Evening Post*, later owned by his son, Oswald Garrison Villard.

SAMUEL WILKESON (1817–89) quit the *Tribune* in February 1865 to promote the sale of war bonds for Jay Cooke and Company, the Philadelphia banking-house which contributed largely to the financing of the war. Wilkeson's ebullience and his many newspaper contacts served him well as a publicist. In 1869 he wrote Cooke after prospecting in the northwest: "Jay, we have got the biggest thing on earth." Subsequently he lobbied the Northern Pacific bill through Congress, paying Forney's papers alone $4,666.66 for their support, and promoted the sale of Northern Pacific stock—"I believe in it as I believe in God." He was secretary of the road, and so remained after his old enemy Villard ("a coarse brute," he once wrote Gay of him) succeeded Cooke in control.

FRANC BANGS WILKIE (1832–92) settled down to a desk job on the Chicago *Times* late in 1863, and for thirty years was one of the town's saltier journalists. His *Pen and Powder*, written in 1888, is among the best reminiscences of the Bohemian Brigade.

JOHN RUSSELL YOUNG (1840–99) joined Jay Cooke as Wilkeson's assistant in 1865. Late that year Young began writing for Greeley, and in June 1866, at twenty-six, he succeeded Gay as managing editor of the *Tribune*. Abounding in vitality, he did well until discharged three years later for slipping Associated Press copy to a non-subscribing paper in Philadelphia. Young went over to the *Herald*, accompanying General Grant on his trip around the world in 1879. He was minister to China, 1882–5, and Librarian of Congress from 1897 to his death.

BIBLIOGRAPHICAL NOTE

As IN THE selective documentation provided in the text, I have imposed certain limits upon the bibliography to keep it within reasonable bounds. There are many omissions; the De B. Randolph Keim Collection in the Library of Congress, for example, and the *Official Records of the Union and Confederate Navies* contain some pertinent material, but are not listed because none of it was used. On the other hand, I have listed a few secondary sources on which I have not drawn, but which belong on any list that is to prove useful to researchers in related fields and to readers who care to delve further.

In this category, mention should be made of Bernard Weisberger's *Reporters for the Union*, a zestfully written, highly satiric study in which the frame of reference is political rather than military or journalistic. In Mr. Weisberger's view, the reporters were not much better than political pamphleteers. While I would dispute this with him, to say nothing of his interpretation of the successive attempts at censorship as forming "a stockade of regulations" that drastically restricted the right to report, there is much of interest in his provocative volume on matters which I have neglected or passed over lightly. Battle reporting is ignored. There are no other books on Civil War newsmen save their own memoirs. Robert S. Harper's *Lincoln and the Press* is of value for editorial opinion.

I have often wondered, in perusing these solemn tabulations in the backs of books, how thoroughly the newspapers listed have been examined by the researchers, as it is practically impossible to read *in toto* even one file covering a four-year period. In the present case, the papers deprecatingly known at the time as "provincial" sheets— all of those outside New York—were only spot-checked; most issues of the four major New York papers were examined throughout, along with such of their extra editions as were available; and the weekly periodicals were checked issue by issue.

The section devoted to correspondents' books omits the many they wrote which are not primarily concerned with the war and their own experiences in it.

360

BIBLIOGRAPHY

Manuscripts

James Gordon Bennett Papers, Library of Congress, Washington.
Sylvanus Cadwallader: *Four Years with Grant*, MS, Illinois State Historical Library, Springfield.
Simon Cameron Papers, Library of Congress.
Salmon P. Chase Papers, Library of Congress.
William Conant Church Papers, Library of Congress.
——, New York Public Library.
Sydney Howard Gay Papers, Butler Library, Columbia University.
Horace Greeley Papers, New York Public Library.
Greeley letters to Sam Wilkeson, in possession of Ralph G. Newman, Chicago.
Frederic Hudson diaries, scrapbooks, and MS by Woodward Hudson, in possession of Mrs. Wesley P. Wilmot, Concord, Mass.
Robert T. Lincoln Collection, Library of Congress.
Manton Marble Papers, Library of Congress.
John G. Nicolay Papers, Library of Congress.
Edwin M. Stanton Papers, Library of Congress.
Henry Villard Papers, in possession of Henry H. Villard, Garden City, N.Y.
John Russell Young Papers, Library of Congress.

Civil War Newspaper and Periodical Files

Army and Navy Journal
Baltimore *American*
Boston *Evening Transcript*
Charleston *Mercury*
Chicago *Tribune*
Cincinnati *Commercial*
Cincinnati *Times*
Frank Leslie's Illustrated Newspaper
Harper's Weekly
New York *Evening Post*
New York *Herald*
New York *Illustrated News*

New York *Leader*
New York *Sunday Mercury*
New York *Times*
New York *Tribune*
New York *World*
Philadelphia *Inquirer*
Philadelphia *Press*
The Round Table
Vanity Fair
Washington *Chronicle*
Washington *Star*
Wilkes' Spirit of the Times

I have also made occasional use of the Thomas Seaman Townsend Collection, comprising over one hundred volumes of clippings on the war from all of the New York papers and some others, in the Butler Library, Columbia University.

Bibliography

Published Letters, Diaries, and Contemporary Records

Agassiz, George, ed.: *Meade's Headquarters 1863–65: Letters of Colonel Theodore Lyman*. Boston: 1922.

Baker, George E., ed.: *The Works of William H. Seward*. Boston: 1884. 5 vols.

Bancroft, Emily Adams, ed.: *Memorial and Letters of Rev. John R. Adams, D.D.* Cambridge, Mass.: 1890.

Basler, Roy P., ed.: *The Collected Works of Abraham Lincoln*. New Brunswick, N.J.: 1953. 8 vols.

Beale, Howard K., ed.: *The Diary of Edward Bates, 1859–1866* (Annual Report of the American Historical Association 1930, IV). Washington: 1933.

Beatty, John: *Memoirs of a Volunteer*. New York: 1946. Despite its title, this is a diary.

Blake, Sarah Swan Weld, ed.: *Diaries and Letters of Francis Minot Weld, M.D.* Boston: 1925.

Castleman, Alfred L.: *The Army of the Potomac Behind the Scenes: A Diary of Unwritten History*. Milwaukee: 1863.

Congressional Directory. Beginning with the 36th Congress, 1st session (1859–60), members of the House and Senate press galleries are listed.

Craig, Daniel H.: *Annual Report of the General Agent, N.Y. Associated Press, for 1861*. Copy in New York Public Library.

Dennett, Tyler, ed.: *Lincoln and the Civil War in the Diaries and Letters of John Hay*. New York: 1939.

Haskell, Fritz, ed.: *The Diary of Colonel William Camm 1861 to 1865*. Journal of the Illinois State Historical Society, Vol. 28, No. 4, January 1926.

Holloway, Emory, and Adimari, Ralph, eds.: *New York Dissected by Walt Whitman*. New York: 1936. Selections from Whitman's early newspaper writings.

Howe, Mark A. DeWolfe, ed.: *Marching with Sherman: Passages from the Letters and Campaign Diaries of Henry Hitchcock*. New Haven: 1927.

Howe, Mark DeWolfe, ed.: *Touched with Fire: Civil War Letters of Oliver Wendell Holmes, Junior*. Cambridge, Mass.: 1946.

Jones, Jenkin Lloyd: *An Artilleryman's Diary*. Madison, Wis.: 1914.

Lyon, Mrs. Adelia C., ed.: *Reminiscences of the Civil War: from the War Correspondence and Diaries of Colonel William Lyon*. San Jose, Calif.: 1907.

Marshall, Jessie A.: *Private and Official Correspondence of General Benjamin F. Butler* . . . Norwich, Mass.: 1917. 5 vols.

Meade, George Gordon, 2nd, ed.: *The Life and Letters of George Gordon Meade*. New York: 1913. 2 vols.

Moore, Frank, ed.: *Rebellion Record*. New York: 1861–8. 11 vols.

Morse, John T., ed.: *Diary of Gideon Welles, Secretary of the Navy under Lincoln and Johnson.* Boston: 1911. 3 vols.

Nevins, Allan, and Thomas, Milton Halsey, eds.: *The Diary of George Templeton Strong.* New York: 1952. 4 vols.

Norton, Oliver Willcox: *Army Letters 1861–65.* Chicago: 1903.

Perkins, Howard Cecil, ed.: *Northern Editorials on Secession.* New York: 1942. 2 vols.

Raymond, Henry W., ed.: "Extracts from the Journal of Henry J. Raymond," *Scribner's Monthly*, Vol. 19, 419 ff., November 1879, January 1880, March 1880.

Reports of Committees of the House of Representatives, 2nd Session, 37th Congress, Vol. 3. Washington: 1862.

Report of the Joint Committee on the Conduct of the War. Washington: 1864

Ropes, John Codman, and Gray, John C.: *War Letters 1862–1865.* Boston: 1927.

Rusk, Ralph L., ed.: *The Letters of Ralph Waldo Emerson.* New York: 1939. 6 vols.

Thompson, Robert Means, and Wainwright, Richard, eds.: *Confidential Correspondence of Gustavus Vasa Fox.* New York: 1919. 2 vols.

Thorndike, Rachel Sherman, ed.: *The Sherman Letters.* New York: 1894.

Trow's Directory of New York City. New York: 1861. This provides the home addresses of residents as of May 1, 1861.

Van Alstyne, Lawrence: *Diary of an Enlisted Man.* New Haven: 1910.

War of the Rebellion: . . . *Official Records of the Union and Confederate Armies.* Washington: 1880–1901. 128 vols. Cited in the footnotes as *O.R.*

Weld, Stephen Minot: *War Diary and Letters.* Cambridge, Mass.: 1912.

Whitman, Walt: *The Wound Dresser:* . . . *Letters to His Mother from the Hospitals in Washington* . . . New York: 1949.

Wood, Lindsay Lomax, ed.: *Leaves from an Old Washington Diary* . . . *by Elizabeth Lindsay Lomax.* New York: 1943.

Books and Articles by Civil War Reporters

Brooks, Noah: *Washington in Lincoln's Time.* New York: 1895.

Browne, Junius: *Four Years in Secessia.* Hartford: 1865.

Burnett, Alf: *Incidents of the War.* Cincinnati: 1863.

Coffin, Charles C.: *Four Years of Fighting.* Boston: 1866.

——: *Stories of Our Soldiers: War Reminiscences by "Carleton"* . . . Boston: 1893.

Conyngham, David P.: *Sherman's March Through the South.* New York: 1865.

Bibliography

Croffut, William A.: *An American Procession 1855–1914: A Personal Chronicle of Famous Men.* Boston: 1931.

Crounse, Lorenzo L.: "The Army Correspondent," *Harper's Monthly*, Vol. 27, 627–33, October 1863.

Davis, Theodore R.: "Grant Under Fire," *The Cosmopolitan*, Vol. 14, 333–9, January 1893.

Dicey, Edward: *Six Months in the Federal States.* London: 1863. 2 vols.

Fiske, Stephen Ryder: "Gentlemen of the Press," *Harper's Monthly*, Vol. 26, 361–7, February 1863.

——: Article in *Lincoln Among His Friends: A Sheaf of Intimate Memories*, Rufus Rockwell Wilson, ed., Caldwell, Ohio: 1942.

Gobright, Lawrence A.: *Recollections of Men and Things at Washington.* Philadelphia: 1869.

Hinkle, Thornton M.: *Some Observations of an Army Correspondent.* Cincinnati: 1879.

Hudson, Henry Norman: *General Butler's Campaign on the Hudson.* New York: 1864. Pamphlet.

Knox, Thomas Wallace: *Camp-Fire and Cotton-Field.* New York: 1865.

Lawrence, George Alfred: *Border and Bastille.* New York: 1863.

Page, Charles A.: *Letters of a War Correspondent.* Boston: 1899.

Poore, Ben: Perley: *Perley's Reminiscences of Sixty Years in the National Metropolis.* Philadelphia: 1886. 2 vols.

Richardson, Abby Sage, ed.: *Garnered Sheaves: From the Writings of Albert D. Richardson.* Hartford: 1871.

Richardson, Albert Deane: *The Secret Service, the Field, the Dungeon, and the Escape.* Hartford: 1865.

——: *Personal History of U. S. Grant.* Boston: edition of 1886. (First published in 1868.)

Russell, William Howard: *My Diary North and South.* New York: 1863.

Sala, George Augustus: *My Diary in America in the Midst of War.* London: 1865. 2 vols.

Shanks, William F. G.: *Personal Recollections of Distinguished Generals.* New York: 1866.

——: "How We Get Our News," *Harper's Monthly*, Vol. 34, 511–20, May 1867.

Smalley, George W.: *Anglo-American Memories.* New York: 1911.

Stedman, Laura, and Gould, George M., eds.: *Life and Letters of Edmund Clarence Stedman.* New York: 1910.

Taylor, Benjamin Franklin: *Mission Ridge and Lookout Mountain, with Pictures of Life in Camp and Field.* New York: 1872.

Townsend, George Alfred: *Campaigns of a Non-Combatant.* New York: 1866. (Republished, 1950, as *Rustics in Rebellion.*)

——: "A Winter Among the Peripatetics," *The Galaxy*, Vol. 1, 57 ff., May 1866.

——: "Recollections and Reflections," *Lippincott's Monthly*, Vol. 38, 515–22, November 1886.

Truman, Ben. C.: "Old Time Editors and Newspapers I Have Known," *Pacific Printer*, Vol. 6, 338 ff., December 1911.

Villard, Henry: "Army Correspondence: Its History," *The Nation*, Vol. 1, 79 ff., 114 ff., 144 ff.; July 20, July 27, August 3, 1865.

——: *Memoirs*. Boston: 1904. 2 vols.

Webb, Charles Henry: *John Paul's Book*. Hartford: 1874.

Wilkie, Franc Bangs: *Walks About Chicago and Army and Miscellaneous Sketches*. Chicago: 1869.

——: *Pen and Powder*. Boston: 1888.

——: *Thirty-five Years in American Journalism*. Chicago: 1891.

Williams, George Forrester: Articles, *The Independent*, Vol. 53, 1860 ff., 2397 ff.; Vol. 54, 210 ff.; August 8, October 10, 1901; January 23, 1902.

Winchell, James M.: "Three Interviews with President Lincoln," *The Galaxy*, Vol. 16, 34 ff., July 1873.

Wing, Henry Ebenezer: "Stories of a War Correspondent," *The Christian Advocate*, Vols. 88–90, February 6, March 27, May 22, October 2, October 30, November 27, 1913; April 2, May 21, October 1, 1914.

Young, May D. Russell, ed.: *Men and Memories: Personal Reminiscences by John Russell Young*. New York: 1901.

Biographies, Newspaper Studies, and Related Works

Aldrich, Mrs. Thomas Bailey: *Crowding Memories*. New York: 1920.

Andrews, J. Cutler: "The Pennsylvania Press During the Civil War," *Pennsylvania History*, Vol. 9, 22 ff., January 1942.

Atkins, John Black: *Life of Sir William Howard Russell*. London: 1911. 2 vols.

Aubrey, Cullen B.: *Reflections of a Newsboy in the Army of the Potomac*. Milwaukee: 1904.

Baehr, Harry W., Jr.: *The New York Tribune Since the Civil War*. New York: 1936.

Bates, David Homer: *Lincoln in the Telegraph Office*. New York: 1907.

Bowman, S. M., and Irwin, R. B.: *Sherman and His Campaigns*. New York: 1865.

Brigham, Johnson: *Iowa: Its History and Its Foremost Citizens*. Des Moines: 1918.

Brinton, John H., M.D.: *Personal Memoirs*. New York: 1914.

Brown, Francis: *Raymond of the Times*. New York: 1951.

Brucker, Herbert: *Freedom of Information*. New York: 1949.

Bullard, F. Lauriston: *Famous War Correspondents*. Boston: 1914.

Bibliography

Carlson, Oliver: *The Man Who Made News: James Gordon Bennett.* New York: 1942.

Carpenter, Francis B.: *Six Months in the White House.* New York: 1866.

Congdon, Charles C.: *Reminiscences of a Journalist.* New York: 1880.

Cortissoz, Royal: *The Life of Whitelaw Reid.* New York: 1921. 2 vols.

Cox, Jacob Dolson: *Military Reminiscences of the Civil War.* New York: 1900.

Cummings, Amos J.: "How Newspapers Are Made," *Packard's Monthly,* Vol. 1, 87 ff., 105 ff., October, November 1868; Vol. 1 (New Series), 16 ff., January 1869.

Curry, Roy Watson: "The Newspaper Press and the Civil War," *West Virginia History,* Vol. 6, 226 ff., January 1945.

Dana, Charles A.: *Recollections of the Civil War.* New York: 1913.

Davis, Elmer: *History of the New York Times.* New York: 1921.

Downes, William Howe: *The Life and Works of Winslow Homer.* New York: 1911.

Gilmore, James R.: *Personal Recollections of Abraham Lincoln and the Civil War.* Boston: 1898.

Grant, Ulysses S.: *Personal Memoirs.* New York: 1885. 2 vols.

Hale, Edward Everett: *James Russell Lowell and His Friends.* Boston: 1899.

Hale, William Harlan: *Horace Greeley: Voice of the People.* New York: 1950.

Harper, Robert S.: *Lincoln and the Press.* New York: 1951.

Hassard, John R. G.: *The Fast Printing Machine.* New York: 1878.

Hebert, Walter H.: *Fighting Joe Hooker.* New York: 1944.

Hertz, Emmanuel: *Lincoln Talks: A Biography in Anecdote.* New York: 1939.

Hesseltine, William Best: *Civil War Prisons: A Study in War Psychology.* Columbus, Ohio: 1930.

Hindes, Ruthanna: *George Alfred Townsend.* Wilmington, Del.: 1946.

Hudson, Frederic: *Journalism in the United States.* New York: 1873.

Isley, Jeter Allen: *Horace Greeley and the Republican Party, 1853–1861: A Study of the New York Tribune.* Princeton, N.J.: 1947.

Kinsley, Philip: *The Chicago Tribune: Its First Hundred Years.* New York: 1943. 2 vols.

Kirkland, Frazer: *Reminiscences of the Blue and the Gray.* Chicago: 1895.

Leech, Margaret: *Reveille in Washington.* Garden City: 1945. (First published 1941.)

Lewis, Lloyd: *Sherman: Fighting Prophet.* New York: 1932.

Meredith, Roy: *Mr. Lincoln's Camera Man: Mathew B. Brady.* New York: 1946.

Mott, Frank Luther: *A History of American Magazines.* Cambridge, Mass.: 1939. 2 vols.

——: *American Journalism.* New York: 1945.

——: *The News in America.* Cambridge, Mass.: 1952.

Oberholtzer, Ellis Paxon: *Jay Cooke: Financier of the Civil War.* Philadelphia: 1907. 2 vols.

O'Brien, John Emmet: *Telegraphing in Battle.* Scranton: 1910.

Paine, Albert Bigelow: *Th. Nast: His Period and His Pictures.* New York: 1904.

——: *A Sailor of Fortune: Personal Memoirs of Captain B. S. Osborn.* New York: 1906.

Parry, Albert: *Garrets and Pretenders: A History of Bohemianism in America.* New York: 1933.

Parton, James: *The Life of Horace Greeley.* New York: 1855.

——: "The Newspaper," *North American Review,* Vol. 102, 376–419, April 1866.

Phillips, Melville, ed.: *The Making of a Newspaper.* New York: 1893.

Porter, Horace: *Campaigning with Grant.* New York: 1897.

Pray, Isaac C.: *Memoirs of James Gordon Bennett and His Times.* New York: 1855.

Prescott, George B.: *History, Theory, and Practice of the Electric Telegraph.* Boston: 1860.

Reid, Whitelaw: *Ohio in the War.* Cincinnati: 1868. 2 vols.

Rosebault, Charles J.: *When Dana Was the Sun.* New York: 1931.

Sandburg, Carl: *Abraham Lincoln: The War Years.* New York: 1939. 4 vols.

Stevens, Walter B.: "Joseph B. McCullagh," *Missouri Historical Review,* Vol. 25, 3 ff., 247 ff., 425 ff.; October 1930, *et seq.*

Stoddard, William O.: *Inside the White House in War Times.* New York: 1890.

Tarbell, Ida M.: *A Reporter for Lincoln: The Story of Henry E. Wing.* New York: 1927.

Trollope, Anthony: *North America.* London: 1862. 2 vols.

Weisberger, Bernard A.: "McClellan and the Press," *South Atlantic Quarterly,* Vol. 51, 383 ff., July 1952.

——: *Reporters for the Union.* Boston: 1953.

Wilcox, Julius: "Journalism as a Profession," *The Galaxy,* Vol. 4, 796 ff., November 1867.

Wilkeson, Frank: *Recollections of a Private Soldier in the Army of the Potomac.* New York: 1887.

Wilson, James Harrison: *The Life of Charles A. Dana.* New York: 1907.

——: *The Life of John A. Rawlins.* New York: 1916.

INDEX

Index

Becker, Joseph, *Leslie's*, 227–8

Beecher, Henry Ward, 77, 357

Bellew, F. H., *N.Y. Illustrated News*, 9, 204, 210

Bennett, James Gordon, 9, 67, 69, 75, 78, 79, 176, 195, 234, 235, 240; described, 23–4; discharges Hanscom, 80; Lincoln and, 157, 159; on *Tribune* beat, 308

Benson, Eugene, *Leslie's*, 10–11, 354

Bentley, Henry, Phila. *Inquirer*, 110; captured, 101

Bickham, William D., Cincinnati *Commercial*, 115, 183, 251, 257

Bigelow, John, 8, 56, 145, 245

Biglow Papers, 99

Blair, Gen. Frank, 177, 178

Blair, Montgomery, Postmaster-General, 94, 127, 325, 327

Bodman, A. H., Chicago *Tribune*, 241

Bohemian movement: origins, 4; tenets, 5; appeals to reporters, 7, war correspondents, 62–3, artists, 253

"Bonaparte," N.Y. *World*, 210, 212–13

Bonwill, F. C. H., *Leslie's*, 255

Booneville, Mo., action at, 58–9

Booth, John Wilkes, 268

Boston, 31, 220

Boston *Advertiser*, 228, 291

Boston *Courier*, 332

Boston *Herald*, 31

Boston *Journal*, 37, 94, 306

Boston *Traveller*, 275

Bowerem, George, N.Y. *Tribune*, 239

Bowers, Col. Theodore S., 279

Bowles, Samuel, Springfield *Republican*, 6, 23

Bowling Green, Ky., 79

Boyd, Belle, *CS* spy, 122–3

Brace, Charles L., N.Y. *Times*, 43

Brady, John A., N.Y. *Herald*, 295

Brady, Mathew, 44, 168–9, 272

Bragg, Gen. Braxton, *CSA*, 135, 164, 191, 270

Bridgeport, Conn., 220

Bridgeport, Tenn., 237

Brigham, Charles D., N.Y. *Tribune*, 106, 293; in Charleston, 19–20; and *Merrimac*, 91–2; m.e. Pittsburgh *Commercial*, 291

Brockway, Beman, 54

Brook Farm, 15

Brooklyn *Eagle*, 315

Brooks, Erastus, N.Y. *Express* publisher, 319

Brooks, Noah, Sacramento *Union*, 83, 151, 156, 311, 333, 337; and Lincoln, 157–8, 200–1

Brough, John, 191

Brown, John, 6

Browne, Charles F. ("Artemus Ward"), 4

Browne, Dunn, *see* Fiske, Samuel

Browne, Junius, N.Y. *Tribune*, 62, 100, 250, 274, 276; Fort Donelson, 87–8; captured and imprisoned, 185–93; fakes battle dispatch, 247–8

Bryant, William Cullen, N.Y. *Evening Post* ed., 6

Buchanan, James, 26; on "telegrams," 9; Pike deplores, 17

Buckingham, L. W., N.Y. *Herald*, 131, 195

Buckner, Gen. Simon Bolivar, *CSA*, 88

Buell, Gen. Don Carlos, 79, 100, 102, 161, 164, 183

Buffalo, N.Y., 16–17, 68, 333

Buffalo *Courier*, 327

Bulkley, Solomon T., N.Y. *Herald*, captured, 189

Bull Run, Battle of: genesis, 34–6; reporters at, 43–4; action and aftermath, 45–51, 173

Bull Run, Second Battle of, 130–3, 151, 155

Burlington (Iowa) *Hawkeye*, 33

Burnett, Alf, Cincinnati reporter, 259–60

Burns, George H., censor, 42, 48, 49, 50

Index

Index

Graffan, Charles H., N.Y. *Herald*, 210

Graham, "Wash," sutler, 284

Grand Gulf, Miss., 184

Granger, Gen. Gordon, 238

Grant, Gen. U. S., 83, 85, 86, 103–4, 184, 192, 270, 335; Shiloh, 101; Lincoln on, 161, 162; and Knox case, 175–82 *passim;* in Washington, 272, 288–9; as seen in newspapers, 273–5; and by reporters, 275–9; Cadwallader and drinking spree, 280–6; Wilderness, 293–308 *passim;* Appomattox, 339–46 *passim*

Greeley, Horace, 32, 69, 70, 77, 99, 100, 116, 195, 234, 235, 239, 266, 292; Clapp mot, 4; on news, 6; Georgia editor on, 8; fame of, 14, 17; relations with Dana, 15, 18, 19, 53, 96–7; Emerson on, 18; "On to Richmond," 34, 35*n*, 52–4; on slanting news, 53; on Frémont, 71*n*; on Shiloh, 100, 104; relations with Gay, 117–18, 129, 348–9; Hill on, 124–5; Lincoln seeks support of, 127, 159; "Prayer," 128; Lincoln on, vs. Bennett, 157; softens Villard dispatch, 166; for mediation, 169, 196, 289; draft riots, 221–3; Hill and Villard quit because of, 291; and 1864 election, 312, 314, 323, 326–7, 333

Greene, Gen. George, 142

Grey, T. C., N.Y. *Tribune*, 204, 205; Gettysburg, 210, 211–12, 216; Wilderness, 294, 298, 306, 308

Grimes, James W., 124

Grover, Gen. Cuvier, 330

Gunn, Thomas Butler, N.Y. *Tribune*: in Charleston, 20–1; on Peninsula, 106, 107

Gurowski, Adam, 75

Hagerstown, Md., 144, 145

Hale, Charles, Boston *Advertiser*, 228, 230

Hale, Edward Everett, 99, 350

Hall, E. S., *Leslie's* artist, 111

Halleck, Gen. Henry W., 79, 162, 188, 205; bans reporters on Corinth campaign, 118–19; orders Pope to expel reporters, 130–1; ban dies, 138

Halpine, Charles G. ("Miles O'Reilly"), 9, 64, 312

Halstead, Murat, Cincinnati *Commercial* ed.: on New York press, 12; and Sherman "crazy," 71; Fredericksburg lead, 256; on Grant, 275

Hambleton, James B., *Southern Confederacy* ed., 190, 191

Hamlin, Hannibal, 320

Hammond, James B., N.Y. *Tribune*, 197, 294, 306–7

Hannam, Charles H., N.Y. *Herald*, 329, 330

Hanover, Pa., 209, 216–18

Hanover, Va., Battle of, 249

Hanscom, Simon Parker, 159, 162, 272; as *Herald* bureau chief in Sumter crisis, 25, 26; on censorship, 67, 69; discharged, 80; edits Wash. *National Republican*, 116; and Lincoln, 153

Hardenbrook, N.Y. *Tribune*, 120

Harding, William W., Phila. *Inquirer* ed., 241–2

Harper Brothers, publishers, 7, 10

Harper's Ferry, 208, 209

Harper's Monthly, 232, 263

Harper's Weekly, 12, 37–8, 147, 254, 273; South toward, 8; on Anderson, 11; censored, 105; artists on Peninsula, 111; accuracy of, 252–3

Harriet Lane, U.S.S., 29

Harrington, Henry W., 203

Harrisburg, Pa., 25, 68, 137, 203, 205, 206, 209

Harrison's Landing, Va., 114

Hart, George H., N.Y. *Herald*, 210; captured, 189

Harvard College, 98, 124, 139, 354; Law School, 121, 124

Harvey, James E., N.Y. *Tribune*, 27, 32

Index

Index

Index

Index

☼ *A NOTE ON THE TYPE* ☼

This book was set on the Linotype in JANSON, *a recutting made direct from the type cast from matrices (now in possession of the Stempel foundry, Frankfurt am Main) made by Anton Janson some time between 1660 and 1687.*

Of Janson's origin nothing is known. He may have been a relative of Justus Janson, a printer of Danish birth who practiced in Leipzig from 1614 to 1635. Some time between 1657 and 1658 Anton Janson, a punch-cutter and type-founder, bought from the Leipzig printer Johann Erich Hahn the type-foundry which had formerly been a part of the printing house of M. Friedrich Lankisch. Janson's types were first shown in a specimen sheet issued at Leipzig about 1675. Janson's successor, and perhaps his son-in-law, Johann Karl Edling, issued a specimen sheet of Janson types in 1689. His heirs sold the Janson matrices in Holland to Wolffgang Dietrich Erhardt.

The book was composed, printed, and bound by THE PLIMPTON PRESS, *Norwood, Massachusetts. Designed by* HARRY FORD.